AMERICAN STUDIES – A MONOGRAPH SERIES
Volume 224

Edited on behalf
of the German Association
for American Studies by
REINHARD R. DOERRIES
GERHARD HOFFMANN
ALFRED HORNUNG

ANNE MIHAN

Undoing Difference?

Race and Gender in Selected Works
by Toni Morrison
and Jeanette Winterson

Universitätsverlag
WINTER
Heidelberg

Bibliografische Information der Deutschen Nationalbibliothek
Die Deutsche Nationalbibliothek verzeichnet diese Publikation
in der Deutschen Nationalbibliografie;
detaillierte bibliografische Daten sind im Internet
über *http://dnb.d-nb.de* abrufbar.

UMSCHLAGBILD:
© Kerstin Gürke
unter Verwendung eines Fotolia-Motives des Autors: onlinebewerbung

ISBN 978-3-8253-6025-2

© 2012 Universitätsverlag Winter GmbH Heidelberg
Imprimé en Allemagne · Printed in Germany
Druck: Memminger MedienCentrum, 87700 Memmingen

Gedruckt auf umweltfreundlichem, chlorfrei gebleichtem
und alterungsbeständigem Papier

Den Verlag erreichen Sie im Internet unter:
www.winter-verlag.de

Contents

Acknowledgments

Undoing Differences? Race and Gender in Selected Works by Toni Morrison and Jeanette Winterson was presented to the Philosophical Faculty II of Humboldt-Universität, Berlin, as a doctoral thesis in the field of North American Literature and Culture; I defended my dissertation in June 2010. My Ph.D. project was partly financed by the NaföG program of the *Land* Berlin.

I am grateful to the following mentors, colleagues, friends and relatives for their guidance, encouragement, generous support and manifold assistance during the process of my working on this book: My academic advisors Günter H. Lenz and Eva Boesenberg of the Department of English and American Studies at Humboldt-Universität; Alfred Hornung as an editor of "American Studies - A Monograph Series"; Thomas O. Haakenson, Stephanie Remlinger and Annette Lahrius, who were among the first to discuss my ideas with me; Matthias Leuthold, who helped funding the beginnings; members of the American Studies research colloquium at my department, especially Antje Dallmann, Sladja Blazan, Suncica Ozretic-Klaas, and Katja Linke; Stephan Breidbach, who gave me time when I needed it; Carsta Busch, my untiring helper in many rounds of formatting; my parents, who sponsored my work over long stretches of time and calmly supported me through all of it; and Ulrike Mihan, who helped me in more ways than I have words for.

Introduction

> Race does not exist. But it does kill people.
>
> Colette Guillaumin

> [N]ot only is it unclear what gender is and how we should go about understanding it, but whether it is anything at all.
>
> Sally Haslanger

> [T]he very notion of the subject [is] intelligible only through its appearance as gendered [...].
>
> Judith Butler

The concepts of race[1] and gender have kept scholars of the natural and social sciences as well as the humanities engaged in vigorous discussions for many decades. Today, we are nowhere near an end to these academic disputes, nor should we wish to be, given that many questions still remain unanswered and new inquiries bring up more questions. Also, and even more importantly, race and gender continue to be major sources of social injustice, discrimination, and exploitation and thus provide ample reasons for serious research into and debates about these concepts, which determine our reality like few others.

Scholars of both fields have pointed to the ontological gulf between contemporary academic discourse on the constructedness of race and gender and the deep-rooted folk beliefs in essential, biologically grounded

---

[1] Frequently in academic discourse, race is placed in inverted commas "to signify its questionable status" (Youngs 26). Following Youngs and in the interest of limiting the number of words in quotation marks, however, I will dispense with this indicator when I refer to race in this study. Toni Morrison herself uses inverted commas infrequently, and I hope to show clearly in the following that I question this concept in my own thinking about race as well as in my analyses of Morrison's contributions to the race discourse.

racial and gender differences. Thus, Judith Butler notes that "academic debate seems woefully out of synch with the contemporary political usage of [terms such as gender, sex, homosexuality]" ("The End" 183). Indeed, "[g]ender is so much the routine ground of everyday activities that questioning its taken-for-granted assumptions and presuppositions is like thinking about whether the sun will come up. Gender is so pervasive," as Judith Lorber emphasizes, "that in our society we assume it is bred into our genes" (13). With regard to race, Sally Haslanger writes that "[t]he self-evidence of racial distinctions in everyday American life is at striking odds with the uncertainty about the category of race in law and the academy" (32). "Because individuals are so deeply invested in gender, and, at least in the US, race categories, it remains of crucial importance to be and to be perceived as a 'woman' or a 'man' and as a member of one of the standard races" (48).

Novels and other works of literature that receive a wide readership can work to bridge this gap between folk conceptions and academic discourses of race and gender, as they are capable of illustrating complex theoretical insights, developing them further, and contributing valuable ideas to the race and gender debates. With their texts Toni Morrison and Jeanette Winterson both actively participate in these debates; their thinking and writing about race and gender have motivated this study and form its focus.

Race and Gender – What are we talking about?

At the end of the twentieth century Colette Guillaumin stated that "[t]he idea of race is one of the most contradictory and violent in our world today" (355), and this continues to be the case in the first decade of the twenty-first century, as will be shown later. Both the contradictions and the violence inherent in the idea of race have their roots in the history of this concept. Invented at the dawn of imperialism as a system to classify colonial subjects on the basis of their geographical origins and perceived physical characteristics, it already started out evaluative in character. Ian Hacking states that, "[r]acial classification is evaluation. Strong ascriptions of comparative merit were built into European racial classification and into evaluations of human beauty from the beginning" ("Why Race" 109/2). Furthermore, Guillaumin describes how the idea of race was constructed as a natural phenomenon, built up (and slowly, at that) from elements which might equally well be physical traits as social customs, linguistic peculiarities as legal institutions, lumped together and homogenized according to the precept that they must ultimately all be biological phenomena. This idea carries a great deal of weight in a society obsessed with the sanctity of 'Science,' which has been invested with the power not only to unveil and understand natural phenomena, but to establish what actually constitutes those phenomena themselves. (358)

In colonial and imperialist societies, like the American South during the Jim Crow system of racial segregation, the "idea of race" became a legal category and thus was "turned into a concrete social fact" (358). The folk conception of race as a biological essence that causes distinct intellectual, social, legal, and economic differences between people who are grouped into different races has proved so persistent that even decades after race was widely understood within the academic community to be an arbitrary invention,[2] "the races ... are treated as if they were essential characteristics of people" (Hacking, "Why Race": 112/1). Haslanger, who calls for a concept of race that takes existing folk beliefs about this idea into consideration, suggests that "race ... could be fruitfully understood as a position within a broad social network" (43). She offers the following definition of a race and racialized groups:

A group is racialized iff$_{df}$ its members are socially positioned as subordinate or privileged along some dimension (economic, political, legal, social, etc.), and the group is 'marked' as a target for this treatment by observed or imagined bodily features presumed to be evidence of ancestral links to a certain geographical region. [...] [R]aces are groups demarcated by the geographical associations accompanying perceived body type, when those associations take on evaluative significance concerning how members of the group should be viewed and treated. (44)

Race, for Haslanger, thus is a matter of social positioning, of assigning characteristics and actively racializing people. Race is a doing, an active constructing, and as such it is real, even though it has no scientifically verifiable biological foundation. Like Haslanger, Joshua Glasgow argues

[2]Guillaumin quotes a declaration of the American Psychological Association of 1938 which states that "[i]n the experiments which psychologists have made upon different peoples, no characteristic, inherent psychological differences which fundamentally distinguish so-called 'races' have been disclosed" (qtd. on 358).

that "[t]he discourse relevant for the race debate is folk racial discourse, and analysis of folk racial concepts (and conceptions) should be informed by empirical study" (9).[3] Glasgow's analysis of empirical studies of folk racial discourse underlines that "[t]he relevant racial concepts (and conceptions) are composed of biological, and sometimes social, elements" (10).[4] He points out that "biological realism has been gaining ground in recent years" (84), although, as he stresses, its representatives do not entertain essentialist notions of race, or connect the physical or ancestral with moral, intellectual, cultural, or other characteristics in order to create hierarchies. Glasgow's general critique of biological realism is that of arbitrariness. He writes that all in all "it remains likely, if not decided, that if we line up humanity, we can group ourselves in various ways without being required to say that those groupings reflect genetically or ancestrally discontinuous distinctions" (107). Still, as Guillaumin states rather matter-of-factly, "simply showing that a category of this type has no scientific basis is insufficient to remove it from the mental universe not simply of the majority of people, but even of those who are intellectually convinced that it does not exist as a 'natural' reality. It is a necessary operation, but not a sufficient one" (361). Therefore, the constructedness of race, the mechanisms of the "doing" of race and the consequences of racialization for all people involved need to be investigated in order to effectively challenge the folk belief in essential racial difference.

In folk conceptions of gender – in analogy to folk racial conceptions – a person's gender identity is firmly attached to a naturally given, pre-discursive sex. Even transsexuals who transition from male to female or female to male and reconstruct their bodies by means of surgery and hormone therapy are assumed to do so because of an innate maleness or femaleness which their physical bodies paradoxically do not match so that these bodies need to be adjusted. In folk conception of transsexuality as well as in some academic conceptions, this adjustment, or sex re-assignment, reaffirms the assumed essential difference between men

---

[3]Glasgow's argument is that "contemporary folk discourse fixes the meaning of racial terms for the race debate" (51).

[4]Apart from the outdated Classical Racialism Glasgow identifies three biologically realist theories: the Superficial Theory of Armand Marie Leroi, Genetic Racial Realism, represented for instance by Sarich & Miele, and the Populationism of Andreasen, Arthur, Kitcher and others (cf. Glasgow Ch. 5, "Breaking Nature's Bone").

and women.[5] In contrast to folk beliefs, however, research in the fields of ethnography, sociology, history, and psychology has provided ample evidence that "[g]enders ... are not attached to a biological substratum" (Lorber 18), be it physical, hormonal, or otherwise 'natural.' Rather, they are social constructions "constantly created and re-created out of human interaction, out of social life, and [are] the texture and order of that social life" (Lorber 13).

Yet, as Lorber emphasizes, in a society that "[takes] ... for granted" that gender is "all biology, or hormones, or human nature," it is "difficult to see how gender is constructed" (18), especially so, since "the process [of religious, cultural, and legal construction of gender] is made invisible" (26). Moreover, Judith Butler has argued that even the theoretical juxtaposition of a natural, biological-bodily sex and a discursively constructed, social gender not only reinforces the notion of the body as a "ready surface awaiting signification" (*Gender Trouble* 44), it also exchanges the received biological determinism to which the folk conception of gender adheres for a social or discursive determinism with regard to the construction of gender:

> Gender ought not to be conceived merely as the cultural inscription of meaning on a pregiven sex (a juridical conception); gender must also designate the very apparatus of production whereby the sexes themselves are established. As a result, gender is not to culture as sex is to nature; gender is also the discursive/cultural means by which 'sexed nature' or 'a natural sex' is produced and established as 'prediscursive,' prior to culture, a politically neutral surface *on which* culture acts. (*Gender Trouble* 11)

Butler develops a concept of gender that allows us to investigate not only the construction of bodies "through the mark(s) of gender" (*Gender Trouble* 13), but also the hegemonic norms and what she calls "regulatory practices" of the production of "intelligible genders," i.e., genders "which in some sense institute and maintain relations of coherence and continuity among sex, gender, sexual practice, and desire" (*Gender Trouble* 23), and which reproduce and confirm structures of binary oppositions – male vs.

---

[5]Lorber suggests that "[t]ransvestites and transsexuals do not challenge the social construction of gender. Their goal is to be feminine women and masculine men" (20). For her, "bending gender rules and passing between genders does not erode but rather preserves gender boundaries" (21). In my readings of Jeanette Winterson's novels I hope to complicate this rather generalizing view.

female, masculine vs. feminine – that are traditionally and universally accepted as rational.

Butler has theorized the body as the site of the forcible materialization of the "ideal construct" of sex in the interest of a heteronormative social matrix: "It is not a simple fact or static condition of the body, but a process where regulatory norms materialize 'sex' and achieve this materialization through a forcible reiteration of those norms" (*Bodies That Matter* 1f.). Stressing the performative quality of discursive constructions of sex, gender, and sexuality, Butler argues that "the regulatory norms of 'sex' work in a performative fashion to constitute the materiality of bodies, and, more specifically, to materialize the body's sex, to materialize sexual difference in the service of the consolidation of the heterosexual imperative" (*Bodies That Matter* 2).

In hegemonic regimes genders are "manufactured" as internal essences through what Butler calls "a sustained set of acts, positioned through the genderized stylization of the body" ("Preface" xv). We are the actors, the performers of "certain bodily acts" which produce, "at an extreme, an hallucinatory effect of naturalized gestures" that we take for essential genders ("Preface" xv). Our normative gestures of gendering create "masculinity" and "femininity" which are then taken for natural expressions of "maleness" and "femaleness."

Butler discusses gender as a phenomenon that changes in different contexts, which therefore "does not denote a substantive being, but a relative point of convergence among culturally and historically specific sets of relations" (*Gender Trouble* 15). Thus, rather than being the natural psycho-social consequence of a biological essence that determines male and female bodies, gender is a construct, "the repeated stylization of the body, a set of repeated acts within a highly rigid regulatory frame that congeal over time to produce the appearance of substance, of a natural sort of being" (43f.). Butler emphasizes the complexity of gender and questions the possibility and wisdom of trying to develop a simple definition of the concept that can be applied to all human beings in all contexts. Rather, what is important is "the ability to track the travels of the term through public culture" ("The End" 184).

Desire is regulated as decisively and sometimes violently as gendering; just as the binary opposition of "male" as that which is not female and "female" as that which is not male is necessary for the heterosexual matrix of our society, so is the regulation of sexuality, the "heterosexualization of desire" (*Gender Trouble* 23). Through a system of "prohibitive laws" in Lacanian or "regulatory practices" in Foucauldian terms normative gender is directly linked with normative sexuality: Someone who *is* a man must not *desire* a man but must desire a woman and vice versa. "[U]nder conditions of normative heterosexuality," Butler writes, "policing gender is sometimes used as a way of securing heterosexuality" ("Preface" xii).

These "highly gendered regulatory schemas" are the preconditions for the appearance and existence of what Butler calls "intelligible bodies" (xi), bodies that fit into and make possible the heteronormative setup of society. However, for gender identity to become intelligible, identities are needed that do not fulfil the laws of gender following from sex and desire following from sex or gender and are therefore "unintelligible" in terms of the hegemonic cultural matrix.

The laws of compulsory heterosexuality thus also produce "the domain of unthinkable, abject, unlivable bodies" and with them lives that are threatened by social invisibility, marginality and psychosis (Butler, *Bodies That Matter*: xi). Therefore, the hierarchical notion of gender not only privileges men at the expense of women, it also creates a hierarchy of intelligible and abject bodies. Thus, gender needs to be questioned as to "what will and will not constitute an intelligible life, and how do presumptions about normative gender and sexuality determine in advance what will qualify as the 'human' and the 'livable'" (Butler, "Preface": xxii).

Concepts that Matter

Race and gender are no less real for being discursive constructions. The reality of race includes both the "pervasive tendency to apply the category of race" that Hacking bemoans ("Why Race" 104/1), and the fact that race is "a legal, political and historical reality which plays a real and constraining role," as Guillaumin insists (361), who describes the role of race as that of a "social category of exclusion and murder" (362).

However, since the 1980s, the political right as well as neo-conservative intellectuals such as Dinesh D'Souza have claimed that the United States has reached a postracial era in which racial differences – if they are noted at all – no longer determine a person's chances of success and in which, therefore, affirmative action or programs designed to curb inner-city poverty and violence are not only redundant but also repre-

sent a "reverse discrimination" (cf. D'Souza, *End*).[6] Yet, the comparative
economic success of the Black middle-class in the past decades and the
election of the Barack Obama as the first Black president of the United
States in 2008 have not rendered racial difference and racism non-issues
in this country. After Obama famously proclaimed in his speech at the
2004 Democratic National Convention that "[t]here is not a black America and a white America and Latino America and Asian America – there's
the United States of America" (273f.), he has often felt the need to refute
claims that Americans "have arrived at a 'postracial politics' or that we
already live in a color-blind society" (275):

> We know the statistics: On almost every single socioeconomic indicator,
> from infant mortality to life expectancy to employment to home owner-
> ship, black and Latino Americans in particular continue to lag far behind
> their white counterparts. In corporate boardrooms across America, mi-
> norities are grossly underrepresented; in the United States Senate, there
> are only three Latinos and two Asian members [...], and as I write today
> I am the chamber's sole African American. To suggest that our racial at-
> titudes play no part in these disparities is to turn a blind eye to both our
> history and our experience – and to relieve ourselves of the responsibility
> to make things right. (275f.)

In order to illustrate the extent to which African Americans suffer from
the socio-economic and psychological effects of being racialized "black,"
Obama reminds his readers of the catastrophe that ravaged the Gulf Coast
and the city of New Orleans in the summer of 2005 in the shape of Hurricane Katrina: "[I]t was obvious that many of Katrina's survivors had
been abandoned long before that hurricane struck. They were the faces
of any inner-city neighborhood in any American city, the faces of black
poverty – the jobless and almost jobless, the sick and soon to be sick,
the frail and the elderly" (271). In the wake of Katrina, neoconservative
proclamations of a postracial America reveal a mentality of blaming the
victims of racism for the effects of racialization, rather than highlighting
the failure of political and ethical efforts to tackle racist oppression and
marginalization in the United States.

Categories of race not only remain relevant in the face of persistent
racial inequality, but also because racial identity continues to be a source

---

[6]See for example the Hoover Institution, a think tank that funded not only
D'Souza, but also neo-conservative politicians like Condoleezza Rice and others.

of pride and empowerment for many members of minorities in the US, including many descendants of former slaves whose ancestors' struggle to end slavery and whose own fight for political equality and economic prosperity form a treasured history of liberation. For good reasons as well as bad, therefore, race still matters in the United States.

Scholars from fields as varied as critical legal studies, sociology, anthropology, philosophy, psychology, cultural or literary studies who have contributed to a critical theory of race believe that the attempt to eliminate the notion of race and racial difference from thinking, language, and politics would not be an appropriate response to this prevailing relevance.[7] Rather, Critical Race Theory, understanding race as socially and historically constructed instead of a bio-psychological essence, explores mechanisms and dynamics of the construction of racial groups and identities and enquires into hierarchies of power that are created and maintained through racial classification as well as in interaction with other categories of identity.[8] Here, race is accepted as a socio-economic, psychological as well as cultural reality; indeed, critical race studies regard this concept as a primary structural element of US society, an element which historically was designed and until today continues to promote and secure White supremacy. What is challenged and rejected, therefore, is the belief in essential differences between groups defined as races, a belief that is grounded in myths of biological, social or psychological differences that justify the subordination or privileging of certain groups. Critical race scholars and civil rights activists fight racism and promote an intersectional approach in the study of race in the United States; unlike neoconservative strategists, they do not eliminate racial categories and certainly do not declare race a thing of the past.

Just as a postracial America has been proclaimed in neoconservative quarters, a conservative backlash against feminism has been accompanied by claims about a postfeminist age following the alleged arrival at complete equality between men and women. Yet, while in the Western world women's rights have undoubtedly been strengthened over the course of the

---

[7]For a representative collection of essays from different academic fields that have been influential for Critical Race Studies, see Crenshaw et al.

[8]There are also critical race theorists who call for a complete abandonment of race talk. Glasgow identifies Anthony Appiah and Naomi Zack as "eliminationists" who "seek a broader rejection of a network of folk ideas, conceptions, and meanings, including intensions, associated with race" (128).

past three or four decades, gender boundaries have become more porous, and the normative binary of maleness and femaleness is being contested from multiple directions,[9] our societies continue to be patriarchal hegemonies based on hierarchical gender systems that subordinate women. Regardless of international efforts to emancipate women and to safeguard their human rights as well as successful steps taken towards gender equality in many societies, violence perpetrated against women all over the world still abounds, as the women's fund of the United Nation points out: "Globally, up to six out of every ten women experience physical and/or sexual violence in their lifetime" ("UNIFEM"). Likewise, murderous attacks against lesbian women, gay men, and transgenders in the recent past are shocking reminders of homo- and transphobia still rampant in the United States.[10] Moreover, we continue to live in hegemonic regimes in which prescriptive gender norms are used to violently regulate social interaction in ways that secure hierarchical set-ups that privilege maleness and heterosexuality.[11] The project of gender studies, therefore, continues to be an exploration and calling into question of the binary gender system together with its regulatory rules and laws.

Doing Gender, Doing Race – Performativity and Agency

If gender and race are constructions, who does the constructing and how is it done? Butler explains in *Gender Trouble* that femininity and masculinity are performatively produced and obey the laws and regulations that ensure gender coherence. They are produced in expectation of the eventual revelation of their "interior essence," an expectation, as Butler

[9] Among the causes of this development are an increasing political democratization that was used and perpetuated by poststructuralists, feminists, scholars and activists of gender studies as well as queer theory in conjunction with lively gay, lesbian, bisexual and transgender communities which have acquired a significant amount of visibility through their political activism and its coverage by the new media world-wide.

[10] See the stabbing to death of Sakia Gunn in 2003, the murder of Matthew Shepard in 1998, or the rape and shooting of Brandon Teena in 1993.

[11] See the controversy about Proposition 8 or the California Marriage Protection Act of November 2008 in which the definition of marriage was restricted to heterosexual couples, withdrawing the constitutional right to marry from same-sex couples.

points out, that "ends up producing the very phenomenon that it anticipates" ("Preface" xiv). Apart from creating the ideal of "sex" and the gender binary, performativity also produces the domain of abjection which
forms the "constitutive outside" of cultural intelligibility (Butler, *Bodies
That Matter*: xi).

As performativity, "gender is always a doing" (*Gender Trouble* 33).
However, this does not mean that individuals have a conscious choice
over how to "do gender" or that they can decide to produce gender in one
way today and in another tomorrow, as no subject exists prior to the deed,
which here means prior to gendering. "[T]here need not be a 'doer behind
the deed,'" Butler analyzes, "but ... the 'doer' is variably constructed in
and through the deed" (*Gender Trouble* 181). Yet significantly, the fact
that there is no un-constructed subject that "does gender" does not condemn us to being passive objects of a social determinism that precludes
collective or individual agency, because "performativity must be understood not as a singular or deliberate 'act,' but, rather, as the reiterative and
citational practice by which discourse produces the effects that it names"
(Butler, *Bodies That Matter*: 2). How, then, can the performativity of
gender contain the potential of agency within the matrix of a compulsory
heterosexuality that produces not only intelligible bodies but also a domain of abject ones?

Agency is made possible through what Butler calls "the iterability of
performativity," i.e., the fact that "performativity is not a single act, but a
repetition and a ritual, which achieves its effects through its naturalization
in the context of the body, understood, in part, as a culturally sustained
temporal duration" ("Preface" xxiv f.). In *Gender Trouble* Butler spells
out that

> all signification takes place within the orbit of the compulsion to repeat;
> 'agency', then is to be located within the possibility of a variation on that
> repetition. If the rules governing signification not only restrict, but enable
> the assertion of alternative domains of cultural intelligibility, i.e., new pos-
> sibilities for gender that contest the rigid codes of hierarchical binarisms,
> then it is only *within* the practices of repetitive signifying that a subver-
> sion of identity becomes possible. [...] [T]he very injunction to be given
> gender takes place through discursive routes: to be a good mother, to be
> a heterosexually desirable object, to be a fit worker, in sum, to signify a
> multiplicity of guarantees in response to a variety of different demands all
> at once. The coexistence or convergence of such discursive injunctions

produces the possibility of a complex reconfiguration and redeployment. (185)

Agency therefore can occur in required acts of fulfilling the regulatory law and to identify with the norms of the hegemonic cultural matrix. Where there are norms and rules that regulate the production of gendered bodies, failures to comply with their each and every aspect are bound to occur. These "instabilities, the possibilities for rematerialization [of bodies] opened up by this process," Butler argues, "mark one domain in which the force of the regulatory law can be turned against itself to spawn rearticulations that call into question the hegemonic force of that very regulatory law" (*Bodies That Matter* 2).

As gender is produced in countless rituals and reiterations, it allows for possibilities of construction. These possibilities also stretch to the sphere of sexuality and sexual practices, because "sexual practice has the power to destabilize gender" (Butler, "Preface": xi). Consequently, while "normative sexuality fortifies normative gender," "non-normative sexual practices call into question the stability of gender as a category of analysis" ("Preface" xi), adding pressure and producing psychic problems for those who fail to perform in accordance with the norm. To open up possibilities of gender and sexuality, thus presents an emancipatory project for those whose sexualities, sexual practices and indeed gender identities do not conform to heteronormativity leading to their classification as unintelligible, abject.

Haslanger proposes a concept of gender that takes up the idea of multiple possibilities: "Gender can be fruitfully understood as a higher-order genus that includes not only the hierarchical social positions of man and woman, but potentially other non-hierarchical social positions defined in part by reference to reproductive function" (43). For Butler, too, gender and gender practices are "sites of critical agency" (*Bodies That Matter* x), and a goal of that critical agency must be to "alter the very terms that constitute the 'necessary' domain of bodies through rendering unthinkable and unlivable another domain of bodies, those that do not matter in the same way" (xi).

The idea of construction through performative reiterations and citations has also become a corner stone for Critical Race Theory. In her article on Nella Larsen's novella *Passing*, Catherine Rottenberg quotes Mirón's and Inda's notion of race in order to declare her theoretical perspective: "'[R]ace does not refer to a pre-given subject. Rather, it works performatively to constitute the subject itself and only acquires a naturalized effect through repeated or reiterative naming of or reference to that subject'" (436f.). Linking Butlerian gender theory with Critical Race Theory, Rottenberg proposes that "race performativity is the power of discourse to bring about what it names through the citing or repetition of racial norms" (437). This adds an important aspect to the notion of race as an effect of the ascription of attributes, behaviors, and values onto an individual as expressed by Stubblefield and Appiah, who propose that "racial identities result from criteria governed practices of racial classification through the application of racial labels" (paraphrased in Gooding-Williams 241). Robert Gooding-Williams differentiates between "being black" and "being a black person": Racial classification racializes a person, for example as black, but "one becomes a black person by, and only by, acting under certain descriptions" (243). Gooding-Williams argues further that "individuals classified as black contribute to the construction of their racial identities" (241) and insists that there is "no black personhood apart from a black person's actions to which she or he could be true or untrue in the performance of those actions" (243). Consequently, there are, on the one hand, no essentialist racial selves prior to discursive construction and, on the other hand, individuals participate in their own racialization and the racialization of others as they reiterate racial laws and performatively repeat racial norms.

Yet in race, too, performativity as reiteration and citation contains a potential of agency. Rottenberg points out that "hegemonic regimes . . . cannot completely control the effects of their own discourse" and that, indeed, "the very repetition and circulation of different – and at times contradictory – racial norms create the possibility of subversion." Thus, "gaps and fissures can and do emerge within symbolic orders as subjects strive to embody regulatory ideals" (447). This underlines the palpable importance of a critical analysis of race for the project of racial emancipation and the struggle against doctrines of racial essentialism. As a critical analysis uncovers and indicates "gaps and fissures" within the symbolic discourse, new possibilities of identification open up, subverting essentialist notions of race and empowering the person who exercises a certain freedom of identification.

Reading Ian Hacking, Gooding-Williams notes that "our sense of ourselves and of the possibilities existing for us is, to a significant degree, a fiction of the descriptions we have available to us to conceptualize our intended actions and prospective lives" (242). Moreover, according to Hacking, "what I am deliberately doing depends on the possibilities of description ... [h]ence if new modes of description come into being, new possibilities of action come into being in consequence" ("Making up People" 231).

In her reply to Gooding-Williams, Judith Butler therefore calls for an "agential construction of race" which does not view race as an effect of racism, only:

> The demand for a theory that accounts for race as an effect that is at once lived and transformed in the course of its being lived suggests a move away from those mechanistically formulated versions of old construction to one in which norms are understood to have a revisable temporality. ("Conversational Break" 263)

She expresses doubt as to whether we will be able to do the necessary analytical, critical work on race without altering the notion of race as we know it – the folk concept that is evaluative and fraught with essentialisms. "For 'race' to become a sign of agency and cultural self-affirmation, its historicity must not be fully constrained from its putatively classificatory origins, the possibilities for its meanings must exceed the original purposes for which it was designed" (263).

The categories of race and gender thus have relevant characteristics and mechanisms of performative construction in common. Sally Haslanger summarizes the qualities shared by the two concepts and points out the possibilities for agency and subversion they entail:

> Both gender and race are real, and both are social categories. Neither gender nor race is chosen, but the forms they take can be resisted or mutated. Both race and gender (as we know it) are hierarchical, but the systems that sustain the hierarchy are contingent. And although the ideologies of race and gender and the hierarchical structures they sustain are substantively very different, they are intertwined. (51)

Yet, while "we need to begin understanding race as performative reiteration," as Rottenberg insists, "critics must be careful not to ignore the specificities of race norms" (438). This caution is supported by Butler who warns that "race and gender ought not to be treated as simple analogies" ("Preface" xvi). In her essay on passing, Rottenberg highlights "differences between race and gender as performative reiteration," which she identifies as differences in identification and the "desire to be" (439). Two ideal gender positions are available in the context of heteronormativity, where

> identification with 'being a woman' almost always implies (and is inextricably intertwined with) the desire to 'be a woman,' that is, a desire to live up to the norms of femininity in a particular symbolic order. Femininity is posited as desirable and as something that 'women' should approximate; wanting to 'be a woman' is coded as positive. (444)

"[I]n stark contrast to heteronormativity, where women are never encouraged to live up to norms of masculinity, nor are men urged to live up to feminine ideals," Rottenberg continues, in racist regimes that posit whiteness as the norm, "[t]he forced identification with blackness ... is not linked with a desire to live up to norms of blackness. Rather, black-identified subjects, in order to sustain a nonmarginal existence, are compelled and encouraged to privilege and thus 'desire-to-be white,' that is, to live up to attributes associated with whiteness" (444). Because of this, identification with the "opposite" norm has very different consequences for the regimes of gender and race: "Whereas female-identified subjects (subjects interpellated into the symbolic order as women) who desire to approximate masculinity (active, aggressive, etc.) are threatening to the powers that be, black-identified subjects who attempt to approximate whiteness have often been accepted by hegemony" (444). Significantly, Rottenberg does not mention counter-hegemonic norms of blackness that encourage a 'desire-to-be black' and are by no means embraced by African Americans only.[12] This constellation will be relevant to my discussion of Toni Morrison's *Paradise*.

On the other hand, as Butler states, "[t]he symbolic [...] is also always a racial industry, indeed, the reiterated practice of racializing interpellations" (*Bodies That Matter* 18), and the intersections of race, gender, and sexuality become crucial. Moreover, she argues that "the social regulation of race emerges not simply as another, fully separable, domain of power from sexual difference or sexuality, but that its 'addition' subverts the monolithic workings of the heterosexual imperative" (18). In her own essay on Larsen's *Passing*, Butler investigates the interrelatedness of gender and race:

> [T]he domain of socially instituted norms ... is composed of racializing norms, and ... they exist not merely alongside gender norms, but are artic-

---

[12]I thank Katja Linke for reminding me of this.

ulated through one another. Hence, it is no longer possible to make sexual difference prior to racial difference or, for that matter, to make them into fully separable axes of social regulation and power. ("Passing, Queering" 182)

In a later publication, Butler again stresses that "racial presumptions invariably underwrite the discourse on gender in ways that need to be made explicit" ("Preface" xvi). For her, then, "the question to ask is not whether the theory of performativity is transposable onto race, but what happens to the theory when it tries to come to grips with race" (xvi). This question will be relevant especially for my reading of Morrison's novel *Paradise* in Chapter 4.

However, while the idea of performativity and reiteration is relevant for understanding the construction of both gender and race, there are significant differences with regard to the respective aims and directions of the potential for agency inherent in the two categories. Poststructuralist gender theories, apart from exposing mechanisms of gendering and the regulation of sexuality as well as their consequences for the individual, have been successfully translated into activism and life styles that blur gender boundaries, open up and live new possibilities of gender, desire, and sexuality. In contrast to this, calling into question a supposed race binary and blurring the boundaries between "races" is relevant to critical race studies only in so far as it exposes the constructedness of race and challenges the essentialist folk discourse of the concept. Activism in connection with race critique instead aims on the one hand at complicating crude images of "Blackness," "Asianness," "Whiteness," etc., and to highlight the intersections of race with categories of identity such as gender, class, sexuality, religion. On the other hand, it exposes strategies of racialization that create power hierarchies and lead to the subordination of non-hegemonic groups, causing inequity between social groups and individuals. Moreover, racial identities that have been categorized as less valuable or sophisticated than whiteness are celebrated for their cultural richness and their contributions to US history and culture, thus working toward and calling for a rehabilitation and emancipation of African Americans, Chicanos/as, Native Americans, and other racial minorities. Therefore, while critical race studies and gender studies both call into question the respective categories and investigate their power to create hierarchies in society, the relative diversity of existing racial categories diminishes the urge or necessity to blur the boundaries of race and create alternative racial identities through race performances and subversive citations of regulatory race laws – goals which, in the face of a restrictive gender binarism, are highly relevant and legitimate for gender studies.

Literature and the Politics of Race and Gender

As I explained in the opening paragraphs of this introduction, the initial assumption of my study is that works of literature play an important role not only in the theorization of the concepts of race and gender, but also in the search for subversive possibilities of gendering and constructing non-hierarchical racial identities, in the discussion of perspectives and strategies that challenge hegemonic systems of race and gender. As Barbara Christian stated so passionately:

> [P]eople of color have always theorized – but in forms quite different from the Western form of abstract logic. And I am inclined to say that our theorizing [...] is often in narrative forms, in the stories we create, in riddles and proverbs, in the play with language, since dynamic rather than fixed ideas seem more to our liking. [...] And women, at least the women I grew up around, continuously speculated about the nature of life through pithy language that unmasked the power relations of their world. ("Race for Theory" 38)

The task Henry Louis Gates, Jr., set scholars of US-American literature and culture more than twenty years ago, still informs my discussions of Toni Morrison's work: "We must ... analyze the ways in which writing relates to race, how attitudes toward racial differences generate and structure literary texts by us *and* about us" ("Writing 'Race'" 15).

Apart from being a medium of explorations and discussions of race, literature strikes me also as being a valuable source material for an analysis of mechanisms of gendering and their effects on individuals; I furthermore consider literary texts important tools for the imaginative construction of subversive alternatives of gender. Judith Butler highlights language as a major site of the discursive construction of gender and therefore as a critical instrument of inquiry and innovation: "If gender itself is naturalized through grammatical norms, as Monique Wittig has argued, then the alteration of gender at the most fundamental epistemic level will be conducted, in part, through contesting the grammar in which gender is given" ("Preface" xix). As "literature is, of necessity, political" (Christian, "Race for Theory": 49), Butler points out that "the production of texts can be one way of reconfiguring what will count as the world" (*Bodies That Matter* 19).

However, I do not propose to read Jeanette Winterson's and Toni Morrison's texts as collections of recipes for the construction of gender-equal and non-racist societies. Rather, I consider them part of their authors' intellectual efforts to grapple with gender in Winterson's and race in Morrison's case. With Christian I want to see literature, and the texts of these two authors in particular, as "necessary nourishment for their people and one way by which they come to understand their lives better" ("Race for Theory" 39), rather than "an occasion for discourse among critics" (39).[13] I want to suggest that Morrison's and Winterson's writings become a source of strength for their readers because of their political contents and their powerful questioning of hegemonic notions of race and gender. As Gates underlines, "one important benefit of the development of subtle and searching modes of 'reading' is that these can indeed be brought to bear upon relationships that extend far beyond the confined boundaries of a text" ("Writing 'Race'" 17).

Because of the illusive nature of both gender and race – an illusiveness that does not diminish their pervasiveness as powerful concepts that regulate our realities – I want to adopt in this study an attitude of questioning and querying. After several years of analyzing the notions of gender and sex, Butler comes to the following conclusion:

> Sexual difference is not a given, not a premise, not a basis on which to build a feminism; [...] rather, as *a question* that prompts a feminist inquiry, it is something that cannot quite be stated, that troubles the grammar of the statement, and that remains, more or less permanently, to interrogate. ("The End" 178)

Race, although it is not a natural fact but "an apparition" (Glasgow 155), also wields tremendous power as a performative reiteration, with deleterious as well as empowering effects on individuals and groups of people. The statement Butler formulates cautiously for sex/gender therefore is also true for race: It is "not a thing, not a fact, not a presupposition,

---

[13] I am aware that Christian is writing explicitly about works by African American women authors and their importance for their Black audiences. Yet, in my view, her statement would be just as true for many of Winterson's readers for whom her novels have become "necessary nourishment and one way by which they come to understand their lives better" ("Race for Theory" 39).

but rather a demand for rearticulation that never quite vanishes – but also never quite appears" ("The End" 186). Neither Morrison nor Winterson, I propose, attempt to finally resolve the problematic issue of racial and gender difference, but with their literary texts they question hegemonic regimes and "leave that question open, troubling, unresolved, propitious" (191f.), encouraging their readers to join in their critical reflection on racial and gender identities.

Set-up of the Study

Toni Morrison's and Jeanette Winterson's respective explorations of issues of race and gender in their fictional texts form the primary interest of this study. On first sight, my decision to focus on these two authors might seem arbitrary, if not odd, given the fact that one is American and the other British and that they have hardly ever been the subjects of one and the same study before.[14] Yet there is a remarkable parallel in Morrison's and Winterson's oeuvre which to me seems a compelling reason to discuss their work side by side in this study: Both authors produced texts in which they challenge the very foundations of the concepts they thematize – Morrison's *Paradise* and Winterson's *Written on the Body*. They do so by imagining in these narratives the absence or ineffectiveness of race or gender as a means of social regulation and identification; they investigate possibilities and consequences of "racelessness" and "genderlessness," respectively. How Morrison and Winterson proceed to construct these absences of race or gender, to what critical effects, and whether they are in fact suggesting that we should eliminate these categories because they rely on essentialist notions of purity and exclusivity are the overarching questions of this study.[15]

---

[14] Together with works by other contemporary authors who write in English, novels by Morrison and Winterson are discussed as exemplary texts in a number of studies that focus on a particular topos, such as the girl in literature (Saxton), the fantastic in contemporary women's fiction (Armitt), feminist criticism in literary texts (Felski), monstrous bodies in women's writing (Curti), or the unconscious in works of literature (Terzieva-Artemis). These studies are not devoted to the two authors specifically.

[15] As mentioned earlier, Glasgow identifies Anthony Appiah and Naomi Zack as "eliminationists" who "seek a broader rejection of a network of folk ideas, conceptions, and meanings, including intensions, associated with race" (128), while

This closely defined research interest presents a novel perspective on Toni Morrison's work in so far as it brings into critical focus the author's struggle with and fundamental questioning of the notions of race; earlier work on Morrison has concentrated on her celebrations and examinations of Black identity in connection with African American traditions, culture, and community (Bryce Bjork; Christian, *Black Feminist Criticism*; Harding and Martin; Kella), her exploratory rewriting of US history from an African American point of view (Kubitschek; Lehmann; Tally, *(Hi)Stories*), or her dissections of the mechanisms and the traumatic effects of slavery on Black men and women (Mori; Sollors and Diedrich; Bryant; Durrant). My focus on Morrison's raising and scrutinizing the "troubling, unresolved, propitious" question of race and racial identities, to transfer Butler's words into the context of race, must necessarily include a discussion of some of the topics mentioned above, particularly those that concern the intersections of race and gender. Yet the author's uneasiness with the category of race is the motivation and driving force of my inquiry.

My perspective on Jeanette Winterson's work is influenced by Butlerian theories of gender which, in my understanding, engage in a dialogue between feminism and lesbian-feminism and a poststructuralist questioning of hegemonic power structures. Winterson has been read as a lesbian author (Farwell, "Lesbian Narrative"; Griffin; Hinds; Moore; C. Allen; Palmer, *Contemporary*; Stowers, "Erupting"), she has been viewed through a feminist lens (González; Pearce, *Feminism*; Quadflieg), and was criticized for allegedly betraying her feminist politics to lesbianism or a postmodernist relativism (Wingfield; Pearce, "Emotional"; Armitt; Duncker). Winterson has been analyzed as a postmodern writer (Burns, "Fantastic Language"; Gade; Lee; Maagaard; Palmer, "Postmodern Trends"; Rubinson, *Fiction*; Taylor Merleau; Belsey), as well as a postmodern lesbian author (Farwell, "Postmodern Lesbian Text"), and she has been approached from the perspective of queer theory (Harris; Lanser; Langland; Ramsey). However, I have no interest in trying to categorize Winterson either as a feminist or lesbian-feminist author, or as a poststructuralist/postmodernist who cannot at the same time be committed to

Haslanger proposes as a goal for "the project of feminism" the eventual elimination of the notion of women – and, per analogy, men – though not of "females" and "males" (47).

feminist, lesbian-feminist, or queer politics. Rather, by investigating her far-reaching critique of the notion of gender and her envisioning of new possibilities of gender, sexuality, and identity this study follows those critics who discuss from various theoretical perspectives Winterson's experiments with the notions of time and space (Lemke; Bengtson; del Mar Asensio Arostegui), the body (Curti; Lindenmeyer; Kilian; de Zordo; Rubinson, "Body Languages"; Palmer, "Foreign Bodies"; Haslett), love and romance (Belsey; Andermahr; Pearce, "Written"; Ganteau, "Fantastic"), as well as narration and identity (Fludernik; Kauer). Like Doan, Nunn, and Stevens, I emphasize the critical, deconstructive potential of the possibilities of gender and sexuality explored in Winterson's works of the 1980s and early 1990s, but I consider the writer's early work – and *Written on the Body* in particular – as more radically challenging to hegemonic norms and notions of identity than earlier criticism has granted. Indeed, I want to suggest that in this work the author is ultimately toppling the category of gender as we know it.

In order to make transparent the theoretical and political perspectives from which Morrison and Winterson engage in their literary explorations of race and gender, I begin with analyses of the authors' public statements and essayistic writing on these concepts in Part One: The Power of Fiction. My sources will be interviews with the authors, literary and theoretical essays by Toni Morrison and Jeanette Winterson, as well as newspaper columns and radio broadcasts, of which Winterson makes frequent use. In Chapter 1, I will consider Winterson's productive juxtaposition of her quasi-modernist passion for art, words, and canonical literature in English with her feminist politics, her ambivalent stance toward radical lesbianism, and her experiments with postmodern notions of ruptured space, discontinuous time, fragmented bodies and identities. This chapter aims to extrapolate the author's belief in art and literature to change realities and enhance human existence, and to spell out the enormous task she sets for fiction in general and her own writing in particular.

Chapter 2 is dedicated to Morrison's complex relationship with the concept of race. I trace the author's fascination with African American history and reverence for Black culture, her trust in the empowering quality of Black identity, and her longing for a home in US-American society for people of African descent. Moreover, I aim to elucidate Morrison's acute awareness of the tension between the importance of racial identity as a source of empowerment and the history of race as a phantasmal construct designed to evaluate and subjugate colonial and imperial subjects. The author's own race debate culminates in her essay "Home," a text in which she discusses how race matters and must be unmattered at the same time and outlines how she approaches both of these tasks in her writing.

The results of my analyses in terms of the authors' thoughts on the power of art and literature to contribute to and thereby influence theoretical discourses and effect changes in social realities, as well as of Morrison's own notion of race and Winterson's specific notion of gender, provide the framework for my readings of a number of key texts. In particular, I will juxtapose the authors' theoretical stances and the aims they profess to follow with their writing and their fictional narratives. For this endeavor, I selected works I consider especially suited to illustrating their authors' respective inquiries into the notions of race and gender, to demonstrate the development of their arguments and of questions they raise and to highlight possible discrepancies between beliefs or politics the writers express in nonfictional text and meanings transported by their fictions. These key fictional texts include Morrison's short story "Recitatif" and her novel *Paradise*, furthermore Winterson's novels *Oranges Are Not the Only Fruit*, *The Passion*, *Sexing the Cherry*, and *Written on the Body*.

Part Two of the study, Questioning the Notion of Race, is dedicated to the two Morrison texts. My analysis of "Recitatif" in Chapter 3 aims to highlight what I take to be one of the text's strongest messages, which nevertheless has received comparatively little critical attention so far: Rather than trying to assign to the protagonists racial identities which Morrison carefully withholds (Rayson), or attempting to decode text passages that are purposely ambiguous in their potential to racialize (Goldstein-Shirley, "Race and Response"; Abel), I want to examine Morrison's critique of race as a dominant marker of difference in the United States. When the obtrusive question of the uncertain racial identities – the bait laid out for the readers by the announcement of the racial difference of the protagonists – is allowed to remain unresolved, what other differences will move into focus? What shared traumas will be uncovered, what individual or shared dreams become visible? A discussion of these questions will lead to a reappraisal of contributions Morrison makes to the race debate with her short story "Recitatif."

In *Paradise*, Morrison's seventh novel, I see the author's most radical interrogation of the concept of race to date. Chapter 4 analyzes the ritualistic construction in this fiction of what amounts to a religion of pure blackness in the town of Ruby. Taking as a theoretical point of reference Clifford Geertz' notion of religion as an important means of structuring the life of people in chaotic situations, I explore the myths that found this "religion" and the creed that follows from them, asking which rites structure its exercise, and how its structural integrity is safeguarded. The intersection of race and gender will be discussed here in the context of the all-Black town, where women are at once worshipped as the reproductive vessels of racial purity and subjected to violent regulation as potential agents of racial pollution. Furthermore, Ruby's gender norms and gender relations influence the relationship between the citizens of the town and the women in the neighboring Convent.

This community of women will be understood and analyzed as a contact zone (Pratt; Lenz), a heterogeneous borderland community (Anzaldúa) grounded in an eclectic, uninstitutionalized spirituality. One of the most striking characteristic of the women's spirituality is what I regard as their renunciation of race as a marker of difference. Yet, does the woman-centered, raceless Convent represent simply the opposite of patriarchal, racialist Ruby, as has repeatedly been suggested by more unsympathetic reviewers (Kakutani; Bent)? Is there not a much closer – and more complex – connection between the town and its neighbor than may appear at first sight? According to Butler, "it seems crucial to rethink the scenes of reproduction, and hence, of sexing practices not only as ones through which a heterosexual imperative is inculcated, but as ones through which boundaries of racial distinction are secured as well as contested" (*Bodies That Matter* 18). Drawing upon theories of race and gender as performative citations and reiterations, I aim to illustrate how in *Paradise* Morrison explores normative regulations of gender and sexuality as major building blocks of racial essentialism and the concept of race as such. Moreover, by analyzing the ways in which the Convent women build their community and interact with one another I hope to delineate the alternative idea of race which I suggest Morrison envisages in *Paradise*.

Part Three: Questioning the Notion of Gender, returns to the work of Jeanette Winterson. In Chapter 5 I will be looking at her first three novels, *Oranges Are Not the Only Fruit*, *The Passion*, and *Sexing the Cherry*. I am interested in the author's exploration of the capacity of lesbianism to subvert heteronormative conceptions of gender and identity constructions. Furthermore, what possibilities of gender does Winterson open up in her fiction? In what ways do non-normative sexual practices and reiterations of gender norms call into question the meaning of "woman" and "man" in her three early novels? How do postmodern notions of time, space, and the body contribute to alternative forms of gendering and to what effect for those who fail to conform to the laws of hetero-patriarchal regimes? As Winterson's texts also probe the function of genre rules for the regulation of gender performances in the interest of the preservation of heteronormativity, in what ways are they exploring modes of bending rules of genre in order to de-essentialize gender?

In my view, *Written on the Body* presents the zenith of Winterson's inquiry into gender; Chapter 6 therefore is dedicated entirely to this fiction. While her first novels, despite the radicalism of their depiction of subversive interpretations of gender norms and gendered bodies, retain the bipolarity of maleness and femaleness as a frame of reference, her fourth, I want to argue, calls into question the very notion of a fixed gender identity through the invention of a genderless protagonist in a romance narrative. But what are the consequences of genderlessness? Butler claims that it is "as important to think about how and to what end bodies are constructed" as it is "to think about how and to what end bodies are not constructed" (*Bodies That Matter* 16). She furthermore highlights the importance of asking "how bodies which fail to materialize provide the necessary 'outside,' if not the necessary support, for the bodies which, in materializing the norm, qualify as bodies that matter" (16). In my analysis I aim to show that Winterson's narrator in *Written on the Body* not only requires the expulsion of gender markers from the English language in a linguistic construction of genderlessness such as Wittig called for. The genderlessness of the protagonist, the narrator's unintelligible, abject body, also has substantive effects on relationships with other human beings, on the concept of love, as well as notions of identity.

One of the basic assumptions of this study is that the writing of Toni Morrison and Jeanette Winterson is characterized by a decidedly political impetus; with their public statements, their interviews, essays, and fictional narratives the authors engage in the theoretical and political discourses of race and gender, respectively. In 2000, Sally Haslanger claims that "it is our responsibility to define gender and race for our theoretical purposes. The world itself can't tell us what gender is. The same is true for race" (52). She continues to outline her goal with the suggestion that "rather than worrying, 'what is gender, really?' or 'what is race, really?' I think we should begin by asking (both in the theoretical and political sense) what, if anything, we want them to be" (52). As I hope to show in this study, Winterson and Morrison have been doing this work already since the 1980s. Not only are they investigating and not so much "worrying" about, as Haslanger puts it, what our traditional concepts of gender and race entail, how they shape our realities, and what consequences follow for whom from these regulatory processes – analyses that contribute to the efforts to denaturalize gender and race that Butler calls for (cf. "Preface" xx). With their literary texts, in ways that are at times clearer and more radical than their theoretical statements, they have also begun to re-define these concepts by opening up possibilities of gendering and racializing that "force a radical rearticulation of what qualifies as bodies that matter, ways of living that count as 'life,' lives worth protecting, lives worth saving, lives worth grieving" (Butler, *Bodies That Matter*: 16). The following examination aims to trace this work in its theoretical and artistic aspects and to gauge its critical scope.

Part I

The Power of Fiction

1   Gender and the Art of Fiction

Since the instant critical and public success in 1985 of her first novel, *Oranges Are Not the Only Fruit*,[1] Jeanette Winterson has become a well-known writer on the threshold to the literary canon who is blessed with a faithful and numerous multi-national readership.[2] However, the work she produced after her first three fictions has received both the highest compliments and damning criticism.[3] Two of the more severe accusa-

---

[1] Some editions of Winterson's books quote the veteran US-American author and literary critic Gore Vidal who said after the publication of *Oranges* that he considered Winterson "the most interesting young writer [he has] read in twenty years" (see e.g. *The World and Other Places* with reference to *Oranges*). *Oranges* won the 1985 Whitbread Award for First Novel, and the TV series of the same title, to which Winterson wrote the screenplay, was awarded the BAFTA (British Academy of Film and Television Arts). *The Passion* won the John Llewellyn Rhys Memorial Prize of 1987, and in the wake of the publication of *Sexing the Cherry* Winterson received the E.M. Forster Award from the American Academy of Arts and Letters. In 2006 Winterson was awarded the OBE (Order of the British Empire) for services to literature.

[2] In 1992 *The Guardian* praises her as "the most highly esteemed writer of her generation" (Messud). Harold Bloom in *The Western Canon* considers *The Passion* a modern classic.

[3] Throughout much of the 1990s, Winterson had a tense, difficult relationship with the media, especially with newspaper journalists and reviewers, but also with the literary establishment. As a young and little-known writer she openly expressed pride in her own work, confidently stressing its innovative linguistic and narratological potential, and berating reviewers who did not share her enthusiasm. Such attitude and behavior quickly earned her a reputation of indulging in hubris and self-aggrandizement (see e.g. Lainsbury, Lambert's "I don't," and Gerrard's "Ultimate"). In combination with accounts she volunteered of early affairs with wealthy married women, this resulted in mean-spirited caricatures of her, as well as caustic criticism of her work. Winterson experienced this period as a witch-hunt against her as a gifted working-class lesbian author, orchestrated by the

tions leveled at Winterson and her writing concern an alleged proneness
to elitism and escapism, which supposedly derives from her affinity with
modernism. Ironically and yet understandably, given Winterson's presumed agreement with the elitist ideology of more conservative modernism, these charges are tied to the very characteristics that earn the author enthusiastic praise from her admirers: her poetically intense language
and the innovative form of her narratives.[4] In the following, I will therefore discuss Winterson's own views on the tasks she understands art in
general and her own writing in particular to fulfill in society.

1.1 The Mind-Altering Possibilities of Art

Jeanette Winterson has always professed enormous faith in art's ability
to achieve change in society. "The power of art is so immense that even
its dilutions are homeopathic," she writes in her essay collection *Art Objects* in 1995 (*AO* 66).[5] This faith is as deeply rooted as her conviction that
Western society of the late twentieth century must change, poisoned as she
sees it to be by "the spirit, that [life] is pointless and mean" (*AO* 20). Journalists and critics attribute much importance to her working-class origins

---

(male) establishment and eagerly executed and perpetuated by the sensationalist
media. In 1995 she left London to live in comparative seclusion in the country-
side. She returned to the city, to a less hermitic lifestyle, and to a more relaxed
relationship with the press only toward the end of the decade. At different times
Winterson has had columns in *The Guardian*, in *The Times* of London, as well
as in other dailies and journals in Britain and France. In 1992 she founded the
publishing company Great Moments Ltd. with Margaret Reynolds and took the
management of her professional affairs into her own hands. Since the year 2000
she has run a popular official website, www.jeanettewinterson.com designed by
Pedalo Limited, taking charge of the construction of her public image and the
marketing of her texts.

[4]Thus, while some critics praise Winterson's poetic style of writing (cf. e.g. Berch;
Hancock; Jaggi), her fellow-writer Michèle Roberts is quoted with the remark
that her "middle period was about art for art's sake, language for language's
sake; she became suspicious of storytelling" (Jaggi). It is this "middle period"
culminating in *Written on the Body*, on which the main focus of my engagement
with this writer lies.

[5]Jeanette Winterson, *Art Objects: Essays on Ecstacy and Effrontery* (London:
Vintage, 1996). All further reference is to this edition.

in the Northwestern English mill-town of Accrington and to her outspoken lesbianism.[6] But while all of her writing more or less overtly addresses issues of classism, sexism, and homophobia,[7] the changes which she believes and wants art to work in society are aimed at a general, psycho-philosophical level. They are meant to affect the human soul and people's perception and interpretations of reality.

In contemporary Western society two conflicting conceptions of art exist. They could be summarized as the idea of art as cheap entertainment for the masses on the one hand, and the notion of art as luxury available only to an economic and/or educational elite on the other. Winterson regards these mass culture and high art approaches as equally far removed from the truth. With regard to the former she writes: "Art is not amnesia, and the popular idea of books as escapism or diversion, misses altogether what art is. There is plenty of escapism and diversion to be had, but it cannot be had from real books, real pictures, real music, real theatre" (*AO* 111). Her reactions to the latter are brief to the point of being brusque: "I don't understand why people talk of art as luxury" (Jaggi); "[a]rt is not rarefied or elitist" (Campbell-Johnston), because "art leaves nobody out" (*AO* 20).

But when Winterson speaks of "real art," which characteristics does she assign to it? "I believe art is about changing the way people think," she affirms in an interview (Ivry). In a later, more cautious statement

---

[6]Indeed, the curiosity of journalists in the sex life of Jeanette Winterson has often surpassed their interest in her art, and even authors who in the late 1990s express admiration for her writing and respect for her perseverance in the face of an adverse press, are unable to resist the temptation to slip in the occasional reference to alleged sexual services to bored housewives in her early London years (cf. for example Brooks; Hancock; Lambert, "Winterson"). Winterson's own attitude toward lesbianism and the label of lesbian literature will be discussed later in this chapter.

[7]Chloë Taylor Merleau's study of postmodern ethics in Winterson's novels presents the most thorough and affirmative examination to date of the author's efforts to protest through her writing against the marginalization of what Taylor Merleau calls "the carious other of society: [...] women, lesbians, animals, the homeless, the illegal, the abjected, and the poor" (102). Her analysis focuses on *Art and Lies* (1994), the novel Winterson published after *Written on the Body* and the very text which occasions Gerrard's critique that due to her "cocooned seclusion" the author "cares about the word, not the world."

she slightly moderates this view of art as a meaning-bestowing, quasi-religious institution to the suggestion that "[art is] a mind-altering possibility" (Jaggi). Whether she phrases her conviction with vehemence or caution, Winterson believes that art, if it is to deserve this name, alters the society in which it occurs, because it alters the people who encounter it. "True art, when it happens to us, challenges the 'I' that we are," she writes in an essay (*AO* 15). Art that is sincere – and I suggest that this is what she means by the seemingly essentialist attributes of "true" or "real" – questions the art consumers' long-held beliefs, prejudices, and ready-made answers to inquire about what we perceive to be the realities of our existence.[8] When, in an essay that seems to repeat many of the more conservative tenets of the modernist movement with regard to the dangers urban modern mass culture allegedly poses to high art, she insists that "art objects" to the "primitive doomsaying" of the money culture of the market economy, to the impersonality of industrial society, to the confinement to narrow boundaries" (*AO* 19), Winterson does not mean that art should distance itself from the "masses." Rather, her idea of art is clearly interventionist. She argues that, contrary to what she regards as the shallow, insincere entertainment promoted by the media, real art cannot leave us undisturbed. It will unsettle our sense of orientation in the realities we have constructed for ourselves and nudge us on to discomforting explorations of new ground. Winterson calls this interventionist quality the "riskiness of art," and explains: "The riskiness of Art, the reason why it affects us, is not the riskiness of its subject matter, it is the risk of creating a new way of seeing, a new way of thinking" (Bilger 71).

Winterson tasks literature, her means of artistic expression, with providing a forum for innovative ways of seeing and thinking. Against charges of escapism and in defiance of what she believes to be neo-Victorian, neo-realist trends in contemporary English-language literature, she asserts that the purpose of literature is "to open up spaces in a closed world" (Reynolds, "Interview Winterson": 11), spaces that will afford the reader "[f]reedom, not escapism," and "the chance to push the spirit past the confines of the everyday" (Winterson, "Books and Family"). From the worlds offered in books readers will take to their usually hetero-patriarchally structured everyday realities something that will empower

---

[8] In her Winterson profile of the year 2000, Helen Brown calls the author "a knight in quest of essential art."

them to render that reality less hierarchical. Winterson has a very distinct notion of what in her own books it shall be that stays with the readers to help them alter their ways of seeing and thinking and thus affect reality. Convinced that art can achieve change, she sets her own writing ambitious assignments.

1.2   The Riskiness of Art

Spurred on by the "extraordinary releasing power" Winterson feels to be present in art (79), she sets out to work on her readers' mind. Almost defiantly she declares: "I don't want to please the reader, I want to change them, to expand their imaginations, seduce them, free them, take them to a place they haven't been before" (Jaggi). There is indeed a certain amount of didacticism in Winterson's work; it is strong enough to provoke a critic's comment that "her texts seem to demand that the reader/critic listens hard for an Authorial voice," and her advice to consider that "in spite of the death of the Author," in Winterson's writing "there is the intention of the text to reckon with" (Humphries 14, 15). In order to achieve her goals and to make her texts succeed in fulfilling their intentions, Winterson develops and pursues in her writing a long-term program that she started in her very first fiction, and which she continues to pursue through all of her works, including *Lighthousekeeping* (2004), *Tanglewreck* (2006), her first fiction for young readers, and *The Stone Gods* (2007), her most recent novel.[9]

Two seemingly contradictory concepts form the poles between which she develops her theoretical and artistic standpoint: "reality" and "imagination." Importantly, Winterson's interest in what is understood to be "real" differs from what she sees as the interest of mass education and the mass media in reality. "Art," she writes in *Art Objects*, "is not documentary. It may incidentally serve that function in its own way but its true effort is to open to us dimensions of the spirit and of the self that

---

[9]Ganteau also works with the assumption that Winterson has a "consistent programme" ("Hearts Object" 170). In his analysis he concentrates on the author's methods of "breaking the canon open, of breaking away from it so as to achieve an ethical breakthrough, ultimately" (165). Winterson's ethics and of her innovative use of the canon will be of interest at various points in this chapter as well as in the next.

normally lie smothered under the weight of living" (*AO* 137). Instead of
turning away from "the weight of living," however, Winterson takes it as
an anchoring to her writing. The world of the everyday becomes a starting point for her efforts to get at and express a reality that is beyond – and
more powerful – than the superficial, obvious reality of objects and rules
that surround us. She explains to an interviewer:

> I believe in art as the true means of not telling the truth. You're not setting
> out to deceive. You're setting out to find an ultimate reality. Lies are just
> lies. [...] What art tries to do is cut through all that and come up with
> something that really is objective, and which is trying all at once to deal
> with the mundane tables-and-chairs world of the everyday and also with
> imaginative psychic worlds which we know are there and which we so
> often split off. (Brooks)

The "ultimate reality" Winterson has in mind is the reality of human imagination, intimately related to the material facts of our existence, but forcefully separated from it in contemporary Western society and in consequence scandalously neglected. To get at imaginary reality, however, she
does not set her fictions in outer space, nor does she situate her characters
in utopian social systems of the past or the future.[10] Rather, her characters
find themselves in very specific historic eras; we can place them in recognizable geographic locations, and we usually get to know their socio-
economic circumstances. Jeanette in *Oranges* grows up in a working-class
environment of the 1960s in north-west England;[11] Villanelle and Henri
in *The Passion* live in Venice and roam the steppes of Russia during the
Napoleonic wars.[12] Villanelle works in a Venetian casino and is later sold
into prostitution in the Grande Armée by her husband; her friend is the
son of poor French farmers and joined Napoleon's army as an assistant to

---

[10]There are significant exceptions to this rule, but they are not in the focus of this
study: *Boating* and *Art & Lies* are set in a pseudo-Old Testament society and in
a dystopian London around the year 2000, respectively. *Tanglewreck* connects
contemporary London with inhabited planets and black holes, and the narrative
of *The Stone Gods* explores the effects of human intervention into nature on an
earth-like, barren planet in the future and on the Easter Islands in the eighteenth
century.

[11]Jeanette Winterson, *Oranges Are Not the Only Fruit* (1985; London: Vintage,
1994). All further reference is to this edition.

[12]Jeanette Winterson, *The Passion* (London: Vintage, 1996). All further reference
is to this edition.

the cook. In *Sexing the Cherry* the Dog-Woman experiences the Puritan Revolution in seventeenth-century London, where she lives on the banks of the Thames from the proceeds of her breeding of racing dogs.[13] Her adopted son Jordan joins King James's gardener on his travels to explore the globe and bring back exotic fruit.

As we read about the lives of these characters in their specific situations, we also witness the realities of their imagination. While these realities are closely connected to their "real-life" experiences, they allow us insights into worlds of fears, wishes, intimate thoughts, and into imaginative alternatives created in the minds of the characters. Jeanette's reality in north-west England, her struggle to free herself from the powerful influence of her Pentecostal mother and their homophobic church is paralleled by the reality of her imagination in which Winnet Stonejar is confronted with the strong emotional ties that bind her to the sorcerer to whom she is apprenticed. On his way home from Russia, Henri gets to know Venice as the illusive, shape-shifting "city of mazes" as it exists in the imagination of his friend Villanelle (*Passion* 49); and Jordan, while he journeys with the English explorer John Tradescant, follows his longing to discover himself and visits towns and islands that cannot be found on any map.

Winterson describes herself as a writer who is "very much rooted in the everyday," but for whom the everyday is "quite a miraculous experience" (Marvel 168/4). This perception is reflected by her characters: Young Jeanette believes every man to be a pig in disguise and as a youngster frequently converses with an orange demon. The Dog-Woman is of gigantic proportions, and yet she can become invisible to the people around her. Villanelle is born with webbed feet which enable her to walk on water, and Patrick, a defrocked Irish priest in the service of Napoleon, is blessed with eyesight that allows him to watch a woman undress in her house "some fifteen miles away" (*Passion* 22). Reality for Winterson is multi-dimensional, different for every individual, depending on their socio-economic background, their gender identities, on relationships they entertain or are prevented from entertaining, and on experiences that result from them and feed into the worlds of their imaginations. People chance upon more than one reality in the course of their lives; theirs is not

---

[13] Jeanette Winterson, *Sexing the Cherry* (London: Vintage, 1996). All further reference is to this edition.

a universe but a "multi-verse," a term coined by Silver, the protagonist of *Tanglewreck*.

"What art presents is much more than the daily life of you and me," Winterson insists (*AO* 133) and formulates what can be regarded as her artistic creed: "The charge laid on the artist is to bring back visions" (*AO* 148). The "ultimate realities" her heroines and heroes explore in their dreams, journeys of the mind, and emotional excursions into other times and realms show them inner strengths they never knew they had, facets of their personality that had been hidden to them. As they discover the realities of their imagination, new subject positions and possible identities spread before them, offering them alternative choices for their everyday lives and ways out of their personal predicaments. Thus, Jeanette embraces the otherness that sets her apart from her community – an inquisitive and rebellious spirit, coupled with her budding lesbian identity – and finds the strength to escape the narrow confines of the life mapped out for her by her mother. Jordan sets out to become a hero like his mentor, but in the journeys of his mind he searches for the woman he loves and in the course of his travels discovers the female part of him that had been concealed to him by the masculinist conception of heroism in the society in which he grew up.[14]

Winterson seems to promise that, like the characters of her novels, we, the readers, can be saved from the numbing "doctrine of Realism," if we allow ourselves to become sensitive to visions of realities that transcend their origin in our day-to-day lives and expose us to what Winterson humorously calls "bad attack[s] of Otherness" (*AO* 27). In her fictions the author wants to offer such visions by exploring life styles, thoughts, identities, and ways of self-expression that deviate from those that are socially accepted and therefore promoted at the expense of otherness. She identifies a neo-realist trend in much of contemporary literature and journalism which she castigates as viciously as the prevailing Victorian moral and philosophical attitudes she discerns in the British society of the 1990s. It is this blinkered insistence on realism, a refusal to admit the existence of "imaginative psychic worlds" next to "the mundane tables-and-chairs world of the everyday" (Brooks) which the author holds accountable for

---

[14] Kilian describes the travel motif as an organizing principle endowing continuity and coherence (cf. 132f). For Jordan, it is his imaginary journeys rather than his real ones that lend continuity and coherence to his life-story.

the "primitive doomsaying" that chokes sincere artistic expression in post-industrialist societies (*AO* 19).

"The artist need not believe in God," Winterson stresses, "but the artist does consider reality as multiple and complex" (*AO* 136). With the notable exception of the Dog-Woman, who is very much at home in the reality of the stinking banks of the Thames, in the company of her dogs and fighting the bigoted representatives of Puritanism,[15] the heroines and heroes of her three major early novels seek these multiple and complex realities by giving their imagination space in their lives. As they delve into strata of reality that are cordoned off by the conventions of normalcy of the hetero-patriarchal societies of their day and age, they teach readers to explore for themselves "new space[s] of possibility," as Zucker calls Winterson's imaginative realities (5/2), spaces that offer alternatives to the limited possibilities of self-creation and modes of self-expression available in our society. These alternatives are to be valued even if they appear to lead into self-isolation and madness, as with Henri in *The Passion*. Henri, who "want[s] the freedom to make [his] own mistakes" (*Passion* 157), prefers to remain a prisoner in a lunatic asylum where he is incarcerated after murdering Villanelle's husband. There he lives the life he has chosen for himself, in the company of the ghosts of people that are important to him. "For many people, to step out of the normal confines of society is a way of seeming mad, of dissolving one's own identity," Winterson contends, "[b]ut it's important that people should make the choices for themselves. And it may well be that those choices will lead them to a place that is so outside society, and outside any coherent framework as we know it, that they seem utterly crazy. However, I think that's a valid choice" (Marvel 168/3). Winterson's texts present "the inner life of the imagination" and thereby challenge fixed representations of the outer life (cf. Gade 29). "Reality is continuous, multiple, simultaneous, complex, abundant and partly invisible," the author writes. "The imagination alone can fathom

[15]The Dog-Woman is one of the most ambiguous characters Winterson has created. Although unable to understand her son's yearning to travel and incapable of engaging in journeys of her own mind, she nevertheless respects his choices and where possible assists him in the execution of his plans. I will examine the Dog-Woman more closely under the focus of Winterson's subversion of the binary gender construction in 5.2.

this and it reveals its fathomings through art" (*AO* 151).[16] Her fictions unfold multiple possibilities, thus encouraging readers to make their own choices, on the basis of visions brought back to them through literature.

Winterson approaches art with a quasi-modernist reverence that most people would reserve for religion.[17] This attitude has caught the attention of reviewers and interviewers, who searched for its roots in the writer's religious background. There are few profiles of the author that do not remind readers of the fact that Winterson was brought up to become a missionary for a small evangelical church and that she wrote her first sermons before she reached the age of ten.[18] And indeed, when she talks about her work, Winterson readily agrees with suggestions that this training effects her writing.[19] "I was driven by a need to preach to people and convert them which possibly I still am, except that now I do it for art's sake, and then I did it for God's sake" (Reynolds, "Interview Winterson": 11). Now she "preaches" that salvation lies in art rather than in the Second Coming, and the podium she uses for her preaching is the fiction she produces. Winterson's self-assigned task as a writer is to convert her readers to believing in art as a force of liberation and social change.

Rubinson criticizes this fervent belief in the power of art when he argues that "to suggest that art can effect the kind of change necessary to revolutionize the problems of postmodern society – to propose it as a source of salvation – is to overstate its potential" (*Fiction* 140).[20] Yet this is indeed Winterson's deepest conviction. "People are taught to compromise, to be afraid, to marry young. But I think a lot of them think there's more to it than that," she says. "One of the places things can be utterly

---

[16]The most radical rendition of this idea occurs in *Tanglewreck*, where the protagonist encounters parallel realities that depend upon the choices she has made or will make in her life. In this novel for young readers Winterson turns into a plot element a philosophical idea she expressed already in *Oranges*.

[17]Cf. Rubinson who links Winterson's sacralization of art with that practiced by the modernists (*Fiction*).

[18]See e.g. J. Turner, Bilger, Hancock.

[19]In her interview with Marvel, Winterson herself suggests that she substitutes the miracles of healing she performed as a teenager with those she performs through her writing (Marvel 168/2).

[20]Rubinson's argument recalls Linda Hutcheon's warning against "any attempt to romanticize the postmodern (however ex-centric) into the necessarily oppositional" (217).

changed, where new worlds can be started from scratch, is fiction" (Anshaw 17). Through her writing, Winterson "hope[s] in some way to transform people's lives," as an interviewer suggests (Bilger 86). But she does not use the moralistic tone and language of religious tracts of the uplift tradition, nor does she explicitly bill-board her intention of writing novels "with a particular seriousness or a relevancy to today's gender issues" (86). Rather, Winterson aims to effect an openness in her readers' minds that would allow her to "smuggle" ideas and images "across the frontiers" of the readers' imagination and to pave the way for a transformation (86).

"The writer is an instrument of transformation," Winterson states in *Art Objects: Essays on Ecstasy and Effrontery* (25). But how is this transformation achieved, and of what does it consist? Her starting assumption is that "[a]rt opens the heart" of every individual who engages herself in it (*AO* 7). Art touches and stirs people's emotions, making them susceptible to strong feelings which in their everyday lives they would carefully monitor and censor. She furthermore assumes that art in general and literature in particular induces in a person a state of rapture in which his or her mind is excessively open – to an imaginative reality that presents new possibilities of interpreting reality and of living one's life:

> I think people are often quite unaware of their inner selves, their other selves, their imaginative selves, the selves that aren't on show in the world. [...] I think literature is one of the best ways back into that. [...] You find that your defenses drop, and as soon as that happens, an imaginative reality can take over because you are no longer censoring your own perceptions, your own awareness of the world. (86f.)

Reading has the power to change the readers' perception of everyday reality, of themselves and of their relations with other human beings. Fiction provides readers with imaginative drafts of alternatives to their (heteropatriarchal) reality. As it opens the heart of the readers and enraptures them, transformation can occur. During stolen hours of secretive reading in her childhood Winterson discovered a truth for herself that colored her attitude toward writing and has influenced all her literary production to date: "Books were [...] kinetic forces; they did not write down the world, they altered it forever" (Winterson, "Second Hand": 3). In her understanding, books possess the ability to alter the world, because the rapture they induce "is a state of transformation" (*AO* 94). Literature, therefore, for her can be instrumental in effecting lasting social change.

Winterson argues that in order to have the ability to transform people and change society, texts must create for the readers a world in which they will feel safe enough to let go of the worries of their daily reality. She admires and has learned from fictions that present "authentic closed worlds that run by their own laws and are wholly believable" (Ivry).[21] Accordingly, her own writing is shaped by the aim "to create a space free from the problems of gravity. A place of escape. Free from the content of the everyday, or so it seems. [...] It's not frightening" (Scott and Constantine 25/1). Statements like this would seem to justify the accusations of escapism leveled at the author mostly by critics who argue from a standpoint influenced by lesbian-feminist agendas (cf. for example Duncker), but also by others who are less eager to find fault with Winterson (cf. Pearce, *Dialogics*). By introducing a strong fantastic element into her fictions, they argue, Winterson weakens both her feminist and her lesbian agendas. But during the 1980s and '90s, Winterson neither writes science fiction or fantasy novels nor has she ever expressed the intention of cultivating problem-free literary spaces in her fictions. Rather, from the seemingly safe space of dreams, fairy tales, or myths she "gradually [begins] to challenge the very things they [the readers] thought they were escaping from" (Scott and Constantine 25/1). Far from avoiding pressing issues of the everyday, such as the marginalization of individuals or groups on grounds of gender or sexuality, the imaginative realities she creates for her protagonists force them to get to the roots of their difficulties, often at great distress. Jeanette's lesson in *Oranges* illustrates this very well: During her ordeal of exorcism and exclusion from her church she realizes that underneath all the pious protests against her "unnatural passions" the true reason for her fall from favor is the power over the word she wields in a community that usually reserves the right to speak and preach in public for its male members.

"The true artist is after the problem," Winterson maintains. "The false artist wants it solved (by somebody else)" (*AO* 12). As will be discussed in detail in the next chapter, the alternative realities to which the heroines and heroes – and with them the readers – "escape" in the fictions of Jeanette Winterson open the view onto a variety of options where tradi-

---

[21]Winterson was "enthralled" by Ursula K. Le Guin's Earthsea trilogy. She credits Le Guin with being "the first person since Tolkien to create an authentic habitable world" (Ivry).

tionally there is only one that is deemed acceptable. The transformation in the readers' minds in which the writer is instrumental, then, consists in the challenging of "one totalizing vision" of reality (Burns, "Powerful": 376), and in the creative envisioning of plural identities and subject positions in their own everyday experiences.

The goals Winterson describes for her own writing, therefore, stand in stark contrast to the accusations of escapism and lack of critical engagement with issues of social inequality expressed with particular disdain by lesbian-feminist critics. Although she does not want to present herself as a political writer and resolutely rejects attempts to label her work as either lesbian or feminist, her view of the work of a writer has distinctly political connotations. However, in all her statements referring to politics she is careful to phrase her intentions as broadly as possible, an attitude of which statements like, "I do have a very vigorous attitude to life and I want to chance things," is indicative (Bilger 78). This stance seems vague and non-committal, but Winterson needs to phrase her intentions so broadly in order to harmonize them with the ambitious nature of the changes she wants to achieve through her art. "I'm hoping all the time that it will challenge people, both into looking more closely at these things they thought were cut and dried and also, perhaps, into inventing their own stories," she tells an interviewer after admitting that her writing and rewriting of stories is indeed a political act (Marvel 168/4).

Winterson sets high standards for herself. Through her writing she wants to change nothing less than her readers' uncritical acceptance of some of the core concepts on which Western society rests at the end of the twentieth and the beginning of the twenty-first century. In *Oranges* she "bash[es] away at three cherished idols" (168/4): the sanctity of the heterosexual family, the idea that love is the foundation of the church, and the notion of normalcy and desirability of heterosexual sex. *The Passion* rewrites one of the grand narratives of Western history and undermines the concept of a binary gender system. This continues in *Sexing the Cherry*, a novel that also breaks with the conceptions of linear time and the materiality of reality. Winterson creates worlds that, on the whole, resemble our "table-and-chairs-world" at different points in history and geography, but in these worlds the values of the hetero-patriarchal Western society are all but suspended. She encourages her readers to imagine themselves as somebody different, in an unfamiliar state of being, thinking, and feeling that would shake up their received value systems, to endeavor to explore and embrace other possibilities. "Winterson's fiction forces the reader to work at reading: to reconsider the relationships of things and people in the world, and to recognize the multiplicities in things rather than their singularities," the editors of one of the first essay collection on the work of this author suggest (Grice and Woods 10).

Indeed, Winterson's belief in the practicality of her agenda can only persist because of her conviction that reading is a process that requires the readers' active engagement with the universe the writer has imagined, a "wrestl[ing]" with the text and a "pin[ning] down" of it (cf. "Digital"). Literature for Winterson is "a hands-on experience" ("Digital"); the experience of reading a text that is "true art" will never allow a person to remain uninvolved. During reading, the "energetic space," the text created by the writer, "begets energetic space" in the imagination of the active reader (*AO* 114). This "private dialogue [...] between reader and book cannot be controlled by the State, the media, or even another person," Winterson enthuses; she calls the activity of reading "an exercise of freewill" [sic] ("Digital"). The sources of this author's confidence in the success of her political agenda, however broadly defined it may be, are her confidence in the political quality of the writing and reading of literature and her trust in the power of art to bring about social change.

1.2.1   The Politics of Writing

Jeanette Winterson's texts have almost unanimously been labeled post-modern.[22] Lyn Pykett's calling attention to Winterson's use of postmodern techniques and thinking in form, language, and thematic concerns is emblematic for this increasingly stable consensus among Winterson scholars. Pykett, with recourse to Hutcheon's study on the poetics of postmodernism of 1988, identifies as postmodern devices Winterson's use of

---

[22]*Oranges* is an exception to this rule; it has repeatedly and reductively been read as an autobiographical coming-out or coming-of-age story. Winterson has argued many times that *Oranges* is not an autobiography. She insists that with her first fiction she re-writes this genre by recreating herself as a fictional character and presenting just one version among many possible versions of what we are used to calling reality (cf e.g. Farrar; Marvel). *Oranges* is one of many examples of postmodern fictional texts that problematize and blur traditional boundaries of genre.

parody, irony, pastiche, a generally self-reflexive mode in her writing, her playful approach to the task of narration and to the stories she narrates, a sense of multiplicity, fragmentation, and instability of meaning that permeates all her texts, as well as her apparent distrust of grand narratives and of the traditional mapping and measuring of space and time (cf. Pykett 54 ff.). *The Passion* and *Sexing the Cherry*, in particular, can be regarded as exemplary historiographic metafictions in that they re-visit a historical period and/or historic personages, but narrate "history" from the perspective of social outcasts: the "neck-wringer" of Napoleon's chickens, a prostitute to French officers, and a gigantic, fiercely loyalist dog-breeder during the Puritan revolution. These novels expose the power structures inherent in the formation of "history," and they explore the discursive, narrative quality of our notion of the past.[23]

Regrettably, however, critics who choose to concentrate on Winterson's postmodernism often overlook her commitment to feminist and lesbian political goals, while those who measure her work by the standards of "lesbian writing" blame her for allegedly watering down any feminist political drive with her postmodern form and thinking.[24] As I pointed out above, Winterson, in best postmodern manner, investigates and questions supposed truths of contemporary Western society: that time is linear; that there is one reality which can be represented "as it is"; that there are two genders only that sort human beings neatly into male and female; that these gender categories are oppositional and mutually exclusive; that there exists a canon of attributes, knowledges, emotions, and possible relation-

---

[23]Linda Hutcheon coined the term "historiographic metafiction" which she considers to be the typical narrative form of postmodern fiction: "Historiographic metafiction incorporates all three of these domains [literature, history, theory], that is, its theoretical self-awareness of history and fiction as human constructs (historio*graphic* metafiction) is made the grounds for its rethinking and reworking of the forms and contents of the past" (5).

[24]The difficulty of defining lesbian literature without reducing either lesbians or lesbian writing to essentialist categories is addressed by Farwell. She argues that "the lesbian narrative is not necessarily a story by a lesbian about lesbians but rather a plot that affirms a place for lesbian subjectivity, that narrative space where both lesbian characters and other female characters can be active desiring agents," and points at the disruption caused to the Western narrative "when female rather than male desire dominates the plot" (Farwell, "Lesbian Narrative": 157).

ships appropriate to men and a different one for women, and that from this canon results the superiority of men; that women fulfill their destiny by loving, marrying, and serving men. This list indicates where the author's priorities lie: Among the "givens" that govern social interaction in our society, the concept of gender in its relation to sexuality and – ultimately – identity captivates her attention most firmly. It continually provokes her desire to challenge and subvert it. The central focus of all of Winterson's fictions, I therefore want to argue, is the arbitrary and ultimately restrictive nature of a binary gender system. When she investigates different modes of conceptualizing time and space and explores different ways of narrating "realities," she does so with the larger aim of throwing light upon the way in which individual subject positions and relationships between human beings are governed by conventional notions of femaleness and maleness and by certain codes of behavior designed and enforced to shore up this binary.

My reading of Winterson is informed furthermore by the conviction that her deconstructive postmodernism pursues a feminist political agenda which calls for and celebrates women's autonomy and self-determination. As Laura Doan points out, "asserting that anything can 'rise above' such oppositions [of male and female] is an act of cultural intervention, revealing those oppositions as cultural fictions" (144). Thus, like Doan, I disagree with scholars who follow Hutcheon's argumentation about the inherent inability of postmodern theory and art to be politically committed, who claim that Winterson's postmodern art is incompatible with feminist aims and consciousness and merely indulges in deconstruction for its own sake.[25]

---

[25] From her argument that "postmodernism is a contradictory phenomenon, one that uses and abuses, installs and then subverts the very concepts it challenges" (3), Hutcheon concludes that while postmodernist theory and art are in themselves "inescapably political" in that they render problematic the social and political tenets of society (4), they cannot be committed to any specific political objective, as they would automatically challenge the ideological master narrative which drives its activism. With this conclusion, however, she implicitly agrees with critics of postmodernism such as Eagleton and Jameson who criticize the movement "for not having been a politics, for not providing, perhaps, a platform to replace the ones it was tearing down" (Lee 218). Hutcheon's arguments are taken up by Palmer, who argues in "Postmodern Trends" that postmodern thinking and theory are counterproductive for the feminist agenda. In

Palmer argues that Winterson's work is characterized by a "precarious balancing act" between postmodern notions of decentered, constructed subjectivity in a society in a state of constant flux on the one hand, and on the other the feminist belief in individual agency and collective political action, in working toward goals and maintaining the gains that have been achieved, and in the contributions of literature to political objectives (cf. Palmer, "Jeanette Winterson"). While I agree that there is this tension, I suggest that Winterson is aware of it and makes it a covert focus of her explorations and experiments. Her texts, therefore, are not only political in their deconstructing and subverting the gender-political status quo of Western society. They also testify to the author's dedication to social change and work to induce a political commitment in their readers that is compatible with feminist and queer theory and the political goals of these movements.[26] Accordingly, in the following chapters and subchapters I will frequently return to the politics of Winterson's postmodern poetics.

1.3   Tradition and Re-Writing

> Pirate I was, sailing on the forward momentum of somebody
> else's prose and then tacking on a spits length of my own.
>
> Jeanette Winterson

Jeanette Winterson scandalized the British literary establishment by announcing, or so it seemed, that she was the true heir of Virginia Woolf, Shakespeare's imaginary sister whose advent Woolf foresees in *A Room of One's Own*.[27] In the early 1990s, she presented herself as so enthralled

a more recent article Palmer again thematizes what she sees as contradictions and tensions between postmodern and lesbian/feminist aims within Winterson's work, which allegedly stem from opposed views on the individual's ability to change him- or herself and society in postmodern and lesbian/feminist thinking. Now, however, Palmer concedes that Winterson employs postmodern strategies for feminist ends (cf. "Jeanette Winterson").

[26] Duncker argues that Winterson must be seen as a representative of queer rather than lesbian-feminist writing (cf. 77). Here I agree with her, although I do not share her regret over Winterson's unwillingness to commit herself to the political utopias of radical lesbian feminism of the 1970s.

[27] To Woolf's well-known prophesy – "But I maintain that she [Shakespeare's sister, the woman writer of Shakespearean proportions] would come if we worked

with the originality of her writing that she would only admit the influence of literary figures of the caliber of Woolf, Shakespeare, or T.S. Eliot. Since those days of early and sudden fame, Winterson has become much more ready to acknowledge numerous, disparate sources of influence and inspiration.[28] She has expressed her understanding of herself both as part of a literary tradition and as a writer who connects different traditions with one another in her own work. "I have to respect my ancestors and not try to part company before we know each other well. A writer uninterested in her lineage is a writer who has no lineage," she states (*AO* 172). Humphries rightly points out that "[n]ot only is Winterson's fiction full of theory, it is also full of echoes of literary ancestors. Winterson hates the Canon, but she loves the tradition from which she always writes, and which she would like her reader/critic to pay attention to more than to any abstract theories" (15). While parts of Winterson's project indeed echo styles, ideas, or concepts of literary precursors, others take further, more radical steps in the direction to which the ancestors pointed, and still others parody older works or re-assemble them in pastiche-like, sometimes humorous combinations. Of course, literary texts invariably speak to each other (cf. Langland), and self-reflexivity and the critical exploration of literary traditions are well-known characteristics of postmodern historiographic metafiction. They are, however, particularly useful for the study of Winterson's project, which she herself describes as "a perpetual dialogue, between the one who has written and the one who is writing" (*AO* 181).

In her essay collection *Art Objects*, Winterson places herself in the literary tradition of modernism, the "poet's movement," as she understands it (*AO* 82). She criticizes scholarly views that consider modernism a thing of the past and expresses her commitment to continuing the modernist pro-

---

for her, and that so to work, even in poverty and obscurity, is worth while" – Winterson replied, "That is where I am in history" (*AO* 164). This statement has been widely (mis-)interpreted to mean that Winterson sees herself as Shakespeare's sister, when it could just as well mean that she is doing her part of the work required to bring her forth.

[28] Asked about her early ambitious claims to artistic kinship with Virginia Woolf in an interview with the *Independent* newspaper in 2004, Winterson explained: "I don't think that I'm the direct heir to Woolf or anything like that. I think I'm doing the work, or taking up some of the challenges, and I'm very excited by other writers who are doing it, too" (Field).

gram of renewing a language dulled by commercial over-use. As Pykett has observed, Winterson is contemptuous of postmodern techniques in contemporary Western literature, although she herself uses many of the devices she dismisses as gimmicks in the work of others, designed to catch the attention of potential art consumers. Indeed, in accordance with her self-identification with the modernist tradition, her early texts exhibit some familiar modernist tenets, all of which speak of a longing for essential truths and security in a world that offers little of either: Most of her protagonists believe in the existence of true romantic love, and they hail the superior value of stories to the official records of history. The dancing princess Fortunata in *Sexing the Cherry* teaches her pupils to transcend their human nature in dance and to turn themselves into spinning points of light.[29] And always art, particularly the word-art of poetry, stands aloof as a beacon of purity and a bringer of grace and salvation.

The tension between Winterson's modernist ideals and her postmodern notions of diverse possibilities and multiple, constructed identities is palpable in all of her writing and spelled out in the following statement: "We're trying to get to some truths about people's lives, which by their very nature are myriad, fragmentary and kaleidoscopic" (Reynolds, "Interview Winterson": 19). It encourages some commentators to declare her a modernist at heart, both in attitude and style (cf. e.g. Pykett; J. Turner). I want to suggest, however, that Winterson not only is aware of the tension produced by modernist dreams in her postmodern texts, but acknowledges it as a psychological characteristic of contemporary Western society which she exploits both in her poetics and her politics of writing. The dialogue with the Anglo-British literary canon in which she engages in her writing and her self-association with particular writers stand in the service of the socio-political goals she sets for her work. This means that Winterson loves the modernists not only for the exactness and clarity of their poetic language, but also for their avant-gardist efforts to cross traditional boundaries. Thus, she credits Gertrude Stein's innovative writing in general and her *Autobiography of Alice B. Toklas* in particular for having

---

[29]Note the echoes of the following lines from T.S. Eliot's poem "Burnt Norton": "And do not call it fixity, / Where past and future are gathered. Neither movement from / Nor towards, / Neither ascent nor decline. Except for the point, the still point, / There would be no dance, and there is only the dance" (II, lines 18-22).

inspired her to re-write the genre of autobiography in *Oranges* by creating herself as a fictional character in the guise of Jeanette (cf. *AO* 45-60).
Oranges has also been read as homage to James Joyce, as Winterson's
"*Portrait of the Artist as a Young* working class lesbian" (Pykett 58), in
which she re-invents herself as an artist. Virginia Woolf's fictional biography *Orlando*, too, taught Winterson to play with genre boundaries, but
more importantly, its protagonist provided her with a role model for many
heroes and heroines of her own fictions:[30] Villanelle in *The Passion* woes
her beloved in men's clothes, and in *Sexing the Cherry* Jordan lives as
a woman on one of his mental journeys and cross-dresses in London for
strategic reasons. Also in *Sexing*, besides taking up Woolf's trope of traveling through the centuries, Winterson experiments with ideas about the
simultaneity of past and future in present time that T.S. Eliot expresses in
Four Quartets.[31] She introduces into the narrative two protagonists who
live in the London of the late twentieth century and yet share ideals and
experiences with the Dog-Woman and Jordan of the seventeenth century.
Furthermore, Jordan's journeys of the mind and Jeanette's thoughts about
the life she might have led had she remained in her home town in *Oranges* echo Eliot's musings on the possibility of the different directions a
person's life might have taken.[32]

Winterson wants to continue in the direction her modernists ancestors
indicated; she goes where her forebears did not or maybe rather could not
go at the time of their writing. This is in accordance with her conviction
that modernism is not a "cul-de-sac, a literary bywater" (*AO* 176), but a
movement that can – and indeed must – be extended into contemporary
art, confronted and infused with ideas and insights derived from social

---

[30] I agree with Pykett's suggestion that "it is Woolf's fictional practice – her new
way with words and her concern with sexual and gender politics – which has,
perhaps, most closely shaped Winterson's fiction to date" (59).

[31] In "Burnt Norton" Eliot writes: "Time present and time past / Are both perhaps
present in time future / And time future contained in time past" (I, lines 1-3).
And further: "Time past and time future / What might have been and what has
been / Point to one end, which is always present" (I, lines 46-48).

[32] Again in "Burnt Norton," Eliot thematizes memories of "the passage which we
did not take" and "the door we never opened" (I, lines 12f.). For a more detailed
analysis of Eliotean thought on Winterson, see Pykett, who describes *Sexing* as
"probably the most obviously Eliotean of her works, since one of its clearest
intertextual references is to *Four Quartets*" (58).

movements and scientific discoveries since the days of modernism. For her, to have an intimate, respectful connection with one's literary tradition is to use it creatively, innovatively, and at times critically:

> [T]he calling of the artist, in any medium, is to make it new. I do not mean that in new work the past is repudiated; quite the opposite, the past is reclaimed. It is not lost to authority, it is not absorbed at a level of familiarity. It is re-stated and re-instated in its original vigour. [...] This is not ancestor worship, it is the lineage of art. It is not so much influence as it is connection. (*AO* 12)

In her work Winterson pursues a "double agenda" that concerns the poetics as well as the politics of writing: "I want to push forward what's possible in prose; I'm not content to use what's already there. And I also want to change people's lives" (Messud). It is in the light of these goals that her delight in "ransacking" literary tradition and her ambition to use the Western canon productively for her own innovative writing need to be viewed.

1.3.1   Genre as Form and Subject Matter

For Winterson, form and language are important means of achieving the transformation of her readers for which she aims in her writing. One might say that they orchestrate the tunes her narratives introduce, not only transporting moods and illustrating plot developments, but through their shape rendering intelligible the thematic concerns of a text.

Winterson has a marked dislike of fixed genre definitions; she associates them with what she regards to be the inflexible materialism of Victorian realism, and charges them with contributing to the exhaustion of language and imagination in contemporary industrial societies. Consequently, the "crime" committed by the Modernists to "[question] the boundaries between [novels and poems]" is one of the achievements for which she admires them (*AO* 176). In her own writing she is "interested in finding a relationship between poetic density and narrative possibility – to bring them together and create something which is different" (Field 39/3). The result of these efforts is a lyrical prose language in which the meaning of phrases and sentences are accentuated by the sound units of carefully chosen nouns, verbs, and adjectives.[33] The rhythmic and musical quality of Winterson's prose not only produces very quotable statements; more importantly it achieves an emotional intensity that is traditionally associated with poetry.

This novel quality in the style of prose writing stretches from language to other formal aspects and is also intended to cover the treatment of subject matter in fictional texts: "What I am seeking to do in my work is to make a form that answers to twenty-first-century needs. A form that is not 'a poem' as we usually understand the term, and not 'a novel' as the term is defined by its own genesis" (*AO* 191). The author declares that she "[does] not write novels," because "[t]he novel form is finished," and while we should continue to read and appreciate novels – quasi as representations of a notion of reality that is of historical and theoretical interest – we must "give up writing them" (*AO* 191). Winterson is particularly dissatisfied with texts that reproduce the style of nineteenth century naturalism, i.e., novels designed to represent "life as it really is." The realistic fictions she wants to produce must grow out of the heterogeneous, fragmented realities – material as well as imaginary – with which her readers are confronted on a daily basis; they must be texts that offer analyses, comments, and/or viewpoints on these realities.

For her goal to break up rigid genre divisions the author finds critical inspiration, and indeed role-models, in the writings of European postmodernists, particularly the Italian writer Italo Calvino. Winterson said that

> working off Calvino [in *The Passion*] was a way of aligning myself with the European tradition where I feel much more comfortable. That's a tradition which uses fantasy and invention and leaps of time, of space, rather than in the Anglo-American tradition which is much more realistic in its narrative drive and much more a legacy of the nineteenth century. (Reynolds, "Interview Winterson": 19)

Winterson cites Calvino's *Invisible Cities* (1972) as a major source of inspiration for *The Passion* (Reynolds, "Interview Winterson": 18f.), but it seems very likely that the Italian's experiments with genres and narrative modes in his later books, such as *If in a Winter's Night a Traveller* . . .

---

[33] The following example may illustrate this observation: "The grapes have withered on the vine. What should be plump and firm, resisting the touch to give itself in the mouth, is spongy and blistered. Not this year the pleasure of rolling blue grapes between finger and thumb juicing my palm with musk" (*WoB* 9).

(1979), also influenced and encouraged her in her own experiments with the boundaries of genre.

Winterson weaves a variety of prose forms into her fictions, frequently as stories or memories told by one of the characters in the text, sometimes as a narrator's illustrative comments to events and actions. By borrowing motifs, plot fragments, characters, and/or structural elements from folk stories, fairy tales, epics of quests, and classical myth, as well as from Biblical stories, popular romances of different eras, and canonic texts, Winterson creates intertextual palimpsests with pastiche-like or parodistic qualities.[34] Her borrowing from and referring back to older texts is always critical and interpretive by nature, never merely accumulative or self-congratulatory in the sense of advertising the author's knowledge in literary history. By offering readers the familiar stories that accompanied their socialization in unfamiliar contexts and with altered ingredients, her texts force them to closely re-examine their reading expectations and to position themselves in relation to the ideologies these stories represent. "For me, in the rewriting of stories, of history, of myths, I'm not saying, 'Look, here's the definitive version,'" Winterson explains in an interview. "I'm saying, 'Here's another story about that story, so what do you think?'" (Marvel 168/4). She sees this as a political act, because her readers cannot but consider the ideological undercurrents of fairy tales, myths, and other traditional texts with regard to hierarchies of gender and class, to what they prescribe as "normal" and therefore permissible gender behavior and sexual identities, and to the views of the spatial and temporal makeup of our world transported in them.[35]

In order to spur critical faculties of her readers and to encourage them to mentally engage in the re-writing of stories, Winterson changes the

[34] Winterson certainly is not the first writer who stretches the limits of the novel by including stories of various sorts in a longer fictional text. Yet in her interviews and essays she does not connect her writing with the works of writers such as American authors who re-tell in their texts folk stories and myths, as well as stories arising from historical experiences of people of color in the United States. See for example Maxine Hong Kingston, *The Woman Warrior* (1975), *China Men* (1980), and Toni Morrison, *Song of Solomon* (1977), *Tar Baby* (1981).

[35] Gade also interprets the author's postmodern deconstructions as political subversion of convention. She observes that "Winterson's writing itself is deconstructive: the text undermines the innocence of conventional forms of representation and seeks alternative ways of describing human experiences" (29).

endings of well-known fairy tales, or she narrates tales from the perspective of characters that have a marginal position in the original or whose stories have so far remained untold.[36] The protagonists of her re-written narratives have a wide range of choices as to the professions they want to occupy or to the partnerships into which they enter, a circumstance that leads to a "naturalizing" of lifestyles that have traditionally been declared unnatural or perverse. Often, female characters show an agency that removes them from the status of being the passive prizes fought for by princes and awarded to them for their efforts, to that of empowered actors who decide their own fates. These powerful female protagonists of the stories provide role models for women as well as men in Winterson's fictions.

1.3.2   Feminist Writing

Feminist politics and the works of feminist writers exercise a major influence on Winterson's choices of subject matter and on the creation of her heroines. Her emphasis on the social function of language parallels the traditional concern with language in the feminist movement. Like feminist theoreticians, critics, and authors, Winterson sees language as a system of signs that contains, represents, and transports power and power relations in a society. In her texts she analyzes the workings of this system and imagines constellations in which traditional hierarchies of powers are subverted and alternatives are explored.

Always wary of labels that could curtail the thematic breadth of her writing or endanger her popularity with a broad-based readership, Winterson stresses: "I don't think of myself as a feminist writer" (Scott and Constantine 25/2). Instead, she offers a differentiation between being a feminist writer and being a feminist: "I think of myself as a feminist. I think every woman should think of herself as such – and probably every sane man, too. There is no proper alternative to it. And naturally it informs my whole life, my whole consciousness" (25/2). The thematic scope of her writing and the influences on it, she seems to suggest, are too complex to be subsumed under the label "feminist," but her work necessarily reflects the fact that her general outlook on life is informed by the

---

[36] A recent example of this rewriting of widely-known texts is Winterson's version of the Atlas myth, told from the perspective of Atlas (cf. *Weight*).

tenets of feminism. In a different interview Winterson is less hesitant to associate herself with feminism, but explicitly places herself within the tradition of women writers who participated in the struggle for the emancipation of women: "[F]or me it is vital constantly to use the broadest tradition and to get as much from it as I can. But at the same time, within that, I recognize that strand of women's writing of which I am directly a part and which speaks to me in a very personal way. It has to, because I am part of that struggle" (Bilger 104).

In an interview with *The Guardian*, Winterson pays ample tribute to the Modernists Gertrude Stein and Virginia Woolf, but she also includes in her list of literary ancestors British writers of the 1970s, namely Angela Carter, Michèle Roberts, and Sarah Maitland (cf. Jaggi).[37] Apart from a shared interest in the critical analysis of the construction and preservation of hierarchies of power in patriarchal language, what draws her most to the work of these writers are their portraits of strong women. Of her own work Winterson says: "I would never put a woman in my books who is less than what I think a woman can be. In many ways, these books are about potential – about what people can achieve against overwhelming odds" (Scott and Constantine 25/2). This attitude exposed the writer to the charge of taking an interest only in extraordinary individuals, beautiful, strong women who triumph even though they are initially disadvantaged, and thus of ignoring the struggles of ordinary, weak people – a charge that again denies any political objective in Winterson's writing (cf. Lambert, "Winterson").[38] Not only is this assessment a rather crude simplification of Winterson's complex protagonists, it also ignores the fact that the their stories are invariably the stories of Others: Despite the brutal attempts of the elders of her church to subdue and "normalize" her, Jeanette in *Oranges* retains her voice as an artist and exercises the right to choose her own lifestyle. In *The Passion*, Villanelle remains an autonomous, inde-

---

[37] In Winterson's communities of women in conjunction with the trope of travel Cath Stowers sees a resemblance to Adrienne Rich's representation of lesbian orientation as a "journey back to the mother" ("Communities" 76).

[38] Angela Lambert examines what she considers Winterson's failure to establish herself fully and lastingly in the British world of letters. She comes to the conclusion that "[Winterson] does not, apparently, have the capacity to attribute love to failed, damaged, difficult people. This want of sympathy, rather than her working class origins or her lesbianism, is the real barrier to her admission into the literary pantheon" ("Winterson").

pendent woman in the face of sexual exploitation and the threat of losing herself in a relationship with a non-committal married woman. After his ordeal in the Napoleonic Wars, Henri preserves his right to decide where and how he will live, even if it is in a lunatic asylum on a barren island. All of the dancing princesses in *Sexing the Cherry* manage to either free themselves from forced marriages and to engage in alternative partnerships, or, if these are destroyed because they are considered unnatural, they take up lives of their own choosing, in a community of sisters. In the same text, the Dog-Woman is marginalized because she is poor and of hideous appearance, but still she is in control of her life and very capable of protecting herself and her interests.[39] Winterson seems to be saying to her readers, 'Look what women, what marginalized people can achieve, if they make use of their potential, their capacity to love and the power of their imagination, which will enable them to discover and live multiple possibilities.'

Winterson's interest in and critical re-writing of fairy tales takes up Angela Carter's work, particularly her rendition of well-known fairy tales published as *The Bloody Chamber and Other Stories* (1979), and continues it, albeit with a markedly different objective, as I hope to make clear in the fifth chapter. Also, Carter's engagement with Virginia Woolf's explorations of gender, most obviously in *Orlando*, prepared the ground for Winterson's gender benders.[40] Fevvers in *A Night at the Circus* (1984) presents a powerful example of a combination of the deconstruction of mythic concepts of womanhood with the emancipatory construction of identity by a multiply marginalized female protagonist.

Winterson is said to have asserted that she neither read contemporary theory, nor the works of feminist and lesbian authors of the 1980s, with their startling gender experiments (cf. J. Turner). There are commentators who express strong doubts at this, pointing out parallels between Winterson's fictions and both theoretical insights in the construction of gender

---

[39] See Taylor Merleau for a detailed analysis of Winterson's postmodern ethics of expressing the silence of the victims of a wrong.

[40] Pykett claims that Winterson obscures her debt to Carter who produced "one of the most energetic responses to and engagement with the challenge of Woolf" (59). While it is true that in her interviews and essays Winterson preferably associates her own work with that of Virginia Woolf and the Modernists, it seems only fair to say that she is also quoted in the 2004 *Guardian profile* as explicitly acknowledging Carter among her literary ancestors (Jaggi).

and gender relations, and various writers' earlier engagement with these insights in fictional texts.[41] Indeed, Winterson's protagonists Villanelle, Henri, the Dog-Woman, and Jordan, as well as the narrators of the later works *Written on the Body* and *The Power.Book* do little to hide their connections to androgynous protagonists of earlier feminist writing, such as Carter's Fevvers and gender-changing characters like Kathy Acker's Don Quixote in the book of the same title.[42] How exactly Winterson proceeds in her efforts to subvert received notions of gender difference and the binary opposition of male and female in her texts of the late 1980s will be the focus of Chapter 5.

1.3.3 Lesbian Literature

Winterson's first book, *Oranges Are Not the Only Fruit*, established the author as a promising lesbian writer in Great Britain. It represents the struggles of a young lesbian woman to preserve her emotional and intellectual integrity in the face of violent efforts of her hetero-patriarchal environment to press her into the traditional structures they consider normal. *Oranges* is loosely based on the author's own experiences and it quickly made Winterson a pop icon with many lesbian women in Britain as well as in the United States only a little later.[43] This bill-boarding of the author's lesbian identity was fed by the rumors she strewed liberally of numerous affairs with women in her early London years. What is more, the desire of

---

[41] Jaggi quotes Michèle Roberts who describes Winterson as an "unashamed intellectual, nourished by queer theory, which said even gender was a costume."

[42] Winterson counts Kathy Acker among her friends in 1995 (cf. Bilger; Field). In fact, she commissioned her as an editor at Pandora, but in her interviews or essays I have not found any explicit acknowledgement of Acker as one of the writers who influenced her.

[43] Winterson wrote the screenplay for the successful television drama *Oranges Are Not the Only Fruit*, directed by Beeban Kidron and produced by Phillippa Giles, which was screened on BBC2 in 1990 to great critical and public acclaim. See Hilary Hinds's interesting analysis of the wide-spread popularity in Great Britain of a TV drama that focuses on the experiences of a young lesbian woman in a Pentecostal church. Hinds shows that the topic of lesbianism is de-centered in the mainstream media in favor of universal liberal-humanist themes, such as the conflict between a mother and her teenaged daughter, while it is the central focus for the gay and lesbian audience.

women for other women – whether they identify themselves as lesbians or not – and their relationships form an important and recurring topic of Winterson's writing.[44]

It may come as a surprise, then, that the author objects to criticism that treats her work as lesbian fiction. This is a tradition as a part of which she does not wish to be seen. She insists that, if used in connection with her writing, the term lesbian literature is a misnomer: "There's gay books and there's lesbian books, just like there's crime novels and books about horses. I've got no worries about that. But I don't want to write them" (Farrar). Winterson wants her fiction to reach a wide range of readers, regardless of their sexuality or identification with any specific group. She believes that high quality literature is capable of appealing to diverse audiences, and she is certainly convinced of the quality of her own writing. In fact, Winterson is not only unwilling to be seen as representing lesbians, calling it "a very bad thing" if she became a spokeswoman for lesbians (Bilger 105), she also appears to want to present herself as unsuited to the endeavors of identity politics. "I hate the word lesbian; it tells you nothing, its only purpose is to inflame," she told an interviewer and reiterated her wide-ranging artistic goals: "I don't write for any group – male, female, straight, gay. I write to bring about a change in consciousness" (Jaggi).

Why, then, does lesbian desire have such a prominent space in Winterson's narratives? Why do many of the female protagonists in *Oranges*, *The Passion*, and *Sexing the Cherry* engage in relationships with women, relationships that are always positively connoted? Does the author's own biography determine the thematic focus of her work, as reviewers and critics have so often suggested? Winterson's answer to the question whether her fiction is autobiographical is invariably the same: "Not at all and yes of course," as she writes in the introduction to the 1991 Vintage edition of *Oranges* (xiv). She reacts in a much more irritated manner to intimations that her lesbianism might be the impulse out of which she writes: "I am a writer who happens to love women. I am not a lesbian who happens to write" (*AO* 104). Winterson is well aware of the fact that she can only hope to bring about the change in people's consciousness for which she

---

[44] All of this justifies the observation that "[i]n Britain, at least, it would seem that Jeanette Winterson has come to represent the popular face of lesbian fiction" (Pearce, "Written": 147).

aims if she avoids addressing just one section of the reading public and if she does not allow herself to be made the spokesperson for one particular interest group.

This is not to say, however, that Winterson uses the theme of lesbianism haphazardly or opportunistically. On the contrary, I want to argue that love between women as well as all-female communities play an important part in the politics of her writing. By their very existence they subvert hetero-patriarchal social structures and with alternative concepts of relationships and family constellations they challenge normative notions of appropriate social relations, "normal" sexual behaviors, as well as legitimate identities. Female protagonists who desire women and share their lives with women, who are not only beautiful, but also full of energy and wisdom, and who pursue their professional and social plans independently of men, offer attractive fictional arguments for the belief that there is more than just one possibility of organizing one's life. Furthermore, as will shortly be discussed in more detail, Winterson's lesbians – like other characters who do not confirm the hetero-normative world-view of the majority – never suffer psychically or emotionally because of their deviance from the norm. As I mentioned earlier, this has been criticized as an escapist fantasy of the author;[45] however, I propose to welcome it as a successful attempt to naturalize lifestyles and ways of self-identification that have traditionally been vilified as unnatural and therefore illegitimate. Thus, it is in full accordance with the gender-political ambitions Winterson connects to her work as a writer that she "rejects lesbianism as the key to her fiction" (Humphries 6). For her, lesbian desire is not the "key," the main focus of her writing, but it serves as an important vehicle for her politics of diversity and multiple possibilities.

---

[45] Pearce senses an uncritical universalism in Winterson's early novels. She aims to demonstrate this alleged flaw with what she regards as the fact that the protagonists are not made to suffer the consequences of their unorthodox sexuality or their gender difference. She contrasts this unfavorably with Toni Morrison's uncompromising exploration of the consequences of racial and gender difference in *Beloved* (cf. *Dialogics*).

1.4   Winterson's Investment in Language

Oranges Are Not the Only Fruit, *Sexing the Cherry*, and *The Passion* all
attracted widespread public attention and critical acclaim for their innovative subject matter and captivating plots.   Yet what arguably makes
Jeanette Winterson's writing instantly recognizable is her language, her
idiosyncratic style. The author has been described as a "sound artist,"
whose tools are "rhythm and assonance and association" (Reynolds and
Noakes 8). There is indeed a musical quality in her writing: Reynolds
and Noakes point out a technique of "returns and reinventions" to and
of lines, ideas, images used in other novels, through which "Winterson
has created a universe of her own" (10). Field describes her as an author
who is "acutely conscious of prose rhythms" (39/3), whose way of "fitting
music to prose style" is possibly her greatest accomplishment (39/2).

However, Winterson does not worship language for its sounds and
rhythms only; she fetishizes words for the power they wield over people's
imagination and therefore in their lives – a power which she never tires of
proclaiming and celebrating. Asked about the importance of plots in her
fictions, the self-proclaimed "evangelist for the word" (Bilger 78) replies:
"[M]y loyalties lie completely for language" (Farrar). So for what reasons does the inventor of gripping stories such as Villanelle's and Henri's
privilege language over plot?

Although language in Winterson's mind is a powerful force in contemporary society, it is not *a priori* a force of goodness. Just as she differentiates between "true art" and art that is not true (and therefore is not art in
the true sense), she seems to make a distinction between "true language"
which has healing capacities and language that is not "true" because it
does not live up to its potential. For Winterson, neglected language is capable of corrupting people's minds and through them their society.[46] This
corruption, according to Winterson, occurs through the wearing out of language and imagery in commercialized mass culture, with the effect that
the imaginative powers of individuals and communities of potential art

---

[46]There is a notable contradiction between Winterson's insistence on multiplicity
and diversity with regard to presentations and definitions of reality and her essentialist notions of Art and Language. This modernist penchant for essence –
in spite of numerous declarations and indeed textual examples to the contrary
– surfaces also in Winterson's thinking about story-telling and love, as will be
discussed later in this study.

consumers become dull and numb. Consequently, the artist who wants to effect social change through her art must produce language that will resuscitate the dulled senses of its users. Such language must be precise where mass-produced language is vague and indeterminate. Winterson's writerly credo in 1995 was that "the language of literature is not an approximate language. It is the most precise language that human beings have yet developed" (*AO* 165). This still holds true for her in 2003: "[L]anguage [...] has to be muscular. It has to be agile and quick, it can't be sloppy. Fiction isn't approximate, it's precise" (Reynolds, "Interview Winterson": 22). Winterson's writing, therefore, is determined by a constant struggle for precision.

For Jeanette Winterson, precision in the face of increasing approximation is most directly achieved by the language of poetry: "The poet's method of exactness is a move towards a clearer communication and the more blurred everyday speech has become, the more precise must be the poet" (*AO* 84). The language Winterson wants to employ must have two characteristics: It must be revelatory and affective. In her essay collection she expresses her admiration for Virginia Woolf's "words that cut through the semblance of the thing to the thing itself" (*AO* 95), a seemingly paradoxical statement for a postmodern writer who questions the traditional notion of natural essence. But "the thing itself" for Winterson is rather more than, say, a river. What interests her deeply are questions of the ideological functions to which a river might be put, of who has the power to attribute certain symbolic values to it, of how people attained such power, and what consequences their power has in their society. In addition to revealing what is at the bottom of an image that is employed thoughtlessly at times and sometimes with calculated care, her texts aspire to wresting "the thing itself" from the ideological uses to which it has been put, and to lending it new meaning. Thus, language in a Wintersonian work of fiction attempts "to dismantle, reinterpret and reinvent – rather than repeat – [the structures of existing discourses]" (Maagaard 158); it is revelatory language.

Moreover, by adopting in her fiction poetic language that is "undiluted, unmediated," Winterson wants to "bring back to us starts of feeling that can volt through the thickness of the day" (*AO* 185). Through their language her texts are geared toward producing powerful feelings in those who engage with them. Shaken out of possibly habitual indifference and apathy, readers will rediscover their capacity to empathize with others, to

register injustices and revolt against them – inwardly as well as overtly
and in a politically active manner. "Winterson's aesthetic practice [...]
aims to achieve a new perception of things blunted by habit," writes Jean-
Michel Ganteau, who diagnoses an "ethics of affect" in the author's fiction
("Hearts Object" 184).[47] For Winterson, the particular power which the
emotionally and critically exact language of poetry exerts on the human
mind, accounts for its great social importance: "If we admit that language
has power over us, not only through what it says but also through what
it is, we come closer to understanding the importance of poetry and its
function in a healthy society" (*AO* 76). For her, the function and indeed
the duty of language-as-poetry in our society is to restore and preserve the
human capacity for experiencing and expressing emotions and translating
them into political actions. Thus, even though her disdain for the mud-
dled language of mass-produced pop culture is reminiscent of the elitism
attributed to Modernism, it is ultimately motivated by her conviction that
language at its – poetic – best can be instrumental to achieving very necessary social change.

1.5   The Power of Narration: Identity, Reality, and the Body

Jeanette Winterson's work overtly or covertly proclaims the message that
"[w]ords are very powerful things, [...], [b]ecause they can become realities" (J. Turner). She has an intense interest in the power of language
to sort events into "before," "now," and "later," thus defining concepts
of time. Furthermore, Winterson is fascinated by the performativity of
language, i.e., by its capacity to describe boundaries of and thereby lend
shape to objects, bodies, and landscapes in our minds, to pour memories,
thoughts, and feelings into story-shape so as to present to us, the producers
and users of language, an image of ourselves and others as recognizable
persons. In short, she is interested in the power of language to construct
in the human imagination realities of human subjects in space and time.

  Although Winterson loves the creative power of words, her explorations of this power concentrate on and render problematic the way language has been and continues to be employed by hegemonic forces as a

---

[47]Ganteau focuses on Winterson's use of the romance mode and, in an earlier article, uses the author's work to refute Frederick Jameson's lament of the "waning
   of affect" in postmodern literature (cf. "Fantastic").

tool in the construction of a hetero-patriarchal society. As the preservation of such a society depends on a tightly circumscribed definition of reality, its architects can only be interested in the production of language that represents reality as clearly defined according to the views most suitable to safeguarding the status quo that guarantees their power. In Winterson's eyes, the deplorable effect of language used in the interest of the conservation of extant hierarchies of power is the death of language. The perpetual re-creation and re-affirmation of fixed identities along binary oppositions – male vs. female realized as masculine vs. feminine, translated into strong vs. weak, perpetually complemented and reasserted by the "necessity" to choose partners of the opposite sex – curtails the space needed for the imagination to roam; it leads to an unimaginative use and production of language. Winterson points to her own difference from the norm as defined by hetero-patriarchal Western society as one of the motivating forces for her resistance against unimaginative language and the circumstances that cause it: "In a way I can't [inhabit a narrowness of thought] anyway," she says, "because of my sexuality, because of my gender, because of where I come from" (Kay 29/1). There is "no vested interest" for the author "in the world as it is now structured" (29/1).

Therefore, when Winterson, quasi after deconstructing essentialist gender identities, sets out to infuse language fossilized into rigid forms and imagery with new life, she combines postmodern feminist and queer social critique with visionary ideas of fluid, non-essentialist subject positions. Her (modernist) struggle for precision and her (postmodern) ambition of questioning the foundations of the "world as it is now structured" create a productive tension that permeates all of her fictions.

1.5.1 Narrating Identity

> I feel that I am floating free. I don't really know where I come from and I haven't produced any children. The only me there is, is the one I go on creating through my work which is a curious process but it does leave me with an enormous sense of freedom.
>
> Jeanette Winterson

A central function of the many tales and stories inserted into Winterson's fictions is to feed narrative material into the main narrative of her protagonists. These events in the character's life or accounts thereof – "available plots" as Gade calls them (35) – contribute to the construction of a protagonist's identity. In her characters Winterson illustrates what she has learned about the narrative construction of her own identity as described in the above quotation, the "me" she "[goes] on creating" through her writing in a "curious process" that is still continuing. In order to "know" who they might be, Winterson's protagonists gather details about their existence from their memory, from stories they have been told about themselves, from what they read or heard somewhere about events that occurred at a particular time in their lives or in the lives of others in similar circumstances, from dreams and wishes they have about themselves and their future. Then, in order to present an identity to the world, they piece together an autobiographical narrative from the scraps of stories they have collected over time.[48] Which information to use and which to leave out, whether to present it in chronological order or not, whether to embellish stories with colorful details or strip them of certain facettes is for the narrator-protagonists' to decide, and they make their decisions according to their political intensions as well as their delight in the creative application of story-telling skills. This method of narrative construction of identities they also transfer onto their representation of others.

The young Henri's "invention" of Napoleon as his personal heroic role model and savior of the French nation in *The Passion* illustrates this clearly: Out of his need for a strong father figure, his loyalist mother's religious enthusiasm for kings and emperors, expressions of French nationalist pride, and the impoverished peasants' hopes for a glorious future, he narrativizes a heroic identity for Bonaparte, "invent[ing] Bonaparte as much as he invented himself" (*Passion* 158). This identity cannot survive Henri's traumatic experiences as the neck-wringer of the emperor's chickens during the Napoleonic wars. He acknowledges his image of the emperor as a wishful fantasy, one of a multitude of "truths" about this man, but nonetheless an identity that was shared by many and widely "known" throughout France and Europe. Crucially, however, Henri invents himself in a narrative, just as he invented Napoleon. In his life story he analyzes

---

[48]Cf. Kilian on the concept of narrative identity. Referring to Paul Ricoeur and his "Life in Quest of Narrative," Kilian points out that the life story becomes a critical factor in the identity formation of a subject, and stresses the potential (co-)existence of multiple life stories and therefore narrative identities (118).

historical events from his own marginal perspective; he situates himself within history and constitutes himself as a subject through narrative.

While the narrative construction of identity can be experienced as an emancipatory act, it also highlights identity as a fiction, a subjective selection and interpretation of the "facts" of a person's life. In *The Passion* both narrators repeatedly address their readers with the words, "Trust me. I'm telling you stories." As some of the stories we are told are highly unlikely and some of the narrated identities turn out to be illusions, the reassuringly confident ring of this request, based as it is upon the information lead of one who is "in the know," acquires the quality of a mischievous wink. "Trust me if you dare, because I am telling you stories, and we all know better than to trust stories," the narrators seem to say. With this ironic statement Winterson thematizes a dialectic she explores in many of her fictions: On the one hand, we can only make sense of our realities by means of language and discourse. We depend upon stories, regardless of whether we tell them to and of ourselves, to and of others, or whether somebody else does, and we have little choice but to trust the storyteller. On the other hand, we know we can never be entirely sure of the veracity of the stories we are told; in fact, we are well-advised to question the truths put forth by the storyteller, whoever that may be, including ourselves. "Language always betrays us, tells the truth when we want to lie, and dissolves into formlessness when we would most like to be precise," Jordan in *Sexing the Cherry* warns us (90). Our reliance upon language and our wish to trust narration – indeed, the necessity to trust language, if communication is to be successful – are contrasted with the mistrust of stories we have developed as a result of our exposure to and immersion in postmodern theory and fiction or simply our life experiences.

Although language is our primary means of discourse through which we make sense of our existence, Winterson seems to suggest, we dare not, cannot claim complete ownership of words. Language exists beyond its individual users; it is a complex system of signs and symbols invented long before our time, and since sender and recipient bring a host of different prerequisites to the use of language and demands on communication, complete understanding can never be guaranteed. Moreover, it is an arbitrary system in which words are invested with subjective meanings and employed with conscious or subconscious strategic aims in mind. Words do not depict an essential truth or reality, but the received ideas of a community of language users or individual speakers about "truth" and "reality." Still, even though we sense we might never quite achieve full individual ownership of the word, we always strive for it.

Winterson's response to our "'thrown-ness' into language" (Maagaard 153), and to the task of taking possession of an inherently conservative, hegemonic system with which to create reality, is a ceaseless search for fresh words and modes of expressing emotions, ideas, and convictions. In her writing, the quest for language is an integral part of a continual quest for identity – for the "me" that is created through and perceived as narrative.[49] "Quest is at the heart of what I do [...]," Winterson says; "[t]he holy grail, and the terror that you'll never find it, seemed a perfect metaphor for life" (Jaggi). The structural link between the quest for language and the quest for identity is highlighted especially in *Oranges*, in reference to which the above statement was made: From an early age, Jeanette has connected her sense of self with her ability to use language to capture, persuade, frighten, or amuse her listeners. In the course of the novel she narrates numerous incidents that illustrate this constitutional trait of her identity. When, upon the discovery of her lesbianism, the church elders take away from her the privilege of wielding the word as a preacher in Sunday meetings, during "Glory Crusades," and as a lecturer in bible classes, Jeanette leaves her community and her family. She regains access to language and thus preserves her chance to continue on her quest for identity when she earns a scholarship to a prestigious British university and enrolls in the English program. By telling her story, Jeanette creates a coherent narrative identity for herself through which she presents herself as an empowered subject.[50]

While identity appears to be a potentially stable if constructed entity in Winterson's first book, this stability is radically questioned in *The Passion* and, especially so, in *Sexing the Cherry*. In these fictions Winterson confronts the human desire for foundations and one-ness with the hunger for the freedom that fluid, multi-faceted identities created by oneself can

---

[49]Here, I refer to the notion of "narratological perception of identity" as Gade formulates it (29).

[50]As she tells her own story and constructs an identity through narrative, Jeanette rejects what, in reference to Laura Mulvey's concept of the "male gaze," could be called the "heterosexual gaze" and creates herself as an emancipated lesbian woman.

offer.[51] Within the characters a deep longing for certainty, security, and belonging struggles with a rebellious desire to be freed from social conventions and restrictive manipulations by hegemonic powers. Henri joins the Grande Armée in pursuit of a noble cause to identify and be identified with. When he realizes that Bonaparte's ambitions sully any honorable motivations in the soldiers who give their lives for the emperor's campaign, Henri begins to resent the capricious casualness with which the despot decides upon the fates of thousands of men, his own included. His overwhelming desire to take his life into his own hands, to "make [his] own mistakes" (*Passion* 157), motivates both his decision to desert in Russia and, after killing the cruel cook in Venice, his refusal to accept Villanelle's help to leave the asylum. There, Henri creates an identity for himself by narrating his own story which is also a subversive re-writing of the history of the Napoleonic Wars.

In *Sexing the Cherry* Jordan initially joins the discoverer John Tradescant in the hope of finding through the male-defined activity of traveling the masculine traits he feels he lacks for a clearly-defined gender identity that would guarantee him a secure place in seventeenth century London society.[52] But the voyages of discovery which promise hegemonic masculinity do not engage him sufficiently, nor do they provide him with what he is missing. He has leisure to travel in his mind in search for a dancing princess whom he has grown to love, and embarks on a journey that is literally a quest for the female part of his self. The gender boundaries that once seemed so alluring to Jordan turn out to be too rigid for him, and he dreams of "grafting" his own gender.

In contrast to the male protagonists of *The Passion* and *Sexing the Cherry*, Villanelle and the Dog-Woman are already characterized by complex and flexible gender identities.[53] These are underlined by their asso-

---

[51] Maagaard argues that Winterson's characters are driven by "desire for self-unity and self-transparency, along with a passionate yearning for an other greater than the self" (152). I will discuss the relationships for which the protagonists yearn or into which they enter in Chapter 5 of this study.

[52] On the motif of the journey in Winterson's early fiction see Stowers, "Journeying," and Kilian.

[53] Villanelle and the Dog-Woman differ significantly in their awareness and acknowledgment of the fluidity of their gender identities. I will focus on Winterson's discussion of gender identity in *Oranges, The Passion* and *Sexing the Cherry* in Chapter 5.

ciation with water, an element that symbolizes movement, fluidity, and change:[54] Villanelle lives in the city of Venice and is the daughter of a boatman who passed on to her not only his superior ability to steer a boat through the canals, but also the physical insignia of boat*men*, namely webbed feet. Villanelle feels equally at home in the garments of men and women, and while she experiences love only for another woman, she also has sex with men, voluntarily as well as involuntarily. The Dog-Woman lives on the banks of the Thames and names her foundling son after an ancient river because, knowing that she will not be able to tie him to her, she hopes this name will one day carry him back to her. She clearly sees herself as a woman and attempts to conform to the rules of femininity in seventeenth-century England; yet, she has and embraces so many supposedly masculine characteristics that Jordan grows up thinking that if he wants to be a "real man," he must become like his mother.

1.5.2   Narrating Realities of Time and Space

Winterson's narrativizing of multiple, fluid identities is part of her analysis of the notion of "reality" and the role of "experience" in the construction of it. She locates the origins of the differentiation between experience and imagination, reality and fantasy in the age of rationalism and decidedly rejects "the divide" created then, arguing that "the imagination is just as character forming as the experience, and it's very difficult to separate the two" (Kay 28/1). Her musings about materiality and effects of lived experiences on people's lives and consciousnesses as compared to those of imagined ones lead to critical explorations of the assumed factuality of reality in her work. From the position that our only access to time, space, and matter is via language, a network of signs governed by socio-cultural conventions and power relations between its users, Winterson sets out to question traditional notions of temporal, spatial, and bodily reality, as the list of "lies" presented in Jordan's narrative in *Sexing the Cherry* illustrates:

---

[54]In her reading of *The Passion* and *Sexing the Cherry*, Stowers concentrates fully on the effects of Henri's and Jordan's travels on their gender identities. She neither comments on the relative geographic immobility of the Dog-Woman nor on the lack of effect of Villanelle's travels on her identity, but she mentions their association with water (cf. Stowers, "Journeying").

Lies 1: There is only the present and nothing to remember. *Lies 2*: Time is a straight line. *Lies 3*: The difference between the past and the future is that one has happened while the other has not. *Lies 4*: We can only be in one place at once. *Lies 5*: Any proposition that contains the word 'finite' (the world, the universe, experience, ourselves ... *Lies 6*: Reality as something which can be agreed upon. *Lies 7*: Reality as truth. (83)

Her fictions expose the cultural and historical determination of what we know as "reality," and subversively re-imagine, re-write it as a realm that allows for multiple possibilities for the construction of identities.

Winterson's first novel already dramatizes the unsettling and disorienting effects of the deconstruction of reality. But it also hints at the potential liberation inherent in the idea of life as a pool of possible paths to be taken and identities to be constructed from these paths. In *Oranges* Jeanette pays her hometown a visit after a long absence and goes to the places she had frequented in her childhood and adolescence. She speculates on the life she would have led, had she decided to stay with her mother and their church, and questions the traditional one-dimensional notion of reality:

I was beginning to wonder if I'd ever been anywhere. [...] I have a theory that every time you make an important choice, the part of you left behind continues the other life you could have had. [...] There's a chance that I'm not here at all, that all the parts of me, running along all the choices I did and didn't make, for a moment brush against each other. That I am still an evangelist in the North, as well as the person who ran away. Perhaps for a while these two selves have become confused. I have not gone forward or back in time, but across in time, to something I might have been, playing itself out. (*Oranges* 164)

Winterson explores the idea of going "across in time" instead of "forward or back" and of different selves, resulting from specific choices and existing in parallel layers of reality, in many of her texts, even up to *Tanglewreck*[55] and *The Stone Gods*.[56] Her thinking about time as circular

---

[55] *Tanglewreck* is Winterson's first fiction for young readers. Some of the primary themes discussed in this novel are time as a relative and relational entity, the simultaneity of past, present and future, and the responsibility of each person for the choices he or she has made or neglected to make and which in turn determine parallel realities.

[56] In *The Stone Gods* Winterson continues her enquiry into choices and their consequences on the level of humankind. The author envisions life on planets whose

instead of linear is influenced by the Eliotean understanding of the simultaneity of past and future in the present. In *The Passion*, Villanelle voices
this notion of time:

> The future is foretold from the past and the future is only possible because
> of the past. Without past and future, the present is partial. All time is
> eternally present and so all time is ours. There is no sense in forgetting
> and every sense in dreaming. Thus the present is made rich. Thus the
> present is made whole. (62)

The first of two epigraphs to *Sexing the Cherry* again directs the readers' attention to the question of time: "The Hopi, an Indian tribe, have a
language as sophisticated as ours, but no tenses for past, present and future. The division does not exist. What does this say about time?" (8).[57]
Winterson's own understanding of time is that it is "neither constant nor
straited ... that it is this vast moving thing, entity, energy, that none of us
can fully realise ... " (Reynolds, "Interview Winterson": 24). Jago Morrison and others have convincingly argued that in her attempts to "realise"
time, Winterson draws upon insights of theoretical physics that challenge
traditional views of space and time.[58] The second epigraph of *Sexing the
Cherry* confirms this observation and testifies to the author's engagement
with scientific theory: "Matter, that thing the most solid and the well-
known, which you are holding in your hands and which makes up your
body, is now known to be mostly empty space. Empty space and points of
light. What does this say about the reality of the world?" (8).

The Passion and *Sexing the Cherry* each take on the correlativity of
space and time and their "capacity for curvature and deformation," as described by quantum theory (J. Morrison 105). In *The Passion* Winterson's
mercurial city of Venice radically questions the notion of the measura-
bility of a geographical area, the possibility of meaningfully mapping a
place. The internal boundaries of Venice are as fluid as the water in its
canals; a waterway that has been there for centuries can disappear over
night, a church that has served generations as a geographic signpost can
move to the opposite end of the city. Strangers like Henri are unable to

---

resources have been greedily ransacked by generations of irresponsible humans,
leading to a barrenness that stretches from the natural world to the emotional capacity of the planets' human inhabitants.

[57]Note again the closeness to Eliot's notion of the simultaneity of past and present.
[58]For a book-length study of Winterson's usage of scientific theory see Estor.

orient themselves in this discontinuous, indefinable space. They rely on the help of Venetians whose memories provide the indispensable link between space and time. As the French invaders refuse to cooperate with the natives, they are frustrated in their attempt to mould the ancient city after the linear fashion then current in France.

Sexing the Cherry takes up the motif of mapping and adds the subversive power of imagination to the idea of unstable spatial boundaries.[59] The enchanted cities Jordan visits on his journeys of the mind do not appear on the maps of colonial travelers like John Tradescant, but they are no less "real" for existing in the protagonist's imagination. Both the mapped and the unmapped, imaginary journeys produce material evidence for their existence: From his excursions for the English crown he brings back exotic plants and fruits; from his visit to Fortunata's island Jordan returns with a silver pendant, a gift from the dancing princess, "a woman who does not exist" (*Sexing* 130). The impact of his non-hegemonic travels on his subjectivity, however, is much more significant than that of his travels of discovery. His unlicensed journeying on alternative routes enables him to discover identities he had been taught to ignore throughout his childhood and youth. Thus, Jordan not only undermines colonial modes of describing and charting space, but also successfully challenges masculinist prescriptions of identity and heroic behavior.

Winterson connects both of these political objectives to her explorations of time as a non-linear entity. She complements the fictional universe of *Sexing the Cherry* with two characters who inhabit the England of the late 1980s. Unlike the "chronotopes" Mikhail Bakhtin identified for literary fiction, however, the two time-spaces of London during the Puritan revolution and contemporary London are not separate from one another but intimately related through their inhabitants who pass between them.[60] The Dog-Woman is re-incarnated, one might say, in a scientist who studies the pollution of the lakes and rivers. This scientist had been

---

[59]Thereby it continues Winterson's critique of the (neo-)colonial imposition of hegemonic measures and boundaries upon occupied space.

[60]See Pearce (*Dialogics*), who draws on Bakhtin's theory of chronotopes in order to explain the structure of Winterson's *Sexing the Cherry*. According to Bakhtin's definition, protagonists could neither share chronotopes nor inhabit more than one at a time. Pearce argues that, while Bakhtinian chronotopes were engaged in a dialogue with one another but could never meld together, the time-spaces of Winterson's protagonists are permeable; in the "self-consciously

an unhappy, unwanted girl who had grown fat not from eating too much, but "because [she] wanted to be bigger than all the things that were bigger than [her]. All the things that had power over [her]" (*Sexing* 124). While she lost her superfluous physical weight, she has retained a rage at the injustices of class and gender that to her feels like a weight in her mind. "I had an *alter ego* who was huge and powerful, a woman whose only morality was her own and whose loyalties were fierce and few," she remembers (*Sexing* 125), and fantasizes about storming through the World Bank and the Pentagon unhindered, stuffing into her sack business tycoons and world leaders in order to re-train them and change the world.

The mind-traveling Jordan of the seventeenth century appears to the readers again as the young Navy officer Nicolas Jordan. Like his namesake, Nicolas grew up building ship models and sailing them in ponds, and, like Jordan, he lived with an image of male heroism that did not satisfy his own need for complexity. Nicolas turns to the Navy for the opportunities of traveling it affords and for the heroic masculinity it promises, but he finds heroism in the fight of the ecologist who camps on the mercury-ripe Thames in order to draw attention to the alarming state of the environment.

The eco-feminist scientist and Nicolas Jordan in late twentieth-century London not only show character traits of the Dog-Woman and Jordan or grow up in similar circumstances, however; at times they literally *are* them. The scientist remembers a dream she had as a schoolgirl when she walked home on the Embankment after a school day made painful with bullying:

> I looked at my forearms resting on the wall. They were massive, like thighs, but there was no wall, just a wooden spit, and when I turned in the opposite direction I couldn't see the dome of St Paul's.
>
> I could see rickety vegetable boats and women arguing with one another and a regiment on horseback crossing the Thames.
>
> I had to get on to Blackfriars, there was someone waiting for me. (*Sexing* 128)

In that instance the girl moves out of her reality as an overweight outsider in a school in twentieth-century London into the reality of the Dog-Woman whose identity as a gigantic dog breeder on the banks of the stink-

polychronotopic" *Sexing the Cherry* (*Dialogics* 175), "characters have access to chronotopes beyond their immediate present" (182). Cf. also Jago Morrison.

ing Thames in the seventeenth century she experiences as her own. In a similar fashion Nicolas Jordan finds himself in the body and reality of Jordan while on board an admiralty tug as a naval cadet:

> I heard a foot scrape on the deck beside me. Then a man's voice said, 'They are burying the King at Windsor today.' I snapped upright and looked full in the face of the man, who was staring out over the water. I knew him but from where? And his clothes ... nobody wears clothes like that any more.
>
> I looked beyond him, upwards. The sails creaked in the breeze, the main spar was heavy with rope. Further beyond I saw the Plough and Orion and the bright sickle of the moon.
>
> I heard a bird cry, sharp and fierce. Tradescant sighed. My name is Jordan. (*Sexing* 121)

Thus, by allowing the Dog-Woman and Jordan to live simultaneously in the seventeenth century and in a contemporary London, Winterson creates a short circuit of time that defies the concept of linear time and neatly separable time-spaces.[61] The notion of a circular or cyclical time structure is reinforced on the level of politics. While the Dog-Woman, disgusted with the moral depravity of the Puritan elite, allows a fire to develop that will devour most of pestilence-infested seventeenth-century London, the scientist sets fire to a factory responsible for the dramatically high mercury level that pollutes the Thames and poisons the population of London. She takes this desperate measure after a long campaign fought at great personal loss to raise public awareness of the ecological disaster and to pressurize the government into imposing sanctions on the polluters.

---

[61] Gade stresses the importance of one's personal experience of time as compared to scientifically measured time. She cites the environmentalist as an example for a person whose individual experience of time increasingly takes precedent over "official" time (cf. 33). I would add that this is true for Nicolas Jordan as well. See also Pykett who points out that Winterson's novels repeatedly foreground the subjectivity and cultural relativism of space and time, questioning common sense or rationalistic Western perceptions of time, space, and matter. Pykett regards this as Winterson's taking up the Eliotean preoccupation with the simultaneity of time past and time present.

1.5.3   Narrating the Body

Fluid spatial boundaries and curved time structures in Winterson's writing of the late 1980s must have an impact on the physicality of bodies.[62] As Winterson re-writes time-space inspired by insights of New Physics, she also re-imagines and narrativizes the human body. The most radical sub-version of traditional notions of time and matter is presented in the story of the youngest dancing princess, Fortunata. Like her sisters, she defies gravity as she flies with them from their father's house, but unlike them she does not seem to age. When Jordan finds her on a rocky island, she is just as young as she was when she involuntarily left her sisters' company. Moreover, she now runs a dancing school where she teaches her female students to spin on their toes with such rapidity that their bodies turn into "points of light," producing a tone that is too rich, too strong to be called music (*Sexing* 93).

During his search for Fortunata, Jordan encounters other places where physical rules, rules of logic, and/or rules of cultural conventions are unhinged. At the onset of his journey of the mind Jordan dines in a house with ceilings, but no floors, where people travel from room to room by winch or by balancing on tight ropes. From there he witnesses the youngest dancing princess descend on "a thin rope which she cut and re-knotted a number of times during the descent" (*Sexing* 21). Fortunata later tells him that this was the dancing city to which she flew with her sisters, a city in which people "had abandoned gravity" and in turn "gravity had abandoned them," allowing them to float in the air while they went about their business (*Sexing* 97). Gravity is lent to words in the city of words, where language takes on a materiality that has the power to harm people. Every word uttered there floats to the sky where big word clouds would suffocate the population, if fearless cleaners did not ascend into the sky in balloons and tackle the aggressive crowd with mops. The inhabitants of yet another city habitually destroy and rebuild their houses on a different spot in a single night, thus traveling like nomads with their entire house-holds, while in the city where love is forbidden, generations of people are destroyed by the disease of love. As he experiences realities that contra-dict everything he knew about time, space, and matter, Jordan – and with

---

[62]Cf. Jago Morrison's statement that "questions of time lead inevitably to ques-tions of flesh" (95).

him the reader – wonders just what is "real" and what "reality" actually means.[63] Like Jeanette in *Oranges*, who acknowledges that she might have been someone else if she had made different decisions in her life, he realizes that there is more than one way of interpreting one's experiences, more than one life to live in a lifetime, and consequently more than one possible identity to every person.

Apart from the realities and bodies of Jordan's imagination discussed above, Winterson also peoples her Puritan London with bodies that contest the idea of solid matter and of bodies that can be divided into neat categories. A very obvious example of a body re-written is the Dog-Woman, a being of huge bodily proportions complete with enormous physical strength.[64] Yet, the body of this mountainous woman does not always behave in predictable ways: As a mere baby, she broke both her father's legs when he swung her on his knees to tell her a story, but her feather-light mother was able to lift her up and carry her for miles (cf. *Sexing* 25). The Dog-Woman attributes this to the power of love which gave her mother the strength needed to level out the weight of her daughter's body but which her father lacked; later in fact she kills her father for planning to sell her.[65] To her, love seems like a force of nature, like darkness and water in which she "weigh[s] nothing at all" (*Sexing* 40). This episode also testifies to the uncertainty of matter; it presents the material not "as irrefutable facts but rather as means of representing" (Gade 32). Different individuals – and per extension, societies – will have different notions of size and weight; the description of a woman's body as "huge" or "tiny", in particular, depends on specific cultural conventions of femininity.

---

[63] Pearce suggests that "what Jordan learns in his journeys through the enchanted cities is the *synchronicity of time*: the simultaneity of past, present and future" (*Dialogics* 182). While this is indeed an important lesson for Jordan, it is not the only one. His travels to the enchanted cities have grave implications for his own notions of space and matter as fluid and changeable.

[64] The Dog-Woman has been read as the parodistic inversion of the mythical half-woman, half-beast, of Sin in the Miltonian sense of the monstrous female who with her body represents everything men fear and despise in women (cf. Onega; Haslett 42).

[65] In *Tanglewreck* love defies the pull of gravity and travels faster than light. Winterson's notion of love as an integrative force will be discussed in Chapters 5 and 6.

The solid materiality of bodies is furthermore questioned when the
Dog-Woman mentions in passing that in spite of her bulk she can become
invisible, a paradox that is corroborated in the story of the ecologist who
was "ignored and overlooked" in her childhood in spite of her remarkable
height and weight (*Sexing* 124). Winterson here applies "complementar-
ity" and "uncertainty," key principles of the theory of relativity, to the
analysis of human bodies and their materiality in the field of social relations. These terms "enshrine the idea that no object may be viewed in its
entirety, but instead it presents different qualities to the observer in different circumstances" (J. Morrison 105). Visibility of a body is not something that can be taken for granted, not even if applied to a body of great
size; it depends on the social status of the owner of the body as well as on
the status of the person looking at or overlooking a body, on their positions in the hierarchy, their relevance to the running of the society.[66] The
Dog-Woman does not do well on any of these counts; therefore, in certain
situations – namely if she does not wish to draw attention to herself and
her subversive activities – she proves easy to overlook, while in others her
presence has immediate and shocking effects on those who encounter her.

The Dog-Woman's body has been read as grotesque according to
Bakhtin's definition (cf. Palmer, "Foreign Bodies") and as an exempli-
fication of the carnivalesque grotesque body described by Mary Russo
in *The Female Grotesque* (Haslett 42). Its femaleness, gigantic size, immense strength, and hideous appearance represent a challenge to the patriarchal order that defines women as weak, thin, and pretty. It also poses
an insurmountable obstacle to the assertion of heterosexuality as the norm
and as a structural pillar of society. This is illustrated in hilarious detail
in the account of the pathetic failure of a very willing man to satisfy the
enterprising heroine in her sole sexual encounter.[67]

---

[66]Note the parallel between female invisibility in a masculinist society as described by Winterson and the social invisibility caused by blackness in a white
   hegemony as Ralph Ellison explores it in *Invisible Man* (1952).

[67]Interestingly, this subversively grotesque female body contrasts sharply with the
   down-to-earth interests and desires of its owner. A staunch loyalist, the Dog-
   Woman also entertains decidedly conservative views on traveling and gathering
   knowledge about strange lands, exotic fruits, and – what is most relevant to the
   thematic focus of this study – on distinctions between the genders or the lack
   thereof. In subchapter 5.2. I will focus on this tension in relation to Winterson's
   questioning of the gender binary.

Jeanette Winterson is convinced of the capacity of art and language to create realities of the mind that offer alternative concepts of time and space, the body, and identity. Her early novels in particular radiate this confidence and translate it into powerful explorations of new possibilities of gender.

2 Struggling with Race

Apart from being one of the most widely known US-American writers, Toni Morrison is also an influential public intellectual who does not hesitate to voice her distinctive views on social and theoretical issues that are relevant in the US-American context. Examples of the author's assertive openness over her entire career are her critical remarks on the then-budding (White) women's liberation movement in "What the Black Woman Thinks About Women's Lib," her scathing criticism of race politics of the US administration in the late 1980s and the treatment of Black women in particular in her Pulitzer interview, "The Pain of Being Black." They include her critical view of L.S.C. Justice Clarence Thomas's conduct and his political convictions in "Friday on the Potomac," and the increasing unease she expresses about the condition of race relations in the United States at the end of the twentieth century in an interview with a German newspaper, where she calls racism "the daily catastrophe of this society that is so devastating that I have to cry out – in a lecture, in an article" (Raddatz 34/3). "A Slow Walk of Trees" of 1976, "Rootedness" of 1984, and "On the Backs of Blacks" of 1993 make the author's stance on the issues of racial identity, difference, and race discrimination equally clear: Morrison is as unequivocal in her affirmation of African American culture and Black identity as in her lucid deconstruction and powerful condemnation of racism.

However, these forceful public calls for racial equality and for the continuation of the fight against racist ideas and structures in contemporary US-American society are accompanied by texts and statements that indicate that at the turn of the 21st century Toni Morrison might still have been exploring the ground she moves on when she talks or writes about race and racial identity, that she might have been questioning some of the accepted truths of Critical Race Studies as well as her own assumptions about race.[1] An analysis of Morrison's explorations of this subject in a number of essays and interviews, therefore, is needed to do justice to her struggle with the concept of race and the realities of racism as well as to her goals as a writer and a politically engaged intellectual.

2.1   Race as an Open Question

In 1993, Elissa Schappell asks Toni Morrison in an interview whether she "write[s] to figure out exactly how [she] feel[s] about a subject" (Schappell and Lacour 93). Morrison replies:

> No, I know how I *feel*. My feelings are the result of prejudices and convictions like everybody else's. But I am interested in the complexity, the vulnerability of an idea. It is not: "This is what I believe," because that would not be a book, just a tract. A book is: "This may be what I believe, but suppose I am wrong ... what could it be?" Or, "I don't know what it is, but I am interested in finding out what it might mean to me, as well as to other people." (93)

Asked almost the same question in an interview with a German daily in 1999, she makes a very similar statement: "When I have a set opinion about something, that topic for me is no material for a book. Normally I write about things I do not understand. I ask myself, 'How does that feel? Is there anything in it that I can still use today or in the future'" (Roether 15).[2]

The question of race, I want to argue, is one such contentious issue for Toni Morrison; it is a question she considers still unanswered in the late

---

[1] Frequently in academic discourse, race is placed in inverted commas "to signify its questionable status" (Youngs 26). Following Youngs and in the interest of limiting the number of words in inverted commas, however, I will dispense with this indicator in my text. Morrison herself uses inverted commas infrequently, and I hope to make clear that I question this concept in all of my analyses of her contributions to the discourse on race.

[2] Diemut Roether: "Versuchen Sie sich durch Schreiben klarer über Dinge zu werden?" ("Are you trying to understand things more clearly through writing?") Toni Morrison: "Wenn ich zu etwas eine fest gefügte Meinung habe, ist das für mich kein Material für ein Buch. Normalerweise schreibe ich über Dinge, die ich nicht verstehe. Ich frage mich, wie fühlt sich das an? Gibt es daran etwas, das ich heute oder in der Zukunft noch anwenden kann?" (15). All translations of passages from this interview are mine.

1990s. Racial identity, difference, and racial discrimination in the United States are important themes in every one of her first six novels. In fact, her whole career has been devoted to the exploration of legacies of the notion of race. Yet, during the time she writes *Paradise* and – following the publication of the book in 1998 – gives interviews about it, she questions her convictions and feelings about race, unconvinced of the completeness of her understanding of the precarious relation between the biologically unfounded idea of racial difference and the factual consequences of the social construction of race in everyday life. Morrison's acknowledged difficulty to fully grasp race and its consequences, her uneasy awareness of a tension between constructivist theory and people's everyday experiences with the social practice of racialization, as well as a deep wariness of ready-made answers are important motivators of the author's writing of fiction, but also of semi-theoretical, essayistic texts. Thus, in her texts and interviews around the publication of *Paradise* she explores not only generally shared interpretations and applications of the concept of race, but also – maybe most importantly – her own.

In the following I will analyze Morrison's remarks about matters of race in select essays and interviews in order to explore her perspective on the concept of race and its social relevance in the United States of the late twentieth century.[3] Concentrating on her essay "Home," I will then address the complex nature of the author's struggle to position herself in the discourse on race, to develop for herself a clear understanding of possible merits as well as pitfalls of the praxis of racializing human beings, and to create a mental framework that would allow writers – and readers – to circumvent and finally overcome the devastating effects of racism. Finally, I will discuss Morrison's understanding of the notion of "race-

---

[3]The following essays by Toni Morrison are considered here: "Home" (1998); "Friday on the Potomac" (1992), and "Unspeakable Things Unspoken: The Afro-American Presence in American Literature" (1989). The interviews are: Elizabeth Farnsworth, "Interview with Toni Morrison" (1998); Paul Gray, "Paradise Found" (1998); Fritz J. Raddatz, "Ich bin keine Amerikanerin. Ein ZEIT-Gespräch mit Toni Morrison" (1998); Margaret Reynolds, "Interview with Toni Morrison" (2003); Diemut Roether, "Radikal bin ich nicht, aber unabhängig": Interview mit Toni Morrison (6./7. Nov. 1999); Elissa Schappell and Claudia Brodsky Lacour, "The Art of Writing Fiction" (1993); Denis Scheck, "Im Gespräch: Toni Morrison. Die Aufklärung hat erst begonnen" (2000); Timehost, "Internet Chat with Toni Morrison" (1998).

lessness" and investigate the meaning and possible consequences of her idea of "unmattering race," both as it influences her writing at the turn of the 21st century and as it adds new thoughts to the discourse on race in the reality of contemporary US-American society.

2.1.1   Race as an Empowering Cultural Concept

Morrison's statements on issues of racial identity and difference in interviews and non-fictional publications of the 1990s show how conflicting her emotions about these topics are. In her remarks on the subject of race a tension appears between her embrace of the potentially empowering qualities of racial identity on the one hand and her fervent critique of the reductively essentialist, discriminatory foundations of this concept on the other. A cross-reading of some of her statements on race will serve to illustrate this point.

When asked by an interviewer in 2000 whether she would create human beings all of one color if she could "play God," Morrison replies in the negative:

> No. The diversity of races is just as important among human beings as among animals and plants. Although the consequences of racism were and still are horrible, it is part of the task set for us humans to come to terms with it. We are not born as humans; we have to make ourselves human – each and every one of us. (Scheck)[4]

This answer suggests that Morrison accepts the idea that human beings can in fact be meaningfully grouped together in different races, that they do differ racially – in short, that race exists. Although she does not enlarge upon the statement here, does not explain why the "diversity of races" is as important for humanity as for the rest of fauna and flora, she asserts that the "task" of coming to terms with racism – that is, with the discrimination and oppression of individuals and groups on grounds of their racial

---

[4]Denis Scheck: "Wenn Sie Gott spielen könnten, würden Sie nur Menschen einer Hautfarbe erschaffen?" Toni Morrison: "Nein. Die Vielfalt der Rassen ist unter Menschen genauso wichtig wie unter Tieren oder Pflanzen. So schrecklich die Folgen des Rassismus auch waren und sind, seine Bewältigung ist Teil der Aufgabe, die uns Menschen gestellt ist. Wir kommen nicht als Menschen zur Welt, wir müssen uns erst dazu machen – jeder Einzelne von uns." All translations of passages from this interview are mine.

affiliation or categorization – is a humanizing factor. To put it bluntly: if she where in the position to redesign the world and had to chose whether to create it with or without different races, Morrison says she would opt for a racialized world, although she is painfully conscious of the negative effects of racism on human society. She regards the distinction of different races meaningful in our world, because for her the task of overcoming racist oppression is necessary for the human endeavor of creating a just society. According to Morrison, then, our struggle against racism will render us more human than we are to begin with. She seems to imply that the distinction of races is an inhuman impulse we have within us, as is our willingness to invest racial attributes with the power to qualify or disqualify. What will enhance our humanness, then, according to Morrison, is our will to suppress this impulse. That we struggle to do so points to the fact that we make a conscious effort of it and that it is a process rather than a one-off decision. A society without racism, however, would be a more humane society.

But what does Morrison mean when she refers to race? A passage in her essay "Unspeakable Things Unspoken" of 1989 provides an answer to this central question:

> For three hundred years black Americans insisted that "race" was no usefully distinguishing factor in human relationships. During those same three centuries every academic discipline, including theology, history, and natural science, insisted "race" was *the* determining factor in human development. When blacks discovered they had shaped or become a culturally formed race, and that it had specific and revered difference, suddenly they were told there is no such thing as "race," biological or cultural, that matters and that genuinely intellectual exchange cannot accommodate it. (3)

As this statement clearly shows, Morrison regards race as a cultural concept. Hegemonic White elites in the United States pronounced race the most relevant means of differentiation between human beings. After centuries of social life organized around laws that divided Americans into "blacks" and "non-blacks" or "whites" and forbade the intermingling of the two groups, African Americans became conscious of the fact that they had developed a distinct Black culture. This culture was shaped by historical experiences such as the Middle Passage, the horrific involuntary journey from parts of Africa to North American plantations, as well as personal experiences. It was beaten into shape by slavery and the individual's struggle to survive with an intact sense of self and a sense of community among those who suffered and struggled under the same premises of racial subjugation. Thus, in Morrison's understanding, racial oppression and forced segregation created an African American community that – in line with centuries of official teachings of biologically determined racial differences as well as daily individual experiences of Otherness – began to think of itself in terms of a group, a racial group with features that were distinct from other racial groups.

Morrison underlines the long tradition among African Americans of questioning the doctrine of biological determinism. But far from dismissing all thought of racial difference, she talks about a "specific and revered difference" ("Unspeakable" 3). Furthermore, she explicitly stresses the cultural nature of this difference between so-called races. The knowledge and perception of difference from other individuals and groups is a necessary part of self-definition for every individual and every social group. For Black Americans, whose sense of identity had been systematically attacked during centuries of slavery and racial discrimination, the idea of difference was essential in their effort to establish themselves as individual persons and full members of the society, against the aggressive resistance of the hegemonic powers. The discovery, cultivation, and preservation of cultural differences between Black and non-Black Americans gave African Americans the opportunity, on the one hand, to claim parts of US culture and history for themselves and, on the other hand, to point out their own contributions to this culture. The identity politics of the 1970s and '80s grew out of and fostered this new sense of identity in the African American community.

Morrison values this understanding of race as a cultural concept that developed through external pressure and as a reaction to it. She subscribes to constructivist teachings of the arbitrary, constructed nature of race; but rather than dismissing the construct because of its constructedness, she acknowledges the existence of race in the set-up of US-American society and defines race as "culturally formed" ("Unspeakable" 3). In race as a cultural characteristic, then, she sees a treasure trove of cultural riches for African Americans to use in the process of individuation and self-empowerment, and she values it for herself as an author. In her writing, Morrison, the "celebrated and gifted chronicler of the African American experience" (Bent 145), uses this treasure to bring to life complex and intriguing characters and to illuminate long-neglected and still underrepresented aspects of US-American history and culture. In her interviews with Margaret Reynolds, Morrison asserts:

> I want to scour the official history for the alternate history that exists, sometimes parallel to it, more often underneath it. [...] [A]nd when you cannot find all of the data, you have to imagine it. But I don't want the story, the alternate, or the underneath or repressed story, told in a manner that duplicates the official narrative. I want the speakers, the characters, to assume whatever form they wish. ("Interview Morrison" 11)

One of many vivid examples of her efforts to re-write in her works of fiction US-American history from an African American perspective is her description of the contribution of Black people to the settlement of the West, the history of all-Black towns in connection with this process, and the experiences of African American soldiers during and after World War Two and the Vietnam War in *Paradise*.[5]

Toni Morrison places herself firmly within the African American tradition and within Black culture, which she compares favorably to Anglo-Saxon American culture: "It's richer. It has more complex sources. It pulls from something that's closer to the edge, it's much more modern. It has a human future," she enthuses during her conversation with Schappell and Brodsky Lacour (118). Culture for Morrison mediates between the poles of emotion and factuality with regard to race. Black history and culture to her are intensely "feelable," a great source of pride that contributes significantly to a positive self-image of African Americans. Yet the facts of their emergence in US history and their continuing development also can and must be researched in detail and made available to people of all colors.

2.1.2   "Racelessness" as an Ultra-Conservative Strategy

Aware of a right-wing racist backlash that coincides with and makes use of ultra-conservative denials of the existence of racism in the United States, Morrison is eager to dispel the impression that in her own work she might be promoting the wholesale casting out of the concept of race. At a conference in 1997 she expresses her awareness of the risk of provoking what she calls "charges of encouraging futile attempts to transcend race or per-

---

[5]Cf. Tally, *Histories*.

nicious efforts to trivialize it" ("Home" 8).[6] "It would worry me a great
deal if my remarks – or my narratives – were to be so completely misun-
derstood," she adds ("Home" 8).

The notion of transcending race has become objectionable to Morrison because of its association with ultra-conservative political teachings
and politics that declare the concept of race obsolete in order to do away
with affirmative action policies that seek to bridge the socio-economic
gap between US citizens of European descent and African Americans.[7]
In addition to this, the author also distances herself from specific political
adversaries: In "Friday on the Potomac," the introduction to the volume
of essays she edited about the hearing of Professor Anita Hill's charges of
sexual harassment against Justice Clarence Thomas, she interprets Justice
Thomas's call for a "transcendence of race" as an expression of the desire
of an upper class Black man to blend in with the White male environment
he has chosen as his workplace and social context. Justice Thomas, she
claims,

> could be understood as having realized his yearning for and commitment
> to "racelessness" by having a white spouse at his side. At least their love,
> we are encouraged to conclude, had transcended race, [...]. Expectedly,
> the nominee called for a transcendence of race, remarked repeatedly on its
> divisive nature, its costliness, its undeniable degradation of principles of
> freedom. ("Friday on the Potomac" xxi f.)

Morrison here associates the notion of racelessness with a political strategy employed by hegemonic powers and represented by the conservative
– some might say right-wing – Justice Clarence Thomas to shore up the
status quo that disempowers the majority of non-White sections of US so-

---

[6]Toni Morrison, "Home," *The House That Race Built: Original Essays by Toni
Morrison, Angela Y. Davis, Cornel West, and Others on Black Americans and
Politics in America*, ed. Wahneema Lubiano (New York: Vintage Books, 1998)
3-12. All further reference is to this edition.

[7]Affirmative action policies are intended to level out the unequal chances of Black
and White Americans on the job market by granting African Americans preferen-
tial treatment for example in employment situations. Affirmative action is heavily
criticized by the political right who argues that these laws result in a "reversed
discrimination" of the White population.

ciety.[8] Influential members of Justice Thomas's political faction discredit the efforts of liberal scholars and activists to point out the undiminished relevance of race matters in American society and put into doubt the detrimental effects of a racism that is continuing on an everyday basis. "Suddenly (for our purposes suddenly) race does not exist," Morrison sums up the neo-conservative trend already in "Unspeakable Things Unspoken" (3). When Clarence Thomas calls for "racelessness" in the United States, to her he does so to further the chances of full integration of a formerly marginalized but now assimilated Black aspirant to power into the hegemonic center. Morrison regards this is as an opportunistic, selfish attitude which – devoid as it is of solidarity with those who remain on the margins of society – becomes a treacherous act, especially so if the "traitor" has no intention of using his acquired high position for the benefit of members of his racial group who, as he knows very well, are still disadvantaged because of their racial and socio-economic background.

Morrison's sharp criticism of one of the very few African Americans in a position of power also needs to be viewed in light of her notion of the humanizing qualities of the struggle against racism. Somebody who – in spite of his privileged position – lends himself to conservative forces that deny the existence of racism and thus the legitimacy of political efforts to promote the cause of members of disadvantaged racial groups in the United States in Morrison's opinion sabotages the struggle for a just society. The hypocritical propagation of colorblind "racelessness" by the political right discredits progressivist calls to put a stop to systemic race discrimination and sneers at artists' efforts to point out limits and dangers of classifying people on grounds of their racial identity, all of which explains Morrison's aversion against the label "racelessness." This aversion is heightened further by the fact that in hegemonic political as well as literary discourses "racelessness" had for the longest time simply meant "white" (cf. *Playing*).

Morrison here reacts to a specific political event, to a particular "hate figure" who is involved in right-wing discourses that misappropriate and taint terms like "racelessness." However, as she denies herself the usage of these labels, she leaves valuable ground to the conservative camp in the

---

[8]For an account of Justice Clarence Thomas as a major player in the neo-conservative movement in the United States see People for the American Way, "Buying a Movement."

discourse on race, relinquishing the power to name progressive, nondiscriminatory ideas and visions concerning race matters. In the 1990s, Morrison does not venture to re-appropriate concepts such as "racelessness," "colorblindness" and "multiculturalism" for her own project but refrains from considering them altogether.

2.1.3   Race as a Discriminatory Construct

At the end of the twentieth century, Toni Morrison is struggling with the tension between the knowledge of the constructedness of race and the empowering faculties of race as a cultural concept. A strong emotional involvement complicates and at times sabotages her efforts to come forward with a clear agenda that combines her theoretical, social constructivist views on race and her desire to preserve for the African American community the empowering faculties transported by this construct. Morrison herself has contributed crucially to the deconstruction of race and has repeatedly castigated its liability to abusive employment in the oppression of people. And yet, she insists that the illusory, constructed concept of race corresponds with "race as a social fact" in two ways: Not only does it allow African Americans to feel pride in their rich and diverse culture, it also affects them negatively as those who are considered "raced" – i.e., not White – by allowing the "non-raced" part of the population significant privileges.

This is the reality of race in US-American society: Although it has been known for decades that there is no biological or genetic base for the categorization of human beings into distinct races along phenotypic or even genetic characteristics and that after centuries of interracial mixing there are in fact no pure races, arbitrary physical, psychological and behavioral signals are still used to define people as "Black," "White," Native American, etc., a practice that almost invariably leads to negative economic and social consequences for those racialized as non-White. By criticizing the "racelessness" propagated in a self-congratulatory strategic move by powerful right-wing intellectuals and politicians, Morrison fights the conservative presupposition of "colorblindness." With this notion, affluent, powerful men and, to a lesser extent, women deny the existence of institutional racism and its widespread consequences. One extreme and very successful proponent of this political opinion, Dinesh D'Souza, formerly John M. Olin Fellow of the right-wing American Enterprise In-

stitute and a Robert & Karen Rishwain Fellow at the equally conservative Hoover Institution, may serve as an example. In *The End of Racism*
D'Souza not only claims that the Anglo-American culture and, by implication, race is more advanced than African American culture whose lower,
urban classes in particular are plagued by "black pathologies that are so
flagrant that no one can ignore them" (*End* 482). In a different publication
he also suggests that Black Americans have themselves to blame for racist
discrimination, as long as they are unwilling to acknowledge and therefore unable to close what he regards as the "civilization gap" to White
America (cf. D'Souza, "Racism").

In "Unspeakable Things Unspoken," Morrison remarks with some in-
dignation that "[i]t always seemed to me that the people who invented
the hierarchy of "race" when it was convenient for them ought not to be
the ones to explain it away, now that it does not suit their purposes for
it to exist" (3). The calls for a raceless society by people who aim to
preserve the economic and political privileges of hegemony elicit in Morrison the strong urge to point out the unmistakable effects of racism as it
still prevails in contemporary US society. By arguing against the views
of a specific but unnamed group of people who feature in a contemporary
political discourse – "the people who invented [and now explain away]
the hierarchy of race ... " – she allows practical political states of affairs
to get in the way of her theoretical considerations of the possibility and
of possible effects of dispensing with racial difference and the compromised concept of race altogether. In reaction to Justice Thomas and the
conservative rhetoric of "racelessness," Morrison feels obliged to defend a
construct invented to oppress Black Americans, because the political right
wants to explain it away.

In 1998, Toni Morrison produces a statement in an internet dialogue
that clearly juxtaposes the tension between the affirmation of racial difference as a productive category in economic as well as political spheres and
the author's own critical analysis of race as an oppressive and reductive
concept that affects thoughts and emotions:

> There are racial differences among us. Exaggerated and exploited for po-
> litical and economic purposes. And we have a great deal of baggage, per-
> sonal feelings about other races because the society has been constructed
> along racial divisions. But in fact, when we meet another person one on
> one, and we know or recognize their race, we pull from that large suitcase
> of stereotypical information, of learned responses, of habitual reaction,
> which is the easiest and the laziest way to evaluate other people. The dif-

ficult thing and the important thing is to know people as individuals. So
knowing that an individual is Asian or white or black is knowing next to
nothing. It's knowing some cultural information which one can assume,
but one must be wrong. But one must know much more than simply a
racial marker. Knowing another person's race is like knowing their height
or some other almost irrelevant piece of biological information. (Timehost)

Morrison's comment highlights an aspect of race that makes it so insid-
ious, so difficult to handle appropriately. Race is a seemingly wanton
construct the biological absurdity of which has been demonstrated many
times. And yet it is omnipresent and almost omnipotent in its history of
dividing US society into powerful insiders and subaltern outsiders. It fundamentally influences the perception human beings of themselves and others and their interaction with others. However, in some ways, the author's
statement is rather problematic. Can Morrison be seriously suggesting
that someone's racial affiliation is irrelevant to that person's individuality? Experiences of discrimination, of being outsiders in a society still
dominated by affluent White men are bound to have a strong influence on
the personality of, say, a Chicano/a or African American. In her narratives the author herself has repeatedly problematized the capacity of race
to shape identities. As important as it is "to know people as individuals,"
is it possible to see this individuality as independent of the group identity
of a person? Apart from the difficulty that there might not be such a thing
as one specific individuality to get to know, it seems that Morrison's wish
clashes here with a reality in which racial differences continue to dominate our perception – a reality which the author makes the topic of much
of her writing, but which also continually challenges the practicability of
her theoretical thoughts.

Morrison's struggling with the complexity of race becomes even more
apparent in the following quote. "Forcing people to react racially to another person is to dismiss the whole point of humanity," she writes in
the aforementioned internet chat (Timehost). If we analyze this remark in
light of her other statements on race, we cannot but wonder how the author
can assert that there are racial differences among human beings, as stated
earlier in the interview, and, at the same time, that it is inhuman to force
people to pay attention to these differences when they get in contact with
one another? Here, Morrison contradicts herself. She claims that racial
identity as a cultural identity owned by a specific community of people
can serve to empower the individual and, at the same time, she warns us

of judging people by their racial categorization instead of seeing them as individuals with many more characteristics and identities than racial ones. Moreover, by suggesting that race is as relevant or irrelevant a feature as a person's height, she seems to ignore her own critique of race, which maintains that this concept was invented and is still being used obsessively in order to classify individuals and groups with the purpose of situating them in hierarchies of power. There is a significant difference between the social and economic consequences a person's height might have for him- or herself and the effects of being classified as "black" or "white." Of course, Morrison is aware of the real-life consequences of race, but she seems torn between her own theoretical conviction that race is a potentially harmful, arbitrary construct without which the world would be a more just place, her sharp disapproval of political tendencies to explain away race in order to maintain the status quo, and her wish to preserve the empowering aspects of racial identity in the face of such tendencies.

This tension between Morrison's theoretical convictions – the arbitrariness of the construct race – and her reaction to historical and contemporary political realities in the United States – the impulse to preserve race as a meaningful and empowering identity – is further highlighted by her comment of the year 2000, in which she claims that racial differences are important for humankind and that coming to terms with racism "is part of the task set for us humans," a task that will help us become human (Scheck).

2.2 "Signing Race While Designing Racelessness": The Essay "Home"

Toni Morrison takes up and discusses many of these questions in her essay "Home," a relatively short text that originates from a talk Morrison gave in 1997 at a conference organized at Princeton University on the subject of "Race Matters." In reaction to claims by right-wing scholars and politicians that racism was no longer an issue and therefore race did not matter any more in the United States, participants stressed the pressing need to discuss the nature of race, its interplay with other identities, the need for difference and for policies designed to counter the prevalent reality of racism, as well as other "race matters."

"Home" testifies to the author's difficulties with the construct of "race" in ways earlier essays by her do not; here Morrison addresses race in terms that illustrate her deep ambivalence about this powerful concept. She enters the debate about relevance and significance of race in US-American society and literature in full consciousness of this ambivalence – a circumstance that makes this text a signpost on her intellectual and psychological journey to "clarify [her] thoughts on racial construction," as she writes in "Home" (3). In this speech-turned-essay, Morrison's long-held convictions become apparent, as do her doubts regarding the theoretical background and the social "facts" of racial difference and identity, how they breed color-coded hierarchies of power and discrimination. At the same time, Morrison questions her own beliefs and prejudices and searches for alternative ways of thinking about difference. Ultimately, "Home" illustrates the author's conflicting needs with regard to issues of race: on the one hand her longing for a place where African Americans truly belong, where their specific cultural traditions and historical experiences are appreciated and their contributions to society at large seen as valuable and indispensable for the common good; on the other hand her desire to create a society in which, in coherence with our knowledge about the constructedness and arbitrariness of race, racial identity is no longer considered relevant to the social placing of a person.

Morrison expresses a keen awareness of the fact that she and her readers live in a profoundly racialized society. Presenting herself as "an already- and always-raced writer" ("Home" 4), she asserts that "I have never lived, nor has any of us, in a world in which race did not matter" (3). In "Home" Morrison refers to race as a "death-dealing ideology" to which she feels "tethered" (5). In this text she does not – and indeed does not need to – give explicit examples for the potentially lethal influence of race on herself. Her audience and readers know from her novels and from interviews like the ones mentioned earlier in this chapter how the author is affected by this ideology: as a person who is constantly confronted with racial hierarchies, prejudices and presuppositions as well as destructive psychological and economic effects of racial discrimination in her daily interactions with others; and as a writer living in such an environment, working within a race-inflected language and laboring to produce a different kind of language in her own texts. "Whatever the forays of my imagination, the keeper, whose keys tinkled away within earshot, was race," she points out in "Home" (3). The fact that even her imagination, that most autonomous and most enterprising part of her, is caught within the narrow confines of race illustrates how much of a fact of life this concept is for the author and how burdened she feels by it.

As Morrison paints this picture of the omnipresence of "race" early on in her essay, she is referring to the binary opposition of "black" and "white," meaning marked and unmarked, a binary designed to disenfranchise African Americans and other racial and ethnic minorities. Yet, the discriminatory aspects of race, which she describes through powerful imagery of oppression and imprisonment in the first lines of "Home," affect all members of society, regardless on which side of the racial divide they are situated or situate themselves. They infringe the capacity to see people as complex individuals and to interact freely and without prejudice in social encounters. In the course of her essay, Morrison imagines and designs a scenario in which the notion of race is freed of its corrupting qualities so as to leave us with a concept that allows for difference without prescribing hierarchies.[9]

[9]Morrison's reflections upon the possibility of purging race of its oppressive, hierarchy-inducing qualities while preserving its empowering aspects that lend themselves in positive ways to the process of individuation, call to mind the original meaning of the verb "to discriminate" as it was used in the English-speaking world before 1866. Before it acquired the additional meaning of "make distinction prejudicial to people of a different race or color" (Barnhart, *Dictionary*: 284), the verb only denoted "make or see a difference between," "from Latin *discriminatus*, past participle of *discriminare* to divide, separate, distinguish" (Barnhart, *Dictionary*: 284). Thus, in consistence with its Latin root, "discrimination" originally would not have had the connotation of creating a social and economic hierarchy to the disadvantage of the powerless party. In the context of race matters it would have meant describing differences in people's physical appearance, their style of dress or music, in their cultural practices, and other characteristics that would be noted to distinguish between two or more individuals but which would not have resulted in the denigration of individuals and entire groups of people because of these characteristics – "discrimination" in the sense of "distinction," as it was used before 1866 (Barnhart, *Dictionary*: 284). At first sight it might seem ironic that the verb "to discriminate" acquired its negative judgemental meaning exactly at a time when, after the American Civil War and the Emancipation Declaration, the systematic oppression and dehumanization of African Americans through the system of slavery was declared illegal. Yet, before 1866, the thought that the act of distinguishing – i.e., discriminating – between "white" and "black" could be unjust, probably did not occur to most slave owners, for whom Blacks classified as chattel.

2.2.1   The antagonism of "House" vs. "Home"

Morrison opens her essay "Home" by establishing an antagonism between what she calls "the racial house" on the one hand and "home"
on the other. There is an interesting overlap of the terms "house" and
"home" with terminology of the discourse of transnational feminism:
Constance S. Richards, for example, speaks of the "house of subordination" in which minorities as well as "Third World" communities find
themselves in their relationship with Western societies (27). Referring to
Gloria Anzaldúa's concept of "Borderlands/La Frontera," Richards contrasts it with the "home" whose culture "must be made a conscious part of
[. . .] self-construction" of minority communities (25).

Diaspora Studies and Postcolonial Theory also use the concept of
"home," but there it is a controversial one, as it idealizes and homoge-
nizes the home culture of a diasporic subject. In his introductory remarks
to an edition of the journal *Indian Literature* K. Satchidanandan, for example, argues that for second-generation Indian immigrants to the United
States "home becomes unreal" (8). He continues:

> They construct their homeland from fragments of information gathered
> from hearsay or from the internet. For them, home is not a place to return
> to, but a place to fantasise about, or may be to visit some time as a guest
> or a tourist. [. . .] The idea of home is also related to time that transforms
> it into history or myth. (Satchidanandan 8)

In Postcolonial and Diaspora Studies the concept of "home" thus tends to
be associated with a reactionary, narrow nationalism that disregards dynamics of hybridization, cultural transfer and globalization, but which,
nevertheless, has to be acknowledged as part of the identity of a postcolonial or diaspora subject. Morrison does not refer to either of these
discourses in her essay, but it seems unlikely that she could be unfamiliar
with them. It is interesting to explore how she fills "home" with meaning
and whether she avoids the problematic connotations of the term. The
"house/home" antagonism prepares the ground for this project.

"Racial house" and "race house" are Morrison's terms for the status
quo of US-American society which is characterized by a more or less
subtle but ultimately pervasive racialization of human interaction. She
admits that at one point she felt tempted to create through writing a niche
in the racial house for herself and her readers in which "racism didn't hurt
so much; to crouch in one of its many rooms where coexistence offered

the delusion of agency" ("Home" 4). For her, temptation lay in the illusion of power qua agency as it is involved in acts of creation. She thought that writing promised "the authority, the glossy comfort, the redemptive quality, the freedom" of converting the "race house" into a place where people could ignore the detrimental effects of race – even if only in fiction ("Home" 4). By phrasing these "admissions" in the past tense, however, Morrison indicates that by the time she presents her talk at the "Race Matters" conference and transcribes it as an essay some months later, she has resisted these temptations and views critically the deceptive promise of agency through the creation of racial safe havens in writing. Designing utopian refuges that bracket off racial tensions while outside them a racialized world continues to oppress people would not "transform [the racial] house completely," Morrison is convinced, and nothing less than that is the task she sets for herself ("Home" 4).

Like Jeanette Winterson, Morrison has great confidence in the power of literature to move readers to involving themselves in important discourses. She has repeatedly voiced her readiness to speak out on issues of racial and gender equality in speeches and interviews as well as in her fiction. In the Roether interview, for example, Morrison acknowledges that wonderful art will not turn malevolent and cruel people into good ones. Nevertheless she holds that

> the work of writers is very important. They are the first to be arrested, assassinated, or to have their works excommunicated. This means that something makes them dangerous for violent regimes. It proves that they are powerful, that literature has power. (Roether)[10]

Indeed, Morrison radicalizes the agenda of her writing by setting herself the goal of being instrumental to the complete transformation of racialized US society: "[I]t became imperative for me to transform this house completely" ("Home" 4). This, in her opinion, requires writing "outside the raced house" instead of from a niche on the inside (8), because "[c]ounterracism was never an option" (4).

The apparent radicalism of Morrison's program is challenging in so far as it suggests not only that a complete transformation of society is

[10]"[Ich denke,] dass die Arbeit der Schriftsteller sehr wichtig ist. Sie sind die ersten, die verbannt werden, die umgebracht werden, deren Arbeiten exkommuniziert werden. Das bedeutet, dass sie irgendwas für die Gewaltherrschaft gefährlich macht. Es beweist, dass sie mächtig sind, dass Literatur Macht hat."

necessary but also that it is possible. Given her own ambitious agenda it seems surprising how very critical the author is of utopian desires of social change. She points out the long tradition of the impulse to defer the yearning for social spaces free of racism to the future or to give it a quasi-religious touch. The idea of a raceless world has existed for a long time, but it had not been imagined as a place whose creation is a distinct possibility in our time or in the foreseeable future, she argues. Instead, according to Morrison, it was understood as an Edenesque, utopian, millennial realm that could only be brought about by a messianic figure (cf. "Home" 3). This belief found expression in political speeches and in utopian literature on the theme of raceless social orders. And yet, in Morrison's opinion it presents an escape from a racialized present, an attempt to make that harsh reality livable through the utopian vision of a race-free dreamland. While she acknowledges the tendency to entertain the idea of freedom from racial hierarchies, she criticizes the deferral of this idea to a distant and unattainable future. Morrison suspects such a move to be motivated by a refusal or an inability to engage seriously in a discussion about race in American society and a lack of willingness for social change.

Two aspects of Morrison's argumentation are debatable here. First, she gives "Martin Luther King's hopeful language" as an example for this – alleged – tendency to defer the idea of "a world ... free of racial hierarchies" to the future and thereby evade active confrontation with the racialized present ("Home" 3). She writes that "the race-free world has been posited as ideal, millennial, a condition possible only if accompanied by the Messiah or situated in a protected preserve – a wilderness park" ("Home" 3). It is of course true that Dr. King's well-known speech contains the words "I have a dream," but does not this dream for a future free of racist oppression stem from King's passionate fight against racism during his lifetime? To suggest that he avoided an active struggle by projecting his ideas into a distant and ideal future would mean to ignore the powerful movement he initiated, the price he and others paid for their engagement in it, and the tremendous impact of the Civil Rights movement on American society in the second half of the twentieth century. While I do not want to imply that Morrison thinks little of Martin Luther King's role in the history of the African American community and the nation as a whole, I think it necessary to point out the forcefulness with which, in her effort to come to terms with race, she dissociates her own project from anything that might even remotely allow for the possibility of escapism, of a "pathetic yearning and futile desire" ("Home" 4).

Morrison's implicit condemnation of utopian thought in general and utopian literature in particular – "a literary discourse that (outside science fiction) resonates exclusively in the register of permanently unrealizable dream" ("Home" 8) – is another controversial point in her argumentation. As she urges her audience to focus on the present and refuse to put up with racial prejudices and injustice rather than project their dreams to the future, the author – consciously, I would argue – overlooks the fact that every Utopia has its roots in the present and is nourished with ideas that stem from a direct struggling of their authors with current political and theoretical discourses. Thus, the imaginary "no-place" in the future or in a fictive past can be read as a mirror of the state of discussions of important contemporary issues.[11]

This aspect of utopian literature is characteristic to science fiction, too. I take Morrison's by-the-way exemption of science fiction from the accusation of promoting escapist ideas in the quote above as an excuse for a short excursion into this genre. In the 1976 introduction to her novel *The Left Hand of Darkness* of 1969, the science fiction author Ursula K. Le Guin defends her métier from charges of escapism. Le Guin describes science fiction as a "thought experiment" borrowed from theoretical mathematics, the purpose of which "is not to predict the future [...] but to describe reality, the present world" (Le Guin ii). "[S]cience fiction isn't about the future," she declares (v). "All [writers of fiction] [a]re trying to do is tell you what they're like, and what you're like – what's going on ..." (ii). Simply making intelligent guesses as to what the future might be like thus is neither the goal nor the purpose of science fiction. Its focus rests firmly on the present.

Le Guin imagines in her novel a society in the future in which gender differences have ceased to exist and racial differentiation is divested of its discriminatory potential. There, despite this optimistic image – if seen from the angle of the fight against gender and race discrimination – soci-

[11]"*Utopia* or *utopia* n. 1551, an imaginary island enjoying a perfect social, legal, and political system; coined by Thomas More, from Greek *ou* not + *tópos* place. The sense of any perfect place is first recorded in 1613. [...] The meaning of visionary idealist, is first recorded in English before 1873" (Barnhart, *Concise*: 849).

ety is still in a precarious situation because of conflicts that are grounded in competing political ideologies. Although Le Guin does not juxtapose the present and the future in *The Left Hand of Darkness*, in her thought experiment she plays through scenarios, developments and fears that are familiar to her contemporaries: potentially violent ideological conflicts of the Cold War, first attempts at genetic engineering, globalization and hybridization.

Morrison seems to regard utopian literature and its alleged tendency to imagine optimistic scenarios, "dreamscapes," as significantly different from science fiction, which she assumes to be more realistic – and therefore pessimistic – in its dealing with current issues. If we take Marge Piercy's *Woman on the Edge of Time* as an example of feminist utopian fiction of the 1970s, however, we find that here the author juxtaposes the patriarchal, racist society of the United States of her time with a gender-equal, raceless society in the future. But this future is constantly threatened by an extremely sexist and racist alternative future and the responsibility for achieving and safeguarding the utopia lies in the hands of the protagonist in the present. It depends on her growing political awareness and on the choices she makes about her own life in the present-day US . Piercy's novel can hardly be called escapist, nor does it paint the future in rosy colors. Thus, one could say that while utopian literature discusses and in a way theorizes contemporary social and political issues in a fictitious space and time, science fiction provides the thought experiments with the ideas generated in such a discussion in order to imagine what could be their consequences.

It seems to me that by making – almost on second thought – a distinction between utopian and science fiction writing in her critique of political and literary escapism Toni Morrison betrays a slight uncertainty with regard to her own condemning stance toward utopian literature. A closer look at her concept of "home" and at some contradictions embedded in it will show that this uncertainty is not so surprising.

Morrison's critique of utopian thinking presents a parallel to the critique of an idealized and conveniently distant "home" in Diaspora and Postcolonial Studies. Instead of entertaining dreams of a quasi paradisiacal place free of racist oppression in the past or the future, Morrison, like Satchidanandan in the text quoted above, insists on the importance of reacting to the racialization of contemporary social reality. This focus on the present entails the author's careful exploration of the past from an African American perspective, as she understands historical political decisions and resultant events to be the roots of tense race relations and continuing racism today. Morrison criticizes the transferal of a contemporary problematic of the magnitude of race issues to the future to imagine and play through solutions to these problems. With all of her own texts either set firmly in a meticulously defined historical era or spanning decades from the past into present time, Toni Morrison searches for answers to current questions and explores possibilities of challenging present-day belief systems and attitudes. She does so by asking her readers to contribute their own experiences to their readings of her texts, to question their presuppositions, and, occasionally, suspend their belief in received "truths" in order to allow their imagination to connect with the author's. Morrison wants her readers to share in the work of re-creating society in a conscious engagement with the things we know today, the policies and social systems we experience in reality, and the human interaction we ourselves perform on an everyday basis.[12] That is why she views Utopia and "home" as set in direct opposition to one another:

> Nationhood – the very definition of citizenship – is constantly being demarcated and redemarcated in response to exiles, refugees, *Gastarbeiter*, immigrants, migrations, the displaced, the fleeing, and the besieged. [...] Yet these figurations of nationhood and identity are frequently as raced themselves as the originating racial house that defined them. When they are not raced, they are ... imaginary landscape, never inscape; Utopia, never home. ("Home" 11f.)

And yet, there is, however unintentional it may be, an unmistakable touch of "dreaming" present in Morrison's own conceptualization of "home," and this causes a certain ambiguity and vagueness in her argumentation. The author's awareness of the fact that racial hierarchies, having been deeply engrained into the social framework, have become an integral part of US society leads her to stress "the need to rethink the subtle yet persuasive attachments we may have to the architecture of race" ("Home" 8). This takes us back to the discussion of the empowering aspects of racial identity at the beginning of this chapter. The "architecture of race" – restrictive and oppressive as it is – also offers a feeling of safety, on either side of the racial divide. Not only can it be comforting and reassuring to

---

[12] I will discuss Morrison's call for "response-ability" in greater detail later in this chapter.

know where one belongs, where one's place is in a complex and divers social system, it is an inherent human desire to be part of a group. The certainty of belonging fosters identity, and shared identities build communities, groups that strengthen the position of the individual. Consequently, the intention to change the "racial house" ignites a barrage of unsettling questions in Morrison's mind:

> Could I redecorate, redesign, even reconceive the racial house without forfeiting a home of my own? Would life in this renovated house mean eternal homelessness? Would it condemn me to intense bouts of nostalgia for the race-free home I have never had and would never know? ("Home" 4)

Racial identity is a concept that, like all other identities, is strongly dependent on the notion of difference. Therefore, given the feeling of safety inherent to race, to dismantle the racist foundations of a society which are based on difference harbors the threat of causing feelings of disorientation and homelessness.

However, Morrison seems to assume that redesigning the racial house would invariably mean surrendering her dream of a race-free home. A mere redecoration might cement the production and perception of racial difference, which in turn would render society prone to establishing hierarchies of power, followed by a renewed discrimination and oppression of the powerless. This option would not achieve the ambitious goal the writer sets herself, to "transform [the racial] house completely" ("Home" 4).

Morrison's first cluster of questions culminates in a second one later in the text that accentuates the fundamental schism the author is trying to bridge both in Race Theory and on a very practical, day-to-day level: "How to be both free and situated; how to convert a racist house into a race-specific yet non-racist home. How to enunciate race while depriving it of its lethal cling" ("Home" 5)? Given the author's own devastating assessment of the political state of affairs with regard to race in the US at the turn of the 21st century, can this agenda be considered "realistic"? Is not this rather a dream of Morrison's, something that she herself might call utopian?

Morrison writes that her "engagement with [these questions] has been fierce, fitful, and constantly [...] evolving," and that "they remain in [her] thoughts as aesthetically and politically unresolved" ("Home" 5). Her perception of the pressures of racism in the United States, however, does not seem to have changed significantly during the past decades. In her interview with Fritz Raddatz of the German weekly *DIE ZEIT* in 1998, around the time of the publication of "Home," her verdict on the current position of African Americans in the US is bleak, if not sarcastic, and her evaluation of her own position as a writer is startling: "Blacks do not have a nationality in this country. We are citizens and Blacks. I am not an American writer" (Raddatz 34/1).[13] While she acknowledges with some irony that "in the meantime [she] has become a kind of Honorary American, . . . a billboard, you could also call it" (34/1),[14] she continues in a more pessimistic vein: "We could not develop the self-confidence of a citizenship which for the others is a cheerful casualness. [. . .] They have a country, are part of a nation – we do not and are not" (34/1f.).[15] Morrison goes on to say that with "more than 30 million below the poverty line – that is roughly eleven percent of the population," the United States is riddled with poverty (34/2):[16]

> This country is being torn apart by barbaric social injustice. All in all I can only warn you: The country is in a highly explosive, dangerous situation. After what is called the collapse of communism, capitalism has gone wild, mad. What dies is democracy. Capitalism and democracy do not automatically go hand in hand. [. . .] I do not look to the future enthusiastically. (34/2)[17]

---

[13] "Schwarze haben keine Nationalität in diesem Land. Wir sind Staatsbürger und Schwarze. Ich bin keine amerikanische Schriftstellerin." All translations of this interview are mine.

[14] "[I]ch [bin] ja inzwischen eine Art Honorary American geworden, Sie können es auch Aushängeschild nennen."

[15] "Wir konnten nicht das Selbstbewußtsein einer Staatsbürgerschaft entwickeln, das den anderen eine fröhliche Selbstverständlichkeit ist. [. . .] Die haben ein Land, sind Teil einer Nation – wir nicht."

[16] "Über dreißig Millionen unterhalb der Armutsgrenze – das sind etwa elf Prozent der Bevölkerung."

[17] "Dieses Land ist zerrissen von barbarischer sozialer Ungerechtigkeit. . . . Im ganzen kann ich Ihnen nur beschwörend sagen: Das Land ist in einer hochexplosiv-gefährlichen Situation. Nach dem, was man den Zusammenbruch des Kommunismus nennt, ist der Kapitalismus wild geworden, rasend. Was stirbt ist die Demokratie. Kapitalismus und Demokratie gehen nicht automatisch Hand in Hand. [. . .] Ich blicke nicht voll Enthusiasmus in die Zukunft."

In Morrison's view, African Americans bear the brunt of what to her is a deplorable state of affairs, as they are the ones who are poverty-stricken and who fill the prisons. Her analysis of the national situation shows a conspicuous "them-and-us" mentality, a feeling of "we against the others" that bespeaks the author's sense of the undiminished enormity of the racial divide in US society. She describes her position as an African American writer on a book market that is dominated by white men in similarly alarmist terms:

> We [Black writers] were never part of the institution, always outside of it. We are at war – persuasion does not help there. Sweet-talking would hardly have made England give up her colonies. The colonizers of our time are called Ted Turner or Time Magazine or Wall Street – without a fight they will give up nothing. (34/4)[18]

While one has to keep in mind that Morrison is talking to a German interviewer here with whom she can allow herself to sound less patriotic and possibly more critical of the US-American status quo than with a compatriot, it is nonetheless sobering to see how little credit she gives society in the United States of the late twentieth century for having overcome the racial chasm or even for trying to end racial discrimination. She concludes the interview by drawing a direct connection between the racism she experienced as a child and young woman in the 1940s and '50s and the situation in the contemporary US: "I've known [what it means to be a second-class citizen]: since as a little child I was not allowed to swim in an 'American' lake, since as a young girl I was told 'What, you want to study? Learn how to type'" (Raddatz 34/4).[19]

With neo-conservatives in leading economic and political positions whose policies initiated and fed a racist backlash while they announce the "end of racism" (cf. D'Souza, *End*), Morrison's acute disappointment with the political realities of the United States in the late 1990s overshad-

---

[18]"Wir waren nie Teil der Institution, immer draußen. Wir sind im Krieg – überreden hilft da nicht. Durch gutes Zureden hätte England wohl kaum seine Kolonien aufgegeben. Die Kolonisatoren unserer Zeit heißen Ted Turner oder *Time Magazine* oder Wall Street – ohne Kampf geben die nichts her."

[19]"Vermutlich wissen Sie nicht, was es heißt, ein Staatsbürger zweiter Klasse zu sein – weil Sie es einfach nicht sind. Ich weiß es: Seit ich als kleines Kind nicht in einem 'amerikanischen' See baden durfte, seit man mir als junges Mädchen sagte: 'Was, studieren willst du? Lerne tippen!'"

ows and diminishes in her perception – if only momentarily – the enormous steps forward African American men and women have taken in all walks of life since the Civil Rights era. In her frustration with the growing economic gap between black and white Americans she overlooks, for example, the efforts and positive results of affirmative action policies in the fields of education and employment as well as the fact that, since the Voting Rights Act was signed at the height of the Civil Rights struggle, the number of Black members of Congress has steadily climbed upward.[20]

Therefore, when Morrison proposes the concept of "home," she does so under the influence of two strong, conflicting sentiments: firstly, her deep misgivings about the development of race relations in contemporary US society; secondly, her longing for a place where African Americans can live in their own right, cherish their traditions, and contribute their talents and resources to the well-being of society as a whole. The first sentiment motivates her unrelenting highlighting of racial injustice and discrimination of racial and ethnic minorities in the contemporary United States. It furthermore spurs her desire – backed by Critical Race Studies and Race Theory – to achieve a discontinuation of the use of arbitrary racial markers for the purpose of distinguishing between groups of people and individuals, the ultimate goal being the eradication of racial discrimination. The second feeling feeds her impulse to save the notion of racial difference in order to preserve and celebrate black cultural traditions and to nurture an empowering African American identity. These contradictory motives render her notion of "home" a somewhat vague concept, one that is likely to leave readers confused as to what the author actually means by it.

The concept of "home" in Morrison's understanding "domesticates the racial project, moves the job of unmattering race away from pathetic yearning and futile desire; away from an impossible future or an irretrievable and probably nonexistent Eden to a manageable, doable, modern human activity" ("Home" 3f.). What this activity of "unmattering race" consists of, however, the author does not fully disclose in her essay. Surprisingly, in spite of Morrison's definition of racial identity as a cultural

---

[20] Henry Louis Gates, Jr., writes in his op-ed commentary in the *New York Times* on 23 September 2004 that the number of black members of Congress has climbed from five in 1965 to 39 in 2004 (cf. "When Candidates Pick Voters"). Still, in 2004 Barack Obama was the only Black senator in the United States.

identity elsewhere[21] and her insistence that race remains a meaningful and empowering – albeit problematic – concept for African Americans, in this essay the metaphor of "home" embodies for her "a-world-in-which-race-does-*not*-matter" ("Home" 3). The contradiction between her conviction that "race matters" and her vision of "a-world-in-which-race-does-*not*-matter" is emblematic of the author's divided feelings about race. She contrasts the "home" she envisions – and encourages her audience to also envision and in turn fill with life – with "the father's house of many rooms" ("Home" 3), which, she says, "has troubled [her] writing" (5).

But what constitutes the "radical distinction between the metaphor of house and the metaphor of home" the author wishes to make ("Home" 3)? Should we understand a "racial house" as a society fashioned according to the "separate-but-equal" principle in which an array of carefully differentiated racial identities is tolerated? Such a notion would bear resemblance to the idea of a multicultural society, an analogy that can be sensed in Morrison's presentation of her minimal goal as a writer early on in the essay:

> If I had to live in a racial house, it was important, at the least, to rebuild it so that it was not a windowless prison into which I was forced, a thick-walled, impenetrable container from which no cry could be heard, but rather an open house, grounded, yet generous in its supply of windows and doors. ("Home" 4)

There would be walls – read: racial differences separating people into groups – but they would have windows through which to look out of one room into another, and out of the house at different houses – read, other societies. The house would be grounded, perhaps in cultural and historical traditions that are shared by all of its inhabitants. It would even have doors through which people could go from room to room or leave the house, if they wish to. Yet the author nevertheless warns against adopting the "racial house" as one's "home."

The essay "Home," too, documents distinct traces of Morrison's frustration about the political trend of avoiding direct confrontation with the legacies of slavery and racism, a trend which manifests itself in the assertions of conservative political and economic agents that contemporary US-American society is multicultural by definition and therefore provides

---

[21] See my discussion of Morrison's understanding of race as cultural identity in section 2.1.1 of this chapter.

equal opportunities for all its members already. The author urges her readers to "think about what it means and what it takes to live in a re-designed racial house and – evasively and erroneously – call it diversity or multiculturalism as a way of calling it home" ("Home" 8). As some of Morrison's political hate-figures strategically proclaim the "multicultural society" and present it as evidence for the end of racism with the aim of precluding any further struggle for racial equality, she does not use this compromised concept herself. For Morrison, as for other scholars, "multiculturalism" transports as evasive, as relativistic a meaning as the conservatives' usage of the term "raceless." She holds that by calling a society "multicultural" the hegemonic elites hope to create in the public the false impression that races are the same as ethnicities or cultures, and that all of these cultures are enjoying equal rights as well as shared power in the US and are equally appreciated,[22] in order to camouflage prevailing institutional and economic structures of domination based on the notion of racial difference. Cynthia Hamilton, for example, encourages us "to consider the ways in which multiculturalism has been used as an insti-tutional practice to obscure and thereby help preserve existing relations of domination and power" (167). "Used this way," she warns, "multicul-turalism redirects – even refashions – social conflict regarding racial in-equality" (167). Furthermore, Hamilton points out that "the current use of multiculturalism obscures the historical and ideological role of race. By treating race and ethnicity interchangeably, we lose sight of the historical use of race and ethnicity as a cover for relations of economic domination" (168).[23] In the "racial house," in other words, white supremacy would be cemented through the denial of racial differences and hierarchies of power based on the notion of race. The "father's house of many rooms" is a racial house that proclaims diversity and coexistence but remains racist; for Morrison it represents the threat of "eternal homelessness" ("Home" 4).

In his work on normalism, Jürgen Link, a German scholar of litera-ture and discourse theory, describes what he calls "aporias" with regard to

---

[22]In a similar vein, Homi K. Bhabha has called attention to the "exoticism of multiculturalism" (qtd. in Schmidt-Haberkamp 305).

[23]For an overview of opinions as to the question whether "multiculturalism [is] antiracist or oblivious to racism" see Gordon and Newfield (3f.).

"as-sociations."[24] He argues that in normalistic modern Western societies members of minorities are under the influence of a tension (aporia): On the one hand there is their desire to as-sociate, that is, to form a "community on the grounds of certain characteristics that run counter to specific societal norms" (Mihan and Haakenson 87/1). On the other hand, as individuals they are subjected to a normalizing pull out of those communities into the mainstream which is exercised by society and which leads to "atomization" of the minority in question and the "separation" of individuals from their minority (87/1).

Justice Thomas's ascent to power and his acquiescence with the values of the hegemonic society can be read in light of this theory. Also, Link's theory is applicable to the tension experienced by the African American community. The desire to as-sociate in a community of people whose lives have been shaped by similar experiences of racial discrimination, a community that forms a "home" free of racial oppression and characterized by a common history and culture, is confronted with the demand of many members of such a community to be part of mainstream society, of the "racial house," to stay with Morrison's metaphor.

However, this movement of the African American community toward the center of society, if it is not resisted, could have two consequences, the second of which is potentially painful and therefore difficult to acknowledge for Toni Morrison. The first, welcome consequence could be the re-creation of US-American society as a society free of racial hierarchies; the second, daunting one would be to give up the tight-knit Black community in the process in favor of a greater community of people regardless of racial and ethnic backgrounds. Arguable, this is what Morrison senses and what urges her to tell her audience to "think about what it means and what it takes to live in a redesigned racial house" ("Home" 8).

Morrison's essay is a document to the difficult realization she is forced to acknowledge in her attempt to combine theories of race and practical states of affairs in the United States: that through the Middle Passage and through slavery, African slaves in North America were robbed of their home; that, in order to re-gain self-confidence and take pride in

---

[24]In his German language publications Link hyphenates *As-Sociation* and *associieren* ("to as-sociate") "in order to combine the ideas of a type of community with that of building a 'social body' ("socius" in the terminology of Deleuze and Guattari)" (Mihan and Haakenson 87/2).

their cultural roots, their descendants formed close communities that empowered them not least because these communities suggested to them the existence of a home; and that African Americans not only would have to continue to point out discrimination and racist practices in contemporary US-American society, to fight for equal rights where they still do not have them, they would also have to give up their exclusive, race-based communities, if they wanted to take part in the creation of a society whose foundation no longer consists of a hierarchy of color. While this realization is implicit in Morrison's essay, she hesitates to proclaim it in her analysis. Her painful awareness of right-wing currents in US race politics, her deep desire to counteract them, and her profound love for African American culture may be reasons for this reluctance to relinquish the delusive safety of race.

Toni Morrison worries that the possibility of life in a "renovated [racial] house" would "condemn [her] to intense bouts of nostalgia for the race-free home [she] never had and would never know" ("Home" 4). Consequently, she refuses to relinquish the idea of a "home," which for her means "a race-specific yet non-racist home" where race can be enunciated "while depriving it of its lethal cling" ("Home" 5). It is "a-world-in-which-race-does-*not*-matter" because race would be divested of the power to legitimize dominance or hierarchy, a world where difference is "prized but unprivileged" ("Home" 12). As a strategy of claiming and preserving this complex and seemingly contradictory idea of "home" she develops the notion of "unmattering race."

2.2.2   "Unmattering Race"

Morrison uses the term "unmattering race" in the speech she gave at the 1997 "Race Matters" conference at Princeton University and which was the matrix for her essay "Home." The conference took its title from Cornel West's study *Race Matters* of 1993. West's title alludes to the two usages of the word "matter:" It can be read as a noun, as in "matters of race," and as a verb, like in "race matters," meaning that "race" is – still – an issue and must be taken seriously.

When Morrison takes up West's coinage with her term she also plays with an implicit double meaning. "Unmattering" in connection with race connotes a de-substantialization, that is, a diminishing in substance. This refers to the deconstruction of race as a biologically founded, essentialist category, as it was used for more than two centuries. It includes a critical analysis of the intended function of race, i.e., the perfection and scientific legitimization of the systematic oppression of African Americans for the economic and psychological benefit of White people and the dehumanization of descendants of African slaves in the perception of White US-Americans. In this context, to demand that "race" be unmattered means that its lack of substance, of a scientifically or otherwise legitimate foundation, needs to be highlighted so that the sanity and justification of dividing human beings into different races be radically challenged.

The second connotation of "unmattering race" transports the idea of attacking the race-bound foundation of US-American society by toppling the hierarchies constructed on the basis of racial differences. It works on the assumption that race is an arbitrary construct invented and kept in place to secure the power of the economic and political elite in the United States (cf. Lubiano vii). Both meanings are intimately related; indeed, they grow out of each other. De-hierarchization can only occur if race is de-substantialized and understood to be a social construct devoid of a biological or genetic basis. To "unmatter race" would mean to de-essentialize race and thus to neutralize its capacity to place people in hierarchies of power. Would it also mean the end of racial difference?

Morrison makes it very clear in "Home" that she regards "attempts to transcend race" as "futile" and "efforts to trivialize it" as "pernicious" (8). She knows the race concept to be an indelible part of US history and present. And yet, she sets for herself the task "to take what is articulated as an elusive race-free paradise and domesticate it" ("Home" 8), a task for which "unmattering race" is instrumental. The questions of what linguistic and literary strategies she suggests for this project and what results she envisions are extremely relevant both to the understanding of her views on matters of race and of her literary works.

2.2.2.1   Unthinking Race – Un-racing Language

In the middle section of her essay, Morrison takes great pains to explain to her audience the importance of the right choice for the final word in her novel *Beloved*: "kiss."[25] She changed the original word, which she does not disclose, after her editor had indicated that he thought it too theatrical. In "Home" she expresses regret at having agreed to the change, because the original choice had been deliberate and difficult to attain.

Language is of extreme importance to Morrison's undertaking of "unmattering race." In her Nobel lecture of 1993 the author talks about language that can be alive or dead. Language that is living is to her "[sublime] [w]ord-work," a "generative" medium which "makes meaning that secures our difference, our human difference – the way in which we are like no other life" (321). Thus, language can indicate humanness by highlighting how and where humans differ from other forms of life. "Sexist language, racist language, theistic language," on the other hand, Morrison calls "dead language" ("Nobel Lecture" 319), i.e., language that does nothing to show that we are human, as it denigrates difference and restricts freedom and development. She continues her critique of what might be called "-ist languages" by pointing out the intimate connection between language and hegemony: "[A]ll [of these dead languages] are typical of the policing languages of mastery, and cannot, do not permit new knowledge or encourage the mutual exchange of ideas" (320).

Since Morrison regards language "partly as a system, partly as a living thing over which one has control, but mostly as agency – as an act with consequences" ("Nobel Lecture" 319), she is adamant in her commitment to re-creating language as a non-racist system. In 1998 she tells her German interviewer: "As a Black writer I have the interesting as well as complicated problem to work with and in a language that carries the hidden signs of racial superiority, denigration, and cultural hegemony carved into itself" (Raddatz 34/2).[26] Morrison views this situation as a potentially productive challenge: The fact that the English language too was molded by racist ideology means for her as a writer to acknowledge and point out discriminatory facets of her mother tongue, and to create verbal expressions that make impossible the easy classification of people according to

---

[25]"Certainly no clamor for a kiss" (*Beloved* 275). The very last word of the novel is "Beloved," which Morrison regards as "the resurrection of the title, the character, and the epitaph" ("Home" 5).

[26]"Ich als schwarze Schriftstellerin habe das interessante wie komplizierte Problem, mit und in einer Sprache zu arbeiten, die versteckte Zeichen von rassischer Überlegenheit, Abfälligkeit und kultureller Hegemonie in sich eingeschliffen trägt."

their racial affiliation. She does not express the wish to create a new language, however; what she aims for is to change the imperfect language she lives and works with.

One of the central concerns in Morrison's work, therefore, is to unshackle American English from the abuse to which it has been subjected through its employment in the transportation and insinuation of racist meaning. The purpose of this effort is to "eliminat[e] the potency of racist constructs in language," because, as she writes in "Home," "that is the work I can do" (4). The program the author has set for herself in terms of changing language in her works of fiction is "to carve away the accretions of deceit, blindness, ignorance, paralysis, and sheer malevolence embedded in raced language so that other kinds of perception were not only available but were inevitable" ("Home" 7). These "other kinds of perception" hint at her objective of showing human beings as complex and unique individuals whose identity is composed of a host of characteristics each of which plays a particular and indispensable role.

Early on in her essay, Morrison states that she feels both "liberated and imprisoned" by language ("Home" 3). She considers her mother tongue to be potentially liberating for her as an author by merit of its efficiency as a tool for the critique of racism and for the creative imagination of a world in which race is unmattered. The example of the changed last word in *Beloved* is intended to sharpen our awareness as readers and language users of the limiting, regulatory qualities of any language which result in what Morrison calls the "complex struggle and frustration inherent in creating figuratively logical narrative language that insists on race-specificity without race prerogative" ("Home" 5). This phrase again points to the author's seemingly paradoxical wishes with regard to race: She wants to be specific about racial characteristics because she considers them important aspects of a person's individual identity or of a certain group identity. Yet she resents the potential violence – the possibility of discrimination – that lies in the distinction of races and wants to see it exposed and challenged. There is almost a sense of the author's exasperation in face of this apparently unsolvable task she has set herself. Morrison holds that sometimes, one single word has to do "an extraordinary battle" for the cause of un-racing language and unmattering race, and not always is the author satisfied with her own choice of words ("Home" 7). "It is difficult to sign race while designing racelessness," she writes in "Home" (8).

Morrison seems to regard and employ language as *pars pro toto* for culture: She equates raced language with racialized society, calling for the change of the one in order to achieve the un-racing of the other. Thus, when she notes that language "liberate[s] and imprison[s]" her, we feel reminded of her desire to be both free – of racial discrimination – and situated – in a racial home – in US-American society. It is interesting to notice, however, that in her engagement with language and its role in the preservation and spreading of racisms Morrison exhibits a greater hopefulness with regard to the possibility for change than in her assessment of the situation in race politics in the United States. Her own use of language, the terms she coins, reflects her confidence in the dynamic character of the work of change she vows to do: She writes of the imperative to "develop" a non-racist language, which suggests action that takes time and which seems to allow this process of change a history as well as the time it needs in the present and in the future.

The driving force of Morrison's efforts to "un-race" language thus is her conviction that changing a language will result in a change of society-at-large: "Since language *is* community, if the cognitive ecology of a language is altered, so is the community," she asserts in "Home" (8). Language transports ideas, and without language there is no thinking. A community, however, organizes itself around a compendium of ideas. Thus, Morrison's argumentation assigns language a key role in the creation, development, and preservation of communities. While race is not a biological fact, it is none the less a powerful fact in people's everyday experiences and has become a reality that is firmly installed in their heads, making race a part of their system of thought. So, in order to tackle the race issue, we must change our way of thinking about race, and that is possible only via language. Consequently, according to Morrison, we must "un-think" race if we want to banish racism from our systems.

Morrison expresses an optimism with regard to language that is absent from her interviews mentioned above and also from the parts of "Home" that deal with the struggle for a "home" that is not the "race house." It seems easier for the author to imagine a society that gradually becomes cleansed of racism because its language has been purged of discriminatory elements, than to envision a political scenario in which race is preserved while racism is expelled from administrative and quotidian reality. However, Morrison's nostalgia for a tight-knit racial "home" for African Americans does not stretch to language. In her own writing, Morrison does not use varieties of Black English, does not "take standard English and use vernacular to decorate it, or to add 'color' to dialogue" ("Home" 7). She has a more radical objective than that as a writer: She regards it as "more urgent than ever to develop non-messianic language to refigure the raced community, to decipher the deracing of the world" ("Home" 11). As she calls for a language that reflects and dissects the social and political realities of contemporary US-American society or specific historical eras, the author dissociates herself once more from other – unnamed – writers' or politicians' attempts to postpone the struggle for racial equality to the future or to a utopian dreamland. Morrison does not offer explicit examples of this non-messianic language to be used in the production of literary texts in "Home." She concentrates on stressing the relevance of the task of "un-racing language" and to point out the difficulties such an endeavor entails.[27]

2.2.2.2   Unthinking Race – Un-racing the Plot

In the conclusion of her examination of the ideal of a "racial home," Morrison carries the effort to "unmatter race" from the level of words into that of content, plot, and story of a literary text. In stark contrast to the suggestion that "race does not matter any more," for her race determines every aspect of life in the United States, and it is closely connected with the notion of home:

> [S]o much of what seems to lie about in the discourses on race concerns legitimacy, authenticity, community, belonging. In no small way, these discourses are about home: an intellectual home; a spiritual home; family and community as home; forced and displaced labor in the destruction of home; dislocation of and alienation within the ancestral home; creative responses to exile, the devastations, pleasures, and imperatives of home-lessness as it is manifested in discussions on feminism, globalism, the diaspora, migrations, hybridity, contingency, interventions, assimilations, exclusions the estranged body, the legislated body, the violated, rejected, deprived body – the body as consummate home. In virtually of these formations, whatever the terrain, race magnifies the matter that matters. ("Home" 5)

---

[27]For analyses of Morrison's creation and usage of un-raced language see my discussions of "Recitatif" in Chapter 3 and of *Paradise* in Chapter 4 of this study.

The author aims to make the idea of a "racial home" the topic of novels that have a historically verifiable setting and correspond with the experiences, knowledges, and realities of her readers: "What I am determined to do is to take what is articulated as an elusive race-free paradise and domesticate it. I am determined to concretize a literary discourse that (outside of science fiction) resonates exclusively in the register of permanently unrealizable dream," she writes in "Home" (8) and points to her novel *Paradise* as an example of a narrative that breaks with the belief in race as the eternal divider in US-American society:

> In the novel I am now writing, I am trying first to enunciate and then eclipse the racial gaze altogether. [...] I want to see whether or not race-specific, race-free language is both possible and meaningful in narration. And I want to inhabit, walk around, a site clear of racist detritus; a place were race both matters and is rendered impotent; [...] . ("Home" 9)

Morrison's desire to acknowledge the existence of racial identities corresponds with her experientially founded conviction that race is meaningful as a cultural and historical identity and relevant as a means of identity formation. She combines this desire with the task she sets herself of "unmattering race" by purging it of its capacity to create hierarchical social structures that denigrate and oppress people. Thus, she declares her goal to create "race-specific, race-free language" with which to "eclipse the racial gaze altogether." But how are these three disparate ideas supposed to fit together and form a union in people's mental systems? Can the racial gaze with which US-Americans grow up be eclipsed when race-specific language is still used? Is not the author asking too much of her readership when she expects them to be able to understand the paradox of "race-specific, race-free language"?

In all her works Morrison places enormous attention on the active participation of her readers. Louisa Joyner writes of the author that she "demands a tremendous imaginative effort from her readers" (9). Morrison herself invents the term "response-ability" to describe the attitude with which she wants her readers to approach her texts: "Writing and reading mean being aware of the writer's notion of risk and safety, the serene achievement of, or sweaty fight for, meaning and response-ability" (*Playing* xiii). In "Home" she emphasizes that "narration requires the active complicity of a reader willing to step outside established boundaries of the racial imaginary" (8f.). When dealing with a narrative that develops "a place where race both matters and is rendered impotent" her readers are faced with a twofold task: They need to recognize the importance of race both as an oppressive social construct and as a potentially empowering and liberating identity. Morrison confronts herself and her readers with "the need to rethink the subtle yet persuasive attachments we may have to the architecture of race" ("Home" 8), the desire to as-sociate, as Link calls it, a topic with which she dealt in depth in her short story "Recitatif," as we shall see in the next chapter. Secondly, readers are asked to follow the author in imagining a social space set in the United States in a specific historical era that is free of racist hierarchies, where racial identity exists but does not carry weight to elevate or degrade a person or a group in society. Morrison calls on her audience to imagine with her "not the threat of freedom, or its tentative panting fragility, but the concrete thrill of borderlessness – a kind of out of doors safety" ("Home" 9), connected with and dependent on the state of "race unmattered." This borderlessness in turn is meant to inspire readers to respond critically and constructively to race matters as they become relevant in their everyday lives.

Morrison's call for acceptance and appreciation of racial borderless-ness in "Home" is followed by a passage from *Paradise*, which at that time was still unfinished. There, a woman is described walking the streets of her town at night, full of the safe feeling of belonging and with the sure knowledge that nobody will harass her or deprive her of her home on account of her race. What is puzzling about this exemplary quote is the fact that the passage, chosen, as we understand, to exemplify racial bor-derlessness, is set in an all-Black town in the middle of Oklahoma that is characterized by an almost complete voluntary segregation from the rest of the US population.[28] In this town, racial purity is the all-important fac-tor that determines whether somebody can become a respected citizen or will always be a social outcast. This turns Morrison's image of a racial safe haven into a scenario of complete racialization. She writes that the scene is "meant to evoke [...] the safety and freedom outside the race house" ("Home" 10), but is this possible when the town seems to be a symbol of the "race house," maybe representing one of the clearly defined rooms in it? Is this place the author's metaphor for "home" or rather her critique of a nostalgic and, in its consequence, dogmatic dream?

---

[28] Also unmentioned in the essay is the fact that this scenario is the dreamscape of one of the founders of the town, a patriarchal figure who patronizes not only his wife, but all women in town and outside, as well as the town's young generation.

Morrison herself seems to question the appropriateness of the example she chose. "[T]hese figurations of nationhood and identity are frequently as raced themselves as the originating racial house that defined them," she writes only a few lines further on ("Home" 10f.), and indeed, much of *Paradise* is devoted to the exploration of this paradox. She continues by explaining that "[w]hen [these figurations of nationhood and identity] are not raced, they are [...] imaginary landscape, never inscape; Utopia, never home" ("Home" 11). Again, Morrison pits utopias against home, closing her eyes on any utopian aspects inherent in such an ideal image of a society. And yet, as I hope to show shortly, in the novel from which she quotes she creates a social space that is not raced but still part of the "inscape" that includes the all-Black town, a place that in the course of the novel becomes home to its inhabitants.

2.2.3   Re-Imagining Racelessness

Toni Morrison's essay suggests that through a conscious effort, by "imagining race without dominance – without hierarchy," we can achieve "the world-as-home" ("Home" 11). Thus, while she claims for herself the sovereignty and authority which she feels is "available only in fiction writing" ("Home" 3), she stresses her readers' important contribution of to the task of "unmattering race." The author needs her readers to join her in imagining racelessness while acknowledging that race matters, to let her fiction enable people to begin to abandon their color-coded system of thinking.

Yet, in "Home" we neither find a definition of the society that Morrison chooses to call "home" nor a discussion of explicit strategies that she uses in her writing in order to unmatter race. Clearly, her essay is not intended to be a theoretical contribution to Critical Race Studies, but rather a reflection of Morrison's ongoing struggle to combine her theoretical knowledge and convictions with respect to the concept of race with her daily experiences of racism in the US-American society. She is quite aware of the unscholarly nature of her text, as she tells her audience that "[f]rankly, I look to the contributors of this conference for literary and extraliterary analyses and for much of what can be better understood about matters of race" ("Home" 5).

In her interview with Margaret Reynolds, however, Morrison does explain her theoretical focus as far as race is concerned. She highlights her

efforts to present people in all their complexity, as multifaceted individuals with a limitless variety of cultural influences and personal experiences,
of which racial identity is but one. She explains:

> [I]f you think that your whole identity is your race, because for the larger
> population that is our identity, then somehow you narrow yourself down,
> or you can narrow yourself down into simply being a black girl, or a black
> woman, and that's all you are and all you do, although life contradicts you
> at every moment. So the complexity and the broadening of identity, rather
> than the narrowing of it is much more my focus. [...] What I am primarily
> interested in is how complicated identity is, and that if it is restricted, or
> hampered by one or two definitions – gender, or race, or class, or any of
> the large things – then you are forced to respond, or you become forced
> to respond, in three areas, while your real living life, of memory, of other
> people's stories, of experience, is lost. (Reynolds, "Interview Morrison":
> 13)

Morrison does not question that race, among gender, class, and other categories that she does not explicitly name here, is a "large thing," a concept
with potentially massive implications for the individual as well as the nation. But she refuses to allow it the omnipotent quality it has been given
so often. Nevertheless, it is beyond doubt that the author has important
goals that focus on political reality in the United States. As she clearly
sees herself as a writer whose tools are her texts, rather than an activist
or politician, the question comes to mind of what the connection between
her non-fictional and her fictional goals is. How does Morrison mean to
realize her political agendas through her fiction? Can the language of
imagination alone alter material reality?

When Morrison speaks or writes about "unmattering race," she neither denies the persistence of race as a social and political phenomenon
in American society nor does she relinquish racial identity as a means of
positive cultural identification and socio-political empowerment. Rather,
she attempts to fill the notion of race with new meaning, just as she works
on changing American English – all in the name of her long-term goal of
changing society. Morrison strives to break up restrictive modes of thinking based on binary oppositions like "white and non-white" or "black and
not-quite-black" which result in the creation and successive preservation
of hierarchical structures. At the conclusion of "Home" she writes:

> Beyond the dichotomous double consciousness, the new space this confer-
> ence explores is formed by the inwardness of the outside, the interiority

of the "othered," the personal that is embedded in the public. In this new space one can imagine safety without walls, can reiterate difference that is prized but unprivileged, and can conceive of a third [...] world 'already made for me, both snug and wide open, with a doorway never needing to be closed.' Home. (12)

Morrison envisions a society in which old hierarchies have become meaningless, in which familiar dichotomies – inside and outside, the own and the other, the personal and the public – are destabilized and rendered futile. She is not interested in a simple reversal of the traditional order of power, nor does she want to give up the idea of difference which, without the capacity of distributing the privileges of power, she sees as "prized." "Home," Morrison's metaphor for such a world, is a social system founded on the principle of thinking beyond binaries. This is indicated by the notion of a "third world," which can be read as a world that encourages identities that cannot be grasped by limiting binaries.[29] For reasons explicated earlier in this text Morrison does not argue in favor of polymorphous heterogeneity in a multicultural society. Instead, she imagines a world that is not founded on the extreme poles of essentialism vs. constructivism. She proposes an understanding of race as a concept that permits connection rather than demanding separation, that appreciates difference, rather than creating an Other as a negative projection.

In her narratives Morrison explores subject positions that challenge the hegemonic constructions of race that oppress them. She creates characters who explore and embrace the multiple facets of their being and actively shape their own identities – often in contrast with the racist mold into which a racialized society wishes to press them. Fictional men and women like Sula, Milkman Dead, or Denver testify to Morrison's conviction that human beings must strive to resist categorization, fashion their own selves and be conscious of the impact they have on their fellow-beings. In "Unspeakable Things Unspoken" she writes:

> We are the subjects of our own narrative, witnesses to and participants in our own experience, and, in no way coincidentally, in the experience of those with whom we have come in contact. We are not, in fact, "other." We are choices. (9)

---

[29] In her critique of binary oppositions Morrison does not limit herself to race, but also explores the concepts of gender, class and sexuality. In the interest of my exploration of the idea of racelessness, however, my focus here lies explicitly on race.

Morrison offers fictions that not only encourage their readers to engage in the re-fashioning of their own subject positions – possibly outside hegemonic discourses – but also to participate critically in the very discourses that determine these positions. Her texts urge readers to question their own involvement in the preservation of the racialized setup of society and to train their thinking toward viewing themselves and every human being as complex individuals whose racial identity is one – hopefully prized – facet of their selves.

Yet, a marked discrepancy remains between Morrison's theoretical understanding of race as an arbitrary and potentially lethal construct that has to be deconstructed, subverted, and undone in the interest of equality on the one hand, and on the other hand her desire to affirm racial difference in reaction to political trends of denying racism as a strategy intended to preserve the racist status quo. The author assigns the task of connecting theory with the everyday practice of living in a racialized society not only to the members of the academic conference on "Race Matters" in 1997, but also to her own fictional texts and to the people who read them and respond to them.

Part II

Questioning the Notion of Race

3   Challenging the Matrix of Racial Difference: Toni Morrison's Short Story "Recitatif"

"Recitatif" is the only short story Morrison has published so far. It first appeared in *Confirmation*, Amiri and Amina Baraka's *Anthology of African American Women of 1983*. [1] The discussion of this text among literary scholars has been less intense than one would expect, given the importance and popularity of its author and the extraordinary qualities of the short story. Various explanations for this comparative dearth of critical writing on "Recitatif" have been offered. David Goldstein-Shirley, for example, wonders whether this might be due to the "critical bias against the short story genre," or to "the relative obscurity of the anthology in which it appeared" ("Race/(Gender)" 83). Juda Bennett believes that "the intelligence, authority, and exhaustiveness of Elizabeth Abel's article 'Black Writing, White Reading'" of 1993 prevented much further discussion of the short story in print (211).

There is, I believe, another reason for the fact that scholars seem to think that everything that needs to be said about "Recitatif" has already been said. The few scholars who have written about this dense and complex short story almost exclusively concentrate on one facet of the text, only: They focus on racial difference and the racial identities of the protagonists, Twyla and Roberta, who meet at the age of eight and across the boundaries of racial difference become friends when they share a room at an orphanage.[2] The text tells the history of this friendship over three decades; also, it highlights the fact that Twyla and Roberta belong to different races without ever revealing who of them is black and who is white.

---

[1] Toni Morrison, "Recitatif," *Confirmation: An Anthology of African American Women*, ed. Amiri and Amina Baraka (New York: William Morrow, 1993) 243-61. All further reference is to this edition.

[2] Although Abel and Furman each briefly touch upon the mother-daughter relationship, both are chiefly interested in Morrison's dealing with racial difference.

Elizabeth Abel set the trend with her insightful and influential essay. She integrates her analysis of Morrison's text in her larger effort to investigate how cultural and racial backgrounds of readers influence their interpretation of texts. Abel contrasts her body-oriented White psychological reading with that of her African American colleague Lula Fragd who emphasizes the influence of different cultural practices on a person's reading experiences. Both scholars hinge their interpretations of the short story on the mystery of Roberta's and Twyla's racial backgrounds, and both come to opposite conclusions (cf. Abel 827-32). Ann Rayson attempts to prove that readers who are able to apply "the right contextual tools for decoding the story" will easily recognize that Twyla is the daughter of Irish catholic immigrants whereas Roberta is black (cf. Rayson 44, 40, 42f.). Goldstein-Shirley concentrates on the narrative tactics with which Morrison veils the racial identities of her protagonists as she describes their feelings and opinions and their long relationship in detail. He devotes his attention to the way "[t]hese unusual elements [plot enigmas, language tricks, and story line gaps] push readers to solve the mysteries, fill in the gaps, and thereby complete the story" ("Race and Response" 77). Bennett, in his interpretation of the short story as the staging of the drama of racial passing between text and reader, also seems to be interested only in the topic of racial difference and its construction.[3]

While I agree wholeheartedly that the construction of race is one of the central themes of "Recitatif," I take issue with the exclusive focus of the majority of the interpretations of the short story on the question of racial difference. Undoubtedly, it is important to point out and analyze the way in which Toni Morrison "demystif[ies] [race] – or, more accurately, [leads] her readers to demystify [race]," as Goldstein-Shirley has it ("Race/(Gender)" 87). It is indeed a relevant and interesting task to explore how we employ the category of race to structure not only our social but also our fictional environments, how little we are prepared to accept heterogeneity and ambiguity, and how our own racial fantasies determine our constructions of racial identities of others. Yet, I am convinced that this participation in processes of racialization – even though it occurs with the intention to critique and deconstruct – stops short of and ultimately in-

---

[3]Furman and Nicol are notable exceptions to this interpretive trend, as they fully accept the impossibility to place Roberta and Twyla racially.

hibits a full understanding of the complex critique of the concept of race conveyed in "Recitatif."

If we accept that the author deliberately and successfully veils the racial identities of her protagonists after she has highlighted their difference, the question arises whether she presents other layers of meaning underneath the surface layer of racial difference and identity. What determinants of Twyla's and Roberta's relationship are revealed and discussed apart from their different racial identities? And then, in what ways does race influence these determinants? A discussion of these questions will further clarify Morrison's critique of the effects race has on our understanding of human interaction. It will also show how this short story prepares the ground for Morrison's discussion of issues related to the concept of race in her later work.

3.1 Temptations of Assigning Race

The narrated time in "Recitatif" covers a period of approximately 30 years, beginning in the early 1950s and ending in the mid-'80s. During these decades, particularly during the first two, local and national politics as well as public discussion in the United States were dominated by civil rights issues, so that questions of race discrimination, racial identity, and racial difference were prominent in people's minds. Already on the first page of the short story Twyla, the narrator of the short story, informs us that she and her former roommate do not belong to the same racial group: "It was one thing to be taken out of your own bed early in the morning – it was something else to be stuck in a strange place with a girl from a whole other race" ("Recitatif" 243).

Here, for the first time readers are alerted to the racial difference between the two girls, and further reminders appear at regular intervals in the narrative. Thus, Twyla recalls that the older girls in the orphanage sometimes called her and Roberta "salt and pepper" because of how they looked together ("Recitatif" 244). During their chance meeting at the Food Emporium Twyla is reminded of her unpleasant earlier encounter with her childhood friend at the road side restaurant where she had waited tables: "A black girl and a white girl meeting in a Howard Johnson's on the road and having nothing to say" ("Recitatif" 253). Roberta, trying to explain why she had treated Twyla so rudely that day, refers to the late 1960s as "those days: black – white. You know how everything was" ("Recitatif"

255). While these direct allusions to the racial differences between the roommates indicate the narrator's perception of difference, the protagonists are not conclusively racialized in the narrative. All other references to Twyla's and Roberta's appearance, behavior, actions, and opinions are unspecific with regard to race and are therefore open to interpretation as to their value as racial markers. Abel argues:

> By replacing the conventional signifiers of racial difference (such as skin color) with radically relativistic ones (such as who smells funny to whom) and by substituting for the racialized body a series of disaggregated cultural parts – pink scalloped socks, tight green slacks, large hoop earrings, expertise at playing jacks, a taste for Jimi Hendrix or for bottled water and asparagus – the story renders race a contested terrain variously mapped from diverse positions in the social landscape. (827f.)

Neither the few direct references to racial difference nor the many relativistic ones give away who of the two is black and who is white. Morrison disqualifies race not only as an essential human attribute, but even as a linguistic position.

Given the explicit highlighting of racial difference in the text on the one hand and the fact that cultural attributes are used like racial ones on the other, it seems hardly surprising that the question of who is black and who white has received so much attention by critics as well as readers.[4] In addition to this, the author has expressed her goal to deny readers the codes with which to place the two women racially. In *Playing in the Dark* she explains her intentions with "Recitatif":

> The kind of work I have always wanted to do requires me to learn how to maneuver ways to free up the language from its sometimes sinister, frequently lazy, almost always predictable employment of racially informed and determined chains. (The only short story I have ever written, "Recitatif," was an experiment in the removal of all racial codes from a narrative about two characters of different races for whom racial identity is crucial.) (xiii)

Bennett suggests that "Recitatif" "restructures the drama of ambiguity so that it involves the reader in the impulse to fix racial meaning and to know the racial status of its characters" (211). This desire to determine Twyla's

---

[4] Abel, Rayson and Goldstein-Shirley each conducted surveys among colleagues and students in which they asked which racial status participants assigned to Roberta and Twyla.

and Roberta's racial identities exists in spite of the fact that Morrison explicitly stresses the "removal of all racial codes from [the] narrative." It persists despite – or because of – the fact that the text gives only contradictory and confusing evidence, withholding clear answers as to the racial background of either of the protagonists. Morrison employs the century-old habit of attempting to racially categorizing people at first glance and of judging them on the basis of their presumed racial identity, a habit to which her readers are well-accustomed and which therefore fuels their desire to solve the mystery. This has led to what amounts to a competition in decoding the text for racial codes which the author has skillfully kept out of it. Abel, for example, self-critically confesses to "install[ing] the (racialized) body at the center of a text that deliberately withholds conventional racial iconography" through her reading of the story (829).

Certainly, the desire to "know the racial status" of Twyla and Roberta has led to astute and eloquent analyses of the author's narrative strategies with which she succeeds in alerting her readers both to the mechanisms of the construction of race and to the fact that race is an attribute without rational substance that is applied arbitrarily. Abel contends that "[b]y forcing us to construct racial attributes from highly ambiguous social cues, 'Recitatif' elicits and exposes the unarticulated racial codes that operate at the boundaries of consciousness" (828). Thus, the short story illustrates both the readers' apparent desire to place characters racially and methods of constructing racial information out of characteristics or behaviors that are quite unrelated to race, applied in order to satisfy this desire.

There is general agreement among scholars of "Recitatif" that with her short story Morrison not only "wishes to confound preconceptions of race" (Goldstein-Shirley, "Race/(Gender)": 86), but also that "[b]y using such rhetorical devices to pull readers into meaning-making and self-reflection, [she] pulls readers into questioning their own assumptions, particularly about race" (Goldstein-Shirley, "Race and Response": 77). Yet, does this do justice to the full extent of Morrison's critique of race? Is it altogether feasible that despite her intention to deconstruct this category the author could be satisfied with her readers' re-constructing racial difference, with their racializing of the protagonists of her short story whose racial identities she has deliberately and efficiently left ambiguous?[5] This would hold us imprisoned in the vicious circle of perpetual construction and reconstruction of race, even though we have learned to distrust the mechanisms of creation and conservation of this concept and its questionable qualities as a marker of difference. It would furthermore obstruct our curiosity to investigate other levels of human identity and interaction the short story explores.

3.2   The Scope of "Recitatif"

The mystery surrounding Twyla's and Roberta's racial backgrounds, I argue, is actually a secondary problem in the narrative. Once we have understood the important truth that we can only attribute a specific racial identity to either of the protagonists at the cost of arbitrarily reading general social cues as characteristics of one race or the other, we can – and indeed must – look for a deeper level of meaning in the short story. Bennett seems to suspect such a concealed level when he writes about "Recitatif" that "[s]ome may say that it sets a trap, but perhaps it simply reveals the traps that are everywhere around us" (212). Racial codes in language and culture are one such "trap" and their uncovering occurs on the surface level of critique in "Recitatif." The text introduces central ideas about the notions of race and racial difference which Morrison investigates further in her later works. It transports a radical critique of the obsession with race in modern US-American society, an obsession that manifests itself in the misconception that race is at the heart of every problem between human beings, that difference is always first racial difference, and that racially coded differences are suspected even where none may exist. Thus, when the topic of the supremacy of the concept of race is omitted in discussions of "Recitatif," the question how Morrison in this narrative analyzes and critiques the omnipresence of race as a habitually applied matrix for the explanation of social and personal conflicts in society remains unanswered.

Morrison draws a complex picture of the relationship between two women with different racial backgrounds stretching over almost three

---

[5]In her correspondence with Abel, who actually asked the author whom she intended to be black and whom white, Morrison volunteered no answer to this question but explained that she "substitute[d] class for racial codes" (Abel 81).

decades amidst racial discord and discrimination in US society in the second half of the 20th century; it is a friendship overshadowed by traumatic childhood experiences dating back to the months the protagonists spent in an orphanage. Part of how race structures our society and influences our perception of reality is the tendency to reduce people of color to their racial identities, to project essentialist ideas about alleged racial characteristics onto them and to ignore the variety of identities that interrelate in every individual in complex ways. This characteristic is part of the inherent discriminatory potential of the concept of race the revelation of which occupies a prominent position on Morrison's agenda as a writer.

Mary Madden says about Toni Morrison's fiction that it "challenges not only stereotypes within categories of identity but the categories themselves" (qtd. in Goldstein-Shirley, "Race/(Gender)": 85). With "Recitatif" the author continues her long-term project of challenging the omnipresence race has assumed. In her radical deconstruction of the concept she lays bare the limits of this category and questions its very usefulness for the creation and interpretation of meaning. Morrison first points out our race-focused patterns of reading both literature and reality and then underlines social relations and the complex composition of human identity and emotional make-up that exist underneath the surface layer of race. The restriction of textual analysis to questions of racial difference at the cost of other relevant features of identity and human interrelation would result in a reduction of the critical scope of this short story to one aspect, an aspect that is important, but not exclusively so.

3.2.1   The Trauma of Parental Neglect – St. Bonaventure

Twyla narrates the history of her friendship with Roberta when she is a grown woman, but her adult reflections are shot through with the truths that accompanied her throughout her childhood years. One of the "truths" she learned from her mother as a little girl was that "they never washed their hair and they smelled funny" ("Recitatif" 243), "they" being people "from a whole different race" ("Recitatif" 243). Consequently, Twyla is disgusted when she realizes that her new roommate at St. Bonaventure, the state orphanage where she is to spend four months of her life, will be one of "them." "My mother won't like you putting me in here," she says to the Bozo, one of the women who work in the shelter ("Recitatif" 243).

Roberta does not react to the racist affront. Instead, she asks the other girl if her mother is ill like hers is.

"Mutual need neutralizes race hatred and makes their similarities much more important than their differences," Furman writes in her analysis of the short story (108). The two girls are the only children in the orphanage whose parents are not dead but "dysfunctional" (cf. Furman): Mary, Twyla's mother, "likes to dance all night" ("Recitatif" 244), while Roberta's mother is mentally ill. Both mothers "dumped" their children in a shelter, exposing them to loneliness as well as to the contemptuous harassment of the "real orphans with beautiful dead parents in the sky" ("Recitatif" 244). This sense of having been deserted stays with Twyla for a long time; even as an adult she refers to places that are unpleasant or threatening to her as "dumps": "Howard Johnson's really was a dump in the sunlight" ("Recitatif" 250), and "[a]ll the schools seemed dumps to me, and the fact that one was nicer looking didn't hold much weight" ("Recitatif" 256).

The two abandoned eight-year-olds constantly try to win ground from the orphans, and they are able to do that only by means of their mothers, even though they are incompetent and tend to cause their daughters embarrassment. On visiting day Twyla therefore is under immense pressure to prove to the real orphans that a living parent is better than a dead one. Seeing how pretty her young mother is in spite of the "ugly green slacks" and the "ratty fur coat" she is wearing, Twyla rejoices: "A beautiful mother on earth is better than a beautiful dead one in the sky, even if she did leave you all alone to go dancing" ("Recitatif" 247). Sadly, Mary does not allow her much time to enjoy her triumph. When Roberta tries to introduce Mary and Twyla to her own mother, her mother brusquely turns and walks away, dragging Roberta with her. When Mary protests loudly against this slight in front of and in the church, swearing at Roberta's mother and behaving disrespectfully during the service, Twyla knows that "the real orphans were looking smug again" ("Recitatif" 248). Her advantage of having a living parent is turned only too quickly into a disadvantage by Mary's inappropriate behavior.

Not surprisingly, Twyla's mother compares unfavorably to Roberta's in her recollections. Mary is small, excited, and childlike, while Roberta's mother is big and imposing. Mary comes to the orphanage without food, forcing little Twyla to improvise a picnic out of fur-covered crushed jelly beans from her Easter basket. Roberta's mother brings more than her daughter can eat. Twyla seems to see Roberta's mother as the "more acceptably negligent mother (a sick one rather than a dancing one)" and one who feeds her daughter properly (829). In reality, as Abel points out, Roberta's mother is mentally ill and her capacity to nurture is "largely fictional," imagined by the envious and insecure narrator (829).

Twyla describes her own mother as "simple-minded" and "not too swift when it comes to what's really going on" ("Recitatif" 247). This apparent intellectual deficiency is complicated and rendered even more annoying by a social one. According to Twyla's analysis, Mary's actions and behavior are often inadequate to the situation she finds herself in and greatly out of proportion. Thus, she does not simply like to dance but "likes to dance all night" ("Recitatif" 244). Twyla complains that when her mother set eyes on her in St. Bonny's, she "dropped to her knees and grabbed me, mashing the [Easter] basket, the jelly beans, and the grass into her ratty fur jacket" ("Recitatif" 247). During the introduction to Roberta's mother, Mary did not just smile and offer to shake hands, but "grinned and tried to yank her hand out of the pocket with the raggedy lining" ("Recitatif" 247). Everything about her appears out of key and is embarrassing to Twyla.

Mary's extravagant behavior, in combination with her shortcomings as a mother, causes gravely conflicting feelings in her daughter. Her overflowing affection and her beauty awaken love and a sense of pride in Twyla who wants "to stay buried in her fur all day" ("Recitatif" 247), in the very same fur she had described as "ratty" only a little earlier. Even when Twyla is an adult, the scent of apples reminds her of the Lady Esther dusting powder her mother used, making her "still go soft when I smell one or the other" ("Recitatif" 248). At the same time, Mary's inability to look after her child or to behave appropriately in public is a perpetual source of shame and frustration for Twyla; already as an eight-year-old she felt like Mary "was the little girl looking for her mother – not me" and dreaded the burden of being responsible for this adult ("Recitatif" 246). The situation of having a mother who is unable to perform the maternal role expected of her is deeply troubling and upsetting to Twyla. Within the short sequence about the visiting day she repeats three times that she "could have killed" her mother ("Recitatif" 247, 248) or thought she "really needed to be killed" ("Recitatif" 248). This despair at what she perceives as her mother's massive shortcomings, especially in comparison to the caretaking qualities she believes Roberta's mother to have, exerts a strong influence on Twyla's feelings toward the orphanage and toward Roberta as a part of it.

The first information Roberta exchanges with Twyla is that her mother is "sick" ("Recitatif" 243). On Visiting Day, her mother seems deeply religious, but her religiosity acquires a psychopathic note through the disproportionate sizes of the religious symbols with which she adorns herself. Not only is this woman "[b]igger than any man" to Twyla, but "on her chest was the biggest cross [the girl] had ever seen [...]. And in the crook of her arm was the biggest Bible ever made" ("Recitatif" 247). Twyla remembers that Roberta's mother read to her daughter from this huge bible even during lunch on visiting day, which must have seemed an odd behavior to her even in a place like St. Bonny's.

The refusal of Roberta's mother to shake Mary's hand when Roberta introduces Twyla and her mother to her has been interpreted as an open act of racism (cf. Rayson 42). Yet, it is not Mary, who burdened her daughter with racist views, who slights someone "from a whole other race," but Roberta's mother about whom we have learned nothing that would suggest a racist frame of mind. Rather, this unmotivated, hostile reaction of Roberta's mother, which in its fervor seems wholly inappropriate, indicates a lack of social competence that can be part of a mental illness. As Roberta's mother is mentally ill or in some way psychologically or mentally handicapped, her slighting of Mary might have little to do with racial prejudice, while it could be due to this woman's pathological inability to act adequately in a given social situation. Racial difference, this scene suggests, is not the exclusive motor of the actions and reactions of characters in the short story.

According to Twyla, Mary never stopped dancing; i.e., she never became a competent and caring mother. Roberta's mother takes her child out of the orphanage, but her daughter has to return to St. Bonny's twice, because the mother "never got well," as Roberta later admits ("Recitatif" 261). Twyla's feelings on the day Roberta left the orphanage – "I thought I would die in that room of four beds without her" ("Recitatif" 248) – indicate both the intensity of her terror at having to stay at the orphanage and the closeness of her friendship with Roberta. What Twyla had originally thought to be a rare "important" remark by her mother about somebody from the other race turned out to be neither important nor useful to her. What instead proves essential for Roberta and Twyla at St. Bonny's are the support and friendship of someone who is like them in the only way that matters under the circumstances: namely someone with whom each girl shares the fate of having been abandoned by an incompetent mother and having to stand her ground against a group of "real orphans with beautiful dead parents in the sky." The racial identity of this friend is irrelevant at this place.

3.2.2   The Reluctance to Remember – At Howard Johnson's

As an adult Twyla sees herself and Roberta at the orphanage as "[t]wo little girls who knew what nobody else in the world knew – how not to ask questions" ("Recitatif" 253). At St. Bonny's, Roberta never pressed her friend for embarrassing details after her initial sympathetic inquiry if Twyla's mother was sick, too, and her understanding nod at the answer that, "No, [...] she just likes to dance all day," when they were introduced to one another ("Recitatif" 243f.). The only piece of information the two girls need to establish an alliance that soon turns into close friendship is whether their mothers are dead or alive. Dead parents would have consigned them to the majority group of "real orphans." The fact that both their mothers are alive but somehow unable to care for their daughters sets them apart as outsiders, while it links them with one another.

Twelve years after the time at the orphanage, Twyla misinterprets Roberta's "reluctance" to ask questions as "politeness" and "generosity" ("Recitatif" 253). Indeed, and more importantly, it was part of the girls' survival strategy, both at the shelter and afterwards. They have learned not to voice their questions, fears and worries in order not to touch a hurting wound. The girls meet again at a Howard Johnson's coffee shop where Twyla waits tables and Roberta stops with two boyfriends on their way to California to see Jimi Hendrix. Roberta's interest in her former friend seems to have cooled markedly. She hardly responds to Twyla's attempts to involve her in a conversation, rudely insults her when Twyla's ignorance about Jimi Hendrix is revealed and thinks her too stupid to waste an explanation on her: "'Hendrix? Fantastic,' I said. 'Really fantastic. What's she doing now?' [...] 'Hendrix. Jimi Hendrix, asshole. He's only the biggest – Oh, wow. Forget it'" ("Recitatif" 250).

As Twyla is an employee at the coffee shop and is still wearing her drab waitress' uniform – "Without looking I could see that blue and white triangle on my head, my hair shapeless in a net, my ankles thick in white oxfords. Nothing could have been less sheer than my stockings"

("Recitatif" 250) –, it seems entirely feasible that a hip young woman on her way to Jimi Hendrix would not want to be associated with this decidedly un-cool "small-town country waitress" ("Recitatif" 253). And yet, Lula Fragd reads Roberta's coldness at the Howard Johnson's as straightforward White racism (cf. Abel 830). While this interpretation indicates Fragd's focus on the racial difference between the protagonists, however, it ought not to cancel out the possibility that Roberta's behavior might not be influenced by racist prejudices and a sense of superior hip-ness, but could also be the result of her reluctance to be reminded of her traumatic experiences at St. Bonny's. In fact, the text encourages such a reading. When Twyla spots her former friend in the restaurant, she cautions herself – and thus also the readers – not to feel too enthusiastic about this chance meeting: "Maybe she didn't want to be reminded of St. Bonny's or to have anybody know she was ever there. I know I never talked about it to anybody" ("Recitatif" 249). The thought that a potential lack of warmth and enthusiasm on Roberta's part might be due to the racial difference between her and her friend apparently does not occur to Twyla. An unwillingness to remember the time at the orphanage, on the other hand, would be a plausible explanation for her, should Roberta decide not to acknowledge her.

The reasons for such an unwillingness are powerful: Life at the orphanage was so unbearable for Roberta that she ran away from St. Bonny's as a teenager. Being made to think of the shelter means remembering the lack of mothering she had to endure in her childhood. It forces her to face the negative feelings she has harbored against her mother and also the actions which resulted from these feelings. Twyla knows that all of this had better remain forgotten; after all, she shares with Roberta the experience as well as the emotions attached to it.

Goldstein-Shirley wonders why Twyla herself would want to reveal that she was at a shelter when she had never told anyone so far. His conclusion unwittingly underlines the secondary importance of the issue of racial difference in this scene: "In fact, ostensibly, the sole basis for the encounter between her and the readers/listeners is Twyla's apparent desire to share intimate revelations about such events, some of which she acknowledges to be embarrassing, shameful, or painful to face" (Goldstein-Shirley, "Race and Response": 84).

At this particular time in the narrative, however, Twyla has not yet remembered, let alone told, all the details of an embarrassing, shameful, and painful incident that happened in the orchard of the orphanage and which involved the deaf and mute kitchen help Maggie, some of the older girls, Roberta, and herself. Twyla leaves it till later in the narrative to tell the readers that Maggie was beaten in the orchard. She had never mentioned it to anybody and assumes that Roberta also prefers to leave it unmentioned and unremembered. Yet, in her musings about whether her former roommate would want to speak with her or not, a sense of dread at the pending confrontation with the past is already present. If Roberta's rude treatment of Twyla is read in the light of the incident in the orchard and her unpleasant time at the shelter, it seems implausible that Twyla's cautioning remarks could be referring to her and Roberta's racial difference.

Interestingly, when Twyla asks her to explain her insulting behavior at the Howard Johnson's at their next meeting in the Food Emporium, Roberta tries to defend herself by pointing to the strained race relations during the 1960s: "Oh Twyla, you know how it was in those days: black – white. You know how everything was" ("Recitatif" 255). Twyla, however, calls this explanation into question on the basis of her experiences as a waitress in a throughway coffee shop. She insists that

> it was just the opposite. Busloads of blacks and whites came into Howard Johnson's together. They roamed together then: students, musicians, lovers, protesters. You got to see everything at Howard Johnson's and blacks were very friendly with whites in those days. ("Recitatif" 255)

Goldstein-Shirley sees in this reaction an illustration of Twyla's naiveté and lack of political consciousness ("Race and Response" 80f.). Yet, to me it signals her unwillingness to let Roberta off the hook who wants to call politics to her defense so as not to have to confront her traumatic past. The final scene at the coffee shop indicates that in spite of possible racist resentments there is something else at issue between the two girls:

> I was dismissed without anyone saying goodbye, so I thought I would do it for her. "How's your mother?" I asked. Her grin cracked her whole face. She swallowed. "Fine," she said. "How's yours?" "Pretty as a picture," I said and turned away. ("Recitatif" 250)

Thus, while Morrison reminds us of the issue of race by referring to the civil rights struggles of the 1960s, she also takes care to deflect our attention from racial difference as the only possible motivator for Roberta's rude remarks by pointing out differences in experience, style, appearance between the girls as well as a lack of difference when it comes to their mothers. The reason for Roberta's coldness might have been the racial difference between her and Twyla; yet, crucially, we cannot be certain.

3.2.3   The Issue of Unreliable Memories – At the Food Emporium

Twyla's survival strategy as a child was not only not to ask questions, it also included "to believe what had to be believed" ("Recitatif" 253). And she continued to believe that one's memories should not be questioned. At the outset of the narrative, one such unquestioned memory of Twyla's is that

> [n]othing really happened [in the orchard at St. Bonny's]. Nothing all that important, I mean. Just the big girls dancing and playing the radio. Roberta and me watching. Maggie fell down there once. The kitchen woman with legs like parentheses. And the big girls laughed at her. We should have helped her up, I know, but we were scared of those girls with lipstick and eyebrow pencil. ("Recitatif" 244f.)

In the course of her short meeting with Roberta in the Food Emporium this memory is radically cast into doubt. During their reminiscences about their time at the orphanage Twyla asks: "Remember Maggie? The day she fell down and those gar girls laughed at her?" ("Recitatif" 254). Roberta challenges her memory: "Maggie didn't fall. [...] They knocked her down. Those girls pushed her down and tore her clothes. In the orchard" ("Recitatif" 254). The brutality of this memory of the Maggie incident shocks Twyla whose own remembered version of the event is considerably less violent. She tries to cling to her more benign memories, protesting that "that's not what happened" ("Recitatif" 254). As Roberta insists, telling her that "[y]ou've blocked it, Twyla" ("Recitatif" 254), already doubt is beginning to undermine the carefully kept façade of Twyla's existence, a façade intended to present her as being at peace with herself. "The Maggie thing was troubling me," she confesses ("Recitatif" 254), and concludes that "Roberta had messed up my past somehow with that business about Maggie" ("Recitatif" 255).

So, why is Twyla so upset about this revelation, indicating that the image of her entire past for her hinges upon the question of whether Maggie fell or was pushed to the ground? Did she indeed "block it," i.e., ban it from her memory in order to protect herself? Significantly, at this point in the narrative the much-discussed question of Maggie's ambiguous racial identity is not raised. Early in the short story Twyla describes the kitchen worker as "sandy colored" ("Recitatif" 245), but Roberta claims later that Maggie was a "poor old black lady" ("Recitatif" 257). Initially, the piece of information that is so disconcerting to Twyla is that violence had been done to the small woman with "legs like parentheses" who was deaf and could not speak ("Recitatif" 245). Maggie's racial identity is of no consequence in this first important challenge to Twyla's version of her past and to her self-image as a non-violent person. Rather, the extent of her involvement and the violence of it are at issue. In Twyla's memories no act of physical aggression was perpetrated in the orchard. Maggie fell, and the older girls laughed, revealing malicious joy at the predicament of a handicapped woman at the most and a regrettable lack of sympathy at the least. The two friends were there but did not join in the laughter. And yet, they were watching – initially the dancing older girls and then, almost by accident, Maggie's "fall." Watching meant that they did nothing to help the kitchen worker, and from Twyla's account of the incident it is apparent that she feels a sense of guilt at this sin of omission, a sin that is only slightly lessened by the fact that the two little girls were scared of the older ones.

In Roberta's version, then, the younger girls' failure to help Maggie is a greater sin than in Twyla's; here, the two eight-year-olds were watching an act of aggression. The "gar girls" are still the aggressors and Roberta assures Twyla that they "had behavior problems" which explain the violence to her and Twyla and reassuringly distinguish the perpetrators from them ("Recitatif" 254). Yet, the knowledge that she and her friend had done nothing to help Maggie is also present in Roberta's version, and this knowledge is more uncomfortable in direct proportion to the higher degree of violence perpetrated against Maggie. Roberta, too, feels guilty and by asking, "Remember how scared we were?"("Recitatif" 254), she tries to defend herself and Twyla.

Roberta has "messed up" Twyla's past because with her insistence that Maggie did not just fall but was pushed and they had sat there, watching, she robs Twyla of the illusion that she is not to blame for what had happened in the orchard. Roberta's revelation initiates a process of self-inquiry in Twyla, of questioning her ability to remember things "correctly" and to pass them on to her audience "truthfully." After Roberta is gone, Twyla anxiously asks herself: "I wouldn't forget a thing like that. Would I?" ("Recitatif" 255).

3.2.4   Racial Strife vs. Ideals of Motherhood – The Busing Protests

During her encounter with Roberta at the Food Emporium Twyla feels reminded of their uncomplicated childhood relationship across racial lines: "Now we were behaving like sisters separated for much too long" ("Recitatif" 253). With lower middle-class Twyla buying food she cannot afford in order to appear well off to her now affluent friend Roberta, who is feeling very much at home in the expensive supermarket, the difference of class is problematized more than racial difference in the episode at the Food Emporium.

In contrast to this, when the women meet again some months later during the busing protests, racial identity is indeed a divisive issue: As the newspapers announce, the nation is in the grip of "racial strife" ("Recitatif" 255). Headlines are dominated by protests in favor of or against the desegregation of schools that followed the Supreme Court decision in "Brown vs. Board of Education" in 1954 and lasted well into the 1980s. Twyla is bewildered by the emotional pathos with which the media cover this dispute, conjuring up for her the image of "racial strife" as "a bird out of 1,000,000,000 B.C. Flapping its wings and cawing" ("Recitatif" 255). She tries in vain to develop an opinion on the issue, even though her own son will be bused to a school in a different neighborhood: "I knew I was supposed to feel something strong, but I didn't know what, and James [her husband] wasn't any help" ("Recitatif" 256). The idea that this decision could be influenced in any way by considerations of equal rights for Black and White Americans does not seem to cross her mind:

> Joseph was on the list of kids to be transferred from the junior high school to another one at some far-out of-the-way place and I thought it was a good thing until I heard it was a bad thing. I mean, I didn't know. All school seemed dumps to me, and the fact that one was nicer looking didn't hold much weight. ("Recitatif" 256)

Here, as in other scenes of Morrison's short story, class difference appears as important as race. Joseph will be bused from his lower middle-class neighborhood with its run-down schools to a more affluent school in a suburban upper middle-class neighborhood, while Roberta's children are supposed to attend a less prestigious school than they used to – irrespective of its racial background.

Twyla, regardless of race- or class-related considerations, only positions herself in the dispute when she sees her former roommate in front of a soon-to-be integrated school. Roberta is among a group of women protesting against the busing of their children, which determines Twyla's decision to be in favor of it. The text makes it quite clear that "Twyla's stance stems more from her resentment of Roberta than from her own political opinion," as Goldstein-Shirley points out ("Race and Response" 80), without, however, offering an explanation why this should be so. I want to suggest that Twyla's resentment has its roots not just in the fact that she and Roberta belong to different racial groups, as Abel and Goldstein-Shirley imply (Abel 830; Goldstein-Shirley, "Race/(Gender)": 91), or to different social classes, as suggested by Rayson (45). Rather, it is owed primarily to Roberta's earlier revelations about the violent nature of the incident in the orchard, the shattering of Twyla's memories of the past they caused, and her emotional uncertainty at her and her friend's failure to interfere on behalf of Maggie. Still struggling to come to terms with this new version of her past, Twyla is prepared for a confrontation with her former friend as soon as she sees her among the crowd, even on an issue which so far has failed to stir her emotions: "I circled the block, slowed down, and honked my horn. Roberta looked over and when she saw me she waved. I didn't wave back but I didn't move either" ("Recitatif" 256).

And yet, as Kathryn Nicol observes, with the announcement of "racial strife" in the media "[i]n official discourse the terms of the conflict have already been set. The protest over the school has already been predetermined as racial conflict, both for Twyla and the reader, [...]" (215). Before long a heated discussion unfolds between the two women. Its point of departure is their opposite stance on the issue of busing, and under the influence of the official label of "racial strife" it turns into a verbal confrontation made hostile by racist undertones: "I wonder what made me think you were different" ("Recitatif" 256), says Twyla, meaning 'different from the rest of the members of your race whom I know to be racists/bigots/losers' etc., and Roberta replies with the same sentence and its connotations. One last time Twyla tries to re-establish the old cross-racial solidarity between herself and Roberta by pointing to the other protesters and asking Roberta to "[l]ook at them, ... Just look. Who do they think they are? Swarming all over the place like they own it. And now they think they can decide where my child goes to school. Look at them, Roberta. They're Bozos" ("Recitatif" 256f.). She is using the "them and us" rhetoric of their days at St. Bonny's where "them" were the Big Bozo and the "gar girls," enemies she shared with Roberta because of their own outsider status and from whom they wanted to differ as strongly as possible.

As the busing protest is presented by the media and generally understood as a political dispute with race at its core, it is significant that Twyla tries to re-establish the childhood union across racial differences between herself and her former roommate and against an obstacle with which both of them have to cope, or so she suggests: bossy people who try to interfere with the way she and Roberta manage their lives. But Roberta's caustic remark suggests that she turns down the offer to re-unite: "No, they're not [Bozos]. They're just mothers" ("Recitatif" 257). She refuses to side with her childhood friend and instead affirms her membership in the group of mothers. Twyla in turn accuses Roberta of throwing into doubt her right to belong in that group, as she retorts with a defiant question: "And what am I? Swiss cheese?" ("Recitatif" 257). Now it is Roberta who reminisces about their congeniality at the orphanage: "I used to curl your hair" ("Recitatif" 257). But Twyla, unreconciled, withdraws her earlier peace offering and falls back on the official theme of racial discord: "I hated your hands in my hair" ("Recitatif" 257), implying that she could never could stand the other girl's physical presence because she belonged to a different, despicable race.

Furman attributes the fact that Roberta and Twyla have such a bitter argument now despite their closeness during their childhood to what she reads as the women's acute awareness of the racial difference that separates them in their adult life, whereas it was less important to them at St. Bonny's:

> The orphanage was an unlikely cover of protection for the unfettered intimacy each girl felt with the other. Later, in adulthood, when new alliances are possible – husband, friends, children – the hothouse of intimacy of the orphanage is impossible between a black and a white woman. The utopian past becomes the dystopic present of shattered memories. (110)

And indeed, at this point race is at the top of Roberta's and Twyla's minds because they are conditioned by the media and by public opinion to automatically interpret clashes of interests between individuals with different racial backgrounds in the light of racial difference. Yet, while I agree with Furman that the orphanage as a relatively autonomous, closed off space and, I would add, the outsider status of the abandoned children among orphans facilitated the alliance between the two girls at St. Bonny's, I suggest that questions of membership in different racial groups, of racial equality and of tolerance or intolerance are not at the heart of this argument. At this first stage of the confrontation between the two women we already sense that this argument is part of Roberta's and Twyla's efforts to clarify for themselves and finally come to terms with the extent to which their mothers with their inability to nurture them shaped their lives and their views of themselves, regardless of their racial identities.

The confrontation escalates when Roberta's fellow protesters intimidate Twyla by rocking her car and Roberta does nothing to help her. To hurt Twyla even more, Roberta confronts her with a new revelation about her past, a revelation that owes its wounding power to its connecting class discrimination with an accusation of racist violence: "You're the same little state kid who kicked a poor old black lady when she was down on the ground" ("Recitatif" 257). Thereby, Roberta latches on to the racialized discourse of civil rights and integration that forms the setting for this dispute. Nicol argues that

> Roberta constructs their personal conflict in terms of racial difference, accusing Twyla of attacking an old black lady when she was a child, an act which marks her not as violent as such, but as a bigot, a perpetrator of specifically racial violence. (216)

Aware of this sudden racialization of their dispute, Twyla does not protest against the accusation of having kicked Maggie but against the statement that Maggie was black: "She wasn't black. [...] Liar!" ("Recitatif" 258). Although Roberta's remark again increases the level of violence of her former friend's involvement in the torment of the helpless woman and presents a significant divergence from Twyla's remembered version of the incident, Twyla first and foremost feels compelled to reject the charge of being a racist bigot, not that of having willfully hurt another human being.

However, whereas Roberta tries to politicize and therefore racialize their conflict as the busing protests continue, Twyla refuses to follow suit. "Twyla's reaction to this, and to the protest as a whole, is to turn from the abstractions of racial or class difference to a personal protest that must also be a personal dialogue," Nicol writes (216). It is revealing that this personal dialogue, conducted via the cardboard signs the two women bring to the picket line, does not touch upon the issues of race and racial difference, at all. By choosing a busing protest as setting for this scene Morrison "flag raises" the issue of race, leading readers to expect that this will also be at the heart of the women's dispute.[6] She thus points to and acknowledges US-American social reality where the notion of race is frequently used not only as an organizing principle but also as a means of creating and enforcing hierarchies in society. While the busing protest with its racial focus forms the launching platform for the ensuing confrontation between the two women, Roberta's signs and Twyla's reactions to them indicate quite a different direction of their argument.

Roberta brings one and the same sign to the school every day. It says: "MOTHERS HAVE RIGHTS TOO!" ("Recitatif" 256, 259). In all likelihood she refers to the parental right to decide which school their child is to attend, a right she sees threatened by the new busing regulations in the interest of desegregation. Twyla's first reply to this sign reads "AND SO DO CHILDREN****" ("Recitatif" 258); it offers a counter argument for her opponent and presents Twyla's final effort to play by the rules of political protest. In this sense her sign can be understood as calling for the preservation of the right of children of all races and classes to receive the same quality of education – a demand that corresponds with the Civil Rights movement's call for integration. Yet, seen in the light of Twyla's and Roberta's personal history of childhood neglect, another meaning becomes possible: Twyla could be referring to every child's right to being loved and looked after by a responsible parent. Her cardboard sign thus bridges the gap between the ongoing political dispute and her and Roberta's personal trauma. In her struggle to fight it out with Roberta Twyla separates herself from her fellow protesters and their agenda and communicates solely with her former friend, as she herself realizes: "Actually my sign did not make sense without Roberta's. 'And so do children what?' one of the women on my side asked me. Have rights, I said, as though it was obvious" ("Recitatif" 258).

When Roberta takes no notice of her, Twyla begins to create what she calls "brilliant screaming posters," a series of cardboard signs designed only to catch the eye of her personal adversary ("Recitatif" 258). During their conversation at the Food Emporium Twyla learned that Roberta has four children. She knows also that they are not her biological children but the children of her husband, a widower whom she had married relatively recently. So, when Roberta ignores her first sign, Twyla produces a sec-

[6]Morrison uses this term in an online interview with reference to *Paradise* (cf. Farnsworth).

ond one which is more provocative than the first. "HOW WOULD YOU KNOW?" it screams at the mother of four stepchildren ("Recitatif" 258). Twyla coldly reminds Roberta of the fact that – contrary to herself – she has not given birth and therefore is not a mother in the biological sense. Thus, according to Twyla, she could not know that biological mothers have rights to make decisions for their children. In Twyla's opinion her one son proves her own right to the status and role of a mother much more powerfully than Roberta's four stepchildren do for Roberta.

Motherhood is crucial to these two women whose own mothers were unable to reach the standards of mothering; their traumatic experiences created in them a deep resolve to prove themselves more capable than their mothers. From the very start of their confrontation about the issue of busing it is apparent how much Twyla and Roberta, through their children, identify as mothers. During their first exchange in front of the school Roberta reminds her opponent that this protest action is "not about us, Twyla. Me and you. It's about our kids" ("Recitatif" 256). She attempts to direct the argument away from the "me and you" that is grounded in their childhood experiences toward the political conflict they witness now. And also, Roberta shows that she is determined to stand up for her children who resent having to attend a different school, and standing up for them is what her own mother was never able to do for her. The fact that they are not her biological offspring only hardens her resolution to demonstrate what a responsible mother she is.

Twyla is unwilling to follow Roberta's escape into race politics and deliberately misunderstands her statement as referring to issues of motherhood. Her reply, "What's more *us* than that?" in turn illustrates how strongly she identifies as a mother ("Recitatif" 256). In stark contrast to her memories of Mary, who did not see herself as 'Twyla's mother' but rather as 'Mary the dancer,' she feels she *is* her son Joseph.

In their determination to present themselves as competent, responsible mothers, Twyla and Roberta are each vulnerable to the other's attacks. They both know how difficult the mother-daughter relationship of the former friend was, how precarious a foundation for the attempt to do better. This reading seems to be shared by Abel, who argues that

> Roberta ... is more lastingly damaged than Twyla by maternal neglect, more vulnerable as an adult to its memory, a weakness on which Twyla capitalizes during their political conflicts as adults; the tenuousness of the

adult Roberta's own maternal status (...) may also testify figuratively to
a lack created by insufficient mothering. (829)

However, Abel offers a psychological interpretation of Roberta's experience of maternal neglect only to underline her arguments that firstly by
reading relativistic human characteristics as racial information she has
stepped into the trap Morrison has set in order to illustrate the arbitrary
nature of the attribution of racial difference, and secondly she has presumed Roberta's mother to be black because she had entertained "a white
woman's fantasy (my own) about black women's potency" (829). As Abel
favors a race-focused reading of the tensions between the two former
friends, she is interested in Roberta's emotional wounds and her questionable "stepmother" status only in so far as they are of value to Twyla
who can exploit her adversary's weaknesses to her own benefit in their
political – i.e., race-related – conflict. Morrison's exploration of other
psychological problems between the two protagonists receives as little
attention as her analysis of the way racial difference tends to dominate
readers' attention at the expense of other differences or, indeed, similarities that may determine human relationships. In contrast to this, I regard
Roberta's traumatic experience of abandonment as central to the dispute
of the two former friends. Nicol seems to share this view when she interprets Twyla's "HOW WOULD YOU KNOW?" sign as "commenting on
Roberta's own absent mother" (216). This poster is Twyla's reminder for
Roberta that she knows about her innermost anguish and possibly shares
it. It also presents a merciless questioning of her former friend's claim to
motherhood.

Twyla's last and – in terms of upsetting Roberta – her most effective sign "in queenly red with huge black letters" points most clearly to
the heart of the dispute between the women ("Recitatif" 259). "IS YOUR
MOTHER WELL?" she asks through her poster, systematically and rather
cruelly rubbing in the painful memory of the illness of Roberta's mother
which resulted in the neglect of her daughter ("Recitatif" 259). It forces
Roberta to flee from the location of the protest in order to escape Twyla's
torturous stabs. Clearly, racial difference and desegregation are not the
most burning issues on the two women's minds when they confront
each other across the picket line. Consequently, after Roberta leaves the
protest, Twyla also stops attending. There is no point in her staying on
with her cryptic signs when her only reader who is able to interpret them
is gone. Yet, while Twyla revenges herself on Roberta who destroyed her

mercifully harmless memory of the incident in the orchard and forces her
to ask herself distressing questions, she cannot enjoy her victory. By reminding Roberta of her neglectful mother the narrator has reminded herself of her own mother's excesses that left her just as lonely and abandoned as her friend.

3.2.5 Scapegoating Maggie – The Orchard Incident

Twyla's victory in her dispute with Roberta therefire is only half complete.
For years after the busing protests her thoughts circle around her former
friend and the months they spent together at the shelter – ample evidence
that the process of coming to terms with her childhood experiences is not
concluded, yet. She remembers how she "couldn't help looking for her
when Joseph graduated from high school" ("Recitatif" 259). Nor can she
forget what Roberta said to her at the busing protest:

> It didn't trouble me much what she had said to me in the car. I mean the
> kicking part. I know I didn't do that, I couldn't do that. But I was puzzled
> by her telling me Maggie was black. When I thought about it I actually
> couldn't be certain. She wasn't pitch-black, I know, or I would have re-
> membered that. What I remember was the kiddie hat, and the semicircle
> legs. ("Recitatif" 259)

This short passage exemplifies Morrison's technique of highlighting a certain key condition or situation while appearing to play down its relevance.
In style and logic the sequence follows Twyla's affirmation in the beginning of the narrative that the shelter "really wasn't bad" ("Recitatif"
243), and that "nothing all that important" ever happened in the orchard
("Recitatif" 244). These assertions sharply contrast with the facts that living at St. Bonny's for four months had been awful for her and that the
incident in the orchard gave her nightmares for years. Twyla's insistence
that she is not troubled by Roberta's accusation of violence and that she
is interested only in the question of Maggie's ambiguous racial identity
is one of the author's most emphatic comments on the pervasiveness of
race in our perception of reality in "Recitatif." This statement demonstrates Twyla's conversance with the ideology of racial difference and its
employment in her own narrative once again, as it manifested itself in her
initial stressing of her roommate's different racial background and framed
her confrontation with Roberta during the busing protests.

If the mystery of Twyla's, Roberta's, and indeed Maggie's racial identities or the impossibility of solving it is made the focal point of "Recitatif," Twyla's confusion at the claim that Maggie was black carries enormous importance and must be read as evidence of how necessary a seemingly secure knowledge of Maggie's racial identity is to her. Such a focus, however, again misses important points of Morrison's discussion of the complexities of identity and of human interaction in "Recitatif." Three quite different examples may serve to illustrate this:

In his analysis of Maggie's victimization, Juda Bennett falls into the "trap" of overrating the importance of Maggie's racial status to Twyla and Roberta whose highlighting he previously identified as one of Morrison's aims: "Maggie's role as victim, emphasized by her 'crippled' legs and her treatment by the sadistic 'gar girls,' becomes ultimately less interesting and more invisible than her role as a text for Twyla and Roberta to read race upon" (212).[7] To illustrate his point he cites the passage quoted above, starting with "I was puzzled by her telling me ..." and continuing with

> I tried to reassure myself about the race thing for a long time until it dawned on me that the truth was already there, and Roberta knew it. I didn't kick her; I didn't join in with the gar girls and kick that lady, but I sure did want to. We watched and never tried to help her and never called for help (372). (212)[8]

Bennett does not consider the possibility that Twyla might profess to be puzzled about Maggie's ambiguous racial identity in order to make little of the fact that she is much more worried about her motives for wanting to kick Maggie and never helping her. She tells herself and the readers that she was thinking about "the race thing," which in a society with a history of racing individuals accurately will be considered only normal,

---

[7]Goldstein-Shirley offers an insightful interpretation of the symbolism of Maggie's bow legs: "Parentheses indicate something of secondary importance, which, added to Maggie's muteness, connote a passive, marginalized victim, a cipher; the bow legs conjure the image of a zero itself. Reduced to nothing, Maggie is robbed of agency which leaves for her only the role of pawn in the battle of memories waged by Twyla and Roberta over three decades" ("Race and Response" 82). However, I caution against a tendency to think too little of the importance of the figure of Maggie for Twyla's and Roberta's psychological development.

[8]Bennett works with a different edition of the short story but does not mention which one.

while in fact she tried to solve the question of whether she had kicked the elderly woman or not – a question that arguably is more urgent to her than Maggie's racial identity. Nicol directly contradicts Bennett's view with her answer to the question of why the issue of Maggie's racial status is even debated between Roberta and Twyla:

> While Roberta and Twyla argue over her racial identity, this identity only becomes important when deployed as part of an argument on violence – the violence they may or may not have done to Maggie as children, a violence which is initially hidden beneath the question of Maggie's race, but which resurfaces repeatedly and insistently. (218)

Concentrating on the surface layer of race, Bennett overlooks clear textual hints which suggest that this is indeed what Twyla is worrying about. He stops his citation at the point when Twyla voices her realization that "Maggie was my dancing mother" ("Recitatif" 259). In his further analysis Bennet also does not consider Roberta's confession to Twyla at their final meeting in which she expresses a similar motive for hating Maggie, using some of the same words Twyla used before:

> And you were right. We didn't kick her. It was the gar girls. Only them. But, well, I wanted to. I really wanted them to hurt her. I said we did it, too. You and me, but that's not true. And I don't want you to carry that around. It was just that I wanted to do it so bad that day – wanting to is doing it. ("Recitatif" 261)

While he is right to suggest that "Maggie's ambiguous race is tied to many other unknowns about personal responsibility and guilt" (212), his conclusion overrates the importance Twyla and Roberta assign to the racial identity of the kitchen worker and to their own different racial backgrounds. Consequently, Bennett fails to investigate the actual reasons why this marginal character occupies such a central position in the two women's reflections about their past and thus in the short story. He never starts to investigate the "other unknowns about personal responsibility and guilt" he diagnoses.

Kathryn Nicol, on the other hand, rightly points out that the uncertainty about Maggie's racial identity at first troubles Twyla, until she realizes that it is not Maggie's race that matters but the violence that was done to her. Nicol goes on to argue that Twyla has come to the understanding that Maggie's poverty and physical disability render her vulnerable to violence: "Maggie may be racially indeterminate, but her position as poor (one could also suggest disabled) places her in a position where violence can be done against her, violence without consequences to others" (218). Her interpretation sees race, class, and relative ability as interrelated and insists that "each can be made part of the others by the imposition of the dominant gaze" (218). Nicol also finds a convincing explanation for the kitchen help's general vulnerability as a marginalized person and thus for the fact that the "gar girls" dared raise their hands against her in the first place.

Although these are important insights into Maggie's role in "Recitatif," they leave out one important factor Morrison emphasizes in her short story. Nicol does not draw attention to the parallel between Maggie's inferior status as a poor, disabled, and possibly black woman and the lack of ability, for some of the same reasons, of Roberta's and Twyla's mothers to nurture them. Thus, it is not her racial or class identity or her handicaps which make the girls hate Maggie but her resemblance of their mothers and indeed of Roberta and Twyla in their own helplessness as the young daughters of incapable and marginalized mothers.

Finally, Elizabeth Abel points out that Maggie is the person "who occasions the text's only mention of skin color, an explicitly ambiguous sandy color" (828). She argues that her "racial undecidability" adds to the girls' difficulty in placing and categorizing her which, she writes, is also symbolized by her "legs like parentheses" and her "'never saying anything at all' (245)" (828). By reading "Recitatif" mainly through the lens of race, Abel overlooks tha fact that while Roberta and Twyla lived at St. Bonny's, neither of them thought Maggie's racial identity in any way problematic or even contentious. Roberta interprets her "sandy color" as black whereas Twyla does not see her as "raced," which implies that she regards her as white. When decades later, during race-related protests, they compare their opinions and realize that they disagree, they – like the readers – initially place great importance on Maggie's racial identity; they first insist on the correctness of their original interpretations and then begin to question them. However, when the two women honestly analyze their memories and the feelings they had as girls, they find that it was not Maggie's skin color that had occasioned their wish to harm the woman, but the way she reminded them of their mothers and of themselves. A closer look at the way in which Twyla's and Roberta's lives are connected with the kitchen help will clarify this argument.

Maggie is a central if illusive figure in "Recitatif:" The day of her attack functions as a structuring event in the narrator's memories of her

time at St. Bonny's and provides a focal point in the short story. Twyla
remembers that

> Maggie couldn't talk. The kids said she had her tongue cut out, but I think
> she was just born that way: mute. She was old and sandy-colored and
> she worked in the kitchen. I don't know if she was nice or not. I just
> remember her legs like parentheses and how she rocked when she walked.
> [...] She wore this really stupid little hat – a kid's hat with ear flaps – and
> she wasn't much taller than we were. A really awful little hat. Even for a
> mute, it was dumb – dressing like a kid and never saying anything at all.
> ("Recitatif" 245)

Both girls detect some of their mothers' traits of character and behavior
in this silent woman. They categorize Maggie as disabled because they
only notice her deafness, her inability to speak, her shortness, her bowlegs
that made walking difficult for her, and her childish outfit. They see her
as a pitiful woman unable to defend herself against the tough gar girls'
aggression and draw parallels between Maggie and their mothers whom
they experience as similarly helpless and incompetent.

Twyla's hostile feelings toward the kitchen help show how much the
girl was traumatized by the fact that her childhood was troubled by a
mother who was unable to care for her properly and was permanently
a potential source of embarrassment to her. Maggie's smallness and her
little hat remind her of the petit figure of her mother and her often childlike behavior. Twyla resents Maggie's inability to hear or speak because
it reminds her of her mother Mary's unresponsiveness and Mary's absence when she needed her. Moreover, Maggie's swaying bowlegged walk
brings to Twyla's mind the aspect she hates most about her mother: her
frequent and excessive dancing that keeps her away from home where
her little daughter waits for her. After a time consuming and emotionally
draining analysis of her feelings toward Maggie and cathartic debates with
Roberta, Twyla realizes that

> Maggie was my dancing mother. Deaf, I thought, and dumb. Nobody
> inside. Nobody who would hear you if you cried in the night. Nobody who
> could tell you anything important that you could use. Rocking, dancing,
> swaying as she walked. ("Recitatif" 259f.)

Maggie became the screen onto which the eight-year-old Twyla projected
her frustrations about her mother, whose lack of motherliness forced her
to live in an orphanage she experienced as hostile and alienating. In the
orchard Twyla took revenge on Maggie for having been "dumped" by her

own mother; she tried to soothe her hurt feelings by transferring her anger onto the handicapped kitchen help. But the pangs of guilt at wanting to beat up, to kill her own mother in the guise of somebody who, in the girl's eyes, shares Mary's deficiencies have weighed heavily on Twyla's conscience. They have occupied her thoughts and have given her nightmares well into her adult years. In order to protect herself from the chastising severity of her own conscience Twyla "blocked" her memories of the incident, as Roberta rightly says, creating and believing in a more harmless version of it.

Throughout her entire girlhood Roberta experienced her mother as embarrassing and overtaxed with the responsibilities involved in raising a child. She dreaded and almost expected to become mentally ill like her mother and to end up in the same kind of institution in which both her mother and Maggie had grown up. In a diner, on a snowy evening shortly before Christmas, she confesses to Twyla what had determined her feelings toward Maggie:

> Listen to me. I really did think she was black. I didn't make that up. But now I can't be sure. I just remember her as old, so old. And because she couldn't talk – well, you know, I thought she was crazy. She'd been brought up in an institution like my mother was and like I thought I would be too. ("Recitatif" 261)

Unable to take revenge on her mother for having abandoned her to the Big Bozo and the "gar girls" at St. Bonny's and for planting in her heart the fear of also becoming mentally ill, Roberta projected her fury onto Maggie. Like Twyla before her, Roberta starts her statement by referring to Maggie's ambiguous racial identity. Yet, for her, too, other characteristics were more important than race: Maggie's age, the fact that she did not speak, her assumed craziness. Her racial background is not included in her memories. More relevantly, the kitchen help to her appeared as incompetent as her mother, but unlike her mother she was within her reach and already victimized. Thus, little Roberta willed the older girls to torment the helpless woman, wanting them to hurt Maggie in her own mother's place and thereby avenging herself. When she is confronted with Twyla's differing version of the events in the orchard, Roberta has to re-interpret her own childhood memories and to confront her well-suppressed sense of guilt. In order to lighten her burden she tries to make her former ally against the older girls and the Bozo her accomplice in her fantacized violent attack against Maggie, and even accuses Twyla of kicking the woman.

Yet, the parallels between Maggie and the two girls' mothers are not the only reason why Roberta and Twyla wanted the old woman to be beaten up. The girls also sensed similarities between Maggie and themselves, as Furman also stresses:

> For Twyla and Roberta, Maggie was a symbol of defeat, a reminder of their own helplessness. Being deaf, mute, and a victim is what they both remember about Maggie and what they both hated about her. The burden of their young lives was bearable when pain, transformed to anger, shifted to Maggie. Without realizing it, however, in hating Maggie they hated themselves and each other. (110)

Twyla's subconscious recognition of similarities between Maggie and herself resurfaces in her recollections as an adult of what the woman looked like and what clothes she wore. She remembers that the kitchen help was very small, about the same height as eight-year-old girls, and wore a strange little hat. This hat is a crucial detail in Twyla's memories about Maggie; she mentions it several times, finding varying descriptions for it – "a kid's hat with ear flaps," "a baby boy hat," "a kiddie hat" – all of which underline Twyla's impression that such a garment looked childish and inappropriate on an adult ("Recitatif" 245, 259). As a waitress at Howard Johnson's Twyla also has to wear a hat, and she is very self-conscious about it. When Roberta laughs "a private laugh that included the guys but only the guys" at Twyla's mentioning her place of residence during that first chance meeting, Twyla feels childish and inadequate ("Recitatif" 250). The same attributes come to her mind when she thinks of the kitchen help. Even though Maggie was an adult woman, her smallness, her bowlegs and the child's hat made her look like a child. Furthermore, not only was Maggie's appearance infantile, she also did not act the way children expect and want adults to act: She was not strong, never defended herself when attacked, and "couldn't even scream" ("Recitatif" 258).

How much of herself Twyla recognizes in Maggie also becomes visible in her account of how "those cows on the picket lines across the street" started to rock her car during the busing protest ("Recitatif" 258); they resonates with her descriptions of the kitchen help at various points in the narrative. Twyla recalls of the attack that when the women gently "rocked" her car she "swayed back and forth like a sideways yo-yo" ("Recitatif" 257). Early in her account she describes how Maggie "rocked when she walked" and "sway[ed] from side to side" ("Recitatif" 245).

Furthermore, just as Roberta and Twyla had watched the incident in the orchard without interfering on behalf of the kitchen help, Roberta does nothing to help Twyla when the women threaten her, making her feel like Maggie:

> Automatically I reached for Roberta, like the old days in the orchard when they saw us watching them and we had to get out of there, and if one of us fell the other pulled her up and if one of us was caught the other stayed to kick and scratch, and neither would leave the other behind. My arm shot out of the car window but no receiving hand was there. Roberta was looking at me sway from side to side in the car and her face was still. ("Recitatif" 257)

Thus, Maggie also represents Twyla and Roberta, two girls abandoned by their mothers, outsiders among older and tougher orphans, children who despise themselves for being little, powerless and frightened. Twyla remembers the masochistic glee she felt during the incident in the orchard: "And when the gar girls pushed her down, and started roughhousing, I knew she wouldn't scream, couldn't – just like me – and I was glad about that" ("Recitatif" 260). By letting Maggie be beaten up by the big girls and watching, by failing to "[pull] her up" and to "[stay] to kick and scratch" in her defense as they used to do whenever one of them had got into the hands of the older girls, Roberta and Twyla not only took revenge on their irresponsible mothers, they also unconsciously punished themselves. Or rather, they allowed that part of themselves to be kicked and beaten that was weak and helpless, because they loathed it.

Once the two women acknowledge their ambiguous and guilt-ridden feelings toward Maggie, they can forgive themselves – and each other. Abel writes:

> 'Recitatif' ends with parallel recognitions by Twyla and Roberta that each had perceived the mute Maggie as her own unresponsive, rejecting mother, and therefore hated and wanted to harm her. [. . . ,] [Th]e story concludes with the shared experience of abandoned little girls who, in some strange twist of the oedipal story, discover that they killed (or wanted to kill), as well as loved (or wanted to love), their mothers. (841)

Twyla's resentment of Roberta during the busing protests stems from her sense of guilt about her own wish to harm her mother and herself in Maggie. The same desire also determined Roberta's actions or lack of action in the orchard, and Twyla instinctively knows this; she resents Roberta for the same reasons for which she subconsciously hates herself. After a series of encounters in which the two women are confronted with their differing versions and interpretations of the past and from which they have to extract the roots of their traumas and their attempts to overcome them, they are able to absolve each other from their guilt. During their last meeting around Christmas Twyla and Roberta comfort one another with the fact they were only eight years old when they lived at St. Bonny's together: "'We were kids, Roberta.' 'Yeah. Yeah. I know, just kids.' 'Eight.' 'Eight.' 'And lonely.' 'Scared too'" ("Recitatif" 261).

The last sentence of the short story is a question asked by Roberta: "Oh shit, Twyla. Shit, shit, shit. What the hell happened to Maggie?" ("Recitatif" 261). It is a question full of empathy, of worry about somebody else, tinged with despair at Roberta's and Twyla's own contributions to the misery of the kitchen help. The same woman asks this question who, as a child and just like her friend Twyla, had thought it important not to ask questions. They were afraid of the answers they might get: that they would never be included in the games of the real orphans, that their mothers would never get well or stop dancing and would never be able to look after them properly, that they would be disadvantaged in their later lives because of the bad start they had had. Fear, insecurity, and loneliness made them turn against someone who was as unable to help herself or anybody else as their mothers were, and as timid, insecure, and unwanted as they felt themselves to be. When the women actually stop to worry about Maggie's fate, the possibility of forgiveness is palpable, forgiveness of their mother's inadequacies and of their own unsuccessful efforts to cope with the trauma of abandonment.

Finally, the question of Maggie's racial identity is not important. It remains unknown and is unknowable because, once the significance of Maggie as a symbol for the girls' incompetent mothers and themselves as helpless beings is understood, it is irrelevant to Twyla and Roberta whether she is black or white.

3.3   Identity and the Un-/Realities of Race

With her short story Toni Morrison "not only calls attention to an ideology that seems so natural that individuals fail to recognize it as such, but challenges that ideology," writes Goldstein-Shirley ("Race and Response" 85). Morrison chooses for "Recitatif" a thoroughly racialized setting which affects the protagonists' perception of themselves and their environment and reflects the reality of American society, including readers' expectations, and proceeds to demonstrate that race is not the only motor of social relations, tensions, and crises. In her "psychological narrative that crosses difference" the author dethrones race as the all-important marker of social relations (Abel 841). She highlights and criticizes an obsession with racial difference that results in a shortsightedness, a readiness to blame racial difference for conflicts that have roots quite other than race.

After scouring the text for cues as to who of the protagonists might be black and who might be white, Abel comes to the conclusion that "[s]ameness coexists with difference, psychology with politics. Race enforces no absolute distinctions between either characters or readers, all of whom occupy diverse subject positions, some shared, some antithetical" (840). By flag raising race only to point out that the relationship of Twyla and Roberta developed in spite of and regardless of racial differences, because of shared experiences, feelings, fears, and hopes Morrison reminds us of a frequently forgotten commonplace: that a person's identity consists of a multitude of interrelated facets, one of which is racial identity. It is undesirable and can have disastrous consequences in the larger scheme of political and social life to attempt a hierarchy of these facets, most likely – given the omnipresence of the category of race in the fabric of US society – with racial identity receiving top priority.

Of course the relationship of Twyla and Roberta is influenced by their different racial backgrounds. At every stage of their acquaintance this difference is reiterated, as if to remind readers of it. While a Black and a White girl could be fast friends within the walls of an orphanage, outside of St. Bonaventure race presents a formidable obstacle to the communication between the two women. However, while on the surface of the text race is evoked as the reason for personal apprehensions as well as political unrest, their racial difference itself is never the force that divides the former friends. At Howard Johnson's, the snub and Roberta's coldness stem from her unwillingness to reopen a painful chapter in her life by acknowledging the friend who had shared it with her. At the Food Emporium class rather than race establishes difference between Roberta and Twyla. The busing protests hinge upon the call for desegregation, but to Twyla they present themselves as a matter of being rich and influential or being poor and having to live with the rich people's decisions.

Having grown up and living in a racialized society the women at first read their personal conflict in terms of the politics of race, yet with every new encounter they realize that, contrary to what they had been taught, the information of racial difference is *not* "anything important that you could use" for the task of understanding their feelings and working through their childhood traumas. They must learn not to want to decide on a specific racial identity for Maggie in order to recognize the ultimately more relevant question of why they wanted to hurt the old woman. This is precisely the task Morrison sets her readers with "Recitatif." Like her protagonists, we are encouraged to question the power of race to determine identities and relationships. The critical value of ambiguity is underlined in a short story which challenges the fallacy of thinking identity as monolithic and pre-discursive.

"Recitatif" illustrates the factual materiality of race in people's lives. Yet, it also highlights the limits of race as an explanatory matrix, challenging the authority of racial concepts to regulate quotidian and imaginary realities. In her later work Morrison continues this twofold effort of exploring realities of race while deconstructing mechanisms of racialization. In *Paradise* in particular she perfects the technique of "flag raising and erasing race" in fiction.

4 "The Solace of Home": *Paradise*

I opened my investigation of Morrison's discussion of the notion of race by exploring her thoughts and statements on the subject of race relations and racial identity in the United States as they appear in specific interviews and in her critical writing. I pointed out the dilemma in which Morrison finds herself through her investment in racial essentialism as an empowering concept on the one hand and poststructuralist, constructivist ideas about the non-existence of a racial essence on the other. From this analysis of the author's critique of race in essays and interviews I turned to her fictional writing, suggesting that with her short story "Recitatif," Morrison problematizes an obsessive preoccupation with racial difference at the expense of other, equally important identities, arguing that she regards this characteristic an inherent liability of the concept of race.

In the following, I re-visit the literary battleground of essentialism versus constructivism in the discourse on racial identity as it presents itself to the readers in Morrison's seventh novel, *Paradise*.[1] In her essay "Home" the author refers her audience to this text, rather than explicating what exactly she understands race to mean at a moment in time when this concept continues to be employed regardless of the fact that it has been deconstructed and proven a fiction. In *Paradise*, Morrison suggests, we will find exemplary renditions of the "home" she talks about in her essay, where race is effectively "unmattered:" "I want to inhabit, walk around, a site clear of racist detritus; a place were *race both matters and is rendered impotent* [...]," she writes ("Home" 9, italics mine). The seemingly paradoxical idea of unmattering race even as it still matters to Morrison shows the author's recognition that in spite of our knowledge of the constructedness of race, of its "unrealness," the notion of racial difference continues to create powerful and harmful hierarchies in US-American society. It

---

[1] Toni Morrison, *Paradise* (1997; London: Chatto & Windus, 1998). All further reference is to this edition.

is this capacity of the concept that needs to be highlighted and critically analyzed in order to unmatter race.

Morrison's novel *Paradise* pits two communities against each other that could hardly be more different: the all-Black town of Ruby, founded by descendants of slaves who believe their settlement to be the quasi-paradisiacal home of God's chosen people, and a group of five women who sought and found refuge from a hostile society at the Convent, an old mansion in the vicinity of the town.

Some critics of *Paradise* consider this narrative setup simplistic and unimaginative because of its apparent adherence to polar opposites at a time when binaries have long been deconstructed. Early reviewers find fault with what they regard as rigid oppositions between non-racist and racist attitudes, women and men, and ultimately good and bad. Geoffrey Bent, for example, calls *Paradise* too didactic, simplistic and schematic (148). In her scathing critique, Michiko Kakutani accuses the novel of being a "contrived, formulaic book," "clunky," "leaden," and a "heavy-handed, schematic piece of writing." Duvall, in agreement with Philip Page's reading of Morrison's oeuvre as successfully inverting and thereby deconstructing hegemonic hierarchies, both in plot and structure of her fictional work (cf. Page, *Dangerous Freedom*),[2] points out that "[w]hile [Morrison's] writing at times most definitely challenges certain 'bipolar oppositions,' those same oppositions may return to drive her fictional engines" (9). However, *Paradise* does not work with polar opposites like "Black vs. White" or "Black vs. non-Black." Rather, I suggest that Morrison is interested in the opposition of "race defined" vs. "race undefined," essential vs. non-essential. The social construction of a racial essence in the society of Ruby and the refusal to construct race as biological essence in the Convent are such oppositions; their confrontation drives the plot forward as it creates the potential and ultimately deadly reason for a clash between the two communities. "The tension between identity as a biological essence and identity as a social construction," as Duvall writes, is "perhaps the central motivating opposition" in Morrison's fictional texts in general, (9). In *Paradise*, I argue, the author specifically explores the conflict between a community that constructs racial identity as a biological given and one that does not construct racial identity but leaves it undefined.

---

[2]Published in 1995, this volume does not include a discussion of *Paradise*.

For Morrison, the opposition between racial essentialism and constructivism embodies two conflicting versions of the "racial home" she searches and calls for in her essay "Home:" on the one hand, a home that is a safe haven for African Americans, based on the belief in an essential blackness that defines the moral worth of a human being, and on the other, a home that leaves race undefined and thus avoids color-coded hierarchies as it strives to facilitate its inhabitants' access to and reconciliation with their innermost selves. This focus places the question of the role of racial identity in the construction of individual and communal "homes" at the center of my investigation.[3]

4.1   The Search for Home: Race and Religion

> A man can indeed be said to be "religious" about golf, but not merely if he pursues it with passion and plays it on Sundays: he must also see it as symbolic of some transcendent truths.
>
> Clifford Geertz

From the beginning, the search for a home has been an important issue in the history of African Americans, who, after the Middle Passage, found themselves strangers and outsiders in North America and needed to find their own place there. Asked whether "there [is] something in African-American history that makes [her] especially interested in this separate place," Morrison replies:

> Yes, because only ... African-Americans were not immigrants in this rush to find a heaven. They had left a home. So they're seeking for another home, while other people are doing the same thing, except the other people were leaving a home they didn't want to be in any longer, or couldn't be in

[3]Here, I disagree with Duvall, who claims that "race is not central to the novel" (144). He slightly relativizes this astonishing statement by explaining that "[r]ace matters, but in an upside down, through-the-looking-glass kind of way. The racially pure Black community of Ruby emerges out of the doubled insult of class and colorism" (144). While this is true for Ruby, the suggestion that race is not central to *Paradise* indicates that Duvall, if only for an instance, lost sight of the central point of the novel. He has a point only if he refers to the fact that White-on-Black racism is not the explicit theme of this text – but this is rarely the case with Morrison's novels. It seems blatantly clear to me that race, namely the construction of race, is the central topic of Paradise.

any longer. Native Americans were moved around in their home. African-Americans were looking for a second one and hopefully one that would be simply up to them, their own people, their own habits, their own culture, and to contain themselves in that. So it makes the motive for paradise a little bit different. (Farnsworth)

Paradise is an exploration of the human yearning for a home, especially – but not only – in the case of Black Americans, for a place of safety from persecution, of spiritual and emotional warmth, of liberty to express one-self in spite of one's minority racial or gender identity, of being intimately connected with one's past, present and future. This state of feeling and being at home is "paradise" for Morrison, who considers US-American society essentially "utopian" in so far as it is a society that was conceived as paradisiac (cf. Scheck).[4] This original, strongly religiously connoted vision stands in stark contrast to the contemporary US-American pop-image of paradise which the author describes as crassly materialistic: "In this country, we do not teach people to be citizens but consumers. Our idea of paradise is the ultimate shopping event, a 24 h super-market with-out cash registers. This is banal and kills the soul" (Scheck).[5]

Morrison said about her novel that "[it] is about this important in-tellectual topic, which is religion" (Jaffrey), thereby adding another item to a veritable list of themes compiled by reviewers and critics with which this novel is allegedly concerned.[6] Indeed, she called *Paradise* the only overtly religious novel she has ever written (cf. Donahue). Deirdre Don-

---

[4] In her interview with *Deutsches Allgemeines Sonntagsblatt*, Morrison states that "die USA sind ihrem Wesen nach als utopische, also auf das Paradies hin aus-gelegte Gesellschaft konzipiert."

[5] "Wir erziehen in diesem Land die Menschen nicht zu Bürgern, sondern zu Verbrauchern. Unsere Vorstellung vom Paradies ist das ultimative Shopping-Erlebnis, ein 24 Stunden geöffneter Supermarkt ohne Registrierkassen. Das ist seicht und tötet die Seele."

[6] Besides religion, this list includes love (cf. Menand; Whitton), "the ways in which preconception can determine experience itself" (Storace 64/3), "the com-plex uses of story-telling" (65/1), the re-writing of US-American history from the African American perspective (cf. Tally, *(Hi)Stories*; Bold), the combination of love and violence in Morrison's novels (cf. Staples; Bold); "the troubled his-tory of Black America" (B. Allen 6/1; cf. also Bemrose); conflict and violence between women and men (cf. Donahue; Goldberg; Jones), and "the male scape-goating of sexually unattached women" (Menand 78/3); racism within the Black community (cf. Menzies); the power of language (cf. D. Smith); "racial dignity

ahue explains that "[i]t sprang from her desire to explore in a series of books, 'the various kinds of love.' In *Beloved*, she wrote about the love of a mother for her child, in *Jazz*, she examined romantic love. And now, in *Paradise*, she wanted to understand 'the love of God and love for fellow human beings.'"[7] Morrison, for whom "[n]ovels are always inquiries" (Jaffrey), created a text in which the Christian "experience of life" is "an absolute, one that the book takes for granted," as Marcus explains. In *Paradise*, "questions of God or divine love or forgiveness" are anything but unimportant; in this novel they are "matters of life and death" (Marcus). In what way religion decides over life and death in *Paradise*, how the concept of race becomes an integral part of religion in the town of Ruby, and how its absence shapes and is shaped in turn by the kind of religion practiced in the Convent – these questions are central to the investigation of the idea of a paradisiacal home in Morrison's novel.

In traditional concepts, paradise functions through mechanisms of exclusion of the unsaved, usually at the expense of justice and equality. "All notions of *Paradise* have in common that they are exclusive places," says Morrison. "Only the chosen few have the right of entry. All others are excluded and literally discarded, so that the result is a holy war between the redeemed and the condemned" (Scheck).[8] In a lecture on occasion of the release of the German translation of *Paradise* in October 1999,[9] Mor-

---

and equality" (Barthelme 25/1), our notion of paradise as separatist and exclusivist (cf. Shockley); history turned into myth (cf. Mantel); the individual in a community (cf. Phipps); "the loss of innocence, the paralyzing power of ancient memories, the difficulty of accepting loss, change and pain" (Kakutani E8/1), and the "long-term human consequences of slavery" (P. Turner 1/1). Some reviews with a more negative tenor have accused the author of pursuing too many topics for one novel (see e.g. Kakutani). In my view, however, the critical focus on the construction of racial essence renders these seemingly disparate themes form an indivisible union.

[7] See also Louis Menand who writes of *Paradise* that it is the last book in a trilogy about different kinds of love. "The love in 'Paradise' turns out to be the love of God – God's love for human beings, and their love for God" (78/3).

[8] "Alle Vorstellungen vom Paradies verbindet, dass diese Orte exklusiv sind. Nur bestimmte Auserwählte haben Zutritt. Alle anderen werden ausgegrenzt und buchstäblich verworfen, so dass es zu einem heiligen Krieg zwischen den Erlösten und den Verdammten kommt."

[9] Toni Morrison, *Paradies*, transl. Thomas Piltz (Reinbek bei Hamburg: Rowohlt, 1999).

rison described the conventional image of paradise as dominated by key-concepts such as abundant beauty, boundless plenty, infinite rest, eternity as in avoidance of death already in our earthly existence, and the desire for exclusivity ("Trouble"). This illusory and inherently discriminatory, all too familiar notion called forth in her the urge to "re-imagine" paradise. "The paradise that anybody could get would be no paradise at all but it's in that direction people have to think," she proposes in an interview and continues: "Anyway, it's a more exciting proposition to me than the old paradise, the one where somebody wins by dint of some effort of the will, of some purity they maintain" (Italie).

In her seventh novel Morrison explores two variants of home-as-paradise, one that is founded on the principles of sameness, exclusivity, and continuance, and another that is defined by heterogeneity, openness, and constant change. The home of the founders of Ruby epitomizes the ideas connected with the traditional paradise: It is available only to a small and select group of people who gained the right of entry by virtue of their purity and moral rectitude. Because it is based on the belief that it is exclusively for the chosen, it is ultimately repressive toward outsiders and oppressive toward internal dissidents. Condemned by its very structure to preserve its exclusive status, this version of paradise is increasingly aggressive toward the outside; yet in a world where new technologies and global trade destroy any chance of maintaining a society that is closed toward outside influences, it cannot last.

The Convent, then, embodies Morrison's re-imagined home as paradise that is fundamentally different from the traditional notion of paradise. It is an open, heterogeneous, multi-faceted space that can be created on earth and made available to everybody. It harbors a multicultural society that is liberating, empowering, and provides equal rights and opportunities for its inhabitants. In direct confrontation with the aggressively exclusive society of Ruby and vulnerable because of its very openness, the Convent paradise is an endangered social space. The idea I want to explore in this chapter is that the different approaches to racial identity that these communities have point to the very character of each of these social systems.

The fact of Morrison's adding religion to the already long list of topics her novel explores should not be mistaken for yet another add-on to a different list, namely that of the "et ceteras" accumulating in the discourse on identity. This discourse is marked by the effort to take into account as many concepts that influence identity formation as possible; hence the enumeration of, for example, "race, class, gender, sexuality," which often ends with a treacherous "etc." Rather, I want to suggest that even though Morrison singles out religion as the theme of her novel, race remains at the center of her attention. For, in *Paradise*, the concept of race and racial identity is intimately interwoven with that of religion and religious identity in the sense of ideology and belief systems. In my exploration of alternative notions of race in *Paradise*, I found a useful theoretical tool in the anthropological approach of religion as a cultural system developed by Clifford Geertz. In his essay "Religion as a Cultural System" Geertz defines religion as

> "1) a system of symbols which acts to 2) establish powerful, pervasive, and long-lasting moods and motivations in men by 3) formulating conceptions of a general order of existence and 4) clothing these conceptions with such an aura of factuality that 5) the moods and motivations seem uniquely realistic" (90).

However, while Geertz analyses the social uses to which existing religions are put in the societies that develop them, be they world religions or animist religions little-known in the Western world, my chief interest lies in the religious zeal with which essentialists pursue the construction of racial purity, and how closely related the structures of institutionalized blackness and institutionalized religion are.

In the small Oklahoma town of Ruby, the moral superiority of dark black over lighter skin colors is one of the "transcendent truths" inherent in any religion to which Geertz refers in the statement with which this subchapter opens. In the history of this fictitious all-Black settlement in the American Midwest, the belief in an essential blackness becomes the creed to which all members of the group must confess. Racial purity is a holy commandment, its preservation is the prerequisite for admission into home-as-paradise for any individual, and racial difference effects the exclusion of Others from this paradise. The concept of race in Ruby corresponds organically with the oppressive ideology of the traditional idea of paradise.

By juxtaposing Ruby and the Convent, the only neighbor of the town within a radius of ninety miles, Morrison also explores organized, institutionalized religion in relation to its unorganized, non-institutionalized counterpart.[10] However, she does not do it only for the purpose of investigating the differences between these two religious opposites, say from a theological perspective. I want to argue that Morrison uses religion *quasi* as a simile for race: Institutionalized religion functions similarly and has comparable consequences for adherents as well as heretics to essentialist notions of race and their effects on those considered pure or impure. Thus, the absence of racial codes in the Convent attests to the unwillingness, the unconscious or at least uncommented failure of the women living there to reproduce hierarchies into which people are forced by means of a color-code and to submit to a highly organized and restrictive variety of religion. This un-naming of race is both a linguistic experiment of the author's aimed at expelling racialized elements of language from American English as well as her thought experiment about a social space where a construction of racial essence does not occur. While the Convent, through its interaction with the neighboring town and the world at large, is certainly not a race-free space – after all, we know that the supposed lack of racial purity is one of the reasons for the nine Ruby men to attack the women – race is unmattered within the community of women, cleaned of its potential to create domination and submission. The absence of racism, the fact that the racial background of each person is of no consequence to the others in the group, is indicative of the general openness and the heterogeneity of the Convent community.

Freedom from essentialist notions allows for the evolution of a multifarious, non-institutionalized religion. Consolata's religious eclecticism, the wealth of spiritual influences that shape the religious practices she introduces into the Convent community, and the constantly evolving character of this community are features that contribute to the image of a new paradise. I propose that the idiosyncratic treatment of race by the Convent women is a central feature of this paradise as it highlights and exemplifies the emancipatory faculties of an open, heterogeneous society.

---

[10] See also Morrison in her interview with Elizabeth Farnsworth: "You have a very Protestant religion in Ruby, and you have something that verges on magic that is non-institutional religion in the convent [sic]."

4.2 The Price of Pure Blackness: The Racial House of Ruby as Exclusive Paradise

4.2.1 Fact and Fiction in *Paradise*

Strong links to historical details of cultural or everyday life, historical persons, or specific occurrences in the history of the United States are hallmarks of all of Morrison's fiction. We have observed this already in "Recitatif," where the plot incorporates factual events like protests in connection with the busing of children to integrate the school system and a Jimi Hendrix concert, and uses facts like the state of integration in Fire Brigades or employment policies of soft-ware firms in New Jersey at a particular time to hint at the possible racial and class backgrounds of the characters in a short story set in that time.

For her seventh novel, Morrison again chooses specific historical periods and landmark events as a time frame: the eras of Reconstruction and Post-Reconstruction, the decades of the settlement of the West, the Depression of the 1930s, World War II, the Civil Rights struggle, the Vietnam War, the Black Power and Women's Rights movements.[11] Not all of them carry equal structural importance, but jointly they serve two important purposes: They are historical referents for the ideologies and discourses that engage and shape the fictional societies invented by the author, and they allow Morrison to comment upon mainstream as well as African American historiography, to highlight aspects and details of official US history and historical discourses that have been neglected, misrepresented, or wiped from the records altogether. In *Paradise*, as in her other works of fiction, Morrison foregrounds the experiences of African Americans, relegating those of White Americans to the background. In this novel, the protagonists are Black men and women whose ancestors arrived in North America already before the Declaration of Independence and whose story until the mid-1970s is told.[12] Morrison here puts into practice her own maxims for literary theory and production in the United States formulated in her collection of lectures published under the title *Playing in the Dark*: to acknowledge the existence and to study the forma-

---

[11] See Tally's *(Hi)Stories* for a more detailed and comprehensive analysis of Morrison's engagement with US history in *Paradise*.

[12] Katrine Dalsgård examines the African American variant of American Exceptionalism in the light of the community of Ruby.

tive impact of the "black presence" on the whole of US-American history and culture.[13]

Without making it the main objective of this chapter, I will point out links and connections between fictional and historical events and discourses whenever such a reference seems useful for clarifying a particular view of a protagonist, or to highlight a specific political setting in which a plot development occurs. Historical events, eras, and significant public discourses alluded to in the novel include the history of all-Black towns in Oklahoma, racism during Redemption, Marcus Garvey and UNIA, Alex Haley's *Roots* and the discourse on the notion of home among African Americans, the Nation of Islam, the Black Panther Party, and the *Cato* Case of 1995. However, although these events will be treated as historical "facts," it will become clear in the course of this chapter that in *Paradise*, as in her previous two novels, Morrison always also explores history as something that is vulnerable to manipulation.[14]

Paradise tells the story of the fictive town of Ruby in Oklahoma. With the description of the history of an all-Black town in the Midwest of the United States, Morrison devotes herself to a chapter of US-American history from which African Americans have been almost completely excluded in the public perception, indeed, "a history of Reconstruction unknown to most Americans" (Christian, "The Past": 417).[15] The frontier myth was and often still is the myth of the White American. Regardless of the 1862 Homestead Law which promised free land to any settler, the predominately White population in most of the new western territories of

---

[13] Patricia Storace writes that "in *Paradise*, the story of America's white founding fathers is moved from foreground to background" (65/1). See also Tally's reading of *Paradise* as Morrison's re-interpretation of US history from an African American perspective (*(Hi)Stories*). Cf. also Dalsgård; Lehmann.

[14] This point is stressed particularly in Tally, *Reality*.

[15] Barbara Christian claims that "the subject of all-Black towns in the West is generally not presented as American history and thus is practically unknown even to many scholars of American history" ("The Past" 417). While her grim assessment is true in principle, it can be slightly softened by the following list of publications on the subject: A widely received contribution to the exploration of the history of Black settlement in the Midwest is Painter's study *Exodusters* of 1977. For Black settlers in Oklahoma see, for example, Teall, Tolson, and Franklin. Publications devoted more generally to African Americans in the West include an important study by Katz. Others are Suggs (ed.) and Taylor.

the United States insisted on barring Black settlers from making a home in the West and from participating in the new wealth as well as in the positive self-image the so-called "unassigned land" offered (cf. Johnson; Katz; de León).[16] However, against massive White resistance and for a long time largely ignored by mainstream historians of the frontier, African Americans came to the American Midwest with the Spanish conquerors as early as the sixteenth century, and proceeded to work and live there for example as servants, assistants to land surveyors, or as fur traders. After the end of Reconstruction in the South, large numbers of Black refugees from White discrimination and oppression migrated to Kansas and other more western states in what became known as the "Exodus of 1879." Thus, African Americans contributed to the settlement of the Midwest and West in the nineteenth century, be it as soldiers, as cattlemen, homesteaders or as farmers. Among the 50,000 men and women who rushed out in April 1889 to claim land in the first land-run in Oklahoma's Indian Territory, for example, were 2,973 Black settlers, a number that rose to 7,000 – 8,000 during the later land-runs and added to the number of Black families that had already been living there (Williams 267, 270). By 1910, about twenty-five Black towns had sprung up in Oklahoma (cf. Katz).[17] In the 1910 census the African American population of Oklahoma numbered no fewer than 137,600, making the Black community of this state one of the largest in the West (183).[18]

---

[16]Baskin names Kansas as an honorable exception to this rule. Quoting Painter, he calls Kansas "the Quintessential Free State." Baskin cites the "hospitality of whites living in Kansas" as one of the reason for the initial success of the Exodusters in this state. This view is contradicted by Katz, who writes of a "Western colorphobia" that was universal to the Western territories before and after the abolition of slavery (49).

[17]The number of Black towns in Oklahoma Territory and State differ in publications on this subject. Katz writes of twenty-five (249), Williams claims that there were twenty-seven (268), and Christian, citing K. M. Hamilton, *Black Towns*, gives the number of "Oklahoma towns of predominantly black populations" as "at least 30" ("The Past" 418).

[18]De León points out that compared with the large numbers of White Americans and Europeans who settled on the frontier during a short period of time, African American westward migration was slow and thin. He assumes that the explanation for this relative reluctance to migrate west lies in the fact that African

4.2.2 Constructing Pure Blackness – Ruby, Okl., population 360

In the novel's present, the mid-1970s, Ruby still exists in almost perfect seclusion from the rest of the world.[19] The town's history begins more than one hundred years earlier with a group of freedmen who, after being forced from the responsible positions in the administrations of Louisiana and Mississippi to which they had been elected during Reconstruction and relegated to exploitative share-cropping only a decade later, gather their families and march north-west in search of a place they can safely call home. After being denied entrance into the Black settlements they had set out to join, these Black pioneers found their own, which they name Haven, on former Native American land, far removed from any other town.[20] Haven lasts half a century before it succumbs to economic pressures and demographic change.[21]   After World War II, the grandsons of the Old Fathers pick up their households and travel further west, vowing to fill the vision of their forebears with new life. Inspired by the myths surrounding the beginnings of Haven, the self-styled New Fathers create a new town. They name it Ruby, after their sister who died in a hospital waiting room because no White doctor would treat her. In 1976, the narrative time of the

Americans had little hope to find better economic opportunity there than anywhere else in and beyond the Union (20).

[19]Christian cites *The Black Book* edited by Toni Morrison and published in 1974 as a source of "information on all-Black towns in Oklahoma" for the author ("The Past" 413). She furthermore points out that Morrison found dates and newspaper articles on Black treks west in C. Hamilton's 1991 study of Black towns in the West (417).

[20]Testimonies of Black pioneers of the American West show that many freed slaves who took the risk of going west did so because they were seeking refuge from White aggression and discrimination. The search for a "haven" is often mentioned as a motive for attempting the challenging and dangerous trek to the Western Territories (cf. Katz). Thus, the name of this all-Black town is symbolic for the hopes of many historical Black settlers.

[21]Morrison's fictional all-Black town thus parallels the fate of most of the Black settlements in the Midwest. In contrast to points of view that stress economic and demographic pressures as instrumental to the demise of Black towns in the West, Katz draws attention to the role of White racism. He points out that despite promising beginnings, "[t]he black enclaves of Oklahoma fell victim to the white supremacy they had fled. [...] [B]y 1915 Oklahoma became the first state to segregate its phone booths" (252, 264).

novel, Ruby is exclusive and prosperous, but serious cracks have started to appear in the structure of the once close-knit community.

Morrison develops the story of Ruby through the memories of a number of citizens and their personal interpretations of the events that shaped their town, in a "discourse [that] constantly oscillates between omniscient voices, straightforward third-person narration and indirect free style" (Lehmann 200). These individual narratives are the "official story" of the history of the town and its citizens in the version of the New Fathers of the community, the twin brothers Steward and Deacon Morgan, the women's perspectives on this story as they are expressed by the brothers' wives, as well as illegitimate versions of the town's history presented by the old midwife Lone DuPres and by Patricia Best, the school teacher and Ruby's unofficial historian.[22] While these memories are by no means homogenous, but selective and often contradictory, they move in concentric circles around and collectively form a non-linear narrative about one subject: the construction of racial identity as the foundation of their community.

The narration of the relegation of the once highly respected Old Fathers to menial field labor in the 1880s again firmly links *Paradise* with US-American history, commenting upon it from the perspective of the disenfranchised freedmen and -women. The decades immediately after Reconstruction were a time during which Black people in the South were exposed to structural racism and White vigilantism without enjoying the protection of influential Northerners. With the story of the Old Fathers, Morrison puts into words the anguish and acute disillusionment which she imagines the men felt when their posts were taken from them and given to White Southerners, their incomes diminished, their freedom curtailed, their dignity accosted and their pride deeply shaken. The disempowerment of the Old Fathers set a precedent in the collective memory of their entire generation. It suggested to them that, regardless of the fact that slavery had long been abolished, dark-skinned Americans still – or once again – had to interpret whatever happened to them in the light of the racist color code developed and institutionalized by White Americans during slavery times, more or less secretly preserved during a Reconstruction that was forced upon resisting Southern slave-owners, and collectively reinstalled during a period that in the South was also known as

---

[22] See Lehmann on the interesting topic of narrative techniques applied in *Paradise* and the different narrators in the novel.

"Redemption."[23] "They must have suspected yet dared not say that their misfortune's misfortune was due to the one and only feature that distinguished them from their Negro peers. Eight-rock," Patricia Best assumes in her reflections on the fate of the patriarchs, the original founders of her community (*Paradise* 193).[24] She uses the term "eight-rock" to describe "blue-black people, tall and graceful," who have "clear, wide eyes" (*Paradise* 193). Patricia borrows the term from mining where, so she informs us, it refers to "a deep deep level in the coal mines" (*Paradise* 193).[25] Thus, the Old Fathers learned from these experiences that not only did it make a difference for a person's prospects whether she or he had been a slave or not; apparently it also mattered to those in the position to distribute or withhold power and therefore was of consequence to potential recipients of power whether the former slave had light or dark skin.

This suspicion solidified into conviction, and combined with an acute awareness of increasing violence against and oppression of Black men and women by White Southerners during "Redemption" it urged the Old Fathers to leave their homes. They followed newspaper advertisements encouraging Black people to seize their chance and join others like them in building independent all-Black towns in the still thinly settled regions of the American West.[26] But the incident that would shape their and their descendants' entire outlook on life and was to enter the annals of Haven and

[23] See Storace for a powerful picture of the circumstances under which African Americans had to live during the last three decades of the nineteenth century (64).

[24] Note Patricia's choice of words. It betrays a lack of certainty and is an example for Ruby's unofficial historian's attitude toward historiography. She assumes that the Old Fathers thought their black skin color to be the cause of the rejection they experiences from other Americans and forms from there her conclusions as to the racial ideology of these men. Lucille Fultz rightly points out that "Patricia's history of Ruby must be read with cautious skepticism" (88), but her musings about the Old Fathers are corroborated by the stories of other characters in the novel, notably those of the Morgan twins, the other two unofficial chroniclers in Ruby.

[25] Storace sees a symbolic connection between the term "8-rock" and the landing of the (White) Pilgrim Fathers on Plymouth Rock (65/2).

[26] Morrison might have taken her inspiration for Haven and Ruby from Oklahoma towns like Langston City, one of the first and most successful all-Black towns in the state. It was founded in 1890 by Edwin and Sarah McCabe and had an original population of 600. Today, Langston has about 1.700 residents, 93.3% of

Ruby as the "Disallowing" intensified the racial trauma they had received at the hands of White people. At the gates of the town of Fairly they were turned away by people who had been slaves like them.[27] It did not matter to the shocked migrants that the townspeople cited the newcomers' obvious poverty as sole reason for their rejection. "Come Prepared or Not At All," the advertisement in the *Herald* had warned them (*Paradise* 13),[28] but as intelligent and strong men, as proud, experienced administrators, the Old Fathers felt superbly equipped for whatever their task might turn out to be. They disregarded the fact that the new settlements, focused as they were on the ideal of self-reliance and the desire for acceptance into wider American society, needed and demanded the economic resources of potential newcomers in order to survive in this unindustrialized region, in the face of racism and intense competition from budding White towns in the Midwest and West of the United States in the late nineteenth century. "If we can't get the best class of our people, we don't want any," the Langston City Fathers are reported to have said (Hamilton qtd. in Christian, "The Past": 418). During an internet chat Morrison explained the origins of such Black towns and explicitly stressed sufficient economic means as a precondition for admittance into these towns:

> The towns were made up of ex-slaves completely. What they were asking in that phrase ["Come Prepared or Not At All"] was that the other ex-slaves who came to homestead there, came with enough money and supplies for a couple of years. [...] So it wasn't a question of their slave status, it was a question of their money. (Timehost)

whom are African Americans. For more information, see Katz and, for example, "Langston, Oklahoma."

[27] Note the "talking name" of this settlement: "Fairly" highlights the one feature of the inhabitants of this town that is of importance to both the Old and the New Fathers, the light or "fair" color of their skin.

[28] An advertisement with these words ran in the *Langston Herald* and is cited in Katz (260). One of the earliest Black newspapers in Oklahoma, the *Herald* was a journal that had its largest readership outside the Territory. Described as "propagandistic, inspirational, gossipy and opinionated" (258), the paper encouraged Black mass migration and promoted the organization of all-Black towns by means of which African Americans would be able to command full political sovereignty, or so it was hoped. Cf. Williams for detailed information on the history of the Black press in Oklahoma.

Morrison's imagination was fired when she found a historical report about "200 ex-slaves" who "didn't have enough money, they didn't have enough resources, and were turned away. [. . .] And that was what compelled me to wonder about what might happen to ex-slaves being turned away by other ex-slaves" (Timehost).[29]

However, before the background of the massive disenfranchisement and intimidation of Black Americans in the South after Reconstruction and with their own painful memory of their loss of office the Old Fathers convinced themselves that the real reason to keep their group out of Fairly was the dark skin color of the nine original families in the trek. They felt forced to concede that the difference between "light-skinned against black" was of "serious consequence" not only for Whites but also for Blacks, "serious enough that their daughters would be shunned as brides; their sons chosen last," as Patricia concludes in her historical notes (*Paradise* 194). The Black pioneers reduced the project of the citizens of Fairly to "uplift the race" exclusively to the desire to "lighten the race" – a moment that arguably might have played a role in historical incidents of "disallowing." The narrow focus on racial identity conveyed to them during a lifetime fraught with experiences of race-based discrimination effects their reading of events in which they become involved. The category of race thus blocks out other relevant parameters of social interaction, in this case that of class. This capacity of race to corrupt the perception and dominate the reasoning of women and men is of tremendous interest to Morrison. In "Recitatif," the information of racial differences between the protagonists dulls their own and the readers' sensibility to the significance of psychological issues with which Twyla and Roberta are struggling. In *Paradise*, the difference in skin color overrides class difference in the minds of the Old Fathers, a misreading they pass on to the following generations.

The story of the "Disallowing" becomes the "controlling story" which lays the ground and provides the cornerstones for this all-Black community (*Paradise* 13). Passed on orally from grandfather to grandsons, it

---

[29]This historical case is described in Hamilton's study. See Christian who points out this connection ("The Past" 418). Christian also mentions Hamilton's description of "the ways in which McCabe and his colleagues discouraged poor blacks from coming to the Oklahoma territory even to the point of attempting to deter three hundred destitute blacks on route to the Cheyenne and Arapaho areas" (418).

describes the parameters of the quasi-religious convictions, the articles of
faith, so to speak, of a group of people who regard this narrative as one of
their holy texts. Every year during Advent, the Disallowing is re-enacted
by the children of Ruby as a Christmas pageant rich with biblical allusions: Seven Black holy families ask for admission into a Black town and
are turned away by yellow-faced, money-counting inn-keepers. The "disallowed" families carry on with their search for their home land, a search
on which they are mysteriously guided by a God-like "walking man" who
eventually indicates to them the spot where they are to build their own
town.

The misreading on the part of the "founding fathers" of Haven and
their heirs in Ruby of economic stipulations as racist prejudice resulting
in discrimination can be interpreted as the prime example of preconception that "can determine experience itself" (Storace 64/3). Originally, this
misreading is motivated by the historic experience of racial hierarchies
with which the former slaves grew up. When the Old Fathers and their
families worked as field hands, they had fortified themselves against the
psychological repercussions of their low social position by developing intense pride in their blackness. In their own eyes and minds they enhanced
their status by stressing what they regarded as their racial purity, a concept that was familiar to them as the core of the segregationist ideology on
which the Old South rested and which had engrained itself into their own
minds. In order to retain and bolster their self-respect that was constantly
attacked by hegemonic whiteness in the South, the Old Fathers redefined
racial purity as pure blackness. Through this definition they distanced
themselves as far as possible from whiteness, which they considered inauthentic. This attitude helped them not only to keep themselves separate
from White Americans, their most immediate oppressors, but also from
lighter-skinned slaves. These were often the offspring of house-slaves
and their White masters, and although they were more directly exposed
to sexual and other kinds of harassment, they were said to enjoy certain
privileges because of the comparative lightness of their skin.

Consequently, when light-skinned men and women refused the dark-
skinned travelers entry into their town because of economic pressures, the
latter interpreted this act as motivated by racism because their experiences
during slavery and "Redemption" had fostered in them a preconception
that led them to expect racism – and not discrimination on grounds of
class differences – from anybody with lighter skin, be they former slaves

or not. In the perception of the Old Fathers and their successors race blocks out class.

Yet, perhaps paradoxically, even the trained expectation of racist discrimination does not prepare the original migrants to the American Midwest for the shock they are to suffer when their intense pride in pure blackness is hurt. Geertz suggests that religion comes into play expressly in situations where "chaos – a tumult of events which lack not just interpretations but *interpretability* – threatens to break in upon man: at the limits of his analytic capacities, at the limits of his powers of endurance, and at the limits of his moral insight" (100). "[A]ny religion [...] which hopes to persist must attempt somehow to cope [with] [b]afflement, suffering, and a sense of intractable ethical paradox," he argues further (100). The Old Fathers experience such chaos when their carefully nursed racial pride is attacked in Fairly. With their rejection at the gates of this Black town "[t]he sign of racial purity they had taken for granted had become a stain" (*Paradise* 194). What to them was of high value and in turn made them valuable in their own eyes incredibly turns out to be worthless in the eyes of those they used to disrespect for their lack of racial purity and authenticity. In the course of their direct and indirect experiences of discrimination this founding generation of Black settlers therefore comes to define American society as a society whose history of race discrimination meant that people's well-being was solely and entirely dependent on the degree of lightness of their skin, a society that denies them acceptance and support explicitly because of their dark skin color.

Patricia Best tells us about the leading men of Haven that "[t]heir horror of whites was convulsive but abstract. They saved the clarity of their hatred for the men who had insulted them in ways too confounding for language: first by excluding them, then by offering them staples to exist in that very exclusion" (*Paradise* 189). A bewildering experience like the "Disallowing" defies language. Thus, when the grandchildren of the Founding Fathers are subjected to their own "Disallowing, Part Two" after their return to discrimination and abuse when they came home at the end of World War II (*Paradise* 194), when the experience of their forefathers is matched by their own, they resort to drastic actions. In the late 1940s, the Morgan brothers and a few of their closest friends attempt a new start further west of Haven. They found their new town on the "values inherited at the Disallowing" (Clewell 133), values that are extremely community-oriented; after all, safety, also from racial discrimination, lies in numbers.

The painful experience of being turned away at the gates of Black towns is the "founding trauma" for the communities of both Haven and Ruby, the "historical event, [...], that comes to constitute a group's collective identity and becomes the basis for group members' individual identity" (LaCapra 724). In the minds of the people of Ruby it is supplemented by the knowledge of the Old Fathers' dismissal from their offices after Reconstruction and by the shameful reception the New Fathers suffered at the hands of "gangs of rednecks and Sons of the Confederacy" on their return from the battlefields of World War Two (*Paradise* 194). For the Rubyites the traumatic events of their past are intimately linked through the all-pervasive hegemony of whiteness over blackness: They were caused by White and light-skinned African Americans with the intention to discriminate and oppress people whose skin-color is a dark black.

In order to cope with the chaos the multiple disallowings had caused in their world-view, and in an effort to restore and preserve their feeling of self-worth after the demise of Haven, their first Black home-town, the New Fathers initiate a veritable cult of blackness in their new town, Ruby. They use the color-code system of US society they have internalized but they turn around the scale: "Pure" blackness becomes the "limit position within a continuum of color difference" (Nicol 225). As Nicol argues, "[t]he complexities of color difference rather than straightforward 'racial' differences cannot be contained in normative racial discourse, yet it is this complexity rather than a white-centering black/white difference, which drives racial identification in Ruby" (225). In this "continuum of color difference," the difference between the polar opposites of black and white pales in significance compared with shades of blackness that differ in their closeness to "purity." As a measure to ensure survival and prosperity in spite of what they have learned to consider as a serious handicap, the leaders of this community of dark-skinned men and women create a secluded micro-society whose basis is formed by that very handicap. Pure blackness here counts as the only valid entry ticket, as the only reliable sign of belonging.[30] In Ruby, community and culture come to rest on a

---

[30]Nicol points out that by writing from within Black history and within a Black-identified community Morrison reverses the normative terms of racial ascription. She creates a literary text where to be 'White is to be the racialized Other (cf. 222). This is also true for light-skinned African Americans.

quasi-religious system that elevates racial purity to the level of religious dogma.

But how is this system organized? What are the 'articles of faith' for its members? Who defines these articles? What are the rule set up to keep the system running, and how are these rules implemented? With the cornerstones of Geertz's anthropological analysis of religion as a cultural system in mind, I now investigate creed, ritual and symbol of the "religion" of racial purity in the shape of pure blackness.

4.2.2.1   Creed and Commandment

In the spiritual system of the people of Ruby the Old Fathers occupy a central position. They are the ancestors of this community not only in the genetic but also in the spiritual sense of the word; in other words, they are the founders of the religion. A firm belief in the sanctity of the blood lines of the Old Fathers has its roots in the strong religious connotations race has in this town. The families in the original group of migrants formed a community of outcasts, a "tight band of wayfarers" (*Paradise* 189), because of their unusually black skin and their 8-rock identity. For the Old Fathers such a degree of blackness testifies to purity of a high quality, and they convey this conviction to their descendants who, like them, have to defend their human dignity in a racist, White-centered society. Old and New Fathers derive this dignity from their belief in a racial essence: In their eyes, 8-rock blackness is essential blackness, the true and uncontaminated state of the Black race, comparable to seams of coal that have been buried deep within the earth for millions of years and under extreme pressure have become pure and hard. They see racial purity as treated with envious hostility by the impure, hostility that stems from an unacknowledged feeling of inferiority with which they are beset. Oppression and persecution, however, produce saint-like martyrs who occupy a moral high-ground because of their innocent suffering.[31]   According to this ratio, Zechariah Morgan is the 'holiest' among the Old Fathers, not least because he sacrificed his health for his dignity as a Black man. The conception of the quasi-holiness of the 8-rock blood of the Old Fathers motivates and facilitates their descendants' definition of themselves as a

---

[31] See also Storace who argues that "[t]he incident of persecution becomes a mark of superiority, evidence of the founders' immense significance" (66/1).

community on the grounds of race. The citizens of Ruby "religiously" believe that race is biological essence that determines moral characteristics and that their forefathers bequeathed to them an inestimably precious heirloom: their racial and therefore moral purity.

Seen in this light, the name the citizens chose for their town bears strong symbolic significance. A ruby is a precious stone of deep red color, similar to the color of blood. The founding families of Ruby treasure their 8-rock blood like a ruby would be treasured by its owner. As the value of such a precious stone would be measured by its purity, the Rubyites measure the value of their community – and that of every individual or group – by the purity of their blood. As a ruby would loose value if lesser minerals were to run through it and contaminate it, any mingling of 8-rock blood with blood that had been "racially tempered with" was believed to cause irreparable contamination of the once pure blood.[32] It would result in a loss of racial and moral value of the individual and of the community.

In the hearts and in the mental cosmos of most of the citizens of Ruby, the Old Fathers occupy a position similar to that of the Israelites of the Old Testament. Freed from the deprived state of slavery, they embarked on a long migration to find the 'Promised Land' they needed in order to live in freedom and prosperity. It becomes holy land through the guidance of the divine walking man. For the Rubyites, the founding of Haven was a homecoming of their people after slavery and a period of wandering in a wilderness characterized by frequent instances of uprooting and by a constant struggle for acknowledgment of their human and civil rights. Like Moses and the Israelites, the Old Fathers are assumed to have had a covenant with God: In order to receive and retain land, freedom, and prosperity they had to protect the God-intended purity of their blood, their racial essence. They had to increase their numbers and to preserve their unity.

What Steward Morgan calls "the fathers' law, the law of continuance and multiplication" (*Paradise* 279), demands that the sanctity of the blood lines of the (male) founders of this race-based community be maintained

---

[32]This ideology corresponds closely with Hacking's theory of "pollutions rules" as foundational element of the concept of race (cf. Hacking, "Why Race").

throughout the generations.[33] It is a sacred commandment for all those who want to consider themselves part of this community. The citizens of Haven failed in this project. Many married outside the community of the pure, diluting the holy blood of their fathers and allowing themselves to be "disvalued by the impure" (*Paradise* 194). More and more of them left their promised land in search of prosperity. Like their grandfathers before the gates of Fairly, the Morgan brothers refuse to acknowledge economic pressure as the reason for the dispersal of the community of Haven. They believe that the betrayal of the principle, the commandment of racial purity, led to the downfall of this first safe haven for 8-rocks. As if they acknowledged as the truth Gobineau's teachings on the weakening effect of miscegenation, the New Fathers of Ruby convince themselves that the Havenites let the pure blood of their fathers be watered down and thus allowed their community to slip into degeneration. Steward and Deacon Morgan feel that if the unity of their community is to be preserved, they have to renew the covenant with God: Black racial purity has to be protected, and the pure must remain in the town.

Threatened by a renewed dispersal of its members and shaped by the struggle to escape White domination, Ruby is "a community where shadows are not black but white" (Storace 65/1). The realness of "white shadows," the threat of racist violence against African Americans, remains acute during the Civil Rights era, and again Morrison weaves her fiction around factual events in US history. The perpetual sense of persecution felt by the people of Ruby is exemplified through Soane Morgan. She was happy to see her two sons enlist with the Army to fight in the Vietnam War from which neither of them returned, because "[s]he had thought war was safer than any city in the United States" (*Paradise* 101). The New Fathers consciously or unconsciously utilize the external threat in order to inspire unity among the citizens of the town, a strategy that surfaces in repeated warnings about the dangers lurking "out there," beyond the boundaries of the town. "Out There" is presented as an inchoate wilderness devoid of human order, a hell of violence and discrimination that is

---

[33] In "the fathers' law" an intimate connection between racial purity and issues of gender and the control of women becomes apparent. This will be explicated later in this chapter.

firmly in the hands of White fiends.[34] Using words that bespeak a mixture of fascination and abhorrence, one of the townsmen describes it as

> a void where random and organized evil erupted when and where it chose – behind any standing tree, behind the door of any house, humble or grand. Out There where your children were sport, your women quarry, and where your very person could be annulled; where congregations carried arms to church and ropes coiled in every saddle. Out There where every cluster of whitemen looked like a posse, being alone was being dead. (*Paradise* 16)

To counter the threat of the scattering of their members, the town's leaders especially emphasize the necessity of preserving the original cohesion within the community. As the enemy is defined by whiteness, and whiteness is understood to mean lack of purity and authenticity, pure blackness must be the defining marker of unity among the group of self-described victims of racism. The chasing away at gunpoint of a car full of rowdy White boys hints at the problematic nature of this dichotomy of White aggression versus Black victimhood in the complex context of Ruby. In this incident, in which the action is informed by a deep mistrust if not hatred of White Americans, the roles of (White) aggressors and (Black) victims of violence are not clearly attributable. This episode foreshadows an event later in the history of the town when these roles will be *de facto* reversed. The same men who warn against the horrors of a white-dominated "Out There" will become what one reviewer of *Paradise* has called "a lynching party entirely made up of black men" (68/4).

The strongmen of Ruby are convinced that their town will prosper only if the shadows are held at bay, if the rules they deduct from their historical experiences as 8-rocks in the United States are observed. They interpret the fact that nobody has died in Ruby since the founding of the town as proof for God's willingness to keep his part of their deal. Fully in

---

[34]The idea of a hostile "Out There" has two interesting parallels, one in US-American history and another in the oeuvre of Toni Morrison. When the Puritans founded their "Cit[ies] upon a Hill" they did so with the conviction that these beacons of moral rectitude had to be guarded and defended against a wilderness of corruption, heresy, and heathenism threatening both from their European countries of origin and on American soil. In *Beloved*, Baby Suggs takes up this notion in her sermon in the clearing, where she refers to enemies outside the sheltering Black community who threaten the wellbeing of Black women and men (*Beloved* 88). The story of Ruby thus points to the Puritan inheritance of the African American community. See also Wilt.

tune with this understanding, the players in the annual Christmas pageant threaten the impure White and yellow-skinned inn-keepers of Fairly with God's wrath: "God will crumble you," they shout under the appreciative murmurs of the audience (*Paradise* 211). In the eyes of the leading families of the town the racially pure Ruby is also morally pure, which makes their home "the one all-Black town worth the pain" (*Paradise* 5), a Black "City upon a Hill," and its inhabitants "God's Chosen People," the "People of the Covenant."[35] Their Covenant stems from "the deal" of the Old Fathers of first-generation Black settlers – to earn God's protection by strengthening the group and multiplying its numbers – and it was renewed in the "new bargain" of the third generation. In the research for her project on the genealogy of Ruby Patricia realizes the nature of this new bargain negotiated by the Morgan twins: "Unadulterated and unadulteried 8-rock blood held its magic as long as it resided in Ruby. That was their recipe. That was their deal. For immortality" (*Paradise* 217).

What Patricia discovers is nothing less than the price for racial "purity": The scandalous outcome of her research, "the problem with blood rules," as she calls it (*Paradise* 196), is the revelation of an entangled web of incestuous relations between and within the original founding families. In her home town a self-identification as purely black can only be accomplished and preserved at the expense of a healthy proliferation of the founding dynasties. Ironically, the New Fathers can only keep their forefathers' deal by violating the vital part of it that demanded the proliferation of their sacrosanct bloodlines. Consequently, the three most prominent families are threatened with the possibility of extinction: Steward and Dovey Morgan's marriage remains childless; Soan induces a miscarriage and later she and Deacon lose their sons in Vietnam. The sole remaining Morgan heir is their sister Ruby's son, K.D. Smith, a young man of questionable morals who is universally disliked. The first child he fathers dies shortly after his premature birth, because his young mother Arnette tries to abort the unwanted baby. All four children of Arnette's brother Jeff Fleetwood are severely disabled; the incessant care they require brings their mother Sweetie close to a breakdown.[36] Billie Delia's realization

---

[35]For an analysis of parallels between early American Puritanism and the self-perception of the Old and New Fathers in Haven and Ruby respectively see Wilt.

[36]O'Reilly points out that "[f]or each of the town women, motherhood is associated with loss and harm, pain and suffering" (140). She argues that this proves

that there is "[n]o baby's breath anywhere" in Ruby for Arnette's bridal bouquet at her wedding with K.D. is more than a commentary on the horticultural preferences in her hometown (*Paradise* 149). It is a critique of social conventions in Ruby that have adverse effects on children and on the proliferation of bloodlines.

Far from acknowledging a state of affairs that is profoundly at odds with the strict moral principles they propagate and demand their fellow citizens to follow, the New Fathers fanatically cling to their conviction that pure blackness must be protected at all costs. They attempt this through a system of control over who is allowed to marry whom, always with the aim of keeping alive the 8-rock genealogy. The men who implement the blood rule are direct descendants of the original Black migrants to Oklahoma. Among them, Steward and Deacon Morgan, grandsons of "Big Papa" Zechariah and sons of "Big Daddy" Rector Morgan, consider themselves most closely in touch with the spirit of the Old Fathers.[37] "He and Steward were truer heirs [of Zechariah and Rector]," Deacon insists when thinking of the Morgan sons and daughters who had not been asked to make a new start further west of Haven, "proof of which was Ruby itself. Who, other than the rightful heirs, would have repeated exactly what Zechariah and Rector had done?" (*Paradise* 113). As the "rightful heirs" of saint-like men, however, the Morgan twins inhabit a social position similar to that of High Priests of the Old Testament. Not only are they the wealthiest and most powerful men in Ruby, they also rival the three Protestant ministers of their town in their desire and actual licence to tell their fellow citizens what to think and what to do. Steward and Deacon feel that "everything requires their protection" (*Paradise* 12). As the earthly representatives of the founder of their race-based religion – a twinned pope, so to speak – the two brothers represent the central ideas and convictions of these patriarchs: Race is essence, and pure blackness

"Haven's and later Ruby's inability to sustain a community" (140). Both towns are "modelled ... on patriarchal values of power, status, ownership, and control," which leads to the "marginalization of women and the feminine" and the subsequent "erasure of funk" (140).

[37] The absurdity of the blood rule and the extreme binding power it nevertheless has is demonstrated most vividly when Deacon asks Roger Best to make sure that the body bags that holds the remains of his sons who died in Vietnam only contained "black parts" and to "get rid of the white pieces" before the burial (*Paradise* 112).

is the prerequisite of a race-based home that needs to be preserved and safe-guarded.

The community structure of Ruby strongly resembles that of an institutionalized religion designed for the worship of pure blackness. As virtual priests, the New Fathers provide the members of their community – their congregation – with a creed, namely the sacredness and moral supremacy of pure blackness, and with a set of commandments for moral behavior, the blood rule. They also give the Rubyites a ritual and a shrine for their worship, both part of the second measure employed to protect pure blackness. This measure aims at a repression of otherness within the boundaries of Ruby. It has lasting influence on the town's historiography as well as the set-up of and social interaction within the community.

4.2.2.2   Ritual: Religious Myth Re-lived in the Christmas Pageant

> It is in ritual ... that this conviction that religious conceptions are veridical and that religious directives are sound is somehow generated.
>
> Clifford Geertz

According to Clifford Geertz's analysis, "[i]n ritual, the world as lived and the world as imagined, fused under the agency of a single set of symbolic forms, turn out to be the same world" (112). In Ruby, the ritual that is most important for efforts of community building and the construction of a communal identity is the annual Christmas pageant. When the New Fathers initiate this performance consisting of narrative and epistemological elements from the story of the nativity of Christ and their forefathers' story of the Disallowing they create a bridge between the Old Fathers' lived world and their own – the grandchildren's – imagined world. The lived world of Zechariah Morgan and his peers was dominated by their experience of being turned away at the gates of Fairly, first and foremost because they were too poor to contribute to the "racial uplift" the founders of that town intended.[38] Conditioned as they were to see reality

---

[38] Booker T. Washington's concept of "racial uplift" aimed at an improvement of the economic situation of Black Americans by way of acquiring vocational skills at the expense of social and political equality and civil rights. A racial accommodationist and favorite with the White political elite, Washington argued in favor of racial segregation in the social spheres, as long as African Americans

through the color-lens, the 8-rock patriarchs and forefathers of the people of Ruby overlooked, ignored the economic reasons for a disallowing that in their imagined world only made sense as a racist act. This race-based interpretation of the Disallowing they passed on to the generations after them. In the symbolic re-enactment of the founding drama of their community, with seven exhausted, very Black families seeking shelter and greedy whitish innkeepers denying them entry into their town,[39] the New Fathers fuse the two contradicting worlds into one that establishes and confirms their own worldview year after year. Geertz explains:

> As a religious problem, the problem of suffering is, paradoxically, not how to avoid suffering but how to suffer, how to make of physical pain, personal loss, worldly defeat, or the helpless contemplation of others' agony something bearable, supportable – something, as we say, sufferable. (104)

Through the celebration of the Christmas pageant, the pain and suffering of the forefathers is read as a meaningful, even necessary event. The Disallowing acquires much of its relevance through its religious connotations, and the Christmas pageant explicitly stresses these connotations. "The conflation of stories dramatized by the children's play makes Ruby's history a sacred text of community martyrdom, and as a sacred text the story is God-given truth," as Lisa Krumholz holds (29/2). As the ritual keeps alive an undiminished sense of persecution and martyrdom in the individual and collective imagination, it helps to preserve a sense of unity among the people of Ruby, who feel "bound by the enormity of what had happened to them" (*Paradise* 189).

The members of the third generation of Black settlers in the Midwest identify with their grandparents' experiences to such an extent that they take them to be their own. As racial unrest unsettles the country in the Civil Rights era, the sense of persecution on account of their blackness is ripe among the generation of the New Fathers. And so is their fear of a scattering of their group, not least because of the growing influence that the ideas of the Black Power and the budding women's movement

---

in the South were admitted into crafts and trades and thus were given the chance to make themselves indispensable to White Americans. Cf. Washington, as well as "People & Events."

[39] As if they could not completely deny the economic necessity at the root of the Disallowing, the New Fathers portray the inn-keepers as greedy and fixated on money.

exert on their children. In order to reign in the mildly rebellious fourth generation and to motivate all citizens to strengthen the unity among the townspeople, a threat to unity is being kept palpable through the annual reenactment of the first Disallowing.

With the tradition of the Christmas pageant Morrison documents the processes at work when history is turned into myth, or, in the words of Barbara Christian, how the "mythic stories" emerge "as the basis of people's interpretations of [historical] facts" ("The Past" 417). In Ruby, the Morgan brothers are mainly responsible and firmly in charge of this process; they control the message of an event that is prepared and attended by the entire community. While they are not old enough to have experienced the Disallowing themselves, they profess to "have powerful memories": "[b]etween them they remember the details of everything that ever happened – things they witnessed and things they have not" (*Paradise* 13). What is referred to as "rememory" in *Beloved* – the necessary if painful task of the descendants of slaves to "remember" the traumas of their forebears – is celebrated in Ruby with religious fervor, thereby turning the Disallowing into something like a temple (Storace cf.). Under the leadership of the Morgans, "the nine families who found this all-Black town construct themselves as the descendants of prophets and their founding of their *Paradise* as a command from God, as a veritable divine mission [...]" (Christian, "The Past": 420). This is accomplished with the help of "memories" that render history myth because they are authorized and circulated by the men in power.

The exceptionalist attitude adopted by the New Fathers with regard to their own position within their community and to Ruby's relationship with the outside world thus stems in large parts from the religious connotations of the self-image of these men. As Patricia Storace suggests, "[t]he Disallowing relates the founding families directly to divine justice, giving them a part in deity, and simultaneously enshrining a perpetual appetite for revenge, while becoming a source for further 'disallowings'" (66/1). The closeness the New Fathers feel to the patriarchs of their community and which has been accepted by the vast majority of the townspeople for the longest time becomes the platform for the launching of their exclusivist politics toward outsiders within their town as well as strangers outside of it. In the historiography created and promulgated by the leading men of Ruby, racial purity in the shape of blackness becomes the decisive marker of virtue and righteousness.

Moreover, pure blackness is used by the rich and influential Morgan brothers as a tool in service of the preservation of the status quo that sees them firmly at the top of the social hierarchy of their town. During her research into the family histories of Ruby, Patricia Best discovers that over the years the number of "holy families" participating in the Christmas pageant has decreased from nine, the number of families that left the South and founded Haven, to seven, representing the dynasties in Ruby in the 1970s that are considered pure 8-rock. Because of that, she assumes that "[t]he bargain must have been broken or changed [...] [b]y [t]he Morgans, probably. They ran everything, controlled everything" (*Paradise* 217). Thus, history is censored, be it national, regional or local, made dogma beyond questioning or interpretation. In its mythical, quasi-religious expression it is utilized by the powerful, "the disallowed [who] become the elite disallowers" (66/1), to reduce the number of their potential rivals to economic and political power. How instrumental the ideology of pure blackness is to these new instances of disallowing will be discussed after an analysis of the "shrine" the town fathers set up for the worship of racial purity.

4.2.2.3   Religious Symbols: The Oven as Shrine

The debate over the weathered inscription on the Oven, a communal facility built by the Old Fathers in Haven and carefully reassembled in the center of Ruby by the New Fathers, illustrates an increasing solidification of history into myth and dogma in the new settlement. It also testifies to the degree to which "[t]he present-day Ruby of the novel is a town enmeshed in generational and political conflict" (66/4). This conflict, I argue, is markedly inflected by the religious views and indeed the dogmas of the two opposing parties.

Geertz writes that "sacred symbols function to synthesize a people's ethos [...] and their world view [...], their most comprehensive idea of order" (89). In Ruby, the Oven functions as such a sacred symbol for the older generation of the town: a material fact intended to unify the citizens' ideas of the way their reality is set up ideologically and politically within their physical surroundings. In his anthropological analysis of religion Geertz continues that "the world view is rendered emotionally convincing by being represented as an image of an actual state of affairs peculiarly well arranged to accommodate such a way of life" (89f.). Originally, the

Oven had been designed and was used as a communal cooking and eating place for a group of people who, after fleeing discrimination and repression, arrived impoverished at the location of their future settlement. Its first users not only prepared their food there and ate it together, they also congregated around the Oven to hold town meetings, to discuss matters that required the community's joint action, and to celebrate baptisms, weddings and other kinds of festivals.

In Ruby, however, the Oven has lost its original meaning. In their new "haven," the leading men rebuilt it as a mere icon of the past, or, to be more precise, as an icon of their version of the past, their imagined world. As a consequence, "[a] utility became a shrine," as one of the disapproving townswomen remarks (*Paradise* 103). Here, where cooking stoves are in every kitchen and the men meet in each others' houses to negotiate business interests and otherwise keep to themselves, the Oven at best serves as a memorial to the days of close interdependence among the citizens, of their sense of togetherness in their mutual struggle to succeed against the odds in a hostile natural and social environment. At worst, it is abused by the strongmen of the town to institutionalize their view of history and thereby cement their grip on power in the community.

The parts of the inscription on the Oven that have been spared from the effects of weather – "the Furrow of His Brow" (*Paradise* 86) – present a message which, by virtue of its vagueness, allows for a number of different interpretations. Members of the fathers' generation insist that the original, now missing first word was "Beware." Their claim rests on the testimony of a blind woman who claims to have felt the words with her fingers when she was a five-year-old child in Haven. The young people around the new Baptist minister Richard Misner call into doubt the memories of a five-year-old and instead suggest a different beginning: "Be the Furrow ..." (*Paradise* 87 et al.). Thus they turn a warning into what they regard as an encouraging demand. Outrageously, they dare to spray this new motto on the side of the Oven which has become their hang-out, a meeting place "for other kinds of freedom celebrations going on in its shadows," as Dovey Morgan complains (*Paradise* 88).

The New Fathers are enraged by their children's public proclamations and secret actions for two reasons, one of which is more religious in nature, the other one more political; both carry equal weight. The sinister threat to "Beware the Furrow of His Brow" reflects the elders' belief in an authoritarian God whose command is to be obeyed, the belief in a vengeful, angry God who will destroy the enemies of his chosen people. The citizens of Ruby collectively reaffirm this religious truth once every year during the children's performance in the Christmas pageant. Theirs is a worldview that demands submission, holding still under patriarchal authority.

Misner's young people, on the other hand, are no longer willing to be passive and submissive. They believe their God to be an empowering God and strive to be "His instrument, His justice, [...] His voice, His retribution" (*Paradise* 87). Inspired by what their minister teaches them about the struggle of African Americans against racism and White hegemony, they want to be part of this struggle, fortified with God's power. Thus, while the third-generation Black settlers favor seclusion, practice voluntary segregation – of the leading men of Ruby it is said that "Booker T. solutions trumped Du Bois problems every time" (*Paradise* 212)[40] – and despise the Civil Rights and Black Power movements, their children wish to step out of isolation and shape their community and their country as free agents. With their final version of the motto of the Oven, "We Are the Furrow ..." (*Paradise* 298), they express their new sense of pride in being part of a larger community of African Americans and Black people worldwide.

On a political level, change itself becomes the subject of conflict in Ruby. In the eyes of the New Fathers, the very fact that the wording of the inscription has been changed is sacrilege. Steward is convinced that his grandfather Zechariah, who forged the words for the Oven, did so after divine inspiration; he shaped the words that God had dictated him. Therefore, as a self-proclaimed interpreter and guard of divine order

[40]Misner refers to Booker T. Washington's Atlanta Compromise. Washington argued that the plight of African Americans, particularly in the US-American South, could be remedied through high-quality vocational training, such as was offered at the Tuskegee Normal and Industrial Institute, which would enable them to establish themselves in niches of the American economy and become economically independent. In contrast to W.E.B. Du Bois, who emphasized equal rights and the complete inclusion of Black Americans in the social and political life as prerequisites for economic success and indeed as superior aim to it, Washington encouraged his fellow-African Americans to accept segregation and discrimination. He believed that the respect and acceptance of their White compatriots ultimately could be won through diligent work and cultured manners. Cf. Washington, Du Bois.

in his hometown, Steward feels fully justified in threatening the young Rubyites with severely violent measures:[41] "If you, any one of you, ignore, change, take away, or add to the words in the mouth of that Oven, I will blow our head off just like you was a hood-eyed snake" (*Paradise* 87). What looms large in these words is Steward's and his generation's fear of change. Change, particularly of the non-physical, the mental or emotional kind, is not part of the plan the patriarchs of Ruby entertain for their town, because "[c]hange is the enemy of utopias," as Barbara Christian writes ("The Past" 421), and we might add, of paradises of the traditional kind. History and the interpretation of its present-day consequences have taken on the character of the Oven's unchangeable "words of beaten iron" (*Paradise* 99). The Morgan brothers once vowed to create their 'haven,' their utopian exclusivist home out of their firm commitment to virtues of continuity and sameness. They do not intent to let young people, "those puppies" in Steward's words (*Paradise* 99), introduce new ideas into their community.

It is no coincident that this debate takes place in one of the three churches of Ruby. Rather, this circumstance reflects a kinship between a community that rests on the foundation of the ideology of racial essence and one that relies on religion in its institutionalized variant as its communal basis. The ideology of racial purity and religion both depend on laws and commandments and can thus be used as structuring principles in a community. In Ruby, the chief ideologues of racial essentialism not only rival the ministers of their town in their spiritual influence on the

---

[41] Steward's and Deacon's given names echo their father's and grandfather's command to them with regard to the future well-being of their community. Indeed, both of the brothers seem to regard their names as something close to job descriptions. Morrison has been criticized for her choice of names, particularly for Steward and Deacon, with the suggestion that names carry too much symbolic significance in *Paradise*, thereby coarsening the characterization of the novel's many characters (cf. Bent; see also Kakutani). However, such criticism overlooks the fact that the heads of families in Haven and Ruby choose names for their children with a precise purpose in mind: Their names are meant to carry symbolic weight; they are personal assignments as well as prescriptions of approved standards of behavior, of attitudes and views on life that correspond with fixed gender roles and social positions which the children are presumed to assume in their adult lives. I will return to this point in my discussion of the situation of women in Ruby later in this chapter.

townspeople. The reverends Pulliam, Carey, and Misner also take sides in the dispute over the meaning of history for the town; they participate in or – in Misner's case – criticize the marginalization of the "impure" in the town and their persecution in the vicinity of it. As Storace points out in her review of *Paradise*, "[Morrison] also explores [exclusivism's] necessary alliance with religious creed" (65/3). "[A] society designed to perpetuate itself unchangingly," she continues, "needs to propose its self-perpetuation as divine obligation" (65/3). God is presented as wielding this exclusivist and pious society as a tool for his purposes, "so that its refusal to examine its hostility to outsiders, its unamendable laws and customs, its permanent social hierarchy can be seen as obedient instead of wanton, arbitrary, or aggressive, a reflection of a divine and necessary order" (65/3). Thus, religion lends creed and structure to the idea of exclusive, homogeneous blackness.

In her study on the possession of history in Ruby, Elizabeth Yukins interprets the Oven debate as a memory debate. Like Christian, who sees "[m]emory" in Morrison's earlier novels "as the repository of suppressed history" which "becomes a key to the possibility of liberation in the future" ("The Past" 416), Yukins identifies a new approach to memory in *Paradise*. She notes a shift from the "devastation of excessive forgetting at the end of *Beloved* to the destructiveness of excessive remembering in *Paradise*" (239). Used excessively and in service of an exclusivist ideology, memory, so necessary and important for the never-ending process of identity formation, can also present a formidable obstacle to the development of free individuality. The prescribed ways and official events of commemorating "the past as the only legitimate identity for the town to assume" (239) curtail any healthy impulse in the citizens of Ruby to remember their own stories and to develop from those memories individual tales that could then be woven together to form a communal identity. Patricia is aware of the missing desire for self-enactment among the generation of the New Fathers, the retrograde focus from which her hometown is suffering. Her analysis of this state of affairs is precise and damning:

> Over and over and with the least provocation, they pulled from their stock of stories tales about the old folks, their grands and great-grands, their fathers and mothers. Dangerous confrontations, clever maneuvers. Testimonies of endurance, wit, skill and strength. Tales of luck and outrage. But why were there no stories to tell of themselves? About their own lives they shut up. Had nothing to say, pass on. As though past heroism was enough of a future to live by. (*Paradise* 161)

For the young Rubyites, neither the past heroism of the Old Fathers nor the achievements of the New Fathers, who started anew after Haven's failure, are sufficient for creating a promising future. In their eyes, they do not even suffice for a meaningful present. What makes the positions of the old and the young in the debate over the inscription on the Oven so bitterly antagonistic is a lack of understanding between the generations. Yukins argues: "The men and women who experienced the traumas of slavery and its effects created the words as a memorial and a directive, yet time has altered the inscription, and, more important, their descendants no longer have the knowledge of the authority of the traumas that engendered the motto/command" (239). Moreover, the older generation does not trust the younger one with the future of their community, an the New Fathers are not interested in the plans of their children. Not only are the youngsters chronologically too far removed from the traumas that shaped the lives of their parents and grandparents, as Yukins suggests, they are also denied the right to participate in the communal effort to use the past as a means to developing an identity for no other reason than their youth. Deacon Morgan reminds them that "our grandfathers [dug the clay, made each and every brick one at a time with their own hands, mixed the mortar and carried the hod sic] – not you" (*Paradise* 86). In Deacon's eyes, since Roy, Destry, Lorcas and the others had not only not been there when the Oven was built and have no direct experience of the horrors that gave expression to its inscription, they also have no right to propose any change even to parts of it. As far as Deacon and his peers are concerned, the youngsters "are in long trouble if [they] think [they] can disrespect a row [they] never hoed" (*Paradise* 86). The fact that they never could have "hoed that row" because they were born too late plays no role in the Morgan brothers' reasoning, nor do they consider the possibility that it is respect rather than disrespect for the Old Fathers that motivates these young people.

However, ironically and maybe tragically, what the New Fathers interpret as a betrayal of the traumas and the achievements of the forefathers, for the younger generation is an attempt "to give [. . .] new life" to a stone structure that has lost its practical purpose, but has acquired a symbolic one, as Richard Misner suggests (*Paradise* 86). With their position in the Oven debate they wish to rejuvenate the memory of the Old Fathers, of Black women and men during slavery in general. With an intellectual attitude that bears the signs of critical theory and constructivism, the young Rubyites regard history as open to interpretation and memory as ready to be filled with meaning, while for their fathers these are fixed entities that neither call for nor allow qualification of any sort.

By the time of the attack on the Convent, the New Fathers have copied the belief system of their forbears into the setup of their own society; they reassembled it as meticulously as they rebuilt the old and obsolete stone structure in the middle of their new town. But, dreading to repeat what they regard as the mistakes of their fathers in Haven and risk the scattering of their community, which would also mean their own financial and political ruin, they enforce these beliefs as dogma, install binding rites and set up traditions that are to be strictly observed. By mercilessly enforcing unwritten rules of conduct and an ideological system that severely restricts individual self-expression the New Fathers not only render their own outlook on life solid and unchangeable, but delay, even thwart their town's arrival in the present, not to mention its future prospects.

Opinions that differ from the official reading of past events or contemporary communal politics are not acknowledged as valid voices in the town, even though they do exist, as shall be shown shortly. "Ruby's leaders [...] have avoided the signs of internal difference by attempting to inhabit the past," Clewell states in her study of the different efforts to cope with traumas explored in *Paradise* (141). Over a period of some eighty years, the past of this all-Black town has been pressed into an ossified historiography in the shape of an African American jeremiad narrative that claims American exceptionalism for African Americans:[42] A Chosen People fortified by a covenant with God wanders through the wilderness of slavery and "Redemption" to overcome its adversaries by building their exclusive City upon a Hill. But despite the assumed moral high-ground this people occupies, it lives in constant danger of dispersal and thereby extinction.[43]

When the youngest generation rebels against their home community's enforced self-isolation from the world, a scattering of the once tight-knit community is again feared in Ruby, just as the biblical Jeremiah feared the

---

[42]Dalsgård explores the African American claim to and usage of the narrative tradition of American exceptionalism in the attempt of the leaders of Ruby to realize their vision of a national paradise.

[43]For a more detailed analysis of the use of the jeremiad narrative in the construction of ethnic identity in Ruby, see Fraile-Marcos's instructive study on this subject. See also Dalsgård who raises the question of whether the story of the Convent could be regarded as the first feminist jeremiad narrative.

dispersal of the Israelites. It is no coincident that Grace, a young woman looking for a rock formation that symbolizes eternal love, instead strays upon a town named after a hard precious stone and ruled by "8-rocks." Her desire for eternal love (-making) is confronted with the very real absence of love, tolerance, and forgiveness in Ruby's relationship with Others. For, in an attempt to prevent a new Haven-style failure, driven by the task of keeping their families united in their purity of race and of thought and thereby to save their all-Black enclave from being absorbed into a larger society that is racially impure, i.e., not purely Black, Ruby's leaders exclude dissident individuals from their community and bar outsiders' entry into it. Thus, they join the ranks of "disallowers" that shaped the nation of which they are a part even if against their own wishes.

4.2.2.4   Sinners

The completeness with which the founders of Ruby incorporated into their world-view the racist ideology of White supremacists with which the generations before them and they themselves grew up is reflected in "the fundamental organizing principle" of the town (240), summed up disturbingly precisely by Steward Morgan: "Neither the founding fathers nor their descendants could tolerate anybody but themselves" (*Paradise* 13). Unacknowledged or unrecognized by the leaders of Ruby, the original Disallowing suffered by the Old Fathers for them "is marked by and as [a] loss [...] of meaningful relations to those different from themselves" (Clewell 134).[44] Clewell points out that "the more enigmatic loss" experienced by the people of Ruby and also unacknowledged by them is that of "the passing of time," a sense of loss which is "characteristic of traumatic experience" (134). It can be read as the background for their belief in their own immortality.

   The repression of traumatic loss is also exemplified in the fact that the leaders of the trek away from Haven toward an even more remote district of Oklahoma suggested the name of their sister, Ruby, as a fitting name for their newly founded settlement. Ruby Morgan Smith fell ill on the trek and died untreated in a hospital waiting room. As she was a victim of White racist discrimination, her dying turns into martyrdom and becomes part of the quasi religious history of the town, the founding myth of Ruby

---

[44]For an exploration of the theme of loss in *Paradise* see also Wood.

and thus the ideology the society rests on. Her fate adds to the painful experiences of denied citizenship and human rights of the black settlers that started with the relegation of the Old Fathers to share-cropping and continued with Disallowings I and II. By naming their town after Ruby the New Fathers refuse to acknowledge and accept the traumatic loss of their sister. As long as their town exists, their sister is not dead.[45]

In the wake of the trauma of the original Disallowing and the "Disallowing Part II," pure blackness acquires the status of a mark of holiness, and blackness (rather than whiteness) is regarded as the guarantor of moral rectitude, of the survival of the group, and ultimately of success in life among the denizens of this small town. Racial purity needs to be guarded and aggressively defended against 'polluting' forces in the shape of persons or ideologies. Clewell argues that Ruby's founders attempt to preserve the unity of their community by continuing to avoid the initial loss of their ability to relate to anybody but themselves. Instead of confronting an inability that drains the life-force of their community by making it hostile toward the outside and sterile inside, the New Fathers make a vice of a virtue: Clannishness and intolerance toward strangers are looked upon favorably, because, as Christian puts it, "[f]or [the founders and their immediate descendants] any difference is a sign of the snake in the Garden of Eden" ("The Past" 421). Again racial essentialism shares common ground with religious essentialism; difference and diversity are fought bitterly in both.

As I pointed out earlier, the New Fathers install a "blood-rule" to preserve the racial purity of Ruby and their own prominent positions within the town: 8-rock blood, the sign of such purity as they themselves represent, must reproduce within the confines of the town. Christian emphasizes that "the meaning of freedom and its relationship to identity and community" is of concern to much, if not all of Morrison's fictional and non-fictional work (416); it certainly plays an important role in *Paradise*. The hard-won freedom the Old Fathers passed on to their children and grandchildren as a gift to be treasured and protected is the freedom to define themselves – as autonomous citizens who are free to choose with

---

[45] Significantly, Delia Best, Roger's wife and Patricia's mother, was also one of the few Rubyites to die. Her death, however, is excluded from the town's mythology because she was not 8-rock and because the circumstances of her death smack of deliberate negligence on the part of the New Fathers.

whom to keep company, free to put down the rules that govern their communities and to enforce the implementation of these rules. The story of the
original Black settlers in Oklahoma makes abundantly clear their undeniable right as well as their deep-felt desire to create a society that would
respect their human and citizens' rights and in which they had the power
to define themselves. In Ruby, however, this act of self-definition stretches
only as far as the identity of the group, and this group-identity rests heavily on sameness, in terms of race and of historical experience.

Tragically, the townspeople are unable to use the freedom they inherited from their forefathers and which they believed to protect when many
of them fought on the battlefields of Europe and Vietnam. Instead, and
in keeping with the racist system that has permeated their entire lives,
the New Fathers choose to react to their people's and their own history of
discrimination by subjecting their original "disallowers" and their descendants to their particular brand of racism. This they perfect and make the
very foundation of their community: as semi-religious dogma that is beyond dispute to such an extent that it does not even need to be expressed
as a written rule. The "presence of the unfree within the heart of the
democratic experiment" that Morrison describes in *Playing in the Dark*
as "distinctive in the New World" and "its claim to freedom" is also part
of the social structure of Ruby (Morrison qtd. in Storace 65/3). Pondering
the meaning of the Oven's motto as the older generation reads it, Patricia
writes: "'Beware the Furrow of His Brow,' in which the 'You' (understood), vocative case, was not a command to the believers but a threat to
those who had disallowed them" (*Paradise* 195). As Storace points out,
"Ruby itself is in fact a racist town, as well as an enclave of moral and
physical freedom for its freedmen founders" (65/3).

To judge from the Rubyites' consequent seclusion from and dread of
White America, one might expect these "disallowers" to be White Americans. Instead, the "clarity of their hatred" is aimed at lighter-skinned
African Americans (*Paradise* 189). Morrison explains her motivation to
focus on racist tendencies among African Americans in her novel with her
desire to construct a color-blind mirror for the conditions in the United
States as a whole (Scheck cf.).[46] Race-related prejudice within the Black
community is a great worry to the author: "I think the threat for many of

---

[46]"Es hat mich gereizt, in diesem Buch einen Spiegel für die Zustände in unserem
    Land insgesamt zu konstruieren, einen sozusagen farbenblinden Spiegel. Aus-

our communities is internecine," she says in an interview, and continues by clarifying that "[b]y that I mean the enemy is within, as opposed to being on the outside" (Verdelle). Historically, in the United States the effect of the internalized color-code that privileges light-skinned at the expense of dark-skinned people is that "[w]hole sections of the Black population [are] just totally cut out, dropped like detritus" (Verdelle). With Ruby, however, the author depicts a special variety of racial hierarchies within a Black community: The former victims of a discrimination that favors light skin colors set up their own standards of purity and values, and those standards privilege blackness over whiteness. Here, to be light-skinned is to be on the margins of society; it means to be the victim of discrimination.

Morrison gives her readers several examples of the extent to which this brand of Black-on-Black racial discrimination permeates and guides interaction between the citizens of Ruby. The command not to marry outside the circle of 8-rocks is enforced by the Morgan brothers and their peers through the calculated application of psychological pressure and the threat of violent punishment.[47] It reaches representatives of different

gangspunkt für meine Figuren ist ja die Erfahrung, dass Schwarz nicht gleich Schwarz ist – ich schildere auch den Rassismus der Schwarzen untereinander."

[47] While the most obvious connotations of "eight-rock" in Patricia's definition from coal-mining are purity and high quality as well as hardness, haughtiness, immobility, and relentlessness, the abbreviated version "8-R" calls to mind a very different and highly disturbing connotation: Among international neo-Nazi groups numbers are often employed as codes for the transportation of unconstitutional slogans, but serve as means of instant identification and unpunishable public outing for group members. They are shouted across the street, printed on stickers and distributed in public places, sewed to shirt-sleeves and jackets, or tattooed onto arms and necks. In this code system the number "8" stands for the letter "h" in the alphabet and thus carries special importance for Neo-Nazis: it symbolizes the name Hitler. The code-number "18" then refers to Adolf Hitler, "28" means "blood and honor," and "88" is "Heil Hitler!," the infamous salute of the German Fascists the public use of which is prohibited under the German constitution. International neo-Nazi groups that use this number code, such as "Blood and Honor" and "Combat 18," define themselves through an extremely racist attitude and a high propensity to violence, directed especially against members of non-European ethnic groups, lesbians and gay men, as well as people with leftist views. The visual similarity between "8-R" and "88," in combination with Patricia's critique of the eight-rock leaders of Ruby as racist, autocratic, and ruthless makes a connection between the New Fathers of Ruby

groups of people that differ in their extent of racial purity: The first group consists of men with blue-black skin, i.e., members of the ruling faction and thus potential rivals of the New Fathers to influence and power in Ruby. They were among those who decided to leave Haven with their families and start a new Black town, but at some point in their lives they had had a relationship with a light-skinned woman. Theirs are the families that Steward and Deacon Morgan, the secret directors of the play, struck from the script of the Christmas pageant, thereby deleting them from the official history of the town.

Roger Best was "the first to violate the blood-rule" (*Paradise* 195). When he returned to Haven after World War II, he brought with him his baby daughter and a "cracker-looking" woman, a "wife with no last name, a wife without people, a wife of sunlight skin, a wife of racial tampering" (*Paradise* 197), as Patricia sarcastically recalls the abusive terms given to the light-skinned stranger who was her mother. As a consequence of Roger's breaking the unspoken rule, as a punishment for "bringing along the dung we leaving behind" as Steward phrases it (*Paradise* 202),[48] he is slighted by the men of power in Ruby, overlooked when it comes to engaging citizens in business deals and creating networks of power and influence. The lifelong penalty for his race-related misdemeanor renders Roger harmless as a competitor to the wealthy Morgans. Such is the seriousness of his race-crime that when his daughter Patricia marries Bill Cato and the couple have a light-skinned child, the 8-rock Cato family,

and the ideologues of Fascism and National Socialism thinkable. This possible implicit comparison seems especially cynical, given the fact that the racist ideology of the Nazis aims at suppressing and eliminating those they considered non-Arian, i.e., not White, and the "8-Rs," who thus get a reputation for being racists, praise themselves for not being White. I am indebted to Stephanie Remlinger who brought the possible parallel between Ruby and the Nazi number codes to my attention. For further information on the use of numbers in Neo-Nazi circles, see, for example, "Zeichen" and "Nazi-Symbole: Zahlen."

[48] The woman whom Steward calls "dung" was much needed by the 8-rock families from Haven on their way further west. Patricia recalls how her mother was sent into white-owned grocery stores to buy provisions for the travelers and to ask the way, while the cars of the trek remained parked out of sight. This forced dependence on a light-skinned woman must have riled and humiliated the proud 8-rock men and doubtlessly contributed to the hatred that Steward felt toward Delia Best.

once one of the revered families on the original trek to Oklahoma Territory, is – secretly but with lasting effect – struck from the cast of the Christmas pageant by the Morgan twins as well. A family that is unable to produce "racially pure" children is not considered worthy of being part of this sanctified tradition.[49]

Menus Jury is another 8-rock man who disregarded the blood-rule when he became engaged to a "pretty sandy-haired girl from Virginia" after his return from Vietnam and is made to pay a heavy price for it (*Paradise* 195). Menus is a son of one of the major families in Ruby, a family that helped set up the town after the demise of Haven but has grown critical of the amount of power and influence amassed by the Morgan brothers. Steward first uses his influence in the council of elders in Ruby to pressure Menus into breaking his engagement with the Virginian. He then forces him to give up the house he had bought for himself and his fiancée, leaving him to drown his sorrow in alcohol. It becomes the "town house" of Steward's wife Dovey and is later passed on to K.D. Morgan, heir to the Morgan clan.

Apart from these men who had the "right" skin color but had not adhered to the commandments set up to maintain the racial purity of the community, there are individuals whose very existence gives away the racial crime of their parents. Roger Best's wife and her unborn child died in childbirth, ostensibly because the men of Ruby were slow to call medical help. Patricia, Ruby's school teacher, is the surviving older child of this union and, as she sarcastically writes, "some of [the dung]" that

---

[49]Patricia muses about the identity of the other family that was dropped from the original cast of nine 8-rock families in the Christmas play. In terms of the commandment of racially pure reproduction the hopes of the Morgan clan rest solely on K.D., but the arranged marriage of this young man with Arnette Fleetwood creates the basis for the survival of this family. In fact, extinction is warded off from the Morgans when a son is born to K.D and Arnette. The second clan in question is that of the Floods of whom a single heir exists: Anna Flood who has returned to Ruby and runs her father's shop. Patricia speculates that the Flood line might be saved through the union of Anna with the Reverend Richard Misner who, although he is a newcomer to the town, is at least of sufficiently dark complexion. But this seems doubtful, since the men who wield most of the power in Ruby are deeply distrustful of the reverend and are unlikely to leave the care for the purity of their community to one who regards all African Americans united in an African diaspora, as will be explicated shortly.

is "still aboveground, instructing their grandchildren in a level of intelligence their elders will never acquire" (*Paradise* 202f.). The light-skinned woman cannot remove the stigma of her father's disrespect of the blood-rule even by marrying an 8-rock man.

With Patricia's situation Morrison comments on a pivotal event in US history that falls into the time of the writing of *Paradise*. There is a parallel between the teacher's fate in Ruby and the most famous of the slave reparations lawsuits in the US. Yukins points out that Patricia Best Cato

> attempts to marry into the Cato family to gain greater community legitimacy, but after her husband dies the town refuses to remember or authorize this name in the long term. In the *Cato* decision (1995), [...] the Ninth Circuit Court refused to recognize the Cato family history as legitimately traumatized and legally entitled to recognition and reparations by the federal government. (223, fn. 3)

Both cases, the factual *Cato* case and the fate of the fictional Patricia Best Cato of Ruby, are concerned with the effects of the past on the present and with contestations over collective memory. When Bill Cato dies, light-skinned Patricia loses her only link to the 8-rock community and her right of belonging which was tied to her 8-rock husband. The name of the old and revered family, still unsullied in the eyes of the New Fathers, is taken away from her; as a widow she is commonly referred to as "Pat Best." Rather than being allowed to reap the benefits of the moral superiority attributed to her husband because of his pure blood, she is condemned to being an outsider in her own home town because her body bears the sign of her father's supposed defilement of the holy blood of his forebears. Patricia becomes the unmarried schoolmarm whose efforts to compile a genealogy of Ruby are routinely frustrated as prominent people do not trust her with relevant details of their families' histories. In the case of her daughter, for reasons that will be explored later in this chapter, social exclusion reaches proportions of ostracism.

4.2.2.5 Heretics and the Discourse on Home

In a society that takes extreme pride in the unity among its people as well as in its aloofness from other societies, marginalized individuals can be taken as indicators of the central values that hold the majority community together and shut out those who appear not to share these values to the fullest. In Ruby, two important outsiders are Patricia Best Cato and

Reverend Richard Misner – Patricia, as I explained above, for her father's sin against the commandment of preserving the purity of 8-rock blood and for her own light complexion, and Richard because neither he not his forefathers belonged to the group of original Black migrants to the Midwest. He has only lived in the town for a few years, but during this short time-span he acquired the reputation of being a troublemaker among his conservative congregation whose spokesmen are the Morgan twins. Both outsiders are educated, critical thinkers at potentially influential positions in the community, Patricia as the school teacher and Misner as minister of the powerful Baptist congregation. These attributes and the position of these characters at the edge of their community make their enlightened attempts at deconstructing the core values of the town and the social system driven by these values highly informative for the reader.

The way in which Patricia completes her notes and the chief motivation behind her efforts bear a strong resemblance to the work of an author who imagines the personal fates behinds dates and facts, of a historiographer who explores possible links between certain events, speculates upon motives and interests of the actors involved, and interprets the outcome. The passage describing Patricia's history project for the town of Ruby illustrates this:

> It began as a gift to the citizens of Ruby – a collection of family trees; the genealogies of each of the fifteen families. [...] When the trees were completed, she had begun to supplement the branches of who begat whom with notes: what work they did, for example, where they lived, to what church they belonged. Some of the nicer touches [...] she gleaned from her students' autobiographical compositions. [...] The trees still required occasional alterations [...] but her interest in the supplementary notes increased as the notes did, and she gave up all pretense to objective comment. (*Paradise* 187)

As shown earlier, Patricia uncovers "the deal" the New Fathers negotiated with their God, the "blood-rule" that governs social interaction in Ruby during her work on the family trees of the fifteen families who left the South and came to settle in Oklahoma. Yet, the story she tells of Ruby is incompatible with the official story of her hometown. Patricia is what Yukins refers to as a "bastard daughter," one of the women in the contemporary African American community who are descendants of survivors of the founding trauma of American slavery. Although they have not experienced the traumas of their forebears because of their temporal distance to slavery, they also suffer from the effects of slavery on the emotional and physical life of African Americans, and they feel responsible for recording and preserving the memories of past generations. It is bastard daughters rather than sons, because in patriarchal societies daughters are not only barred from passing on the family name but "are also denied the legitimacy of their own history" (Yukins 227).

Patricia as *Paradise*'s bastard daughter struggles with a double sense of illegitimacy: Firstly, as the too-white child of her light-skinned mother Delia she is marginalized among Ruby's race-conscious Black citizens. Secondly, as Delia died when her daughter was a still child, Patricia feels isolated from her mother's inheritance of memories and experiences. This feeling of isolation is enhanced by the fact that the town shrouds Delia's history in silence. Tortured by her "bastard consciousness," an "anxious understanding of matrilineal alienation," Patricia feels "an intense, disorienting, and at times debilitating sense of being cut off from and denied rightful claims to previous generations' memories" (Yukins 226f.).

However, bastard consciousness does not only torture Patricia, it also acts as a stimulus for her. Like Du Bois's "double consciousness," it empowers the individual to critically observe the society that denies her membership, although she has grown up in it and intimately knows it. The sense of illegitimacy and marginalization, in combination with her insider knowledge of the town and the lives of its citizens, drive Patricia's longing to record a history of Ruby. Yet, because of her bastard position, her story turns out to be an illegitimate, transgressive history that would be unacceptable to the New Fathers. Moreover, it is also unacceptable to Patricia herself, who has grown up with the version of the history of her hometown and the conclusions drawn from the experiences of her ancestors as told and promulgated by the leaders of the community. In this confusion of feelings she burns her genealogical notes and thus actively wipes out parts of her town's history. This act testifies both to the bastard daughter's disillusioned rejection of the history of her home town Ruby, a history that does not acknowledge her as a legitimate component, and to her desperate desire to be part of it. Moreover, it highlights the power of the official story to curb and suppress illegitimate knowledges.

Patricia Best and Richard Misner both refer to the people of Ruby as "they," verbally underlining their own peripheral position in this community in full consciousness of their outsider status. Nevertheless, they differ in the extent to which each of them is willing to live in that exclusion and embrace the status that has been assigned to them – as part of their exclusive community, but kept at the margins of it, a fact that bears witness to Patricia's precarious position as bastard daughter in a patriarchal society that leaves to men a certain amount of freedom to choose allegiances. The difference between the two protagonists surfaces most distinctly in their concept of "home." When Patricia thinks of home, she thinks of Ruby: "This is their home; mine too. Home is not a little thing" (*Paradise* 213). Despite the bitterness the teacher holds in her heart against the leading men of Ruby and those who follow them uncritically, making her life and that of her father and daughter difficult with their dogmatic attitude toward racial purity, she regards the town as her home.

In contrast, Reverend Misner, although he recognizes and understands the need his parishioners have of a home, locates his own far outside Ruby: "Africa is our home, Patricia, whether you like it or not," he tells her (*Paradise* 210), underlining not only his own claim to membership in the community of African Americans, regardless of the degree of blackness of their skin, but also the claim of every individual in Ruby, whether they regard other Black Americans as racially "impure" or not. For Misner, Africa represents the world. By locating his roots in Africa he claims citizenship of the world, something that has been denied Black US-Americans for a very long time and that in their desire for exclusiveness the people of Ruby deny themselves:[50] "We live in the world, Pat. The whole world. Separating us, isolating us – that's always been their weapon. Isolation kills generations. It has no future" (*Paradise* 210). Richard does not restrict his wish for Black unity to the level of the nation, but implicitly emphasizes the link between Black people in the United States as well as in other countries and Africans on the African continent, thus weaving a racial bond between Blacks of every nationality who live in the African diaspora and in the motherland. With this – idealized – motherland in mind, he warns Patricia that "[i]f you cut yourself off from your roots, you'll wither" (*Paradise* 209).[51]

---

[50] Page describes Misner as an "outsider with a critical perspective on the town who thus parallels the reader's likely position" ("Furrowing" 644/1-2).

[51] Via the reverend's views Morrison not only expresses pride in the African ancestry of her people, but joins scholars such as Paul Gilroy in celebrating the Black Atlantic (cf. Gilroy).

Miner's and Patricia's discussion of the roots of Black Americans in Africa establishes yet another link between Morrison's fiction and an event in US-American history that was relevant for the Black community, in this case the publication of Alex Haley's seminal novel *Roots*. Although *Roots* did not appear as a complete novel before the fall of 1976, it was excerpted in the *Reader's Digest* in 1974. In the summer of 1975, the fictional present of the scene analyzed above, the protagonist Richard Misner moves within a factual discourse contemporary to him and uses ideas and terms from that discourse. The serial publication of *Roots* occurs at a time of growing interest of African Americans in their family histories, particularly the part of history that goes back to pre-slavery times. As Barbara Christian pointed out, during the early 1970s "[t]he excavation of black history and the celebration of literature from the perspective of African Americans [...] resulted in scholarship that laid the bases for important literary works" ("The Past" 413), one of which was Haley's novel. It initiated a veritable trend in the African American community of people traveling to countries along the African west coast, investigating their genealogies in order to find African ancestors and recover their origins. *Roots* helped substantially to boost African American self-esteem and pride in their historical and cultural background,[52] a historical reality that is reflected in Reverend Misner's enthusiasm for Africa.

A dispute unfolding between Patricia Best and Richard Misner from these initial positions allows insights into the discourse on the concept of "home" within the African American community in the 1960s and 1970s; it represents Morrison's fictional commentary on and contribution to this historical discourse. Furthermore, it sheds light on the self-image of the population of Ruby. Patricia accuses the reverend of "looking for [...] just some kind of past with no slavery in it" (*Paradise* 210), a past, this means, which is not an insult to his honor as a Black man. Her remark implies that he should embrace that painful period as part of Black history as

---

[52]Haley's fame and the reverence paid to the novel by the African American community have remained undiminished even after the publication of information that Haley did not in fact fictionalize the history of his own family, as he made believe, but plagiarized substantial parts of the novel *The African* (1967) by the White author and historian Harold Courlander. He was also brought to court by Margaret M. Walker who accused him of infringing on the copyrights of her novel *Jubilee* published in 1966. For more information on the issue see Crouch, Fetterman, and "Alex Haley."

well as his own history. In his reply Richard points out that "[t]here was a whole lot of life before slavery. And we ought to know what it is. If we're going to get rid of the slave mentality, that is" (*Paradise* 210). In his mind, a clear understanding of their past is exactly what modern African Americans need in order to become self-confident and proud citizens who are able to assert themselves against the White majority in their demand for equal rights in US society. In a nation with a population whose majority has some kind of migration background, not knowing one's genealogy or at the least the history of one's immediate forefathers for Misner is a sure sign of lacking in identity, of being insignificant as settlers and builders of the nation.

In the 1960s and '70s, getting rid of the "slave mentality" was high up on the political and personal agenda of many African Americans. So-called African Societies sprang up as early as the 1890s, parallel to the movement to encourage Black settlement of the Western territories, when disheartened Black settlers followed calls to leave for Africa in pursuit of full citizenship and the right to determine their own lives. Katz gives the example of Blacks who "had been ordered out of several Oklahoma communities" where "in some cases white threats had been backed by guns." They followed Bishop Henry M. Turner who "repeatedly and with some success urged Oklahoma blacks to migrate to Africa" (Katz 252). In the second and third decade of the twentieth century, Marcus Garvey and his Universal Negro Improvement Association (UNIA) worked toward their goals of bettering the socio-economic situation of Black Americans and the foundation of a Black nation on the African continent by creating employment opportunities and encouraging identification with the African "homeland."[53] A decade later, Wallace Fard Muhammad took up Garvey's ideas of a Black nationalism when he founded the Nation of Islam in the 1930s. In the 1960s, particularly under the leadership of Fard Muhammad's successor, Elijah Muhammad, with his spokesman Malcolm X, this African American religious organization experienced its first heydays. Apart from condemning the Christian religion as main tool of White hegemony at the expense of the non-White world population, and apart from presenting Islam as the liberating religion for all suppressed peoples, the Nation of Islam taught the moral and cultural superiority of

---

[53]For more information on Marcus Garvey and UNIA, see for example, Cronon and "Unia History."

Black over White Americans, encouraging and fostering a new and strong
sense of community for people of African descent in the United States.

This strengthened feeling of being part of a group was meant to culminate in the creation of a separate Black nation for African Americans
on American soil. Malcolm X's teachings in particular had a strong influence on the founders of the Black Panthers Party (BPP), Huey Newton
and Bobby Seale, and their goal to advance social, political, and economic
equality between Black and White US-Americans. In the years between
the founding of the BPP in 1966 and its decline into insignificance after
several shoot-outs with the police and the incarceration or exiling of its
leaders in the mid-1970s, the Black Panthers organized a variety of relief
programs for the most disadvantaged among African Americans. Thus
they were instrumental to the development of a Black consciousness and
a growing pride in Black culture and identity.[54] Although the non-violent
Civil Rights movement led by Dr. Martin Luther King, Jr., achieved major improvements of the legal situation of African Americans, in the 1970s
the ideology of the militant, radically socialist BPP proved particularly attractive to young Black men and – to a lesser extent – women who were
disillusioned by the continuing structural and individual racism in US-
American society.

We learn of Reverend Misner that he "would happily have taken the
sword" in Dr. King's stead after the assassination of Martin Luther King
(*Paradise* 212). Together with the black fist painted on the Oven by
members of his youth group as well as Patricia's accusation that Richard
teaches militancy in his Black History class, this can be taken as a hint that
the reverend's attitude to the emancipation struggle of African Americans
might not always have been non-violent. We learn further that he spent
time in jail for his participation in the Black protest movement. In Ruby,
much to the chagrin of the bank-owning Morgan brothers, Misner initiates
a cooperative bank that works on non-profit principles. Thus, his convictions combine traces of the strong sense of membership in the community
of African Americans and all people of African ancestry preached by the
Nation of Islam, with Malcolm X's Black nationalist teachings and the
militant socialism of the Black Panthers. But his idea of "home" is most
of all Afro-centric and romantic in character, as is typical for Garveyism.

---

[54]For further information on the Black Panther Party see for example Robinson.

Patricia is suspicious of Misner's opinion not least because of the romantic undertone it has to it.   Indeed, Morrison herself is aware of a tendency among African Americans to "romanticize [Africa] too much," but she also gives a reason why that is so. In an interview she said that "maybe [it is important for African Americans to journey to Africa] [...] [b]ecause we're so easily drawn [...] into the myth of [...] whatever – a history – a useful little test story" (Jaffrey). Patricia, in contrast to this, for once is completely in tune with her fellow Rubyites in her attitude toward Africa. It "doesn't mean anything" to her, for whom Africa is "fifty foreign countries" (*Paradise* 209, 210).[55] This sentiment is echoed and even fortified by Soane Morgan, a representative of the leading families in Ruby. Soane assumes that "[s]he had the same level of interest in Africans as they had in her: none" (*Paradise* 104). She resents the fact that some young people around Misner "talked about [Africans] like they were neighbors or, worse, family" (*Paradise* 104).[56]

In a direct reversal of Misner's ideas, Patricia's concept of African American history effectively excludes everything that happened before Western colonialism in Africa and slavery in the Black Atlantic. In reply to her interlocutor's appeal to "get rid of the slave mentality" she maintains that "[s]lavery *is* our past. Nothing can change that, certainly not Africa" (*Paradise* 210). With this statement Patricia puts herself in line with a generation of well-known writers and reputable scholars of African American history and culture whose work aims at establishing and underlining the importance of the experience of slavery to that culture and to

---

[55] Although Patricia knows from her own experience what it feels like to be marginalized, she participates in the town's practice of withholding information from the newcomer Reverend Misner, always behaving non-committal when town politics or residents are concerned and thus making him feel strange and unwelcome in Ruby. As will become clearer in my analysis of her treatment of Billie Delia, her own daughter, Patricia has internalized the exclusionary ideology taught and perpetuated in her home community over several generations. She is aware of the effect exclusionism has on her and condemns herself for conniving in the marginalization of Others.

[56] Ruby's attitude toward Africa is indicative of what Christian, using the phrase coined by W.E.B. Du Bois, called "the problem of 'double consciousness'" ("The Past" 414): They feel not American enough to seek participation in mainstream US politics and culture, but too American to acknowledge their bond with the African peoples from which their forefathers and -mothers descended.

the image Black people in the United States have of themselves. These include among others Toni Morrison herself with her Pulitzer-Prize winning novel *Beloved*, Margaret M. Walker with *Jubilee*, Fred D'Aguiar with *The Longest Memory*, as well as the afore-mentioned *Roots* by Alex Haley.

Yet, Patricia's willingness to recognize slavery as part of her people's history is not matched by an equal interest of her neighbors' in this historical period. The relationship of the citizens of Ruby to their great-grandparents' slave status is a very ambivalent one. During the Oven debate, Deacon Morgan reprimands one of the young men under Reverend Misner's tuition for calling the Old Fathers "ex-slaves:" "That's my grandfather you're talking about. Quit calling him an ex-slave like that's all he was. He was also an ex-lieutenant governor, an ex-banker, an ex-deacon and a whole lot of other exes, ..." (*Paradise* 84). Deacon is of course right to point out the fact that Zechariah Morgan, "the man who put the words in the Oven's black mouth" (*Paradise* 13), and his peers had all occupied respectable positions in their towns and districts in the late 1860s and 1870s and therefore should not be reduced to their status as former slaves. But he cringes at the thought that they had in fact all been slaves when he says that "[e]verybody born in slavery time wasn't a slave. Not the way you mean it" (*Paradise* 84). This word has such dishonorable connotations for Deacon that he feels the need to defend his grandfather against what to him sounds like a mean-spirited accusation, an act of heresy.

The town fathers have a schizophrenic position toward the slave status of their ancestors: On the one hand, they take great pride in the fact that their families had inhabited North America already more than two centuries ago. Deacon and the other New Fathers are proudly aware that these men and women were among the founders of the American nation, whether as slaves or as governors. On the other hand, while they exclaim that "[t]hey were extraordinary. They had served, picked, plowed and traded in Louisiana since 1755, when it included Mississippi; and when it was divided into states they had helped govern both from 1868 to 1875, after which they had been reduced to field labor" (*Paradise* 99), they do not mention or acknowledge how their ancestors had arrived on the American continent and for what purpose. Deacon and his peers have internalized the racist doctrine of the first half of the twentieth century to such an extent that they suspect the young generation of disrespectfully equating being a slave with having a weak and servile character. For these men and women who regard the Old Fathers as saint-like patriarchs, this is nothing short of blasphemy.

Thus, three opinions compete among the citizens of Ruby on how far back into the past African Americans should orient themselves in their quest for a history, and these views of the past of the people of Ruby reflect their respective images of "home." For the founders of the town, the history of their families begins only with their exodus from the South after Reconstruction. It is less a history than a semi-religious myth of perseverance and final success against the odds. Its episodes are codified, their interpretation having been turned into dogma. Patricia, in comparison, wishes to include the centuries of slavery in the history of Ruby, recording her people's history from the time of their arrival on American shores onward. Yet, Ruby's history for her does not extend to pre-colonial Africa and thus excludes Africa as a possible focus of identification. "Home" for Patricia is her community with its rich and changeable history on the American continent and with its ancestors, regardless of their racial backgrounds. Finally, Richard Misner searches the roots of African American genealogy and culture in African soil. For him Africa allows Black Americans the same wealth of history other cultures have, one that stretches far back into prehistoric times and is uncorrupted by conquest, oppression, or servitude. His "home" is the African diaspora, with the continent of Africa as its source and center.

However, for those who dominate the discourses on home, identity, and community in Ruby, the New Fathers around Steward and Deacon, the boundaries of their town and land represent the borders of their universe. They are virtual walls that keep those inside safe and protected while they shut out the enemy Out There. Walled in through fanatic self-segregation and separated from the rest of American society through their belief in the moral superiority of pure blackness, the Rubyites have thus created the very "race house" from which to distance themselves Morrison urges her listeners and readers in "Home." This "house" community rests on racial essentialism coupled with the idea of moral superiority of Blacks over non-Blacks. Steward's vision resembles the suffocating narrowness of the traditional notion of *Paradise* that functions through mechanisms of exclusion of those considered unsaved at the expense of justice.

Consequently, the New Fathers insist on regarding the town of Ruby as a paradisiac site for Black people, as Steward's self-satisfied evaluation shows:

> Unique and isolated, his was a town justifiably pleased with itself. It neither had nor needed a jail. No criminals had ever come from his town. And the one or two people who acted up, humiliated their families or threatened the town's view of itself where taken good care of. Certainly there wasn't a slack or sloven woman anywhere in town and the reasons, he thought, were clear. From the beginning its people were free and protected. (*Paradise* 8)

Steward's satisfaction with the orderly, seemingly peaceful atmosphere in town, however, stands in sharp contrast to the history of overt and covert repression of those in Ruby who do not blend in with the majority in every respect. The freedom Steward claims for his people is the freedom from White-on-Black discrimination only, and it has been achieved through strict voluntary segregation. Ruby's freedom does not stretch to the human right to free self-expression and self-determination of the individual. Under the protection of their leaders the inhabitants of Ruby live like under the reign of feudal monarchs or in a patriarchal, highly institutionalized religious community. As long as the citizens submit to having vital decisions taken for them, such as whom to marry, with whom to associate, and where to live, they will enjoy the protection of the powerful. If they insist on making their own choices, they will be ostracized at the least and killed at the worst. The result of this Black Puritan experiment is a static African American mini-nation whose ethnic and quasi-national identity rests on an essentialist racist ideology. It is a highly prescriptive monoculture based on the idea of institutionalized racial purity.

4.2.3   Racial Essentialism and Patriarchy

> [E]verything that worries them must come from women.
>
> Toni Morrison

This examination of the social set-up of the all-Black town of Ruby reveals a close interaction between racial essentialism and restrictive gender roles and relations. The "fathers' law" that demands the proliferation of 8-rock blood within the walls of the town does so by imposing strict rules for procreation. First of all, men are in charge of "regulating marriage ties" in order to prevent the cultural taboo of incest (cf. Lacan 185). In the patriarchal setup of Ruby, men are active while women remain in the passive position. Men choose their partners; women – sometimes warily – wait to be chosen. A telling example is the town's watchful curiosity about Reverend Misner's choice of partner. Patricia Best and Anna Flood present the alternative; none of the two women is expected to hasten the reverend's choice, least of all to take it from him and into her own hands.

The effects of regulation of the gender relations within the community manifest themselves already in Haven, the settlement of the original Founding Fathers. There the systematic political and social control of women was already practiced and the subjugation of Ruby's women indeed has its roots. As Patricia has found out, in Haven, "young girls who had no prospects" could be "taken over" by older men who either had lost their wives or were unmarried (*Paradise* 196). There were instances when men "took over" women who were related to them, so that they were their own children's uncles. Not only is the objective of avoiding incest through regulation of marriage ties not met – Margaret Homans points out that "while the Law of the Father prohibits incest between mother and son, it authorizes incest between father and daughter" (653) –, but such marriage negotiations also reduce female members of the community to objects. In Ruby, the arrangement between the Morgans and the Fleetwoods over Arnette Fleetwood is the prime example for the objectification of women. The union between K.D. and Arnette is wanted by the patriarchs of the two rivaling families and becomes part of the power-play between them. It seems the more desirable because of Arnette's proven fertility which promises the continuance of both the Morgan and the Fleetwood lines.

As soon as the women of Ruby lose their subjecthood in this way, official historical records subsume them under the names of the male heads of their families. "Who are these women, who [...] had only one name?" Patricia asks in frustration at the sparse bits of information about female ancestors she can contrive from the denizens of her hometown. "Who where these women with generalized last names? Brown, Smith, Rivers, Stone, Jones. Women whose identity rested on the men they married – if marriage applied: a Morgan, a Flood, a Blackhorse, a Poole, a Fleetwood" (*Paradise* 187f.). While in the general US-American context "the law of the Mother" became powerful "only and precisely because legal enslavement removed the African-American male not so much from sight as from *mimetic* view as a partner in the prevailing social fiction of the Father's name, the Father's law" (Spillers 671), in the context of secluded, patriarchal all-Black Ruby the name of the father overpowers that of the mother and effectively expels it from official records.

In Ruby maybe even more so than in Haven the reason behind the effectiveness of the Law of the Father is the powerful objective of maintaining what is regarded as foundation and prerequisite for the survival of the community: pure blackness. Whosoever endangers this foundation dishonors the covenant of the Old Fathers with their God and breaks "the deal" of the New Fathers. It is no coincidence that Big Papa, the founder of Haven and revered ancestor of the Ruby community, changed his given name Coffee to that of Zechariah. He saw a strong parallel between the precarious situation of the Israelites and that of his own people and felt an intellectual and emotional kinship with this biblical patriarch. According to scripture, Zechariah was the prophet chosen by God to lead the Israelites to a New Jerusalem, "if they followed the edicts of their patriarchal God who warned them about the evils that women set adrift represented" (Christian, "The Past": 420).[57] In the Old Testament's prophecy of Zechariah, woman is the measure of iniquity and the symbol of wickedness. If Zion is to be blessed by the Lord and the scattering of the people is to be prevented, the measuring basket with the wicked woman must be closed with a lid of lead (cf. Zechariah 9:5, 5-11). The Old Fathers passed on to their sons and grandsons this dread of women who are beyond the control of righteous men. Patricia remarks with a certain amount of cynicism that the biblical Zechariah's visions "would fit nicely for Zechariah Morgan," including that of "the women stuffed into a basket with a lid of lead and hidden away in a house" (*Paradise* 192).

Influenced strongly by this ideological inheritance, Ruby's leading men develop a very contradictory notion of women. Before the background of their biologistic definition of race they see women as sacred vessels that carry future generations of racially pure individuals, whereas in their patriarchal understanding of society they see them as the weak link in the 8-rock chain, always liable to polluting the holy blood they inherited from their fathers in their potential alliances with racially impure men. Thus, women are regarded as epitomes of the racial purity of their town, but also as the most serious threat to it.[58]

---

[57] Morrison remarks that the town of Ruby "has the characteristics, the features of the Old Testament," that "[i]t's patriarchal" and that "[t]he men are very protective of their women, very concerned about their role as leaders" (Verdelle).

[58] Note that the only light-skinned people in Ruby, Patricia Best Cato and Billie Delia Best, are women. Note again, however, that only Black men choose light-

This conflict leaves the female citizens of Ruby with the awkward task of trying to come as close as possible to the visions their men have of them, indeed to fill these visions with life, in order to escape disciplinary measures and live as feely as possible. Storace suggests that the town of Ruby can itself be read as "a kind of ideal woman constructed by men for themselves and their companion women, who are above all responsible for enacting and representing the ideals of men" (66/2).[59] It is these ideals that shape Steward's understanding of Ruby as a place where

> [a] sleepless woman could always rise from her bed, wrap a shawl around her shoulders and sit on the steps in the moonlight. And if she felt like it she could walk out the yard and on down the road. No lamp and no fear. A hiss-crackle from the side of the road would never scare her because whatever it was that made the sound, it wasn't something creeping up on her. Nothing for ninety miles around thought she was prey. She could stroll as slowly as she liked, think of food preparations, war, of family things, or lift her eyes to stars and think of nothing at all. Lampless and without fear she would make her way. (*Paradise* 8)

In the New Fathers' plan for their pure town founded, as they think, at God's behest and according to His commands, the image of ideal Black womanhood plays a prominent role. Fed out of a pastel-colored teenage memory of the Morgan twins of "nineteen Negro ladies" on a summer day in a Black town, this image presents a male utopia that is reflected in the names of some of Ruby's girls: "Hope, Chaste, Lovely and Pure," the "allegorized virtues treasured and codified by men" (Storace 66/2). For Steward, the memory of a group of beautiful, chaste women in a thriving Black town acquires the significance of a god-sent revelation. As such this memory, too, becomes a sacred text, the measuring rod for the entire community, and a vision that has to be defended at all costs.[60] The town's women are expected to live the paternalistic dream scenarios of their husbands, fathers, brothers: They are confined to their roles as wives and mothers, and ignored when it comes to deciding upon the fate of their community. The former expectation is embodied by Miss Mabel and Sweetie Fleetwood, mother-in-law and her daughter-in-law, who are

skinned women as potential partners. None of the 8-rock women has taken a light-skinned man.

[59]Fittingly, the Oven is the townsmen's "symbol of the ideally functioning woman" (Storace 66/3).

[60]Storace likens the zealous New Fathers to "Crusaders for the Cross" (67/1).

engaged in the care of four severely handicapped children. Their "tippy-tappy steps" on the upper floor accompany the men's negotiations about Arnette, but the women themselves are "nowhere in sight" (*Paradise* 61). Patricia sums up the latter characteristic of the fate of Ruby's women: She explains the insolence with which, after sneering at Roger Best's decision to marry a light-skinned woman, Steward dismissed his wife's and his sister-in-law'a admonitions as well as Fairy DuPres' curse with the fact that "they were just women, and what they said was easily ignored by good brave men on their way to *Paradise*" (*Paradise* 201f.).

Ruby's women are revered as 'angels in the house,' with but a slightly larger radius of movement allowed to them than to their Victorian sisters: Their "house" is the town within which they move unmolested as long as they go about their womanly duties. Any venturing outside the confines of Ruby on private business – into the Convent as the only neighbor of Ruby, for example – is frowned upon. Lone DuPres' visits there feed a festering suspicion against her; Deek Morgan sees in his wife Soan's friendship with Connie the source of a growing distance between Soan and himself; Arnette's and Sweetie's voluntary stays with the women are deliberately misinterpreted as forced imprisonment; Billie Delia's flight there is understood to be the first step toward her complete estrangement from her home town. Furthermore, besides having to cope with restricted mobility, the sleepless woman in Steward's vision is also a silenced woman: If she disagrees with her brothers, fathers, or husbands at all she will do so only in the privacy of her own mind, never openly. In a figurative sense that highlights the unworldliness of Steward's vision these women are indeed "lampless," as they remain unenlightened and un-emancipated through their acquiescence in the narrow corsage of housewifery.

For the image of the virtuous and saint-like Black woman to unfold its full power in the *Weltanschauung* of the Morgan brothers, the counter-image of the "loose woman" as source of corruption and moral decay must be constructed. Indeed, as Patricia Storace remarks, "Steward's moral world actually requires prostitution, without which virtue cannot be identified nor recognized" (68/2). Inside the town, the image of Patricia's daughter Billie Delia, who in the context of Ruby is burdened with the light skin of her mother and grandmother, is moulded to fit that of a prostitute. The 8-rock families readily interpret the lightness of her skin as a signal of deficient morality, as a perversity believed to be inherent in racial impurity. From the age of three, when Billie Delia innocently pulled down her Sunday knickers before she climbed on a horse's back, she is accused of licentiousness and sexual irresponsibility, becoming the very symbol of uncontrolled female wickedness that potentially threatens the town. Patricia, who "ever since Billie Delia was an infant, [...] thought of her as a liability, somehow" (*Paradise* 203), joins in ostracizing her own daughter by believing the unfounded rumors and brutally punishing her for a behavior of which she has never been guilty. Faced with such uniform disapproval in her home town, Billie Delia seeks refuge at the Convent and later moves to a larger town. After her departure from Ruby, the symbolic function of this young woman as "the purely imaginary threat [...] to the community" passes on to the five women in the old mansion outside the town (Storace 67/2), women who also do not meet the norms for female virtue and goodness reigning in town.

Steward's conviction that the women of Ruby are able to move in their home town "without fear" is a telling example for the discrepancy between this leader's paternalistic assumptions about lives of peace and harmony available to everyone in this all-Black paradise and the women's actual situation whose precariousness he fails to grasp. Those who disagree openly with the rules, orders and viewpoints disseminated and enforced by the New Fathers are silenced or silence themselves through social exclusion. Patricia Best burns her research papers after discovering the racism governing social interaction among the citizens of Ruby – herself included – and with larger society, thus destroying even this secret channel of self-expression and autonomous opinion she has created for herself. Billie Delia leaves Ruby and becomes a distanced and bitter observer of her home community. People who forbid themselves any complaint – like Sweetie Fleetwood, who devotes her life to the care of her four handicapped children or Soan Morgan, who lives with the knowledge of her husband's affair with Consolata and her own heavy conscience over the loss of her two sons and her foetus – live with the risk of falling into depression and emotional and mental illness. Stereotypical Victorian 'female illnesses' thus correspond with the Victorian-style social roles assigned to women by their men.

Thus, the new founding fathers' protectiveness renders the safe haven they intended for their families a prison in which they are rendered powerless and excluded from the rest of the United States. Finally, the men's protective impulse turns aggressive, and what had remained a violent threat against the youngsters during the Oven debate, is transformed into bloody reality against the unarmed women at the Convent by Steward and his accomplices. According to Reverend Misner's analysis the attackers

> think they have outfoxed the whiteman when in fact they imitate him. They think they are protecting their wives and children, when in act they are maiming them. And when the maimed children ask for help, they look elsewhere for the cause. [...] Unbridled by Scripture, deafened by the roar of its own history, Ruby, it seemed to him, was an unnecessary failure. (*Paradise* 306)

From all the character in the novel Morrison expresses the greatest affinity to Richard Misner, who, she says, "is closest to my own sensibility about moral problems. [...] He is struggling mightily with the tenets of his religion, the pressures of the civil rights, the dissolution of the civil rights [...] [a]nd the young" (Jaffrey). Misner's words can therefore be read as the author's verdict on the actions of the New Fathers.

4.2.4   The Essentialism of the Race House

After the publication of *Paradise* Morrison explained in an interview:

> I pursued the question why honest people can work themselves into a state of seeing in a stranger only an enemy that must be killed. This is basically the essence of war. And surprisingly this readiness to kill has a lot to do with the idea of a paradisiac state of being. (Scheck)[61]

Patricia's disillusioned analysis of the killings at the Convent, stubbornly upheld against a number of conflicting accounts of the raid circulating in the town that seek to exonerate one or the other person involved, is the short version of Morrison's answer to this question. It sums up the cornerstones of the social order installed by the New Fathers:

> [N]ine 8-rocks murdered five harmless women *(a)* because the women were impure (not 8-rock); *(b)* because the women were unholy (fornicators at the least, abortionists at most); and *(c)* because they could – which was what being an 8-rock meant to them and was also what the "deal" required. (*Paradise* 297)

---

[61] "Ich bin der Frage nachgegangen, warum rechtschaffene Menschen sich in einen Zustand hineinsteigern können, der sie im Fremden nur noch den Feind sehen lässt, den es zu töten gilt. Das ist im Grunde die Essenz des Krieges. Und überraschenderweise hat diese Bereitschaft zum Töten sehr viel mit der Idee eines paradiesischen Zustands zu tun."

In exclusivist Ruby the hegemony of pure blackness reigns almost unchallenged, marking individuals of mixed racial background as lesser beings and those indifferent to lineage, let alone to purity of race, as blasphemers who must be eliminated for the good of the pure. Racial essentialism is supplemented by an ideology that assumes the existence of pure, virtuous womanhood and demands female members of the society to submit to the strictures of demureness and self-sacrifice. The prize for female purity is the same as for the purity of race: the attributes of holiness and sanctity. Religion in its institutionalized variant thus is used to disguise the schemes of power-hungry despots, men "whose power to control was out of control" (*Paradise* 308), as devout executions of divine commandments and eschatological designs. However, although much of what the Morgan twins think and do is motivated by their desire to shore up their prominent position in their hometown, I am not suggesting that the abuse of religion I describe here is committed by them quite consciously and with the intention to oppress or harm their fellow-citizens. Rather, the New Fathers turn to patriarchal religion – as did their own fathers – in order to explain and justify actions of whose necessity they have convinced themselves. Whether they argue in favor of the old Oven motto or promote and lead the attack on the Convent, they feel themselves to be tools in God's hand. Robed in the garments of religion, essential blackness and essential womanhood therefore both assume the status of holiness. The purest are the most powerful not only because they may adorn themselves with the most virtuous partners, but also because they are surrounded with the attributes of saintliness. Thus, because of its religious undertones, the "deal" the New Fathers struck with their God rewards racial purity with status and power – power, that is, over the lives of others.

A society that systematically reinforces the primacy of sameness with the aim to forge a monolithic and static group identity based on race perceives difference and heterogeneity as threats to its very core and essence. Therefore it will not tolerate it. As Soane Morgan remarks to her sister Dovey with reference to a possible massacre of the five women in the Convent, being different "[has] been enough before" to motivate oppression and violent expulsion from the community (*Paradise* 288). In the interest of constructing a uniform racial identity which they believe to be the precondition for the survival of the group, Ruby's leaders turn personal and communal history into myth and limit its possibilities of interpretations to one dogma. They curtail individual self-expression through rigid gender roles and forced allegiances in town and hamper the development of the community by prescribing inbreeding and restricting contacts with the outside world.

Over the years and in reaction to centuries of racist politics in the United States, a town whose existence was informed by the legitimate desire for freedom and safety of its founders who had been imprisoned by slavery and racism has itself deteriorated into the "windowless prison," "a thick-walled, impenetrable container from which no cry could be heard," against which Morrison warns ("Home" 4). In *Paradise* the author presents essentialized racial identity and, in this specific case, pure blackness as constructs with a tremendous and deadly potential to restrict the development of individuals as well as communities.

4.3   The Convent: Race Unmattered in a Heterogeneous Social Space

The Convent, a former Catholic school for Native American girls now inhabited by women who drifted in there over the years on their flight from abandonment and mistreatment, has at times reductively been read as the Other of Ruby, juxtaposed to the town as its polar opposite.[62] Schur, for example, holds that "[t]he story of the Convent [...] offers a counter-history to that of the town" (282), and Dalsgård regards the narrative of the Convent as a counter discourse to the Ruby master narrative, as Morrison's ideal alternative to African American exceptionalism. The only neighbor of the all-Black town has also been interpreted as part of a problematic binary Morrison develops as an structuring principle of her novel: While Ruby is patriarchally organized and run along strictly conservative moral guidelines, the Convent is female-dominated and exhibits comparatively liberal ethics. The town has neither a diner nor a motel and systematically keeps out anybody whom it considers racially impure, whereas the Convent community does not care about purity and is hospitably inclusive. Finally, the all-female community becomes the innocent victim of an aggressive assault by righteous Ruby men.[63]

---

[62]Cf. for example B. Allen, Donahue.

[63]Cf. especially Kakutani. This critique is countered among others by Messmer who observes that "[t]hrowing into relief the problematics of absolute binaries and clear-cut dichotomies in general, the Convent [...] at no point becomes

There is some truth in this; with regard to Ruby the constellation of opposites is part of a familiar thematic interest of the author's of which Barbara Christian reminds us: "The question as to whether communities are defined by and are held together by those designated as outlaws, as pariahs – as to whether in order to have a 'we,' there must be a 'they' – is a perennial one in [Morrison's] work" ("The Past" 415). However, I want to argue that to stop there and be content with a reading of the Convent community as a mere tool employed in order to illustrate better what is going on in Ruby would mean to agree – at least partly – with the accusation leveled at Morrison that *Paradise* works with schematic binaries and presents complex issues in an over-simplified generalized manner.[64]

Instead, I propose an analysis of the Convent that on the one hand investigates the history and evolution of this community for its own sake, as that of a model community, so to speak, with which Morrison envisions an example for a home free of hierarchization and exclusion on the basis of race. On the other hand, my analysis will honor the interaction between the Convent as a representative of a racial home and Ruby as the epitome of what Morrison calls the "race house," their interwoven histories and interdependent existence in a fictional version of racialized US-American society. With visitors and refugees from the town moving in and out of the Convent, the fate of this community is inseparably linked with the occurrences in Ruby and the history of the town. In turn it exerts a strong influence on the present and future of its neighbor. I suggest a break with the ideal of a polar opposition between "self" and "other" that is created and maintained by the elders of Ruby with regard to the outside world in general and to their neighbor in particular, an opposition that some reviewers of the novel seem to reproduce. At the same time, by moving the Convent from the position of a prop or second to Ruby to that of one of two leading protagonists in the novel, I want to give this fictional social space the attention I believe it is due. A close analysis of the community of women in the old mansion promises insights in Morrison's vision of "race unmattered" and the novel's contribution to the debates on the position of the concepts of race and racial difference as well as their intersections with gender in contemporary US-American society.

---

a one-dimensional antithesis to Ruby" (233). I also hope to develop a more differentiated reading of the Convent in the following.

[64] See again Kakutani, Bent, also Klinghoffer.

Starting with the working assumption that with the Convent Morrison has created a social space where race is "unmattered," my analysis of the community is governed by the questions of how she achieves this, and what impulses her readers receive for their own critical participation in the discourse on race and a conscious engagement with the idea of an inclusive, transdifferent community. One of the characteristics of the notion of racial difference that Morrison explores in "Recitatif" is its capacity to eclipse other levels of social interaction and other, equally important experiences that contribute to processes of identity formation. This insight provides the background for my discussion of the Convent and analyses of individual and social characteristics as well as specific interactive constellations that move into view when race is "unmattered." I suggest that by exploring the history of the Convent community, its spiritual life, its composition in terms of the social, economic, gender, and racial backgrounds of its members and their individual experiences an understanding of Morrison's notion of a racial home can be achieved.

4.3.1   The Convent as a Contact Zone

During the roughly fifty years of its existence, the mansion known as the Convent repeatedly and radically changes its purpose and character.[65] The great house begins its existence in the early 1920s, as an "embezzler's folly" adorned with pornographic pictures, marble figurines, and bathroom fixtures, in which pleasure-seeking men indulge themselves with abundantly available "food, sex and toys" (*Paradise* 3, 71). About ten years later, a pious benefactress, as if to utterly wipe out what she regards as its morally objectionable origins, converts the building into "CHRIST THE KING SCHOOL FOR NATIVE GIRLS" (*Paradise* 224). A boarding school for Arapaho girls is founded to "bring God and language to natives who were assumed to have neither" (*Paradise* 226); it is run by

---

[65]Dalsgård speaks of the Convent's perpetual indefinability which she links to Cixous's definition of the feminine other as that which perpetually escapes definition. However, she goes on to argue that Morrison is satisfied with marking this indefinability and does not assign any other textual function to the women than that of a "destabilizing supplement [to the narratives of the people of Ruby] with no distinct identity of their own" (244/2). This is the kind of reading of the Convent I want to challenge with my discussion.

Roman Catholic nuns. After the demise of the school and years of languishing without aim and purpose, the Convent evolves into an ad-hoc refuge, something that Morrison in an interview called a "crash pad" for traumatized young women and occasional visitors from neighboring Ruby (Farnsworth). Another decade later it enters its last and most short-lived state of being, as it finally becomes home for its residents.[66] These are Connie, formerly a servant to the nuns and factotum in the school, and four young women who had arrived there independently of one another over a period of eight years: Mavis, Grace who calls herself Gigi, Seneca, and Pallas.

Remarkably, at none of the stages of its existence has the Convent kept the promise that its exterior, the statement of purpose of its management, or the names given to it seem to make. Thus, the embezzler who designed the mansion shaped it "like a live cartridge" (*Paradise* 70). It was to guarantee him maximum security from his persecutors so as to allow him to enjoy the fruits of his illegal activities in comfort and leisure. The embezzler's plan fails miserably as his stronghold turns into a trap that closes on him when "northern lawmen" find him already after the first grand party he organized there (*Paradise* 70).

The Sisters of the Sacred Cross who take over the deserted building do so with the intention of setting up an "asylum/boarding school for Indian girls" in it (*Paradise* 223f.).[67] Yet, under the colonialist agenda of its pious sponsor the school turns out to be a place where "stilled Arapaho" pupils "learn to forget" their cultural heritage (*Paradise* 10), to unlearn it, as it were, in order to vacate their minds and also their hearts for what the nuns assume to be a culture of superior value, consisting of the English language, Judeo-Christian religion, and of Anglo-American history

---

[66]Matus suggests that Morrison's creation of the Convent community was inspired by "a book of photographs, *Ghost Towns of Oklahoma*," that 'scarcely mention[ed] any of the black ones, but it did include one that was all-female'" (Morrison qtd. in Matus 192, fn. 9).

[67]As will be explicated further within this subchapter, there are numerous references to Native Americans, their land, their fate in Oklahoma, and their interaction with non-Native settlers throughout the novel. They form a significant subtext to the stories of Ruby and the Convent.

and art.[68] For the generations of Arapaho girls who go through "Christ the King," the forced assimilation to the cultural standards of the White majority society has dire effects: They are torn out of their indigenous culture and alienated from it and become drop-outs of their new, Western culture.[69] Soon, confronted with dwindling funds, the school is soliciting "wards of the state" whom it considers "wicked, wayward, Indian girls" (*Paradise* 227). Ignorant of the psychological damage done to American Indians in the name of assimilation and education, the nuns complain that year after year the girls they receive for schooling are more unruly and willful, less pliable and docile, less eager to learn what they need to know in order to become good women and trustworthy US-American citizens.[70] Penny and Clarissa, the last remaining pupils in "Christ the King," spend their days plotting their escape from the school, until they succeed.

Ironically, the people of Ruby have never called their only neighbor a "school." They notice first of all that it is a Roman Catholic project run by nuns, and seeing its inhabitants to be all women, they refer to it as "the Convent," continuing to use this name long after there are no nuns left and the place seems void of purpose. Even when some years later young women move there who have nothing in common with nuns safe their gender, it is still "the Convent" for the Rubyites. The mansion carries its given name with some justification only for a short time, namely when it houses a spiritual community of women. Before this community can thrive and give the Convent a new raison d'être, however, it is blasted out of existence.

Throughout its existence the Convent is a space situated at the boundaries of cultures. Günter Lenz, taking up Mary Louise Pratt's concept and applying it to the study of transculturality in the United States, has described such places as cultural "contact zone[s]" in which "the clash, the

---

[68] In their essentialist notions of culture, truth, and virtue the nuns of "Christ the King" share a frame of mind with the men of Ruby. This point is made by Fraile-Marcos.

[69] Thus, they do not enjoy the virtues and privileges of cultural hybridity that Bhabha praises in *The Location of Culture*.

[70] There is a revealing parallel between the nuns' desire to turn "uncultured" Arapaho girls into good American women and the puritan standards of true womanhood that determine the upbringing and education of female citizens in Ruby.

mixing, and the reconstitution of cultures" occurs (469).[71] The girl school set up in the embezzler's mansion unwittingly ends the monocultural, insular status of this formerly clandestine hide-out. It does so by bringing into contact the Roman Catholic religion and Anglo-American culture of the teachers with Native American cultural traditions of the pupils and the African Brazilian background of their servant, Connie. The nuns try to keep the transfer of cultural knowledges strictly one-directional, believing to Americanize their charges in the process and thereby to save them from their supposedly barbaric state of being. They remain utterly insensitive to the multidirectional exchange of cultural influences that occurs despite their efforts at colonization.

With the founding of the town of Ruby, the Convent receives a neighbor in their sparsely populated Oklahoma plain that contributes yet another set of traditions to the inhabitants of the mansion and exerts an important cultural influence on them. The Convent now lies on the road from Ruby to Demby. This next bigger town represents a permanent threat to the citizens of race-conscious all-Black Ruby because of its allegedly corrupting racial "impurity." Due to its location, the Convent represents a "borderland" between what the citizens of the town conceive of as civilization and wilderness – that is: between Ruby and the rest of the world.[72]

---

[71] Pratt defines "contact zones" as "social spaces where disparate cultures meet, clash, and grapple with each other, often in highly asymmetrical relations of domination and subordination [. . .]" (4). She explains further that the term "refer[s] to the space of colonial encounters, the space in which peoples geographically and historically separated come into contact with each other and establish ongoing relations, usually involving conditions of coercion, racial inequality, and intractable conflict" (6). Lenz's use of the term places more emphasis on the interrelation and mutual fertilization of cultures in contact zones than on the asymmetrical relations between cultures during colonial encounters. In my application of the concept of the "contact zone" to the Convent I therefore follow Lenz.

[72] The term "borderland" goes back to Gloria Anzaldúa's *Borderlands/La Frontera* (1987), in which Anzaldúa describes the border region between Mexico and Texas as an unstable cultural and political space inhabited and shaped by people who grew up in two or three interdependent and at times competing cultural traditions. It has been taken up by postcolonial and feminist scholars and used by writers and critics from marginalized groups in border discourses that focus on the inherently heterogeneous, intercultural, and unstable character of cultures. See also Lenz 74f.

The history of interaction between the Convent and the town commences as soon as the settlers begin with the construction of their settlement. While the nuns use the commercial facilities of Ruby, the townspeople travel to the mansion for bread, vegetables, its famed black peppers, and the barbecue sauce made from it. With Connie staying in charge of food, these commercial contacts survive the demise of "Christ the King" and are extended into the last phase of the Convent's history, a phase that is characterized by the influx of individuals with very different social and cultural backgrounds who are strangers to each other.

Morrison supplies a tight web of details about each of the women who arrive at the Convent to live there for different lengths of time. They form a heterogeneous social group that increasingly comes to reflect the multiple cultural identities that characterize a contact zone. "Culture" here represents an umbrella concept that feeds from and combines different interdependent identities. For instance, there is a considerable age-span among the women, the approximately sixty year-old Connie being the oldest, followed by Mavis who, as a mother of five, is probably in her thirties. Gigi and Seneca could be in their late teens or early twenties, while Pallas at sixteen is the youngest of the women.

Apart from their ages, the socio-economic situations and educational or cultural backgrounds of the inhabitants of the Convent also vary considerably. While Pallas is the daughter of a successful manager in the music business, the other women grew up in different degrees of poverty: Connie spent the first nine years of her life on the streets of Rio de Janeiro; Mavis tried to raise a large family in a run-down neighborhood on the outskirts of a small town, where, in the face of the peeling paint and the sagging porch of their small house, the pompous Cadillac of her husband is greeted by the neighbors with ridicule and incomprehension. Seneca grew up in a dilapidated housing project with her teenaged mother; she spent years in different foster families before she was transferred into shelters. Gigi, abandoned by her mother and with her father on death row, was raised by her grandfather in a trailer home.

Although the Convent is a community of women, there are instances in the novel when the mansion becomes a contact zone of genders. These contacts play a crucial part in the fate of the Convent. In the summer and fall of 1954, Consolata has a passionate love affair with Deacon Morgan, one of the self-named New Fathers of Ruby. Many years later another, ill-fated affair unfolds between Gigi and K.D. Morgan Smith, the young heir of the Morgan dynasty. In contrast to his uncle Deacon, K.D. visits his lover in the old mansion. Furthermore, Menus Jury spends some weeks with the women in an – ultimately futile – effort to control his alcoholism. And finally, Connie is visited by a mysterious stranger. This brief encounter with a male being, be he person, spirit, or god, acquires great importance for the community of women as it causes Connie's emotional and spiritual conversion.

On the level of social interaction the Convent as contact zone is a temporary safe haven, especially for women "migrating" from Ruby to the old mansion for short periods of time. Lone DuPres, Ruby's aged midwife, recalls that "it was women who walked this road. Only women. Never men. [...] Back and forth, back and forth: crying women, staring women, scowling, lip-biting women or women just plain lost" (*Paradise* 270). Soan Morgan walks to the Convent to confront Consolata, her rival to the love of her husband, and later on becomes fast friends with her. Soan regularly receives herbal potions from her friend that make bearable her feeling of light-headedness and nausea after her two sons fell in Vietnam.[73] Billie Delia Best flees to the women after a row with her mother that leaves her badly beaten and emotionally devastated. Fifteen year-old Arnette Fleetwood travels to the Convent after finding out that she is pregnant and receiving a beating from her boyfriend. She wrongly assumes that the women would help her abort her unwanted child. Years later, Sweetie Fleetwood wanders into the Convent during a blizzard in a state of extreme exhaustion and confusion caused by the endless nurturing she gives her four severely handicapped children. Although Sweetie accuses the Convent women of witchcraft after her return to Ruby, she unconsciously chose the mansion as a refuge at a time of acute distress. Lone DuPres purposely does not include Deacon, Menus, and K.D. in her list of migrants to the Convent because, although these men also spend time there or, in Deacon's and K.D.'s cases, with its inhabitants, they invariably drive the twelve mile distance between Ruby and the mansion in their cars.

The Convent also is a racial contact zone, as it houses individuals of divers racial identities. After it was confiscated from the embezzler it was

---

[73] For a more detailed exploration of the connection between contact zones and healing see Elia, Chapter 5: "'Under the Weight of Memory and Music:' Contact Zones and Healing in Toni Morrison's *Song of Solomon* and *Paradise*."

taken over by White American nuns. The people of Ruby label one of the women who drift into the Convent between the late 1960s and mid-1970s "white," and the nuns described Connie's ethnic identity vaguely as "certainly not white" (*Paradise* 223). Since the race-conscious Rubyites do not comment on any other person's deviance from their norm of blackness, we can assume that they regard three of the women as black. Furthermore, the land on which the Convent stands originally belonged to Native Americans of the so-called Five Civilized Tribes.[74] Until funds dry up in the mid 1950s, Arapaho pupils are taught at the Convent, girls of whom we learn that their resistance to the Catholic doctrine and to the values of the US-American variety of Western culture is growing steadily, to the point where the last two of the girls escape on their way to a different state boarding school.[75] Morrison's choice of the Arapaho can be read as a very deliberate one: The colors of the flag of the Arapaho nation are red, white, and black; red indicates that the Arapaho see themselves as human beings, white stands for long life, and black symbolizing happiness (cf. Segar). Thus, in the course of its existence the Convent houses individuals of (South) American Indian, European American, and African American ancestry – people who in racialized Western societies would be classified as "red," "white," and "black."

4.3.2   The Role of Religion at the Convent

As I argued earlier, religion provides the frame of reference for much of the social interaction among the residents of Ruby, most pointedly for the construction of an exclusive, separatist community based on essentialist notions of race and gender, as well as a prescriptive approach to individ-

---

[74]Until 1907, when Oklahoma joined the Union as the 46th state, it was called "Indian Territory" and was set aside for the Cherokee, Choctaw, Chickasaw, Seminole, and Creek who had been "relocated" to the Midwest from their original homes in the Southeast. In six "land-runs" from 1889 until 1895, however, the territory was appropriated by non-Native settlers from the North American East Coast, from Germany, Ireland, Poland and other Slavic countries, as well as by freed slaves and their descendants. See "Oklahoma's History."

[75]The Arapaho (Inuna Ina) belong to the Plains Tribes and are closely related to the Southern Cheyenne. They are strongly religious and adhere to their religious practices, the most widely known of which are sun dancing and the procession of the pipe-bearer (cf. Segar).

ual spirituality. In the Convent, a "wilderness of women abused, confused, drifted together" (Wilt), religion also plays a significant role. But in contrast to Ruby, religion here contributes to and is an example of a general inclusiveness that defines this community. Among the Convent women, I want to suggest, religion is not the vehicle for racial purity but for the embrace and creative appropriation of difference.

4.3.2.1 Roman Catholicism and the Pauline Dogma

For more than fifty years Consolata lives as Connie within the teachings of the Catholic Church as they are represented by the nuns who brought her up and, despite her position as a servant, allowed or required her to participate in the routines of their quasi-monastic life. Saved by the nuns from a miserable life of squalor, humiliation, and prostitution, Connie gratefully and fervently embraces both her immediate benefactress, Mary Magna, and the ideology and teachings the nun represents. During these decades, Connie learns to love not only the language in which the nuns conduct their services and address their God, but also the Catholic conception of this God. Furthermore, she adopts their colonialist frame of mind that declares languages and traditions other than the ones championed by the nuns inherently inferior. While the Arapaho pupils at Christ the King feel close to her because "she was stolen, as they had been" from her original culture (*Paradise* 238), Consolata neither seems to have much interest in them nor a lot of patience with them. For the orphaned Brazilian child and young woman, God is a stern but loving father whose commandments she can disobey only at the risk of her own happiness. The nuns' interpretation renders God's love virtually unattainable – especially for women and for members of ethnic minorities.[76]

Of the convictions with which Mary Magna leaves Consolata, two prove the most troubling for her. The first, which goes back to Saint Paul, is the dogma of the division between body and soul and the primacy of the spiritual over the physical. The former servant to the nuns sums up these teachings in the doctrine of "my body is nothing my spirit everything" (*Paradise* 263). This entails the Pauline "truth" that women, who are pri-

---

[76]In principle, the theological beliefs of the nuns are very similar to those of Reverend Pulliam, the Puritan-minded fire-and-brimstone preacher and direct opponent of Richard Misner in Ruby.

marily regarded as bodily beings, must suppress and learn to scorn their physical bodies because they are the channels through which sin entered the world. In order to prevent the continuing unhindered entry of sin into human society, women must strive to become nurturing, docile, and asexual beings like the Virgin Mary. To achieve this they must expel anything from their personality that would render them "tempting Eves": physical beauty, a public presence that would draw attention to itself, sexual desire – basically any kind of sexuality.

When Consolata meets Deacon Morgan at the age of thirty-nine and experiences her sexual awakening with physical and emotional love the like of which she had never felt before, she knows that she places herself outside the teachings of the Catholic Church represented through the Mother Superior. Convinced that she has severed herself from the love of God, Consolata interprets the abrupt end of her love affair and her corresponding misery as the just punishment for her sinful behavior.

The second burden, with which the Mother Superior continues to oppress Consolata long after she had died, is a deep suspicion of spiritual gifts, be it in the shape of an intimate harmony with nature or of the ability to see inside a human mind or body. She is appalled when she discovers that she has the power to strengthen a person's will to live, to invigorate fading energies in his or her moments of dying. When Consolata uses this gift to prolong Mary Magna's life, the teachings of the Catholic Church place her in an insoluble psychological tension that robs her of self-respect and all will of life and condemns her to a slug-like existence in the cellar of the Convent. In order to save the life of the one human being who loves her, the only mother she ever knew and whom she loves more than herself, she has to disregard everything this woman lived for. After Mother's death, therefore, Consolata is convinced of her utter worthlessness and feels certain that both the Mother Superior and God Father have ceased to love her – that once more she is orphaned. Only when she emancipates herself from the powerful mother figure and thus from the doctrinal teachings of the Catholic Church after the visit of an enigmatic stranger, Consolata is able to embrace the gifts she knew she has but dreaded to use.

4.3.2.2   Loss Unacknowledged and Unmourned

The Convent women belong to different generations and come from different social, racial, and socio-economic backgrounds. Yet, they share two characteristics: They are all women, and each of them is deeply and multiply traumatized. The traumas these women suffered in their past continue to shape their present reality as well as their outlook on the future. None of them has a clear idea of what she is going to do or become, or where she will go in the future; they all "drift," as Connie says, adopting the contemptuous terminology with which the nuns refer to the Arapaho girls in their charge.

For a considerable time, the five women remain unable to acknowledge their emotional injuries and to confront them actively. The old mansion they chance upon in their panicky flights from their pasts grants them respite. It is too remote to attract the attention of actual or potential pursuers, too isolated for any of the big and smaller national events of the 1970s to register there, and Connie, their hostess, is too concerned with her own grief as well being as too uninquisitive and too bored by the repetitive stories of their plights to press them for information. Unable to leave their haunting pasts behind them, the women allow their traumas to torment them. Mavis indulges in dreams of self-sacrifice; she imagines a parallel reality in which she watches her twin babies, whose accidental deaths by suffocation she did not or could not prevent, grow older, believing that now she protects them from potential dangers and hearing their laughter ring through the rooms of the old house. Seneca blames herself for having encouraged her various abusers and tries to still the self-hatred she feels by slicing the skin of her arms and thighs.[77] Gigi tries sex as a

----

[77] The names Morrison chooses for her protagonists often contribute to characterizing them. The name Seneca brings to mind the Roman philosopher Lucius Annaeus Seneca, c. 3 BCE-AD 65, an adviser of the emperor Nero, author of the nine so-called Senecan Tragedies, and a philosopher of the school of stoicism. One of the central doctrines of the stoics was the acceptance of the role one has been assigned by fate and therefore had to play, an attitude that in its most defeatist version is characteristic for the young Convent woman who bears Seneca's name. After falling out of favor with Nero, the philosopher Seneca committed suicide by opening his veins. His honorable image is marred by the accusation of hypocrisy leveled against him because of the contrast between his stoic beliefs in and teachings of the virtues of living a simple life and the great

tool to banish the image of a bleeding boy from her consciousness whose violent death she failed to avert and as a substitute for the deep love she is looking for. This strategy leads her into self-destructive, unsatisfactory relationships with men and cynical bickering with women. Pallas, who is too terrified to speak when she first reaches the Convent, later on flatly refuses to believe what her body tells her more clearly with every passing day, namely that she is pregnant and will have a baby, either by her faithless boyfriend or as a result of a gang rape she probably endured.[78]

There is no need for Connie to press the young women for information about themselves; after the death of the Mother Superior, the last of the

material wealth he had amassed mainly through lending money at horrendous interest rates (cf. "Lucius Annaeus Seneca"). The woman Seneca slices her skin, seeking to punish herself for allowing others to abuse her. She becomes addicted to this kind of self-punishment, using the slicing as a means to alleviate tension or carry her over a difficult phase in her life – an attitude that carries a slightly hypocritical connotation. Furthermore, and in a very different context, Seneca's name also contributes to the Native American subtext in *Paradise*: The Seneca Nation of Indians belongs to the six tribes of the Iroquois Confederacy which has territories in the State of New York (cf. "Seneca Nation of Indians").

[78] Above I tried to illustrate the double and deconstructed meaning of Seneca's name. For Pallas let the mention of Pallas Athena suffice, favorite daughter of Zeus and the Greek goddess of wisdom, household arts, and crafts, as well as goddess of war and champion of justice and civil law. This name seems oddly inappropriate for a teenager who in her lifetime had but little self-confidence. Gigi's given name, Grace, recalls the three Graces, the beautiful daughters of Zeus and Eurynome and attendants of Aphrodite. They are the personifications of beauty, charm, and grace. With its theological connotation of divine grace this name is also an indicator for the important role of religion in this novel. Mavis is another name for the song thrush, a bird that migrates to Scotland and is greeted there as the harbinger of spring. Mavis in *Paradise* appears at one time shod with her oldest daughter's yellow Wellingtons she had hurriedly put on before she fled and visited her mother, Birdie Goodroe. Othow suggests that Mavis also means Ma-Vis, "mother of life" (368), a rather free interpretation which I do not see corroborated by Mavis's story. The names Steward and Deacon connote leadership and the management of money. The issue of naming is important to all of Morrison's novels; it illustrates her claim to and concern with the often denied power of (African American) individuals and communities to define, to own, and to control their realities. In *Paradise* the author at times subverts the meaning of a particular name and sometimes she creates protagonists who are caricatures of the properties or faculties their names evoke.

nuns who once ruled "Christ the King," one by one they visit their hostess in her little chamber in the wine-cellar of the mansion to tell her about the events that will not leave them in peace. Believing Connie to be a "sweet, unthreatening old lady who seemed to love each of them best; who never criticized, who shared everything but needed little or no care" (*Paradise* 262), they burden her with their stories at a time when in fact Connie herself moves deeper and deeper into self-loathing, hopelessness, and powerless rage.

O'Reilly describes the Convent as "a place of maternal nurturance" (164). I agree with her in principle, but I want to argue for a clear distinction between the Convent before the visit of the apple-eyed stranger and after the visit. This is necessary because of the pointed difference in the extent of nurturing that the women receive and give each other before and after this event. While the mansion is at all times relatively more safe and peaceful for the Convent women than the places they fled, it is not free of conflict and fights between its inhabitants until the conversion of Consolata. Likewise, Consolata is not the grandmotherly, warm-hearted old woman her guests think her to be. Before she is sought out by her visitor she at times harbors very unfriendly feelings toward them. Like her lodgers, Connie has become obsessed with her past, and like the younger women she is unable to extricate herself from this obsession by reflecting upon that which she lost and acknowledging her losses.[79] Consolata does not consciously acknowledge the fact that she lost her – undoubtedly miserable – home when the nuns picked her up, "kidnapped" her from filth, deprivation, and abuse in the streets of a Brazilian city and brought her to Oklahoma when she was nine years old (cf. *Paradise* 223). For most of the time span covered in the novel, she searches for a home, and it is a spark of recognition and memory of her childhood home that attracts her to the people of Ruby. She enthuses about Latin, "the gorgeous language made especially for talking to heaven" the nuns taught her (*Paradise* 224f.), denying the loss of her own mother tongue.[80] She despises

---

[79] Clewell sees a strong parallel between the Convent women and the leaders of Ruby in their shared inability to face their losses and allow themselves to mourn them (cf. 137).

[80] I disagree with Schur who argues that Morrison "links this loss of language with gaining special, magical abilities" and thus "[foregoes] essentialist theories of identities" (290 f.). Morrison does not idealize the state of homelessness in which Connie exists before she reclaims her identity as Consolata Sosa, nor

herself for having engaged in physical love-making and at the same time blames herself for the abrupt end of her one love affair, unable to allow herself to grieve over the terrible emptiness in her heart that results from the break-up. After the death of Mary Magna, Connie refuses to face the loss of the only mother she ever knew.[81] Furthermore, she poisons her mourning with self-accusations over having kept the old woman alive against her wishes and in violation of the laws of the Church.

Pallas likewise denies the fact that she lost her mother's love and attention, and she tries to banish from her mind any thought of her spoiled childhood and her unfaithful lover. Mavis does not accept that her twins are dead and that she also lost influence over her other children, as she is searched for with a police warrant after escaping from her abusive husband. Seneca denies that her young mother abandoned her, thereby exposed her to the vulnerable existence of an orphan; she does not confront or rebel against the violence that was perpetrated against her by people who ought to have protected her but who instead took advantage of her vulnerability. Finally, Gigi, trying to stay in control of her emotions, fails to embrace her un-assuaged hunger for the loving attention her parents withheld from her.[82] She does not acknowledge the violation she herself suffered when she was forced to witness the killing of a young boy during a civil rights march, helpless in the face of police brutality.

---

does she romanticize Lone DuPres' history as an orphan and outsider in Ruby. Indeed, the driving force behind Consolata's attraction to Deacon is her wish "to go home" (*Paradise* 240), and Lone strongly identifies with the community, regardless of the fact that she is marginalized by it. While it is true that *Paradise* explores the dangers of essentialist notions of identity, it leaves no doubt about the indispensability of a home, proposing, however, that such a home may rest on a multifaceted, heterogeneous identity.

[81] Higgins sees in Mary Magna a "mother-goddess [...] many of whom were worshipped in pagan religions in Africa" who "becomes the safe haven for displaced and abandoned women" in the Convent (132). This reading is influenced by the passages in *Paradise* that narrate Connie's worshipful admiration and love for the Mother Superior. However, in my opinion it confuses paternalistic authority with selfless charity, and misunderstands as divine light of love the light that emanates from the dying old woman because Connie infuses her with her energy through the practice of "seeing in." Higgins is right in stating that through Connie "more links to paganism are revealed," but Consolata does not inherit her "pagan" powers from Mary Magna, as Higgins seems to suggest (132).

[82] Fultz suggests that Gigi had an incestuous relationship with her father (cf. 85).

Cut loose from the social connections that ought to have given them the support they need in times of crisis, bewildered by the succession of horrible events that shattered their confidence in their future as well as their trust in their fellow human beings, and filled with a smouldering self-hate the Convent women see no purpose in their lives – past, present, or future. Connie's desolation after Mary Magna's death points to another grave handicap of the Convent women: They have "no ancestral figures to turn to" in search for counseling, support, and guidance (Christian, "The Past": 422). Convinced that by prolonging the life of Mother Superior by means that the Catholic Church had taught her to regard as witchcraft and devilment she has forfeited not only the affection of her beloved teacher but also the love of her God, Connie virtually buries herself in the cellar, hoping from day to day that God will let her die. During this period, which spans the gratest part of the young women's residence in the mansion, the Convent allows them a time of respite from the gruesome realities of their lives. But throughout that time they continue to be haunted by their memories from a hellish past which sully their temporary safe haven. With the exception of Mavis, who wants to stay where she believes her twins to be, every one of Connie's guests incessantly devises plans of how to leave the Convent and try to build a better life for herself. Yet, they never get beyond the stage of part hopeful, part frustrating dreaming, planning, and plotting, because they cannot muster enough energy to leave their refuge and their reluctant *ersatz* mother. Pallas, the only one who tries to re-join the world outside the Convent, returns to the mansion dejected; she has proved unable to cope with the onslaught of the meaninglessness of her life "outside."

Evidently, for the greatest part of its existence the Convent community is neither harmonious nor particularly hopeful. The traumatic experiences the women bring with them complicate their relationship to a degree that some of the exclusionary tendencies of mainstream society are carried into this sheltered place. In fact, except for short periods of calm and quiet, the women are bickering and fighting among themselves or trying to mediate among the opponents, depending on their character and their ability to tolerate disturbances. Mavis dislikes Gigi so much that she begrudges the newcomer Connie's hospitality and establishes an "us vs. her" dichotomy that seeks to exclude Gigi from the closeness Mavis believes to have established with Connie. Even sweet-tempered Seneca is not immune to unkind feelings toward the person who arrives after her.

She eagerly wishes Pallas away because the girl's harrowing exhibition of psychic wounds make her feel uncomfortable.

The uneasy peace of the Convent community rests on a precarious equilibrium of shared powerlessness and co-dependence among its members. As each of the women congregated in the old mansion is mostly concerned with her own traumatic past and the resulting impasse in her life, none of them poses a threat to the others. However, the strength of the Convent lies in the feature by which it is most lastingly determined and which I described earlier as the characteristics of a contact zone. Because of its general openness toward anybody who happens to stray into the house and its instant, unconditional readiness to help strangers who reach the Convent in times of distress, this disparate community of traumatized, marginalized women is able to transform itself.

4.3.2.3   Spiritual Awakening and Religious Eclecticism

Connie wrenches herself out of the pitiful state of hopelessness and self-disgust after she experiences or hallucinates the visit of a flirtatious stranger. The man carries some of the physical features of herself as a young person: long "tea-colored" hair and "apple-green" eyes like hers that had made Mary Magna "[fall] in love" with the street-child when she first saw her in the South American city (*Paradise* 223) and that thirty years later Deacon compares to mint leaves.

There are several protagonists in the novel who see and communicate with a mysterious stranger. Dovey Morgan also learns to look forward to the chance visits of a friendly young man on the premises of her townhouse. The conversation that commences between the two at their first encounter and all later ones are so full of trust and understanding that the woman comes to think of her visitor as her Friend whom she tells or plans to tell all that is troubling or delighting her. He first appears to Dovey just as a cloud of orange-colored butterflies passes through her backyard. As in other Morrison novels, "a sign," an unusual natural occurrence, announces the advent of a special person or important event. In *The Bluest Eye* for example, "there were no marigolds in the fall of 1941," the time of Pecola's suffering (3), and in *Sula* the heroine's return to Medallion is preceded by a plague of robins (117). Dovey's Friend and Connie's apple-eyed stranger share the realm of Reverend Misner's "companion" (cf. *Paradise* 161) and the walking man of the founding myth of Haven:

They are representatives of divine love whose presence comforts and encourages those who encounter them.

Connie's visitor one evening calls on her when she climbs up from the cellar for a breath of fresh air. By singling her out from the group of women, by addressing her in a fashion that suggests familiarity, warmth of feeling, and a deep interest in her alone, the apple-eyed stranger gives Connie the strength to transform herself: The dispirited Catholic who is frightened of the wrath of her God and suffers from the strictures of the faith the nuns taught her becomes a consciously religious person who draws comfort, energy, and confidence from the spiritual traditions she has encountered and lived with throughout her life. She combines these traditions and channels them into religious practices that are meaningful and life-saving for herself as well as for the other women in the Convent. She reclaims her full name, Consolata Sosa, and takes responsibility for herself and the four young women in her house.

In the unthreatening environment of an all-female community, under the guidance of a mother-like leader who develops a syncretistic religious practice out of the various traditions that shaped her spirituality all five women are enabled to "[confront] their destructive haunting" (Clewell 137).[83] As Clewell points out, "Consolata determines to take an active role in the women's healing, directing a mourning ritual that encourages the women to acknowledge loss and recreate themselves in light of their haunted lives" (138). After Consolata's spiritual awakening, the group of people who have been thrown together by accident becomes a community whose members choose to live there and actively work on forming a home for themselves and each other.

Religious and cultural traditions carried into a place by groups and individuals who settle there do not automatically vanish with the expulsion of these settlers or with their voluntary departure. Acknowledged or unacknowledged, they live on in the bodies of knowledge and in the practices of those who follow after them. Thus, the knowledge and wisdom of the original owners and cultivators of the land on which Haven and Ruby

---

[83] In her analysis of differing strategies of coping with a traumatic past in Ruby and the Convent, Clewell works with the Derridean concept of "hauntology" developed in *Specters of Marx* in which "the figure of haunting" represents "an unequivocal affirmation of alterity [...] that prevents the closure of any totalizing construction of subjectivity or homogeneous social organizations" (132).

were built lives on in the historiography of the Rubyites. Steward Morgan generally seems to pay little attention to the fate of the nations whose territory was distributed among the newcomers in the late nineteenth century, but his rendition of the story of his forebears does record the fact that the Old Fathers traded their labor for their "Promised Land" which then still belonged to "a band of State Indians" (cf. *Paradise* 98f.). Nathan DuPres' dream and his referral to it in his opening address for the annual Christmas pageant in Ruby is another important example for the continuance of the knowledges of one ethnic group in the traditions of another. The wise words of a Cheyenne that "[t]he tallest cotton don't yield the best crop" move Nathan to extending this warning to his fellow citizens (*Paradise* 205). He connects the wisdom of a Native American about the possibility of a bad and bloody harvest from a seemingly good crop with the inexplicable sadness he feels about his own home town and its people. He comes to a conclusion that is astonishing in its clairvoyant but unrecognized accuracy: "I reckon that sighting is like this here story we going to tell again this evening. It shows the strength of our crop if we understand it. But it can break us if we don't. And bloody us too" (*Paradise* 205).

Quite in contrast to Nathan DuPres, the people in Ruby who listen to his respectful reference to Cheyenne wisdom in his address remain deaf to the truths it contains; they fail to see a parallel between the old man's uneasiness, the dreamed words of the Cheyenne, and their community's dangerous course into totalitarian exclusiveness. In contrast to most of the Rubyites, Consolata Sosa has remained sensitive of the knowledges, believes, and traditions with which she has come into contact, incorporating them in her own worldview and way of living. Consolata's spirituality exemplifies her eclectic approach to cultural and spiritual difference: It unites a variety of influences from which originates her idiosyncratic spiritual identity.

Darroch warns of an uncritical usage of the Western construct of religion with reference to non-Western cultures. "Religion" is shaped by the Enlightenment notion of irrationality and powerlessness opposed to the power of rationality and science, and thus "appeals to [. . .] Western imperialism" (205). In postcolonial cultures, and specifically in the writing of Toni Morrison, religion, religious practice, and spirituality carry the potential to empower subjects as well as groups who then use their power to the benefit or detriment of others. It is with this concept of religion in mind that I explore Consolata's religiosity and religious practices at the Convent.

The necessary process of Consolata's emancipation from the nuns' dogmatic Catholicism after the visit of the apple-eyed stranger is facilitated by the traditions of Afro-Brazilian *Candomblé* into which Consolata was born and which represents part of her spiritual background.[84] She lived on the "shit-strewn paths" of her home city until the age of nine, when she was "kidnapped" from the ghetto by American nuns and brought to Oklahoma (*Paradise* 223). Candomblé, which was also known as Batuque before the nineteenth century,[85] is a diasporic, syncretistic religion that has its roots in the Yoruba mythology of Western Africa.[86] It traveled to South America and the Caribbean with the transatlantic slave trade from the mid-1500s until the late nineteenth century.[87] The Brazilian sociologist Abdias do Nascimento defines Candomblé as the

> [r]eligion of the Orixàs, brought from Africa to Brazil by the Slaves. Candomblé is the name of the form practiced in [the state of] Bahia especially; it is used as a general term here. It is predominantly of Yoruba origin but incorporates elements of other African cultures such as Bantu, Ewe and Fon. (212)

In Brazil these West African religious traditions encountered common ideas and practices in the spiritist religions of native Brazilian Indians.[88]

---

[84]In the late 1980, Toni Morrison made a trip to Brazil where she heard the story of "a convent of black nuns who took in abandoned children and practised *candomblé*, an Afro-Brazilian religion. The local populace considered them an outrage and they were murdered by a posse of men" (Matus 192). Although this story later turned out to be untrue, it seems likely that it inspired the creation of the Convent with its violent history in *Paradise*. See also D. Smith.

[85]Both terms may derive from a Bantu language.

[86]On the characteristics of Candomblé as a religion of the African diaspora, see Harding.

[87]In some regions of Brazil, notably in Rio de Janeiro, Candomblé may be called Macumba, even though the latter is also a distinct cult with elements from Vodun and European witchcraft. Candomblé should not be confused with South American Umbanda, Haitian Voodoo, Cuban Santería, and Obeah practices of the Caribbean, all of which developed independently of Candomblé and are of minor importance in Brazil. Cf. "Macumba/Candomblé."

[88]Spiritism is the term used for religious beliefs based on the assumption that the spirit of a human being survives the death of that person. Spiritists believe

Some of these practices, as well as some of the Indian gods who were regarded as the local Orixàs, were incorporated into Candomblé.

Specific strands of Catholicism were also adopted into Candomblé. Brazilian slaves outwardly worshipped under the Catholic faith. They associated their gods with Catholic saints in order to be able to continue to practice their African religion and used *irmandades*, fraternities set up in the eighteenth and nineteenth centuries by the Catholic Church, to hold meetings and slave reunions which were officially forbidden. These brotherhoods were organized along ethnic lines to allow participants to preach the Christian gospel and practice religion in their native languages; their members embraced this offer to practice their African traditions. Thus, the Catholic Church, which persecuted Candomblé as paganism and witchcraft, may have inadvertently helped to develop and spread this religion. Nevertheless, many of the central teachings of Candomblé stand diametrically opposed to those of the Catholic Church. They include the convictions that human beings have both a physical and a spiritual body; that discarnate entities constantly contact the physical world; that humans can learn to contact and incorporate the spirits for the purposes of healing and spiritual evolution.

This discrepancy between the religion of Consolata's childhood and the faith she adopted later in her life very likely contributed to her mental and emotional devastation after the death of her mentor. The friendly visitation of the stranger who claims to know her and is uncannily familiar to her, as if he stepped out of her former life, enables Consolata to re-claim her connection to her native religion and to fuse it with those parts of the traditions and teachings of the nuns that are compatible with it. In the eclectic spirituality of Candomblé lies a new direction for Consolata Sosa and the women in her house.

The cultural and spiritual heritage Consolata received in her childhood in Brazil gives her access to both American Indian and West African spiritual worlds. It also prepares the ground for the admittance of a third religious influence into her spiritual cosmos: African American folk spirituality and religion. Ruby's midwife Lone DuPres passes this tradition

that the spirits of the deceased seek to communicate with the living and can be contacted through mediums, for example in séances. Many African religions have spiritist elements, as do Native American religions. Since the middle of the nineteenth century, spiritism also has a large following in Western, Judeo-Christian societies.

on to Consolata, just like Lone's motherly teacher Fairy had conveyed her spirituality and knowledge to her. In many African traditions as well as the African American tradition the transmission of spiritual gifts from one bearer to another ensures the potency of these gifts for the community. In contrast to Lone, the New Fathers "[have] nothing to say, pass on [about themselves]," as Reverend Misner observes (*Paradise* 161). They have cut themselves off from the African part of their history and tradition. As I will demonstrate in the following section, Lone and Consolata are closely related, both in terms of their spiritual gifts and deeds, and in terms of the social position that results from them.

The French surname of the DuPres's suggests that they might have been among the families that joined the trek of the Old Fathers from Louisiana, where members of the African diaspora had preserved much of their forefathers' religion in the tradition of Vodun/Voodoo (cf. Othow 370). Lone came to the trek as a toddler; like Consolata she was a "stolen [baby]" (*Paradise* 190). Merciful and compassionate Fairy had picked her up by from the doorstep of the hut in which her dead mother lay and had taken her into the care of the group.[89] Consolata's and Lone's first meeting is fraught with symbols of birthing, midwifery, and baptism: When Lone enters the Convent garden in search of one of the nuns Consolata begins to sweat profusely and faints. She experiences the symptoms of her beginning menopause,[90] but her breaking out in sweat recalls Sethe's urgent need to urinate when she first sees Beloved, as if her waters were breaking and she were again giving birth to her daughter (cf. *Beloved*). This particular instance of "breaking of waters" also signifies a birthing, one of a spiritual kind. It is Connie who, as she fully regains consciousness, is covered in water – like a newborn baby. This water has baptismal qualities; the midwife's appearance in her life marks the beginning of Consolata's "practicing," of her new life as a healer and spiritual leader.

---

[89]Wilt points out that the two "stolen children" come to represent the most honorable and valuable qualities of their respective communities – Lone of Ruby and Consolata of the Convent, both under the nuns and when it functions as an ad-hoc shelter for traumatized young women.

[90]In her study of the fate of wise women in the Western world, Barbara Walker states that "the original Crones of the matriarchal community were women past the age of menopause, in whom the blood of life no longer appeared outside the body" (49). Menstrual blood was regarded as wise blood and, if retained within the body, a source of wisdom.

Lone DuPres initiates, baptizes the younger woman into an awareness of divine power within nature, and fosters in her an understanding of her own spiritual powers. Thus, Consolata's first meeting with the midwife is similar in character to the visit of the apple-eyed stranger and has comparable effects. In both instances she encounters a spiritual force gifted with the love of God and capable of passing it on; each time she enters a new phase in her spiritual development and gains access to faculties of healing and teaching that hitherto had been hidden from her.

Lone's faith rests on the belief in an unbreakable union between God's spirit and the spiritual side of life and material creation. When Connie, under the influence of Roman Catholic doctrine, at first refuses to acknowledge and embrace Lone's teachings, the midwife warns her not to separate God from His creation: "You need what we all need: earth, air, water. Don't separate God from His elements. He created it all. You stuck on dividing Him from His works. Don't unbalance His world" (*Paradise* 244). A further cornerstone of Lone's teachings of African American spirituality is the understanding that, first of all, God is a "liberating God. A teacher who [teaches] you how to learn, to see for yourself" (*Paradise* 273), who endows human beings with specific gifts that are meant to be used. Ruby's "wisewoman" encourages the younger woman to accept and apply a specific gift she had noticed in her:[91] to practice what Lone calls "stepping in" and what Consolata – in an effort to legitimize a practice that is uncanny to her – prefers to call "seeing in." It is the gift of reviving people who are dying by focusing one's energy on the "pinpoint of light" in their soul, nursing it back to life. With Lone's encouragement and her admonition not to "[despise] [God's] gift" (*Paradise* 246), Connie is able to save Soan Morgan's son after a road accident, thereby earning Soan's lifelong gratitude and friendship. She also prolongs Mary Magna's

[91] The term 'midwife' is derived from the Anglo-Saxon *med-wyf*, M.E. *mid-wyf* which means literally 'with woman.' Because the old midwives commanded an extraordinary amount of experience with women's bodies and sexuality, with the stages and possible complications of pregnancy, and with the process of giving birth, they were also regarded as 'wise women' or 'wisewomen,' so that the terms 'midwife' and 'wisewoman' could be used synonymously. Barbara G. Walker connects the midwife/wisewoman with the Crone, the old woman who represents the third aspect of the Triple Moon Goddess. Among the many things Lone DuPres shares with the Crone is her desire and ability to teach and mentor other women in order to spread her wisdom to the larger community.

life when the old Mother Superior falls ill. The connection between West African religious thought in the guise of Candomblé and these elementary teachings of the Black Church is a distinct one; it lies in the belief in the unity of spirit and body, of creator and creation.[92]

It is indicative of the exclusivist religious mixture of Puritanism and religious fundamentalism practiced by the New Fathers in Ruby, that Lone is viewed by them with growing suspicion. As a midwife she needs the knowledge of an experienced herbalist: As she smells rain draw near, reads nature's signs expressed in the flight of birds, knows the animals and plants in her environment and what their powers are, she is in touch with nature. Lone is a healer, particularly of women; as she helps to bring babies into the world, she knows about the secret of life. The men of Ruby fear her and are wary of her knowledge, because during the hours of birthing the midwife stands between death and their wives and children. Women in Lone's profession need to be in tune with the innermost thoughts and emotions of those they are called upon to heal. Therefore, if they do not already have it, they must develop the ability to hear the thoughts behind what people say. Lone seems to have been born equipped with this and other extraordinary faculties; already at the age of two she instinctively placed herself in the way of the people who were able and willing to save her life. In her old age, however, she understands this gift to be "another liability" that the men and women of Ruby have come to regard as "a gift from something that, whatever it was, was not God" (*Paradise* 272).

Since the rise to power of the patriarchal Christian Church in the Western world and the destruction of indigenous nature-worshipping, animist religions during the second half of the first millennium after Christ, midwives and wisewomen have moved on a perilously narrow path between veneration as healers and condemnation for practicing witchcraft. Old women in particular, who were in tune with nature and the human psyche, were in danger of being decried as hags and witches, of being marginalized, disempowered, and destroyed. Lone experiences a withdrawal of trust by the men and women of Ruby – and a transferal of that trust to male (White) gynecologists in Demby – when she finds herself literally

---

[92]The status of the body in the teachings and spirituality of the Black Church have long been of interest to Morrison. In *Beloved*, Baby Suggs chooses the love of the God-given body as the main topic of her sermon in the clearing (88f.).

unemployed after the four children in one of the leading families are born with severe physical and mental handicaps. But although she is forced to eke out a living from the sale of medicinal herbs and from donations she receives, although she has to endure the mockery of the mothers who once needed her and the mistrust of the fathers who preferred "a place where other men were in charge instead of some toothless woman" (*Paradise* 272), the old midwife feels a close union with God and creation. She knows herself to be "within His time, not outside it" with everything she ever did and still does (*Paradise* 272). Her deeds include calling on the more moderate in Ruby to save the Convent women, after she eavesdrops on a secret night-time meeting of the New Fathers and understands – "sees" – their murderous intensions.[93] Lone wields God's gifts with the certainty that she is fulfilling God's will. For that reason she sharpens Consolata's perception of nature's bounties and the voices of the human psyche, and encourages her to think of God as a loving, multifaceted, and empowering force.

It is not surprising, therefore, that Ruby's men in power extend their fearful suspicion of the midwife to Consolata, the wisewoman in the Convent, who shares many of Lone's gifts and contributes some of her own to the picture the New Fathers have of her. It is the picture of an old, unfathomable "outside woman" who fends for herself (*Paradise* 279), i.e., without the help of men, but with the help of ungodly powers, whose evil influence stretches not only to the four younger women in the mansion, but also to the impressionable women and young people in Ruby, corrupting and maiming them. Consolata's faculties of healing and spiritual midwifery are misread as destructive powers of evil; the men imagine abortions rather than births taking place in the Convent.

Lone's teachings, the spirituality she passes on to the initially reluctant Consolata, already echo aspects of African religions as they are practiced in Brazil, of Native South American and North American Indian spiritist religions, and of Judeo-Christian religious traditions. After her vision of the apple-eyed stranger the spiritually emancipated Consolata combines these traditions in a religion that is driven by the conviction that the divine expresses itself in creation, including human beings. Her religion explores

[93]Lone's ability to see in the dark and to understand the unspoken thoughts of the men gathered by the Oven further identify her as a close relation of the ancient figure of the Crone. She shares both of these gifts with Consolata.

and fosters the bonds between humans and their natural environment and aims to achieve a state of spiritual purity that culminates in and celebrates the union with God.

The central religious and philosophical idea Consolata teaches the women in her charge is that "[the spirit] is true, like bones. It is good, like bones. One sweet, one bitter. Where is it lost? Hear me, listen. Never break them in two. Never put one over the other. Eve is Mary's mother. Mary is the daughter of Eve" (*Paradise* 263).[94] She renounces the conservative Catholic doctrine that declares the mortal human body inferior to the immortal soul, thereby inducing in believers an estrangement from their bodies and physical needs as well as their spiritual, psychic live. Consolata suffered from the effects of this body-demeaning hierarchy during her affair with Deacon which she tried to keep secret from the nuns, and especially after it had been ended by her lover. The tension she felt then between her physical and emotional needs on the one hand – intimate contact with another human being, an end to her lonely homelessness among stern, distanced nuns and withdrawn Arapaho girls, the excitement of being alive that she senses in the "sha sha sha" of Deacon's movements and which reminds her of the "glittering black people" dancing in the streets of the loud city of her childhood – and the spiritual, bodiless devotion to Christ on the other, filled Consolata with shame and self-contempt. Her horror at her "gobble-gobble love" for "the living man" made her "crawl back," "scuttle back" into the narrow but comfortingly familiar ideological confines of Mary Magna's religious teachings – only to realize with horror that by celebrating physical love she had sullied her soul and offended her Lord (*Paradise* 240).[95]

---

[94] I expressly disagree with Aguiar who suggests that "[u]nlike literary texts that emphasize the union of body and spirit, *Paradise* argues instead for an ultimate *division* of body and spirit" (518/1). In her effort to prove her reading of the Convent women as lifeless but death-denying spirits who are finally released into death by the initially begrudging midwife Consolata (cf. 517/2), Aguiar neglects those – in my view central – passages that celebrate life and convey the Convent women's rejoining of their physical as well as their spiritual selves with the help of Consolata's teachings.

[95] Fraile-Marcos describes Connie's disconsolate attempt to return to the folds of the Church after her disastrous affair with Deacon Morgan as "a 'conversion' by Puritan standards" (25).

The unexpected visitation of the mysterious stranger shakes Consolata out of the slug-like existence into which she has descended. Or should we assume that her dawning realization of the genuine attention and infinitely merciful love of God saved her, or her sudden acknowledgement that she was able and called upon to save Pallas's unborn baby? Morrison leaves the explanation of the nature of this visit to the imagination of her readers. The stranger has very definite human attributes: his long, "fresh" hair, his round eyes of a child, his garments, even his mirror sunglasses. This is a man whose movements, voice, and words have a seductive power over Connie, like those of Deacon Morgan, the "living man" who had once ruled her emotions so completely. On the other hand, there is also something super-natural about this stranger, and this, too, is seductive: He seems to come to her without moving; his voice "lick[s] her cheek" (*Paradise* 252), his language has an almost hypnotic effect on her; and his smile – "like he was having (or expecting) such a good time" – seems utterly infectious (*Paradise* 252). But this flirtatious, god-like man is also like Connie herself, as she was when she was nine and an innocent child and also as she is now in adulthood. He has her hair, her eyes, he speaks the way she does, he wears the aviator-style sunglasses she prefers, and in the course of their short conversation he is giving her the feeling that she too "could move, if she wanted to, without standing up" (*Paradise* 252). Thus, when the visitor claims familiarity with Connie, he reminds her of herself, whom she is in danger of forgetting. When he expresses an interest in her and flirts with her, he demonstrates how loveable and precious a person she is. And Connie laughs, like she has not laughed since her affair with Deacon.

Through the encounter with a stranger who combines features of herself and her former lover with those of God, she understands that through her passionate and very physical love affair with a mortal man she has not betrayed her sincere spiritual love for God. With the realization that love in every guise is God-intended, Consolata acquires a critical distances to the legacy of her beloved and revered teacher, Mary Magna. In consequence, Eve loses the stigma of bringing sin into the world for her inquisitiveness, of burdening all women and men with God's punishment for it in the shape of pain, toils, and death. The union of body and spirit – both of God and god-like – manifests itself in the intimate relationship between mother and daughter.[96] The spiritually awakened Consolata is able to appreciate her human love for the Mother Superior and to forgive herself for prolonging the old nun's life with her gift of seeing in. She recognizes herself as the Eve who lovingly, in a birth-like constellation, released her mother Mary into death, "Eve rescuing Mary to the body as Mary had rescued Eve from the body" (Wilt 288).

4.3.2.4   Religious Rituals at the Convent

Consolata's reconciliation of body and soul enables her to take responsibility not only for herself, but also for the women whose presence in her house used to be loathsome to her and whose traumatic stories had left her unmoved. She devises a therapy for herself and her young housemates that bears the traits of a religious ritual. Not unlike the people of Ruby, the Convent women develop an approach to their traumas that is intensely religious. Yet, it is decidedly more active in character than Geertz' description of suffering as "making sufferable" pain, defeat and trauma with the help of religion implies. It is also less ideologically loaded than Ruby's Christmas pageant. Led by Consolata, they use religion as a way to acknowledge and mourn their own suffering and that of their friends in the Convent, to integrate it into their lives, and to live on – despite of it, even strengthened by it and by the fact that they have overcome it.

The rituals practiced by the Convent women reflect the religious influences that have shaped Consolata's spirituality. They highlight the eclecticism of a faith that delights in the multitude of expressions of religiosity, in the many ideas of the divine that exist in different traditions. Its central, all-important idea is: God is love. The ritualistic preparation of food that heralds the spiritualization of the Convent community after Consolata's spiritual awakening is reminiscent of traditions in Candomblé. The first part of the Candomblé ritual (*toque*) comprises the preparation of gar-

---

[96]Consolata's new or recovered understanding of the divine union of body and soul poses an interesting parallel to stoic teachings: Zeno, the founder of Stoicism, believed in the interconnectedness of all things in the universe. God links everything, because God is the soul of the world; the physical aspects of the world, on the other hand, represent God's "body." Such pan-theistic thoughts are also present in many African as well as American Indian religions. See the connection with Seneca and connotations of this name.

ments, decoration, and food for the second part, a public "mass" and a banquet. Consolata prepares two chickens, the preferred food of the goddess Yemanjá, mother of the orixás.[97] Later in the evening the Convent women gather to eat the food which Consolata lovingly prepared, thus performing the second part of the Candomblé ritual.

Food also plays a major role in the religious life of the Black Church, where church picnics after the Sunday service were and still are common features. The Eucharist-like communal eating of the food, with the four young women sharing the food that Consolata – the founder of their religion, so to speak – has prepared, reminds us of the meals taken together by nuns in any real convent, and of the Lord's Supper itself, both as the original act performed by Jesus and his disciples according to the New Testament and as its repeated re-enactment during mass and services in the Christian Church. It also harks back to the afore-mentioned picnics. The consumption of sacred food in communion with the four young women stills Consolata's "gobble-gobble love" that made her bite Deacon's lip and lick his blood many years back.

After this first *agape* of the community of women,[98] Consolata starts the practice of loud dreaming, a mixture of confessions, free association and conversational therapy developed and used by psychoanalysis, and also of religious testimonials as they are common in Pentecostal churches. During loud dreaming, all of the women are at the same time parishioners and confessors, the one testifying to a religious experience and the congregation witnessing the testimony, client and therapist, as they tell and listen to "half tales and the never dreamed" (*Paradise* 264). During the sessions in the cellar of the Convent, the women speak about traumatic events in their pasts and thereby rid themselves of them. They confide to each other their greatest fears, their dearest memories, and their most trea-

---

[97] Yemaya, from Yey Omo Eju: "Mother Whose Children Are Fish." She is the mother goddess of the Yorùbá people of Nigeria. As the patroness of birth Yemaya is worshipped primarily by women (cf. Took). In Brazil she is addressed as Yemanjá, also Imanje, and worshipped as the mother of all and powerful orixá of the ocean.

[98] *Agape* from Greek $\alpha\gamma\alpha\pi\eta$, Latin *caritas* "love," means one's love for one's neighbor or for God, and God's love for human beings. In early Christianity *agape* was used synonymous for the Eucharist, while nowadays the term refers to the meal taken by a Christian congregation after the service.

sured dreams for the future; they listen to each other, comment on what has been said, question motives or decisions, give and receive advice.

In the first, constituting session of loud dreaming, Consolata asks the women to undress and lie naked on the cellar floor, onto which she then draws their silhouettes.[99] In the succeeding sessions, they fill these "templates" with painted renditions of painful and happy events in their lives, with symbols of their fears and wishes, with images of people they love or loathe. By capturing in the templates everything that harmed them and is still harming them, the women bring a safe distance between themselves and these events and/or things and curtail their inherent dangerousness. Thus, they gain power over them and thereby enable themselves to step out of the vicious circle of victimization, self-accusation, guilt, and self-punishment. "The experience of literally being beside themselves with their losses [...] allows the women to move from destructive to constructive experiences of haunting" writes Clewell (138f.). When the necessary distance from past terrors is achieved, the women in a second step proceed to integrate these terrors into their life stories. They make them part of their newly found, wholesome self-images.[100]

In this respect the Convent women's way of dealing with the experiences and memories that terrify them differs strongly from the one practiced by the Rubyites. The New Fathers externalize their fears and project them onto the Out There, anything that they define as alien from themselves and their community. By destroying the Convent they hope to destroy these fears as well as those features of their own that terrify and embarrass them. While the women's inclusive approach – their "non-violent acceptance of the threatening Other" as Messmer calls it – is successful (238), the massacre of the Convent women committed by the New Fa-

---

[99] Arguing from the perspective of postcolonial theory and critical race studies, Schur reads this as a "redefining [of] the body and the mental constructs that give the body meaning," which is the beginning of the process of decolonization (292). While I agree that racism is responsible for some of the traumas the women seek to overcome, I do not view all their troubles exclusively from the angle of race. Instead, I take a more broadly psychological stance on the templates, in keeping with my line of argument explicated in my reading of "Recitatif" that the holding back of racial markers may facilitate the analysis of human interaction as influenced also by experiences other than that of racial difference.

[100] On the subject of the work of mourning in Morrison's oeuvre see Durrant.

thers fails to solve any of Ruby's internal problems. Rather, their violence ricochets off the women and wounds the attackers and their town who were unable to work through their own racial traumas and those of their forebears.

In the sessions of loud dreaming and with the therapeutic painting of templates the Convent women begin to accept their traumatic experiences as part of their lives. They recreate themselves as individuals who survived their traumas as complex, loving, and lovable women. In order to find the love each of these four young women is searching for, they must learn to love and embrace all aspects of themselves. During the emotionally draining and physically uncomfortable purgatory of loud dreaming they succeed in achieving what Othow describes as "a marriage or union of the women's mental, physical, and spiritual selves" (371), or a form of paradise.[101] "With Consolata in charge, like a new and revised Reverend Mother, feeding them bloodless food and water alone to quench their thirst, they altered" (*Paradise* 265). Consolata takes on the majesty and benevolent power of an ideal loving mother who nurtures her children and passes on knowledge and traditions, giving the younger women the nurturing they lacked before.

Consolata becomes to the Convent women what in *Beloved* Baby Suggs, holy, is for the Black men and women who escaped across the Ohio River from Southern plantations: "an unchurched preacher, [. . .] [u]ncalled, unrobed, unanointed, she let her great heart beat in their presence" (87).[102] Gifted with the "in-sight" of wisewomen, Consolata early on diagnosed the problems with which her lodgers are struggling. Each of the women fled from circumstances they could no longer endure: neglect, abuse, betrayal, loss of love and loved ones, the absence of a sense of purpose. They came to the Convent during a quest for love and for home, a place where they would belong, where they would be able to catch their breath in order to find out who they are, where there are people who loved them the way they are, and where they would find a meaningful task in their lives and fulfill it. Consolata, who was singled out for the visit – or personal contact – with God, is the one who devises and safely conducts

---

[101] The notion of the Convent as "Purgatory, the space that for Catholics allows a soul tainted by sin to purify itself before joining God in Heaven," is explicated by Fraile-Marcos (23).

[102] There are also similarities between Consolata and Pilate in *Song of Solomon*.

the religious therapy for the women to prepare them for such contacts of their own; she designs structure and purpose of their community, and thereby creates an environment in which haunted women become "holy women" (*Paradise* 283).

The women's religious awakening culminates in spontaneous, trance-like dancing. Roused from sleep by the arrival of long-awaited rain, they leave the house and enter the "hot sweet rain" (*Paradise* 283). Dancing is an established part of religious practice in many traditions. While it may be frowned upon in conservative Christian circles and certainly would have confirmed the negative opinion the Rubyites have of the Convent, it is firmly integrated in the worship in African American spirituality, in Candomblé, and in Native American cultures of the North and the South of the continent. When the women dance in ecstasy in the Convent garden, worship is combined with an act of initiation. The water, Yemanjá's element as well as sacred liquid in the Christian ritual of baptism, is cleansing and healing to them "like lotion on their fingers," "like balm on their shaved heads and upturned faces" (*Paradise* 283). The warm rain washes off self-accusation and victimization; in it the women are reborn holy. Consolata, who initiates the dancing, becomes "fully housed by the god who sought her out in the garden" (*Paradise* 283).

As the women dance with her in the rain, they are like novices who have committed themselves to their order and follow their beloved abbess. They shave their heads, but, crucially, they do not take the veil, do not hide their individuality behind restrictive doctrines and rules of conduct of a patriarchal institution. Instead, they shed the traumas and emotional injuries that veiled their consciousness and barred them from loving themselves and accepting the love of others. Never before has the old mansion come so close to what its given name connotes. After the spiritual journey the Convent women undertook together during their sessions in the cellar and by leading their lives as a community structured by religious beliefs and rites that offers them a home, they "[are] no longer haunted" (*Paradise* 266). The Convent has become their paradise.

4.3.2.5 Uninstitutionalized Religion and Women's Freedom – Endangered Home

My discussion of Consolata as the spiritual leader of this community already points toward the fact that the Convent is still hierarchically structured, even though it is a heterogeneous and social space. However, in contrast to the patriarchal society of Ruby, it is a community that hinges upon women as leader and followers, as well as in its religious imagery.

After her religious emancipation, Consolata, who has always been the hostess in the Convent, if only because she was the only remaining member of the group of former residents, installs herself as the head of the small community. She becomes their High Priestess or a new Mother Superior: "I call myself Consolata Sosa. If you want to be here you do what I say. Eat how I say. Sleep when I say. And I will teach you what you are hungry for" (*Paradise* 262). By reclaiming and publicly announcing her full Brazilian name, she also emancipates herself from the childlike, powerless image symbolized by the name "Connie" in which the "colonialist gaze" of the nuns had fixed her (cf. Schur 291).[103]

Consolata calls onto the women to follow her: "If you have a place ... that you should be in and somebody who loves you waiting there, then go. If not stay here and follow me. Someone could want to meet you" (*Paradise* 262). Again, the syncretistic character of the religion introduced to the Convent becomes apparent. The community of women is turned into a symbolic "family" that occupies a "house," the smallest unit of worshippers in Candomblé. Consolata presides over the house as the head of the family – in Candomblé nearly always a woman – as the *ialorixà*, the "mother-of-saint," who can only occupy this position because the gods approve of her (cf. "Candomblé"). And, like other religious founders who gathered around them a following of believers, Consolata makes the women in the Convent her disciples.

As Consolata takes on the spiritual leadership of the Convent community, she proclaims the equal right of women and men to such a position, a right that was considered a matter of course not only in Candomblé, but also in pre-Christian times, in early Christianity, and in the early Black Church. She underlines the necessity of acknowledging both men's and women's creative potentials, as well as their intellectual, spiritual, and administrative contributions to the community – an acknowledgement that

---

[103] It is important to note, however, that she does not renounce the Catholic part of her identity. She calls herself "Consolata," retaining a name rooted in the official and sacred language of the Catholic Church. Consolata's religious syncretism lets her embrace those parts of the religiosity she inherited from her adoptive mother that do not annihilate teachings and practices she received from other traditions.

has long been denied to women not only by the power-conscious male leadership of the Catholic Church, but also, among other Christian denominations, by American Puritanism, of which Ruby is a late descendant. This sexist policy had long-lasting repercussions for women who were driven out of offices in church and social life and were relegated to serfdom. Moreover, religious persecution cost the lives of millions of women whose spiritual gifts, political influence, or economic prowess were defamed as witch craft. In the course of this patriarchal coup, female symbols, traditions, and wisdom were scrupulously wiped out of ceremonies and places of worship.[104]

Contrary to this, in the Convent community not only are the worshippers women, but their religion is distinctly woman-centered, quasi matriarchal.[105] Consolata's reading of Eve as the mother of Mary challenges the traditional patrilinear model of human genealogy that proclaims the passing on of name, power, material and immaterial wealth from father to son, leaving the daughters dispossessed and disempowered.[106] Her own relationship with the younger Convent women resembles an almost ideal relationship between a mother and her children. The mother, out of love and a sense of responsibility, passes on her religious knowledge and spiritual traditions to her daughters and thereby helps them to recover from a traumatic past.

Granted that Consolata is endowed with special spiritual gifts – she sees what others think and feel and raises people from the dead –, the question of who or what has prepared her for such a role still seems well worth exploring. We know nothing of her biological mother, and Mary

---

[104]On the role of women in the early Church and on the "purging" of woman-centered texts from the canon of Christian writings during efforts to verify an apostolic tradition and establish a Christian orthodoxy see Pagels as well as King, *Gospel*, and King, "Why."

[105]Morrison evokes the notion of the sacred feminine some years before it gained a certain currency in academic circles after the publication of Dan D. Brown's *The Da Vinci Code* in 2003. Since her acquaintance with Elaine Pagels' study of the Gnostic Gospels of 1979 Morrison has been interested in Gnostic texts, especially in "The Thunder, Perfect Mind" from the library of Nag Hammadi, Egypt. This poem is the source of the epigraphs to two of her novels, *Jazz* and *Paradise*. For an English language version of the text see "The Thunder."

[106]See also my summary of Yukins's discussion of Patricia Best as "bastard daughter" in the previous subchapter.

Magna, although she was a deeply loved mother-figure for the orphaned nine-year-old transplanted into a setting that was entirely unfamiliar to her, filled Consolata with restrictive and sexist doctrines that left her emotionally and spiritually empty, truly disconsolate, after the old nun's death. Instead of talking about the legacy of the old Mother Superior Consolata tells the Convent women of another, ultimately more powerful mother-figure she knows and reveres. She is Piedade, a religious matriarch of the Afro-Brazilian culture of her childhood, who seems to unite a variety of spiritual ideas and traditions.

As a title, "Piedade" is often added to the name of Mary, mother of Jesus, meaning "the one who is merciful."[107] As I pointed out earlier, the Virgin Mary corresponds to Yemanjá in Candomblé, the goddess of fertility and mother of the orixás. Thus, Piedade, who is both Mary and Yemanjá, is the mother of God, the divine giver of life, a symbol of the sacred feminine. In Consolata's descriptions her relationship with Piedade is a direct and close, even physical one, like that of a mother and her child. After exhausting sessions of loud dreaming in the Convent cellar she tells the younger women how she interacted with this mother-saint or goddess in the land of her childhood. After fifty years she is still filled with the exhilaration of Piedade's powerful and comforting presence:

> We sat on the shorewalk. She bathed me in emerald water. Her voice made proud women weep in the streets. Coins fell from the fingers of artists and policemen, and the country's greatest chefs begged us to eat their food. Piedade had songs that could still a wave, make it pause in its curl listening to language it had not heard since the sea opened. Shepherds with colored birds on their shoulders came down from mountains to remember their lives in her songs. Travelers refused to board homebound ships while she sang. At night she took the stars out of her hair and wrapped me in its wool. Her breath smelled of pineapple and cashews. (*Paradise* 284f.)

The imagery Consolata uses in her narration illustrates another important aspect of multifaceted Piedade. In addition to her very human, motherly characteristics her features also connote landscapes of the Brazilian coast line, the ocean with its emerald water, the night-sky over loud cities and quiet shores – no less than an earthly Eden. Her body is the beach Consolata used to roam as a child, her famous singing voice is the voices of the birds, wind rustling the leaves, or the sound of the waves crashing onto

---

[107]Piedade means 'mercy' in Portuguese.

or gently lapping the beach.[108] Piedade's hair is the starlit sky that was Consolata's comfort during lonely nights on the streets. Protected by this loving godlike matriarch, the orphaned child survives on the rough streets and retains her spiritual gifts, keeping them safe within her soul to use them for the benefit of others and herself later in her life.

Consolata's often-repeated story of her life with Piedade acquires the force of a sacred text for the Convent community: It is a psalm that sings the praise of the deeds of love and the miracles worked by this divine ancestral mother, a liturgy that – employed at a particular point in the ritual – is part of the women's worship. This 'Gospel according to Consolata Sosa' relates a woman's personal, unmediated experience with her God and bespeaks the human longing for a close relationship with God and creation, or the memory of such intimacy, that resembles the ideal of a union of love between mother and child. Consolata's close relationship with Piedade mirrors her own relationship with the young women in the mansion; her gospel implores and prophesies the reconciliation and reunion of the Convent women with their own mothers and/or daughters.

As I hope to have shown, the religion practiced at the Convent is remarkably different from either the Roman Catholicism of the Sisters of the Sacred Cross or the Black Puritanism of the New Fathers in Ruby. Consolata preaches and lives an unmediated closeness to God that is unthinkable in the institutionalized, hierarchical Church. Her concept of God is a very open one: God is like – and God is – a loving mother, a passionate lover, a flirtatious, warm-hearted male friend, the lovely beaches of Bahia, and the warm summer rain in Oklahoma. Consolata's religion goes back to and recovers a time when early Christians were still aware of and appreciative of the close spiritual links between their own faith and animist or spiritist religions surrounding them.

A self-sufficient community of women as a neighbor, however insignificant in size and economic prowess it may be, is a thorn in the eyes of the New Fathers of Ruby.[109] The Convent is a refuge not only for young

---

[108] Piedade is also the name of a beach that is famous for its natural beauty, the 'Praia de Piedade' in the city of Recife, Bahia, which is also a center of Candomblé in Brazil.

[109] Note again that the Convent as "Christ the King School for Native Girls" had already existed for a number of years before the New Fathers founded their town in its vicinity. While the nuns welcomed their new neighbor and the improved infrastructure their arrival promised, the settlers, with an audacity that

women from various regions of the United States, but also for marginalized members of the self-declared Black City upon a Hill, such as Menus Jury and Billie Delia Best. Moreover, during the decades of neighborly relations it has become a place to which self-righteous men and women of Ruby turn with their illicit needs and desires. "[T]he suppressed part of Ruby's own dark self," Messmer calls the adulterous affairs of K.D. and Deacon, Soan's and Arnette's sinister calls for help with the abortion of their unwanted babies, Sweetie's longing for release from the endless task of caring for her sick children, Sergeant Person's greedy wish to possess the Convent's land, and Menus's undignified struggle with his addiction (236). Because of this, the community of women is perceived not only as a rival to the leading men's claim to power, but also as a liability to many of the townspeople. Therefore, in order to preserve the religious and political status quo on which the power of the leading elite in Ruby depends, the Convent must be turned into a scapegoat, a screen onto which the generational, religious, and gender-related conflicts are projected that threaten to shatter the received notion of a paradisiacal safe haven the town has of itself.

"All paradises are described as male enclaves, while the interloper is a woman, defenseless and threatening. When we get ourselves together and get powerful is when we are assaulted," Morrison notes in an interview (D. Smith). The power of the Convent women lies not so much in their limited economic independence, but in the alternative framework for a community of human beings they have developed and now inadvertently offer to anybody in need of such an alternative. Ruby's social setup, as the Old Fathers designed it and their grandsons cemented it into law, rests on the "blood rule" of preserving pure blackness. The dogma of sacrosanct essential blackness, shored up with the help of patriarchal religious creed and structures, prescribes clearly defined roles for men and women within a male hegemony. Racial essentialism requires and rests on essentialist conceptions of gender roles. The clear difference between the five women's notions of gender and race and those of the New Fathers as well as the spirituality which makes this approach possible, are the features that turn the Convent into a target of the aggression of the patriarchs of Ruby.

stems from a notion of exceptionalism based on pure blackness, have viewed the Convent with suspicion from the very beginning of their coexistence.

When Billie Delia Best leaves her hometown to escape discrimination and to gain the distance necessary for her to decide on one of the two brothers she loves, she unconsciously robs Ruby of the personified negative counterpart to the "good woman" that is the necessary prerequisite for the construction of essential female blackness. With "notorious" Billie Delia in Demby, the town elders need a new adversary against whom to defend their virtuous women and whose existence will serve to justify any restrictive measures the men impose upon their community. As the Convent community is both close enough to play a part in the daily lives of the Rubyites and different enough in composition and way of living to serve as antithesis to the town's righteous moral self-image, the women inherit Billie Delia's unsavory part in the story of Ruby. Thus, while the Convent is a threat to the hegemony of the New Fathers in Ruby, it is also an indispensable component of the construct of the ideal Black town, the abject being that renders intelligible the standard of racial purity. It is a threat that is indispensable.

The absence of male residents in the mansion plays into the hands of those who champion the idea of the inherent inferiority and consequent dependence of women on men. To counter the challenge the all-female community presents to this patriarchal dogma and the hierarchy that follows from it, the evident independence of the five women must be redefined as something that is morally despicable and potentially dangerous for Ruby. Thus, Consolata in Deacon's mind turns into "[t]hat ravenous ground-fucking woman" (*Paradise* 279), and the women are collectively described as "[t]hese here sluts out there" who not only consume marijuana and "drink like fish" (*Paradise* 276), but are also part of the ominously hostile "Out There" that serves as a wholesale threat to the town's safety and integrity. They are labeled as lesbians that "[kiss] on each other" (*Paradise* 275),[110] of having murdered babies, or at the least performed abortions. Unlike the nuns who inhabited the mansion before

---

[110]The charge of illicit sexual practices is partly motivated by two of the accusers' feeling of shame at their own sexual involvement with Consolata and Gigi. For the women, however, the all-female Convent indeed holds the possibility of exploring and celebrating their female sexuality which is stigmatized as illicit in the patriarchal world outside its walls. Pallas senses this opportunity when she describes the homo-social setup of the community as "exciting" (*Paradise* 177), while Gigi and Seneca feel free to engage in a loving sexual relationship with each other that survives the raid on the Convent.

them and unlike the subdued Arapaho girls in their charge, these are "[n]ot women locked safely away from men; but worse, women who chose themselves for company, which is to say not a convent but a coven," as Lone DuPres sums up the thoughts of the attackers-to-be (*Paradise* 276). Because these women ostensibly believe that they do not need men, the New Fathers are also convinced of their heretical belief that they do not need God. After all, the patriarchs know for a religious truth that God created man rather than woman in His image, consequently making man His deputy on earth. Therefore, in the male Rubyite imagination the Convent women are "[b]itches. More like witches" (*Paradise* 276), and the men who gather to prepare their assault on the Convent mutually confirm that they "know they got powers" (*Paradise* 275).

When the attackers find the templates and candles in the cellar and the women's personal items in the rooms, they see their worst suspicions verified, their most carefully groomed charges against them proven beyond doubt. In the eyes of the New Fathers these are women who worship the ungodly body and blaspheme against the innocent soul. They practice witchcraft – nothing that could rival the pure religion of the Rubyites, but no less evil and dangerous for being pagan. They are, therefore, "[b]odacious black Eves" (*Paradise* 18), sinful females that can be and finally are hunted down with impunity like game.[111] Echoes of the persecution of spiritually gifted women as witches in the Middle Ages and Early Modern Time, both Catholic and Protestant, are palpable.[112] But moreover, we are reminded of power politics of the Church that led to the banishment of texts and symbols from the biblical canon which testify to

---

[111] The "sins" of which the men of Ruby accuse the Convent women and the raid on their community call to mind the infamous Salem witch hunt conducted by New England Puritans in the late sixteenth century. However, the "palm leaf crosses" the attackers bring with them to the mansion point to another parallel in history, namely the lynching raids of the Ku Klux Klan against African Americans in the southern states of the US. See also Fultz, who describes ideological similarities between "the founders and followers of colonial New England puritanism, the Klansmen, and the 8-rock dynasties of Haven and Ruby" (98).

[112] While there were also cases of men who were persecuted and/or burned at the stake for heresy, supposedly practicing witchcraft, or serving Satan, they are by far outnumbered by those of women. For more information on motives and effects of the religious persecution of women see Barbara Walker.

the important role of women in early Christianity, thus making possible the era of witch trials.

4.3.3   Race Within the Convent Community

Apart from their violation of gender roles and norms of religious conduct, the Convent women also break the unwritten law of racial homogeneity that forms the foundation of Ruby society. Their community consists of individuals with disparate geographical, socio-economic, and ethnic backgrounds. Among the people of Ruby this is a known fact, and the attackers once more underline the variation which, they believe, makes their own community radically different from the one they set out to destroy. Although the powerful men in Ruby worry about the perceived threat of some of the women's racial impurity seeping into their own town and polluting it, racial diversity within the Convent community is not the sole reason for the raid. Rather, it adds to the catalogue of offences that form the main charge of moral impurity, given that racial homogeneity and "pure" blackness are interpreted as a moral concern by the New Fathers, and thus condemns the women even further.

Yet, while the factor of racial heterogeneity merely contributes to Ruby's damning verdict of their neighbor, I want to argue that it is a crucial facet of the Convent's identity. Here, Morrison envisions a community in which racial difference not only does not result in inequality, but for all we know, it might not even be noted among its members. Human variation, although it is registered and described in detail, is never explained in terms of racial difference. Rather, characteristics that serve as means of creating a hierarchy among the women are either related to external aspects such as the duration of their residence in the Convent – the who-was-there-first factor – or to psychological features, like somebody's self-confidence or lack thereof, their readiness or inability to state their preferences and defend them, or their varying degrees of willingness and aptitude to care for others. The category of race plays no role in the formation of the social space that is the Convent.

That said, I hasten to acknowledge that the readers of *Paradise* learn of the heterogeneous racial composition of the Convent community on the very first page of the novel. In a narrative move that calls to mind the first paragraph of "Recitatif," Morrison highlights racial difference among the Convent women early on.[113] This (non-)information is given in the shocking opening sentence: "They shoot the white girl first" (*Paradise* 3). However, in contrast to her short story the differentiation of the women along race-oriented categories like "white" and "non-white" is performed by somebody outside the community, namely by a narrator, possibly one of the attackers.

Morrison's narrative technique in *Paradise* has been described as an "elision of the [omniscient] narrator's perspectives and a character's language and thoughts" (Fultz 86). With this understanding I read the opening passage *Paradise* as the narrator's representation of the thoughts and emotions of one of the nine attackers, maybe the one who would be most likely to classify the women in racial terms: Steward Morgan. Ron David, in contrast, suggests that the narrator of the opening passage is like the narrator in *Jazz*, presumptuous and – most importantly – unreliable. He cites the discrepancy between the nine attackers who the narrator claims were "over twice the number of the women they were obliged to stampede or kill" and the five women who were murdered (*Paradise* 3), as well as other "inconsistencies" in the novel (David 168f.). David's larger point is that Morrison highlights the unreliability of any narration, the inventive character of any story, history, or myth. This argument implies that we cannot take the racial categorization of one of the Convent women as "white" at face value – a point that underlines the general unreliability of differentiation along racial criteria. In the same vein, Schur argues that "[t]he whiteness may exist only in the imaginations of the men of Ruby, and thus [the woman's] actual identity is irrelevant" (294).

Throughout the novel the racial identities of the individual Convent women remain undeclared. In fact, the topic of the racial composition of this community is mentioned only once again, when, toward the end of the book, the story returns to the massacre with which *Paradise* opens. As one of the victims of the massacre is classified as "white," the different versions presented of this event share the Rubyites' general worry that "white law" will descend on the perpetrators of the crime and their se-

---

[113]In the short story, the narrator, Twyla, recalls her feelings when she was introduced to her new roommate: "It was one thing to be taken out of your own bed early in the morning – it was something else to be stuck in a strange place with a girl from a whole other race" ("Recitatif" 243).

cluded town (*Paradise* 290). Which one of the women is labeled "white," however, remains a mystery to the readers.

Predictably, the question of who among the Convent women is black and who is white engages the imagination of early reviewers of *Paradise*.[114] As in the majority of the few scholarly texts about "Recitatif," some commentators seem to want to prove their keen analytical skills by identifying the "white girl." Again and not surprisingly, they come to very different conclusions. Allen, for example, sees Pallas as "a supposedly privileged white girl" (6/4); Mantel declares Connie "white"; for Bemrose it is Mavis who is "poor, white, and tortured by the memory of how she accidentally smothered her own twins by leaving them in a hot car" (65/3), David also opts for Mavis; and Menand declares Seneca "a white runaway" (79/3). Only Grace/Gigi, for no particular reason that I can see, does not seem to be on anybody's list for the role of the "white girl." Clewell even suggests that the woman in question is a sixth member of the Convent community, "an unnamed white girl whose story is never revealed" (138), who plays no role in the novel and about whom Morrison gives us no details other than the fact that she is "white."[115] Finally, Scheck claims that the author gives away who the white girl is only at the end very of the novel, without, however, letting us in to the secret.[116]

Nicol, by contrast, argues that the identity of the "white girl" is irrelevant compared to the question of "who identifies her as white and why" (222). She skillfully uses the opening passage to lead her readers to her

---

[114]Six years after the publication of *Paradise* McKenzie confidently declares that "there are more questions than the usual one of who is the woman referred to in the first line (...) such as what gave the men the right to believe they had read the lives of the women correctly, that the women were doing anything out at the convent [sic] besides listening to one another's stories, singing, and offering a healing touch to those whose lives had been brutal, torn, tragic" (231).

[115]This view harmonizes with Aguiar's surprising suggestion that "at least some of the women are dead long before the Ruby posse attacks" (515/1). Aguiar explains her idea with the apparently nonsensical declaration in the second paragraph of the novel that the nine attackers are "over twice the number" of women in the Convent, and with the fact that none of the bodies of the women are found after the slaughter.

[116]"Sie spielen in "Paradies" eine Art Blinde-Kuh-Spiel mit Ihren Lesern, in dem Sie über eine Reihe von Frauen schreiben und eine Weiße unter Ihre schwarzen Figuren mischen, aber erst ganz am Schluss verraten, wer sie ist."

discussion of "the linkage between the town's racial difference and its protection of this through a system of gender difference" (223). Yet, in her text, the Convent serves as a mere prompter for an analysis of Ruby. While I agree with Nicol's conclusion that the attacker's identification of the "white girl" reveals the racism that permeates the social foundations of Ruby, I consider an analysis of the absence of racial differentiation within the community of women as imperative – in its own right as well as in its relationship with the neighboring all-Black town. The "raceless" Convent, I argue, must be read as an important contribution of Morrison's to the discourse on the status of racial difference in human interaction and the notion of race in contemporary Western society.

So, apart from highlighting the preponderance of racial characteristics and racist views in Ruby, why is there no distinction of racial difference in the Convent? What is the deeper significance of leaving the identity of the "white girl" to the readers' imagination? Shortly after the publication of *Paradise* Morrison's answers to her interviewers' frequent questions concerning the identity of the white girl emphasize the arbitrary nature of the concept of race, as her News Hour interview on PBS exemplifies:

> Well, my point was to flag raise and then to erase it, and to have the reader believe – finally – after you know everything about these women, their interior lives, their past, their behavior, and the one piece of information you don't know, which is the race, may not, in fact, matter. And when you do know it, what do you know? (Farnsworth)

Undoubtedly, this is an important point Morrison wants to make.[117]   It is also a point that she has made before, most clearly with "Recitatif." In *Paradise*, I suggest, she carries her literary reflections, her experiment about race, an important step further. With the Convent community she imagines a social space which, regardless of the fact that it has been racialized by outside forces, does not use the combination of biological, social, and psychological characteristics we have learned to consider as "racial" to differentiate between individual members of the community. The women come to the Convent from backgrounds that we know to be heavily racialized, as well as gendered and stratified according to socio-

---

[117]Citing the author's 1998 interview in *Le Monde des Livres*, Ashley suggests that by "[violating] . . . the American literary convention that black people must be identified, above all by their speech pattern, Morrison herself played the role of trickster in *Paradise*" (283).

economic aspects. They are themselves racialized, for example by the attacker who labels one of them "the white girl," regardless of whether she would identify herself as "white" or not.[118] Once they live in the mansion, however, the part of their identity that used to be described as their race ceases to exist for the members of their community. These women do not racialize each other's characteristic features; they do not perform the acts that result in the construction of race, whether as a biological essence or as a cultural one – in short, they do not assign race to one another.[119] The Convent is a social space free of racial hierarchy.

As we have seen from the speculations of reviewers and critics over the identity of the "white girl," the issue of race in the Convent has excited much interest, although this community is not organized along the color line. How then is race "flag raised" in this text? The pronouncement of racial difference in the first sentence of the novel, of deviance from the norm which in *Paradise* is blackness, is the most obvious "flag" that is raised. As the story unfolds and more and more details about the massacred women are revealed, we cannot but wonder which one of them was the "white girl" – until we realize that neither are we ever going to learn

---

[118]Note that with the "white girl" Morrison marks whiteness and thereby exposes its constructedness. This is significant because historically, race has been a construct created by the White majority to mark Others as different and deviant from the norm which was (and still is) whiteness. Not only was whiteness not regarded as a race, until recently it was also deemed beyond critical analysis. With her seminal series of lectures published in 1993 as *Playing in the Dark: Whiteness and Literary Imagination* Morrison initiated the critical study of whiteness. Her call has been answered with a flood of theoretical and critical texts examining the construction of whiteness and its effects on human society in literature, films, poplar music, as well as anthropological and sociological phenomena – Critical Whiteness Studies. See for example Frankenberg, Hill, Nelson, Keating.

[119]I disagree with Messmer who suggests that "Morrison introduces one white character into the otherwise all-Black community of the Convent, whose racial identity is perfectly visible and explicit within her fictional surroundings but remains unclear solely to her readers" (225). We only have one opinion on the "whiteness" of the first woman that is shot at the Convent, and that opinion belongs to an outside source, presumably one of the attackers, who is conditioned to distinguish groups and individuals according to their racial backgrounds. Within the Convent, no-one participates in the racialization of individuals. In my opinion, this is what makes the Convent so extraordinary a community.

the answer, nor is this question even relevant for the understanding of the dramatic events at the Convent. But the effect of the first sentence is that we pay attention to details in the description of the women, their verbal and non-verbal communication, all of which we have learned to regard as racial markers. When they reveal information that is at best contradictory, we are confronted with our own involvement in the practice of racialization – from a hegemonic position, if we are White readers – a practice that renders us liable to creating and perpetuating racial hierarchies.[120]

Another means of stoking the readers' attention to racial matters without fixing specific racial attributes to the Convent women is to reduce the potential for difference among them. One of the defining features of this social space is its gender homogeneity. The Convent is an all-female community consisting of individuals who are fleeing physical or emotional violence committed against them by men. This is very clear in the cases of Mavis who is terrorized by her brutish husband and of Seneca who experienced multiple instances of molestation at the hands of various foster brothers and lived in a humiliating relationship with a bullying partner. Pallas was left by her mother, is neglected by her father, was used and discarded by her much older boyfriend, and presumably raped by a gang of young men. Consolata endured what she described as "dirty pokings" as a child (*Paradise* 228), and Gigi encountered male police brutality during a civil rights march as well as violent outbursts of her rejected lover.

It is true that some of the violence and humiliation to which the women were exposed prior to their arrival at the Convent was perpetrated by other women: Mavis was mortally afraid of her daughter Sally whom she – wrongly, as it turns out – suspects of conniving with her husband, and found neither help nor understanding with her mother. Seneca was abandoned by her biological mother, neglected by several foster mothers, and sexually as well as emotionally abused by rich Norma Fox who is old enough to be her mother. Pallas feels betrayed by her own mother, and Consolata was made a life-long servant by the woman she loved as a mother.[121] Yet, the direct violent confrontations, the beating, raping, and

---

[120]There is a close, perhaps inevitable connection between the notion of race and racism that makes it impossible to speak about race and not deal with the issue of racial discrimination.

[121]O'Reilly regards the pain of what she calls "reproductive trauma" or "maternal loss" – the loss of mother love or the loss of a child – as an experience that the Convent women share with the women in Ruby. In both cases, she argues,

killing, are perpetrated by men, not by women. With the exception of Mrs. Fox, who is mastermind and agent of the demeaning games she plays with Seneca during the absence of her husband, women seem to be more passively, reactively violent than men in *Paradise*. This suggests that in this novel the violence of women against women happens within the patriarchal framework of male power and female powerlessness. Women play along with or perpetuate the misogynist attitude toward other women they perceive to be the order of the day in their male-dominated society. Patricia's treatment of her daughter – even though it culminates in an act of violence – underlines this observation.

In the Convent, although for most of the time there is little harmony among the women, they find safety from men's harassment. The mansion is permeated by a "blessed malelessness, like a protected domain, free of hunters," as Pallas declares (*Paradise* 177), a refuge from a hostile male world that threatens and traumatizes the women. Here, as she did with the girls' shelter in "Recitatif," Morrison creates a social setting that is bare of the conflicts and alliances that stem from gender difference. In an all-female community, with gender as a means of categorizing people out of the way, readers concentrate on race for the construction of difference. Yet our desire to assign difference through race is thoroughly frustrated.

The Convent women themselves make no use of racial markers, neither in language or content of their speech, they "miraculously speak no racial discourse of each other *at all*," as Wilt observes (282). Therefore, we have to analyze how race is "erased" and to what effect, in order to find out by what means Morrison creates this raceless space. Consolata Sosa, the cornerstone of this small community of women, provides most of the material for such an analysis. Since "a sunshot seared her right eye" after the abrupt end of her affair with Deacon Morgan (*Paradise* 241), Consolata is growing increasingly color-blind, in the literal as well as in the political sense. In proportion with the degree to which her irises are gradually drained of their grass green color, she loses the ability to distinguish the different hues of skin-color of the people around her, and indeed the interest in this visual difference. To protect her eyes from the force of the Oklahoma sun Consolata takes to wearing aviator-style sunglasses, a habit that stops only after the visit of the stranger. Through her glasses she

maternal loss signifies the large-scale failure of the community to care and nurture, as well as the marginalization of women in a patriarchal social order.

sees everything in accidental colors, colors that are unrelated to the phys-
iological features of the person in front of her that in a racialized society
would be interpreted as racial characteristics. The colors change with the
sunglasses Consolata uses over the years; she wears out such an extraordinary number that her friend Soan, who supplies her with the glasses,
humorously suspects her of "eat[ing] sunglasses" (*Paradise* 43).

As far as her lodgers are concerned, "Consolata looked at them
through the bronze and gray or blue of her various sunglasses and saw
broken girls, frightened girls, weak and lying" (*Paradise* 222). The sunray
that seared her eye also awakened the dormant spiritual, supernatural gift
of "insight" in her. When she looks at the women, she sees their inside,
their souls, and literally their internal, hidden parts. Thus, she perceives
the unacknowledged fetus in Pallas's womb and saves his life like a gifted
midwife, or the carefully concealed scars on Seneca's arms and legs. Finally, "[h]er colorless eyes saw nothing clearly except what took place
in the minds of others" (*Paradise* 248). Collective attributes and willful
projections of presumed group features onto a particular person lose all
meaning under Consolata's gaze. Instead she sees individual fears, sorrow, traumas, and hopes. While these almost certainly have their roots
in multiple personal experiences of injustice and inequality caused by the
racialized, gendered, and classed US-American society of the 1960s and
'70s, they are not expressions of essential racial difference.

The younger women also do not appear to think of themselves or refer
to the others in racial terms. Whenever they give a description of a person, they mention features that point to the inner turmoil of the woman in
question and thus are infinitely more meaningful than arbitrary group attributes: Pallas, the youngest and possibly most disoriented of the Convent
women, is described as having "splintered-glass eyes" (*Paradise* 171);
Mavis's grief, fear, and nervousness surface in her sloppy makeup and
the kid's clothes she had hastily put on when she fled from her violent
husband. Styles of clothing also serve to indicate the emotional and psychological states of Gigi and Seneca. While the former tries to cover up
her bruised self-confidence and lack of orientation under scant skirts and
high heels, the latter hides the physical scars that document her battered
psyche with baggy long-sleeved shirts. For all we learn in the novel, what
happened to these women, then, did not happen to them specifically because they are or are not black. It happened because they were deprived
of loving attention and financial resources or, in the case of Pallas, were

inundated with material goods but starved of parental care. Race most probably played a role in these experiences, but it did so as a factor that determines human interaction just like gender and class do, as well as in combination with these and other social relations, rather than as the sole cause of trauma and distress.[122]

There are, however, passages in the sections of *Paradise* dedicated predominantly to the Convent that explicitly describe physical features of the women, often even parts of the human body that historically have been used as racial markers and are still recognized as such: hair, eyes, and skin. Morrison uses these to highlight the fact that supposedly racial characteristics are neither natural in the sense of being biologically determined nor are they permanent. Rather, they are projections and constructions and therefore open to (re-)interpretation. Pallas' "head thick with curly hair" (*Paradise* 171), for example, might indicate blackness to some and blond curls, the epitome of whiteness, to others. The curliness of somebody's hair is not an attribute that can be defined within clearly drawn limit positions. Although in racialist thinking the texture of hair is considered to convey information about a person's racial background, it must be recognized as a marker of difference that is informed by societal conventions rather than biological or cultural essences. The remark about Pallas' hair, therefore, gives us no information about the girl's racial identity, even though it alludes to a physical feature that readers may consider a racial marker. Certainly, the other women in the Convent do not seem to care about the classifying potential of the texture of Pallas' hair; their fatalistic exclamation of "who knew who or what she was?" (*Paradise* 171), could refer to the girl's unclear past as well as to her racial background.

A third strategy Morrison employs to erase race in the Convent is to give protagonists a decidedly ambiguous racial identity. This is particularly noticeable in Consolata's case, who has "eyes like mint-leaves" (*Paradise* 228), "smoky, sundown skin," and "tea-colored hair" (*Paradise* 223). While the text conveys explicit information about physical features of this protagonist, it does so without offering conclusive cues as to her racial identity. The color of a person's eyes and skin has been and still is

---

[122]Race often eclipses other relevant social and psychological factors of human interaction in the perception of people who grew up and live in a racialized society. Morrison makes this point expressly in "Recitatif," as I argue in my discussion of the short story in Chapter 3.

interpreted as a strong marker of racial difference, but it is utterly unreliable: Green eyes are not exclusive to so-called Caucasian types and "sundown" as a shade of skin-color is as unspecific and open to interpretation as is the "tea-color" of Consolata's hair.[123] Moreover, South-American by birth and adorned with physical attributes that could easily be read as "white," she is nonetheless considered to be "certainly not white" by the nuns who bring her to the United States (*Paradise* 223). There, as a young girl she feels drawn to the newly arrived "glittering black people" of Ruby (*Paradise* 226), not least because they remind her so much of home. Yet, she is not black enough for Steward Morgan, whose rage at the thought that his twin brother's love affair with her could have produced "a mixed-up child" makes him pull the trigger and shoot her (*Paradise* 279). Her lover Deacon, who thinks that he knows the difference between "black" and "white" and clings to this knowledge with just as much fervor as his fanatical twin, admits to her his confusion: "I've traveled. All over. I've never seen anything like you. How could anything be put together like you?" (*Paradise* 231). Clearly, Consolata defies fixed racial categories.

In the context of race and racial difference, skin is the physical marker most often referred to. Morrison, however, succeeds in writing about the tone of people's skin without assigning a specific racial identity through it. In the lengthy passage that describes Seneca's careful and determined acts of self-mutilation, we cannot guess the color of the skin that she slices. Dee Dee, Pallas' artist mother, in her attempt to paint a portrait of Pallas, almost despairs of the fact that "the skin tone [of her daughter] eluded her" (*Paradise* 311).

The apple-eyed stranger is another character who can hardly be racially placed. Apart from having Consolata's eyes and hair, he wears clothes whose colors bear a mixed message in terms of his racial background: "a green vest over a white shirt, red suspenders hanging low on either side of his tan trousers, shiny black work shoes" (*Paradise* 251).[124]

---

[123] Interestingly, except for the reference to hair color, Consolata features reappear two years later in Coleman Silk of Philip Roth's *The Human Stain*. There, a green-eyed, tanned classics professor re-designs his Black ethnic identity as Jewish and is professionally and emotionally undone through the unfounded charge of racism against two African American students at a New England college (cf. Roth).

[124] The description of the clothes Consolata's visitor is wearing relates him to the walking man of the founding myth of Haven.

The colors red, black, and green form the flag of the Pan-Africanism of Marcus Garvey and his UNIA. The Universal African Flag is also used by the Black Nationalist movement.[125] According to Garveyite philosophy, red stands for the "color of the blood which men must shed for their redemption and liberty," black is "the color of the noble and distinguished race to which we belong," and green symbolizes "the luxurious vegetation of our Motherland" (McGuire qtd. in "Red, Black and Green"). The ideology of Black Nationalism – albeit minus its strong identification with the African "Motherland" – calls to mind some of the teachings of Ruby's New Fathers: It stresses economic and political independence for African Americans as well as separatism from other ethnic groups and entertains an essentialist view of racial identity that hinges upon the notion of "black blood."

Moreover, the stranger's obtrusive white shirt, in combination with the green vest, red suspenders, and black shoes, on the one hand, can be read as undermining the aims of Black exclusiveness, racial homogeneity, and racial strife with which the Black Nationalists and Ruby are jointly associated.[126] Consolata's visitor assembles such a colorful variety of conflict-

---

[125] Usually, the Pan-African colors are presented by the color combination of red, gold (yellow), and green. These colors derive from the national flag of Ethiopia to which many newly independent African nations looked up because, except for a short period of Italian occupation during World War II, Ethiopia has never been colonized by a European nation. It is also the country of origin of Rastafarianism, a movement that was instrumental for the development of Pan-Africanism. The Garveyites and their ideological descendants, however, insist on the use of black in combination with red and green for their Universal African Flag.

[126] The additional white transforms the Pan-African colors into the Pan-Arab colors; they form the flags of the Arab states of the Middle East and Africa: Iraq, Jordan, Kuwait, Sudan, Syria, the United Arab Emirates, the territory of Western Sahara, and the Palestinian territories. The pan-Arab colors originate in the Arab revolt against the Turkish Ottoman Empire in the first quarter of the twentieth century. They represent the movement of pan-Arabism aiming at the union of all Arab nations. This movement rests on the idea of ethnic nationalism and a secular, socialist government. The goal of establishing a union of secular Arab states was never reached. In fact, with the US-American support of Saudi Arabia and the ousting of the Ba'ath regime in Iraq, Islamist forces now lead the political affairs of most if not all Arab states. This brings to mind

ing racial markers and symbolic colors that he attests to the impossibility of racial essence while citing one of the sources of this idea.[127]

Morrison continues her critique of racial essentialism in general and Black Nationalism in particular through the use of symbolic colors in yet another scene. When Anna Flood and Richard Misner inspect the empty Convent after the massacre, they return from the henhouse with five brown eggs and from the overgrown garden with "long pepper pods – green, red and plum black" (*Paradise* 305), all of which they gather together in a white handkerchief. Again the author uses Garvey's Pan-African colors, but by putting them in the non-racialized context of a vegetable garden she empties them of their separatist, racist symbolism. In Richard's hands, the pepper pods are just that: multicolored, spicy vegetables. Grouped together like a still life, the brown eggs, the white handkerchief, and the green, red and black peppers are a monument to the possibility and the potential richness of a multicultural society.[128]

the Nation of Islam and Malcolm X to whom the New Fathers in Ruby disrespectfully refer as "a nigger name of X" (*Paradise* 65).

[127] On the other hand, the tan color of the stranger's trousers could represent Morrison's critique of the racial essentialism of Black Nationalism. Light brown
is the color of fascism and its most powerful faction in Europe, the National
Socialists of Hitler's Germany. Nazi ideology, also in its US variety, insists on
the existence and proclaimed the superiority of pure Arian blood and creates
an elaborate hierarchy of races which declares those at the bottom degenerate
and unworthy of inclusion within the community of human beings. The possible textual allusion to ideological similarities between Black and White racial
essentialism and racism by means of a color code is supported by the historical affiliation of Marcus Garvey with the Ku Klux Klan. Garvey expressed his
approval of the separatist ideology of the Klan which he contrasted favorably
with what he regarded the unrealistic aim of W.E.B. Du Bois's NAACP of inte-
grating African Americans within US-American society. In 1922, Garvey met
with Edward Young Clarke, Acting Imperial Wizard of the Ku Klux Klan. This
meeting provoked protests both from the NAACP and from the Klan.

[128] However, the brown color of the eggs once more allows the association with
fascist racism. Together with the symbolism of "8-R" and the strangers' tan
trousers the brown eggs form an associative chain that leads me, a White German reader, to the blood-worshipping racial essentialism of National Socialism. Twice, brown and white are added to the Pan-African colors, thereby
confronting Black Nationalism with its White counterpart.

Although Toni Morrison withholds the information of who among the Convent women is "white," thus questioning the notion of racial difference in this community, readers receive a wealth of intimate details on every individual and are therefore well equipped to distinguish the five women. The detail concerning the racial background of the women is shown to be an arbitrarily constructed extra with but little informative substance. And yet, it is at least partly responsible for the destruction of the Convent community.

4.3.4   Home as Transitory P/paradise

Because of its geographical situation at the border between all-Black Ruby and the racially mixed settlements in the vicinity and by virtue of its history as a contact zone that attracts and is open for individuals from different regional, ethnic, spiritual, and socio-economic backgrounds, the Convent becomes an inclusive, heterogeneous social space. In the short time span between the visit of the apple-eyed stranger and the New Fathers' raid of the mansion, it is unequivocally "home" to the five women who live there. It is home because each woman, regardless of her background, is welcome to spend however much time she wants in the house, and because anyone who comes by from neighboring Ruby is given shelter, whether they come as a visitor, as a guest, or as someone looking for help and staying for an indefinite period. Much of the Convent's character as "home" is determined by the presence, teachings, and actions of Consolata Sosa. Her multifaceted spirituality combines and unites religious traditions from different cultures; it enables the women to acknowledge and let go of their traumatic pasts and helps them to discover and explore new perspectives in their lives.

However, is the Convent the racial home Morrison talks about in her essay "Home"? Is it a social space where human beings of diverse ethnic and cultural backgrounds live together without a hierarchy to regulate their interaction along physical differences with the psychological and social characteristics arbitrarily attributed to them? If we understand this to be the meaning of Morrison's "home," the small community of women, which does not interpret physical differences in terms of racial categories, indeed represents an exemplary "racial home."

Therefore, when at the height of the Civil Rights and Black Power movements the young generation in neighboring Ruby rebels against their town's enforced self-isolation from the world and a scattering of the once tight-knit community is feared by the elders, the New Fathers, in their grim resolve to avert the fate they believe has destroyed the town of their fathers, do not hesitate to lay the blame for this development on the Convent women. To put an end to the willful corrupting of the young and the pollution of their racially pure Black community of which they accuse the Convent, nine heavily armed men shoot their way into the mansion on a July morning in 1976, killing Consolata and the other women. Monocultural society violently breaks into vulnerable transcultural space.

In the face of the bloody destruction of the Convent, the question arises whether *Paradise* champions the idea that modern society is unable to survive without tools such as the notion of race with which to differentiate between human beings and around which to structure itself. Is an exclusive, racialized social order presented as being stronger – even though not necessarily better – than an open, non-racialized one? Is the sacrifice of the Convent necessary in order to salvage the laudable and difficult experiment of an independent, self-segregated, and homogenous Black community in the United States?

At first sight, the massacre of the five women indeed appears to have put off the breaking apart of Ruby. Since the bodies of the murdered women cannot be found, nobody plans to inform the authorities of the violent events. Clearly none of the victims will be searched for, so the attackers do not have to fear retribution for their actions. For some time, the townspeople are divided over what really happened at the Convent. Explanations range from attempts to persuade the women "to leave or mend their ways" that resulted in a fight and in the women's "tak[ing] other shapes and disappear[ing] into thin air" to the explanation that some of the men had been attacked by the women and had accidentally shot Consolata, while the other women "took off in their Cadillac" (*Paradise* 296, 297). Lone DuPres, who in the night before the massacre had read the men's minds and knew what they intended to do, despairs of her people as she realizes that Steward, Fleet and the most hardened of the attackers will always deny any wrongdoing and that even the critics of the New Fathers will do nothing to bring the ringleaders to justice. Although Ruby is shaken by the occurrences at the mansion, when no retributions must be feared people continue with their routines, some of them with relief, others with stubborn self-righteousness. Lone interprets the apparent absence of consequences of a crime in which the entire community is implicated in some way as a show of divine mercy: "God had given Ruby as second chance" (*Paradise* 297). In spite of and in contrast to the loveless teachings of Reverend Pulliam she feels that the love of God redeems even sinners who do not repent.

And yet, there are signs of a new beginning in the town after the Convent raid, signs that testify to significant changes in the core values and ideas of this community. The union in spirit and deed between the Morgan brothers Steward and Deacon is broken from the moment that Steward raises his gun to shoot Consolata and Deacon does too little too late to prevent the murder. While Steward continues in his efforts to further the wealth and influence of the Morgans by grooming K.D. as his heir and successor, Deacon slights his nephew, who has become despicable to him, and disassociates himself from his twin. Driven by a sense of guilt by what he and his brother did to the Convent women, Deacon turns to Reverend Misner for a pastoral conversation. He tells him about a woman he once loved and abandoned and talks about his grandfather who disowned his twin brother because the twin danced for some White men rather than taking a bullet in his foot.

Deacon's barefoot walk to the reverend's house – in itself an exhibition of remorse and repentance – and his incoherent confession of his own cruelty and that of his grandfather mark his moving away from the doctrine of essential truth and purity which he and his brother have upheld in Ruby. Much as he now dislikes Steward and wants to sever ties with him, Deacon wonders if he should not try to love his brother despite the ideological differences that separate them. As the twins not only look alike but also used to treasure the same memories and share the same dreams, this would mean that he would have to embrace that which he dislikes most about himself and which he banished deep into his subconscious. With regard to Consolata, Deacon is now able to acknowledge how much he felt attracted to and loved the woman he defamed as dirty and immoral in order to feel justified in discarding her. As one of the two most influential men of Ruby is beginning to back away from the town's self-prescribed corsage of self-righteous exclusivity, a general change of the self-image of the community and their view of others seems imaginable. At least two people are already embracing this possibility: "I got a long way to go," Deacon says to Reverend Misner, who answers, "You'll make it, [...]. No doubt about it" (*Paradise* 303).

Soon after the massacre of the Convent women, Patricia Best also diagnoses the beginning of a new era. For her the death of Save-Marie,
one of the terminally ill Fleetwood children, is a pivotal event in the history of Ruby. Now in "a town full of immortals" (*Paradise* 296), whose
citizens have always proudly proclaimed that "nobody in Ruby has ever
died" (*Paradise* 199),[129] a cemetery is needed – especially so, since the
deaths of Save-Marie's siblings must be expected as probable events in the
near future. Reluctantly, the people of Ruby acknowledge death as part
of life. Very likely their acceptance of change and mortality is facilitated
by the fact that the Oven, symbol of their ossified history, has tilted, its
base washed away by the heavy rain that fell during the night before the
Convent massacre.

In Patricia's reasoning this acknowledgment of death marks an ideological turning point for Ruby. With the dying of the little girl one part of
"the deal" she identified between the New Fathers and their God is broken.
From now on, honoring the "blood rule" will not earn the people of Ruby
exemption from mortality any more. Consequently, pure Black blood
looses its sacrosanct quality. It makes no difference that an 8-rock son
was born to K.D. and Arnette and that Arnette is pregnant again, putting
an end to Steward's fear that the line of the Morgan line might die out.
As racial purity ceases to be sanctioned by divine decree, the human fate
of mortality looms large also for these racially "pure" individuals. Therefore, it is of no consequence whether all members of a family are 8-rock
or not. At the first funeral in Ruby since the – officially unacknowledged
– death of Patricia's light-skinned mother the townspeople break the spell
of the all-powerful past under which they misinterpreted the occurrences
of the present and shied away from the unpredictability of the future.

Richard Misner and his fiancée Anna Flood also come to expect fundamental change to rock their home town, when they return to Ruby from
a journey after the Convent massacre. Their efforts to uncover traces of
the murdered women at the mansion come to nothing, but as they prepare

---

[129]This statement is of course not true. While Ruby, the younger sister of the Morgan twins, and the sons of Soan and Deacon Morgan indeed died outside the
town, namely in the waiting room of the hospital in Demby and the battlefields
of Europe, Delia Best died in Ruby. Because of the lightness of her skin, however, her death is barred entry into the official chronic of the town, allowing the
citizens to cling to the boast that nobody – i.e., nobody who really counts – has
ever died in Ruby. Delia Best was buried by her husband in their garden.

to leave the premises with their load of eggs and pepper pods, they both have a supernatural experience. They sense an opening in the garden that is like an opening in their reality: a partly closed door it seems to Anna, a raised window to Richard. It is a sensation that suggests to the reverend the existence of "another place – neither life nor death – but there, just yonder" (*Paradise* 307). This other realm which Morrison, the "realist" writer, chooses not to enter, not only comforts the two and helps them to accept the inexplicable fate of the five women, it also fills them with optimism: for the women, whether they are dead or alive, as well as for Ruby. Reverend Misner decides to remain in the town, and Anna consents to marrying him – a descendant of one of Ruby's 8-rock family unites with a stranger from Out There. Together they stay "on earth" (*Paradise* 307), in a deeply flawed community.

They return from the mansion with five eggs, symbols of fertility that, I suggest, can be read as an indicator of the fact that the legacy of the Convent women lives on in Ruby, which itself will continue to exist. Unlike the eggs in the hands of the dignified yellow-clad African woman who is so intimidating to Jadine in *Tar Baby*, however, the Convent eggs do not signify the presumed clarity of essential, pure blackness (cf. *Tar Baby*). An important part of the legacy of the Convent women is the unmattering of race which they practiced within their community. Because this inclusive, heterogeneous community has existed and because it has interacted with its neighbor, Ruby will not be condemned to remaining an incarnation of the traditional notion of paradise, "this hard-won heaven defined only by the absence of the unsaved, the unworthy and the strange" (*Paradise* 306).

The changes foreseen by Richard will turn the retrogressive town into a place that moves with the times much like any other small town in the Midwest. He predicts the advent of some of the facilities whose absence mark Ruby most clearly as different from other settlements of the 1970s: television, a diner, a gasoline station, and a paved road that connects the town with the outside world. The elders will be persuaded to trade exclusivity and seclusion for profits; strangers will pass through Ruby, leaving their imprint and possibly taking something or someone from the town away with them; TV and radio programs will inform the young of life beyond the boundaries of their hometown. In fact, through their violence against the Convent the raiders unintentionally hurried along what they wanted to prevent: the gradual and natural evolution of their community.

Without God's redemptive love as described by Lone and felt by Reverend Misner and Anna, however, the massacre of the women would have been an act of self-destruction for Ruby.[130]

Are the Convent women, therefore, defenseless victims of violence or female messiahs who sacrifice themselves for the benefit of flawed humankind? Or are they rather the victorious avengers of injustice done to them and to others who suffered under the oppressive effects of the New Fathers' fanatic belief in pure blackness and virtuous Black womanhood? The latter is Billie Delia's interpretation of the events at the Convent as well as her explanation for the missing bodies. She waits for the women to return to Ruby "with blazing eyes, war paint and huge hands to rip up and stomp down this prison calling itself a town" (*Paradise* 308) – like warrior spirits who return to those who caused their deaths and take revenge for the violence done to them in their lifetime.

And the women return indeed. But instead of wreaking havoc among their attackers they visit people they love or appear to those with whom they need to settle affairs. Mavis reunites with her daughter and they assure one another of their mutual love. Seneca crosses the path of her mother Jean who never stopped looking for the child she abandoned, but she either does not recognize the woman as her mother or does not want to reveal herself as her daughter. Pallas taunts Dee Dee when she returns to her mother's house only to fetch the expensive huaraches she had left there. Gigi renews the contact with her father after he notices and calls

---

[130]Durrant reads the Rubyites' attack on the Convent women as an "act of familial, black-on-black violence" comparable to Cholly's rape of his daughter in *The Bluest Eye*, Guitar's attempted murder of Milkman and his murder of Pilate in *Song of Solomon*, Eva Peace's cremation of her son Plum in *Sula*, Sethe's attempted and executed infanticides in *Beloved*, and Joe Trace's shooting of Dorcas in *Jazz*. He contents that there is a "logic that governs all these acts of (self-) destruction" in Morrison's work: "the black community inflicts on itself – acts out – that part of its history which it has been unable to digest. Each act of self-inflicted or familial violence is a way of remembering – while not remembering – the violence done to the whole race" (82). In the context of *Paradise*, he argues, the "'original' violation" which "comes to function as a prehistory to the events of the narrative" (82), is the Disallowing and, I would add, its precursor, the disenfranchisement of the Old Fathers during Redemption.

her in the park where he and his fellow lifers work. Consolata, finally, reunites with her spiritual ancestress Piedade on the shore.

The passages of the novel which show the Convent women seemingly alive and interacting with members of their families have puzzled some of the reviewers. They particularly nettled those in whose opinion *Paradise* is an overly didactic, moralistic piece of writing that either dims Morrison's deservedly good reputation (Bent; Bemrose), or proves the fact that the Nobel laureate owes her success to the efforts by the international literary establishment to exhibit political correctness, rather than to her talent as an author (Klinghoffer).[131] Critics who take the passages in question seriously read "these 'ghosts' right out of the African belief system" as *revenants* (Tally, "Reality": 40). The belief in revenants exists in various African religions, where this term refers either to the spirits of ancestors who, after their deaths, remain with their families and occasionally appear to them, their good or bad intentions often depending on the quality of the worship that is offered them. Revenants are also the spirits of persons who have been killed or died untimely violent deaths and return to trouble the living and/or to avenge themselves on their tormentors.[132] Mavis's meeting with Sally thus could be read as an ancestral visitation on the living, while Pallas, during her visit at her mother's house, corresponds more closely with the type of the avenging revenant.

---

[131] The fierceness with which some early reviewers condemn *Paradise* is remarkable. Hilary Mantel's self-critical note of caution must be read in this context: "*Paradise* is as much a poem as a story, and it may require a different kind of attention from that which this fly-by-night critic is able to bestow."

[132] Revenants are feared and/or worshipped also in Asian, Southeast-Asian, and American Indian religious traditions. They existed as ghosts in the ancient Celtic as well as medieval European traditions, and appear in Afro-Caribbean religions as their malevolent variant, as zombies. Arguably the most memorable revenant in Morrison's oeuvre is Beloved in the novel of that title. Aguiar associates the Convent women directly with Beloved, not only as they reappear after the massacre, but from their first appearance in the old mansion. Concentrating on the important topic of death in *Paradise*, she contends that – much like the Rubyites who exist in a death-like state of stasis – the women were in fact killed in the traumatic events of which we learn only by way of hints. Because they are unable to accept their deaths and to let go of the past, they continue living as spirits, as "refugees from life" (Aguiar 514/2).

Apart from these spiritist explanations, the reappearance of the Convent women after the massacre can also be interpreted psychologically: The women are seen by those individuals to whom they were close – for good reasons or bad. Their appearance is a result of a sense of longing for people who are gone; it springs from a desire of those left behind to undo the pain and sorrow they caused their loved ones. These "sightings" are part of the attempt to cope with the loss of a child, a mother, or a friend – a loss that is the more painful for the grieving person because it is connected with a strong sense of individual guilt.

However, the question arises whether the grief for these women might also be a reflection of our bitter recognition that an inclusive, open paradise as represented by the Convent community is outside of human imagination, after all. Morrison pointed out in various interviews that the defining feature of the paradises we know is their exclusivity. "Our view of *Paradise* is so limited," she holds. "[I]t requires you to think of yourself as the chosen people – chosen by God, that is. Which means that your job is to isolate yourself from other people" (Marcus). I want to suggest that the passages about the revenants offer an optimistic answer to this question. The manner in which the Convent women show themselves suggests perseverance, even to the point of triumph, in spite of the violence done to them. The Mavis who lunches with her daughter is infinitely more self-secure, dignified and in charge of the situation than the flustered battered wife she had been, who let her babies die in the overheated car. Gigi, who nearly despaired because of her weakness and inability to prevent the violent death of a young Black boy, is wearing army-style clothes when she appears to her father. She calmly comforts and reassures the troubled convict, before she resumes the peaceful life she shares with her female companion. The cuts Seneca receives through a fall just before Jean approaches her in a parking lot are not self-afflicted. There is no need for Seneca to jump at the possibility of reclaiming her mother, because with the help of her friend her minor wounds are quickly cleaned. When Pallas returns to her mother's house she is carrying not only a healthy baby boy whom she named Divine in an act of forgiveness toward her mother. More remarkably, she is carrying a sword and is more alike to her name-sake or patron goddess Athena than ever in her life.[133] It is Pallas's formerly ruthless mother who is unable to utter a clear sound at the sight of her warrior-like daughter. These women are powerful and in control of their lives; they seem comfortable, satisfied, at peace.

Thus, while Ruby is undergoing fundamental changes for the first time since its founding, the Convent community, far from being annihilated through violence, has entered yet another state of being.[134] Change, feared and avoided in Ruby for the longest time, has been a characteristic feature of every one of the stages of the Convent's existence.[135] The

[133]Pallas's association with Pallas Athena is strengthened by the fact that, however hard Dee Dee tries to prevent it, her daughter's hair in her painting "was invariably a hat" (*Paradise* 311) – or Athena's helmet.

[134]*Paradise* is divided into nine chapters, each of which is dedicated to a female protagonist of the novel. In addition to the five inhabitants of the Convent these include Ruby, Patricia, Lone, and Save-Marie. Apart from testifying to the intimate connection between the stories of Ruby and the Convent, the number of the chapters in my view has a symbolic meaning that stems from the realm of female spirituality and pre-Christian religious beliefs, two thematic concerns of the novel. The number nine is the sacred number associated with the Crone, the third aspect of the Triple Moon Goddess – the first and second aspects being Maidenhood and Motherhood. 'Nine' stands for wisdom, sacred magic, as well as completion. The Crone represents the Dark Mother or Dark Goddess of the waning moon, who is the destroyer and taker of life. One of her symbols is the cauldron of life from which death and rebirth originate; the goddess of death also governs the beginning of new life. The two Crone-like protagonists in the novel, Lone DuPres and Consolata Sosa, both preach the interdependence and unbreakable union of life, death, and rebirth. While the New Fathers in Ruby defy the cyclical order of life and death and pride themselves in the achievement of banishing death from their town, the Convent women come to accept loss as an important part of their lives. After their violent deaths at the hands of the Ruby men, they are shown reborn and fully empowered. While the massacre of the women brings death into the consciences of the people of Ruby, the dying of little Save-Marie brings it to their collective consciousness. Ultimately, the Rubyites must recognize the inevitability of death, but the girl's death also marks the beginning of new life inside the walls of this once sealed-off settlement.

[135]Lucille Fultz offers another interesting explanation for the number of chapters of *Paradise*. She describes "Morrison's project of giving voice to nine women" as "a counter and contemporary narrative to the narrative about the nine original families of Haven/Ruby designated by male surnames and male leaders" (82).

community of women evolves even through and after death, and for their former neighbors they become "redemptive agents of change" (Messmer 240).

In *Paradise* Morrison breaks up and complicates binary oppositions or "Manichean polarities" (Fraile-Marcos 24). While she explores the dangers of an excessive worship of the past, she also points out the human need of rites and traditions. She exposes the underlying exclusivist violence of the construction of race and highlights the arbitrary nature of the notion of racial purity, but she also never loses sight of the empowering faculties of racial identity, nor of the continuous prevalence of the notion of racial difference in US-American society.

The dream-like vision of a paradisiacal moment which Morrison gives us on the last page of her novel corresponds with this rejection of binaries and essentialisms. It also presents an alternative to the traditional notion of the *Paradise* of the chosen ones. Piedade, the "coal-black" African ancestress of Consolata's loud dreaming, sits facing the ocean. On her lap lies a younger woman of ambiguous racial identity, with "tea-colored hair," "emerald eyes," and skin in which "all the colors of seashells – wheat, roses, pearl – [fuse]" (*Paradise* 318). She strongly resembles Consolata who, rejuvenated and peacefully united with her spiritual mother, now is indeed "the Consoled One," as her given name announces and implores at the same time.

In this image religious traditions of Afro-Brazilian Candomblé and Roman Catholicism merge once again. The two women look over the ocean, the element particularly associated with Yemanjá. Piedade's head is framed by "cerulean blue," the symbolic color for both Yemanjá and the Virgin Mary. The goddess Yemanjá is the patron of women, especially pregnant women, and thus venerated primarily by women. As the ruler of motherhood she cures infertility and represents fertility in general.[136] In Catholicism the Virgin Mary receives veneration for possessing similar powers; in a supposedly monotheistic religious system she is the saint who comes closest to occupying the position of a deity, and she is addressed

---

[136]To worship the goddess Yemanjá is to celebrate life and fertility, symbolized in *Paradise* by the rock formation in search of which Gigi comes to Oklahoma. It is supposed to resemble a man and a woman in an incessant act of love-making. Gigi never finds the rocks, but Consolata and Deacon choose as a place for their passionate meetings the remains of a farm where two trees grow entwined as if in a loving embrace.

in prayers for fertility. In the tradition of Candomblé practiced in the north-eastern Brazilian state of Bahia, thanks to the syncretistic nature of Yemanjá and under the pressure of Catholic religious persecution in times of slavery, "the personae of Yemanjá and the Virgin Mary fused" ("Omolu and Mary Star of the Sea").[137] Yemanjá and her Roman Catholic equivalent are both worshipped as Mother of God(s): Mary as the mother of Jesus, Yemanjá as the mother of the orixás.

Furthermore, the position of Piedade and the younger woman presents a Pietà-like constellation familiar to the reader from countless depictions of the Virgin Mary with her son, Jesus, after his crucifixion; Piedade is the Black Madonna with Consolata as a female Christ.[138] The Black Madonna with Child of *Paradise* may be read as an acknowledgement of the ties that connect Christian traditions and iconography with their roots in the religion of ancient Egypt or even with prehistoric forms of Earth Mother worship. The original Black Madonna and matrix of later Christian depictions of Mary and the child Jesus is believed to be the Egyptian goddess Isis who holds her son Horus in her arms.[139] Isis was addressed as Our Lady and The Great Mother, titles that produced the Latin words *mater domina* from which the title "Madonna" derives. Isis was a popular goddess in ancient Rome, and only after the Christianization of Europe were Iris and Horus "re-invented" as Mary and Jesus. In Consolata's psalm-like narration and in the last scene of the novel, Piedade conveys some of the fertility, power, and divine authority which characterize the image of the Black (African) Madonna, an image that stands in stark contrast to the meek and docile Virgin Mary of the Catholic Church. The image of Piedade and Consolata, therefore, is both within and outside of Roman Catholic tradition and doctrine: Consolata represents God's child who sacrifices her own life in order to save all human beings from eternal

---

[137] See also Took.

[138] In Santeria, another syncretistic religion of the African diaspora with direct links to the Yoruba pantheon, the goddess Yemaya is associated with La Virgen de la Regla. Our Lady of Regla is venerated under several names, among them La Virgen Morena, the Black Madonna (cf. Mendoza). The Black Madonna revered in Brazil is Our Lady of Aparecida.

[139] Morrison's Black Madonna is another expression of and link to the author's interest in the Gnostic Gospels, early Christian writings in the Coptic language of Egypt.

damnation;[140] however, God and the savior of the world are both women, and they are not White.

The solace of mother and daughter – Piedade, who reconciles "spiritual" Mary with "bodily" Eve, and Consolata, her spiritual daughter – united in love is a novelty, maybe a homecoming in Morrison's oeuvre which often deals with conflicts between mothers and daughters.[141] It adds to the paradisiacal atmosphere of the last scene of *Paradise*. Both women watch a ship arrive that is full of people who are "lost and saved" and have come to rest a while before "shouldering the endless work they were created to do down here in paradise" (*Paradise* 318).[142] The image of the ship carries connotations of the Middle Passage during which millions of Africans died under horrible circumstances on their way to the Americas and Europe. These slave ships were also the means of creating an African diaspora in the Black Atlantic; they mark the beginning of the African American community in the US and of syncretistic religions such as Candomblé.[143]

Morrison told her interviewer James Marcus that she "tried to make it possible to think that *Paradise* was within our imagination." With this

---

[140]Here Morrison is in line with the traditional doctrine of Jesus Christ's self-sacrifice through which all sin is washed away from humankind which, through this supreme act of mercy, is redeemed in the eyes of God. This theory of divine sacrifice is now questioned by many theologians, both Catholic and Protestant (see e.g. Kuitert, Jörns). The image of a Black Christ that dominates Reverend Misner's mind during K.D.'s and Arnette's wedding ceremony and the messiah-like qualities of Consolata and the Convent women attests to Morrison's critical engagement with mainstream theological discourse. It would be an interesting project to study her ideas about the Christian faith as they are expressed in *Paradise* and her other novels in greater detail than is possible in this chapter.

[141]See Pecola and Mrs. Breedlove in *The Bluest Eye*, Sula and Hannah Peace in *Sula*, First Corinthians and Ruth in *Song of Solomon*, Beloved and Sethe in *Beloved*, May and Christine Cosey in *Love*, the minha mae and her daughter Florens in *Mercy*. For *Paradise* see also Billie Delia and Patricia Best, Seneca and Jean, Sally and Mavis, Gigi and Consolata and the mothers they never knew, as well as Pallas and Dee Dee.

[142]In Brazil, Yemanjá is also the goddess of the ocean and patron of all seafaring people.

[143]With its allusion to the Middle Passage the ship watched by the two women creates another connection with *Beloved*, the first in the loose trilogy of novels of which *Paradise* is the last.

project she takes up an idea she already expressed in *Beloved*, where Baby Suggs teaches the former slaves who escaped to the North about grace: "[T]he only grace they could have was the grace they could imagine. That if they could not see it, they would not have it" (88). The paradise Morrison presents to us in the last image of the novel she finished ten years after *Beloved* is a very earthly one, a flawed paradise spelled with a lower case 'p,' and thus the only paradise imaginable.[144] There is debris on the beach, and the people who inhabit the scene are marked by hardship, possibly slavery. They have "ruined fingers," they "have been disconsolate for some time," and they are created to do hard work (*Paradise* 318). This imagery calls to mind the troubled history of the town of Ruby and the ethics of its founders, and yet Morrison's paradise differs from the traditional, Puritan notion of *Paradise* represented by the town in that it is open to all human beings, regardless of their gender, race, class, or sexuality. The Rubyites will not be barred from it either; in fact, their elders are unable to bar their folk and themselves from this new paradise. All efforts to confine their community through self-segregation within a Puritan African American model nation have been doomed from the start. Their failure could not be prevented even through the scapegoating and killing of the Convent women. Critical minds such as Patricia and Lone understand this, as do open-minded people like Anna Flood and Richard Misner. Perhaps most encouragingly, it is sensed also by the conservative Deacon Morgan. But the violence of the New Fathers and the connivance of most other Rubyites with the aggressive exclusiveness of their leaders are not held against them either; they are redeemed by love.

Paradise is not a pre-defined state of being, or a fixed idea or place that must be defended against alternative visions, Morrison tells us. The only paradise imaginable is a process, constantly evolving, always open to change, never reaching completion. Such an earthly paradise can only be achieved and upheld if the participants in this infinite project continually and incessantly work on guaranteeing its inclusive character. If people

---

[144]Morrison expressed regret over the fact that she did not have enough time to go over the script once more, because the novel had to be submitted for publication at the end of 1997 in order to guarantee its availability during the Christmas sales. One mistake that remained undetected is the last word in the novel, "Paradise," which ought to have been written with a lower-case 'p' (cf. D. Smith). It is a minor typing mistake, but the 'p' contains the gist of Morrison's notion of paradise.

are able to appreciate the heterogeneous diversity that accompanies openness and to integrate it into their lives, earthly paradise will be more than
"memories [...] of reaching age in the company of the other; speech
shared and divided bread smoking from the fire" (*Paradise* 318). Then,
"the unambivalent bliss of going home to be at home – the ease of coming
back to love begun" will be a reality (*Paradise* 318).

Part III

Questioning the Notion of Gender

5 Stretching the Limits of Gender: Subversive Genders in *Oranges Are Not the Only Fruit*, *Sexing the Cherry*, and *The Passion*

> Gender is a template, a beginning, a set of possibilities, it's not a rigid structure and should never be a prison.
>
> Jeanette Winterson

My approach to Winterson's work up to the publication of *Written on the Body* in 1992 is determined by the assumption that issues of gender are absolutely central to it. Winterson interrogates social spaces as gendered spaces and the male-female dichotomy as a patriarchal instrument for the exercise and preservation of power and a restrictive corset for individuals of any gender. She explores ways of subverting strict gender definitions, of imagining and living multiple possibilities of gender. Winterson's project begins with texts that deconstruct existing hetero-patriarchal notions of gender. As I concentrate on the gender identities of select characters from *Oranges*, *The Passion*, and *Sexing the Cherry* in this chapter, my goal is to show how the author's understanding of the gender concept has evolved over the course of seven years and three fictions, and how the discussions of gender in these texts, together with the protagonists' subversive subject positions, pave the way for a radical interrogation of the notion of gender in *Written on the Body*.

5.1 Compulsive Gendering and Dev/fiant Lesbianism

Female protagonists in Winterson's early fiction often are or were at some point engaged in lesbian relationships. Yet, the scope of this author's work easily transcends the bounds of lesbian romance writing. Winterson firmly instals her lesbian protagonists in hetero-patriarchal social setups and views mainstream societies through the lens of perceptions and expe-

riences of women who deviate from the norm in their ways of constructing their gender identities and in their same-sex desire. While some of
the protagonists are marginalized because of their non-compliance with
the laws that safeguard the status quo, others are allowed to diversify the
society they live in as they demonstrate alternative possibilities of shaping
one's life and of creating intelligible and meaningful identities. In every
case, however, lesbianism highlights the mechanisms and consequences
of compulsive bipolar gendering in heteronormative societies and it explores ways of subverting patriarchal gender norms.

5.1.1   Jeanette

Oranges Are Not the Only Fruit starts with one of the matter-of-fact statements characteristic of the first-person narrator, Jeanette: "Like most people I lived for a long time with my mother and father. My father liked
to watch the wrestling, my mother liked to wrestle; it didn't matter what.
She was in the white corner and that was that" (*Oranges* 3).[1] At first sight,
this statement seems straightforward enough, but a closer inspection reveals a conflict that points to the dominant theme of this fiction. "Like
most people" Jeanette grew up in a family of father, mother, and child
– the quintessential kernel of hetero-patriarchal society. She lived with
her parents "for a long time," in the late 1950s and 1960s, as we find out
later. This leads us to assume – most of us from our own experience –
that she thoroughly internalized this normative set-up, including the traditional roles and behaviors of woman/wife/mother/passive object *versus*
man/husband/father/active subject. And indeed, we learn that Jeanette's
father works at the local factory, while her mother runs the household and
takes care of the child, albeit in an unusual fashion.

   This incarnation of hegemonic norms is countered by the information that the factory-working father enjoys the passive consumption of
wrestling matches, whether on TV or in real life, while the mother is doing the wrestling. In the entire text the nominal head of the family never

---

[1] In the following, the titles *Oranges Are Not the Only Fruit*, *The Passion*, and *Sexing the Cherry* frequently will be abbreviated to *Oranges*, *Passion*, and *Sexing*,
respectively, as has become customary with Winterson scholars. Page numbers
refer to the Vintage editions, in case of *Oranges* of 1991, in those of *Passion* and
Sexing of 1996.

makes a decision, utters hardly a word, and, working night shifts, is in bed most of the day, whereas Mother devises ambitious plans for her daughter's future career as a missionary. She is a pillar of strength in the local congregation of her small Pentecostal church and fights bitter, vociferous battles against the "heathens" that surround her community in the ungodly town of their residence. Quite obviously, neither the division of roles between Jeanette's parents nor their behavior in family and community conform to traditional notions of their genders in Western society. Father is quiet and malleable, "deep," as his wife likes to describe him; Mother runs the family and manages various charitable and missionary causes. She takes charge of familial and church affairs because she is convinced that, with very few exceptions, men are incapable of doing so. "We had no Wise Men [in the familial Christmas decorations] because she didn't believe there were any wise men," Jeanette recalls (*Oranges* 4).

The domestic power of Mother is paralleled by the strong standing of women in Jeanette's branch of their church. Although the top posts are invariably occupied by men – Pastor Spratt, the missionary, Pastor Eli Bone of the Society of the Bereaved, Pastor Finch, who is the minister and an exorcist of demons – the day-to-day running of the church is firmly in the hands of women. From ample personal experience Jeanette describes the women in her church as "strong and organized" (*Oranges* 121). Until her fall from grace she is, despite her youth, among the most influential members of the church, and by her own account she "had enough [power] to keep Mussolini happy" (*Oranges* 121). Being a gifted speaker, she is regularly asked to preach on Sundays and during the so-called "Glory Crusades." Moreover, she is responsible for a Bible class that caters specifically to new converts. As a fourteen-year-old, Jeanette is the most efficient and persuasive missionary in her congregation. To the girl, there is nothing surprising in this fact, as she was raised in the certain knowledge that she is special – she had been "dedicated to the Lord" by her mother – and would go on to do great things in her life (*Oranges* 81).

Apart from her parents' inadvertent subversion of classical patriarchal gender roles and her mother's oddly emancipatory convictions, "enlightened and reactionary at the same time" (*Oranges* 126), Jeanette also receives an unconventional education as to the procreative functions of women. She remembers that her mother "had a mysterious attitude towards the begetting of children; it wasn't that she couldn't do it, more that she didn't want to do it. She was very bitter about the Virgin Mary getting there first. So she did the next best thing and arranged for a foundling" (*Oranges* 3). Mother disparagingly refers to Jeanette's biological mother as "a carrying case" (*Oranges* 99), while she likes to think of the foundling as a gift of God, for her to form and prepare for great deeds in His name. Early on, Mother instills in this "child of God" "sprung from her head" the idea that sex was to be avoided at all cost (*Oranges* 85, 10).[2] She condemns the noisy sexual activities of "the Heathen" next door as "fornicating" and retaliates by violent wall-banging and singing of hymns. Their numerous children do not in the slightest redeem the neighbors in Mother's eyes. She dislikes sex *per se*; Immaculate Conception is her preferred method of procreation, as it foregoes physical intimacy with men.

Even love in its romantic variety is suspicious to Mother: She changes the ending of *Jane Eyre*, her favorite non-religious book, which she reads to little Jeanette as a bedtime story.[3] In her version, Jane marries St John Rivers and lives a devout and passionless life with him. Mother takes the onset of her daughter's puberty as an opportunity to tell her "about Pierre and how [she] nearly came to a bad end" when, as a young teacher in Paris, she felt "a fizzing and a buzzing and a certain giddiness" as she succumbed to the courting of this flattering Frenchman (*Oranges* 84f.). When a consultation with a doctor revealed that Mother had a stomach ulcer, she put her dizzying feelings with Pierre down to this condition. "So just you take care, what you think is the heart may well be another organ," is the morale she deduces from this experience. She fortifies her point with a gloomy warning never to "let anyone touch you Down There" (*Oranges* 86).

As a result of her mother's unorthodox teachings and the uninspiring personalities of the men in her vicinity, Jeanette develops a rather unfavorable notion of men and of women's relations with them. As a child she is troubled by recurrent nightmares about her own wedding which end with the husband-to-be turning out to be "blind, sometimes a pig, sometimes [her] mother, sometimes the man from the post office, and once, just a suit of clothes with nothing inside" (*Oranges* 69). Jeanette's growing suspicion that men are really beasts is based upon information she

---

[2]Note Mother's megalomaniac self-identification with Zeus, the highest Olympian god from whose head sprang his daughter, Athena.

[3]Little Jeanette grows up in a household in which very few books are permitted, among them the Holy Bible and *Jane Eyre*.

extracts from fairy tales that plainly spell it out and careless dialogues she overhears between frustrated wives about their pigheaded husbands. She knows that a girl is supposed to find a suitable man at some point in her life, but the question that puzzles her is, "What do you do if you marry a beast? Kissing them [does] not always help" (*Oranges* 71).[4]

Thus, her mother's scandalized reaction to the "fornication" going on Next Door, the wives' remarks about their beastly husbands, and Mother's tale about love as a stomach ulcer make heterosexual love and sex appear strange and undesirable to Jeanette. She tries to avoid back alleys in her town out of fear of having to witness the love-making of young men and women: "I went the long way, so as to miss the couples. They made funny noises that sounded painful, and the girls were always squashed against the wall" (*Oranges* 70). In fact, there is little in heterosexual sex that seems normal or natural to young Jeanette.

Love and sexual intimacy acquire a very different meaning for her when she meets Melanie, a young Catholic whom she recruits to her church. Melanie asks her to be her counsellor, a task which necessitates Jeanette's regular visits to her house. The friendship between the two teenagers becomes increasingly intense, not least because it is the first and only friendship either of them has ever entertained with a person of their own age-group. Jeanette's only friend is Elsie Norris, an ambulance driver of Word War I and former suffragette who is now in her eighties. As the daughter of a single mum Melanie has to work after school and does not have the time needed to entertain friendships. In the night following Mother's warning about the dangers of sex, the friendly embrace of the two girls turns into passionate love-making, the prelude to many nights spent together either at Melanie's home or at Elsie's, who provides a safe haven for the lovers.

For Jeanette, the feelings she has for her friend and the desire the two of them share for one another are pure and natural – "an accident," as she later calls it (*Oranges* 126). They cannot be stopped, even though initially they are frightening to her (cf. *Oranges* 86), and intimacy is "so very dis-

---

[4]This subvertive perspective on heterosexual sex practices is again taken up in *Sexing the Cherry*: Because of the huge size of the Dog-Woman, her only sexual encounter with a man has the effect of defamiliarizing the sex act, making it and the male partner appear absurd (see Palmer, "Postmodern Trends"). By problematizing heterosexual relations in this way, *Oranges* and *Sexing* question the heterosexual claim to naturalness and normalcy.

turbing" to Jeanette who had known so little of it (*Oranges* 101). Their first love-making is presented as a creative act of Biblical proportions: "And it was evening and it was morning; another day" (*Oranges* 86).[5] As the girls experience sexual passion for the first time, and because of the multiple warnings they received from their elders about strong feelings outside the narrow emotional parameters prescribed by their Pentecostal spirituality, they wonder what kind of passion theirs might be. "'Do you think this is Unnatural Passion?'" Jeanette asks Melanie (*Oranges* 86). Only after a thorough reflection does she decide to agree with her lover's argument that it "[d]oesn't feel like it," as "[a]ccording to Pastor Finch, that's awful" (*Oranges* 86). Indeed, at the beginning their relationship appears quite uncomplicated to the two young girls; it seems somehow in tune with the negative image of relationships between men and women that dominates their imagination. As they have only a very fuzzy notion of sexuality and sexual practices in general and have never heard of lesbianism, they are unable to recognize the lesbians who live in their town, let alone conceive of themselves as lesbians.[6] "Melanie and I were special" (*Oranges* 104), Jeanette is convinced because of the purity of their love, because of their unity in spirit, their shared faith in God, and their certainty of belonging into the "white corner" (*Oranges* 3). They feel a secure bond between themselves and their community, which they regard as "[their] family. It was safe" (*Oranges* 86).

Out of this profound sense of safety and belonging and out of the desire to communicate her happiness and find sympathy for it, Jeanette confides her feelings for Melanie to her mother. But she does not mention intimacy, knowing that her mother "wouldn't really understand" (*Oranges* 98).[7] This half-confession, Mother's taciturn reaction to it and her suc-

---

[5] Winterson uses a near-quote from the story of the Creation according to Genesis 1, the recurring phrase at the end of each of the six days of Creation in chapter 1,36.

[6] The two women at the local paper shop are a couple and are duly slighted by the members of Jeanette's church. They have always liked Jeanette and she in turn likes them – as oblivious of their marginal position in the town as of its cause.

[7] Previously, Jeanette had noticed the disappearance of the photograph of a woman that had been included in Mother's photo album under the rubric of "Old Flames," after she had inquired who this person was. Winterson here thematizes the often severe homophobic reactions in people who deny and suppress their own homoerotic experiences or desires.

ceeding state of appearing "caught up in something" produce a growing sense of unease in Jeanette (*Oranges* 100). For the second time, after learning that Mother was not her biological mother and would never allow her to meet the woman who had given birth to her, she experiences uncertainty. This is a deeply unsettling sensation for her: "Uncertainty was what the Heathen felt" and what she should never feel, being "chosen by God" (*Oranges* 98). For a while it remains unclear to Jeanette why she should feel "uncomfortable," when "[k]nowing Melanie was a much happier thing" than anything she had ever felt before (*Oranges* 97). As a consequence of this uncertain emotional state she becomes secretive, not always telling her Mother where she spends her nights and trying to be "more careful" about arranging her trysts with Melanie.

Thus, when Jeanette learns one Sunday morning what exactly the pastor means when he rages against "unnatural passions" and demons that possess those who engage in them, taking her and Melanie as examples, she has already had a vague and confused sense of the illegitimacy of a girl's love for another girl in an evangelical church situated in a conventional mill-town community of the 1960s. Somehow she knows that girls will be women one day and then, whether they like it or not, will marry men in order to have children. Jeanette's solution to the conflict between her cultural knowledge of the convention of heterosexuality and heterosexual reproduction on the one hand and her heart-felt knowledge of her love for Melanie on the other, lies in her trust in God: "Still, [...], Melanie [is] a gift from God," she is convinced, "and it would be ungrateful not to appreciate her" (*Oranges* 102). Despite her own uncertainty, Jeanette questions the conventional belief in the normalcy of heterosexuality and the abjectness of same-sex love, first unconsciously, later quite consciously. While Melanie, panic-stricken, renounces their relationship already during that Sunday service, Jeanette refuses to accept that her love for Melanie is the work of demons and therefore despicable. To her, something that is God-given can never be sinful: When the pastor tells the congregation that "[t]hese children are full of demons," she retorts, "To the pure all things are pure. [...] It's you not us" (*Oranges* 102f.).

One of the strongest achievements of Winterson's first fiction is to question the dichotomy of heterosexuality as natural and pure *versus* homosexuality as unnatural and abject. Little Jeanette's thoughtful observations about the unappetizing strangeness of heterosexual love humorously point our attention to the arbitrariness and artificiality of the notion of what is considered natural and therefore normal. Her mother's confusion of the symptoms of falling in love with those of a stomach ulcer serves to ridicule "the symbolic narratives of heterosexuality" (J. Morrison 99), just as her insistence that she can be a mother without having given birth highlights the restrictiveness of the conventional couplings of 'woman equals mother' and 'marriage as state-sanctioned heterosexual partnership equals parenthood.'

Palmer contends that *Oranges* succeeds to a degree in normalising the lesbian perspective by treating it as if it were an everyday, commonsense matter (cf. "Postmodern Trends" 197). However, while I fully agree that one of the functions lesbianism has here is to challenge heterosexism, I want to suggest that in this fiction Winterson is less interested in "normalizing" homosexuality than in calling into question the notion of the normal itself and in establishing same-sex love and desire as a valid and equal alternative to heterosexuality. Furthermore, in *Oranges* the author explores mechanisms of gendering as well as the struggle of individuals to harmonize their desire to resist normative definitions of sameness with their need for community and belonging.

The divide which Jeanette diagnoses between the church elders on the one side and Melanie and her on the other introduces this second thematic complex of *Oranges*. The feeling of safe closeness to the members of her church she enjoyed when she entered the building that Sunday – "There was nowhere I'd rather be" (*Oranges* 102) – gives way to the horrifying realization that she has just been exiled from this community of like-minded people. After the pastor disputes her faith by pronouncing that she does not love the Lord if she loves Melanie, that she cannot love both, his announcement that "[t]he church will not see you suffer, go home and wait for us to help you," sounds to her more like a threat than an offer of help (*Oranges* 103).

Instead of going home, Jeanette follows Miss Jewsbury to her apartment. Miss Jewsbury also belongs to her church but is marginalized for being an educated, unmarried Scottish woman in a Northern-English working-class community that likes to see its women marry young. She acts as a first link between Jeanette and the lesbian community, even though Miss Jewsbury defines her own identity, her deviance from the norm as problematic: "It's my problem too," she explains to Jeanette before she attempts to comfort the shaken girl by making love to her (*Or-*

anges 104).[8] Through Miss Jewsbury, then, Jeanette realizes that she is indeed different from the other members of her church. Unlike them, she does not comply sufficiently with the norms they set for girls and women. She has heard, and to a degree internalized, the recurring comment of Mrs. White, one of the bigoted church elders and a friend of Jeanette's mother, whenever "that Miss Jewsbury" is mentioned: "Oh, she's not holy" (e.g. *Oranges* 105). After the night spent with Miss Jewsbury, Jeanette understands the nature of the woman's difference which, per analogy, is also her own. She learns that difference in the eyes of the elders means deviance from the norm and signifies absence or loss of "holiness." Yet, importantly, Miss Jewsbury also gives her a sense of the fact that – contrary to what she and Melanie had believed about their relationship – she is not alone in her difference, that there are indeed others like her.

These realizations help Jeanette to make sense of what the orange demon tells her. The demon appears to her during her two days of solitary confinement without food or drink to which the elders condemn her after hours of fruitless praying over her and urging her to "renounce [Melanie]" (*Oranges* 105): She has to acknowledge her difference, embrace it, and make use of it in what would consequently be "a difficult but different time" for her (*Oranges* 107). Jeanette decides to keep her demon and accept her difference. Pretending to repent is "the best way [she] can think of [not getting rid of her demon]," so for a while this is what she does (*Oranges* 107). Thereby she buys the time she needs to find out who she wants to be and how she wants to live.

In the ensuing passages of *Oranges*, Winterson explores through her protagonist Jeanette the mechanisms of gendering in hetero-patriarchal Western society, as well as the consequences of an individual's refusal to submit to prescribed gender norms and behaviors. In a feverish dream at the peak of her crisis, Jeanette arrives with "truckloads of men and women" in the city of Lost Chances, a great round stone area that is "crumbling in places" (*Oranges* 108). They are prisoners with numbers

[8]This is a troubling scene in so far as it allows for a reading of Miss Jewsbury's love-making to Jeanette as being opportunistic rather than altruistically motivated. While she does take advantage of the girl's vulnerability, she also gives Jeanette the affirmative (sexual) contact she needs during that phase of abandonment and confusion: "She bent over me; I could feel her breath on my neck. Quite suddenly I turned and kissed her. We made love and I hated it and hated it, but would not stop" (*Oranges* 104).

around their necks; most of them are "mutilated" (*Oranges* 108). When Jeanette reaches the bookshop at the top of a turret that is to be her new address, she learns that the city is for those "who can't make the ultimate decision," and the bookshop is "the Room of the Final Disappointment," reserved for people who "have made the Fundamental Mistake" (*Oranges* 109). In the bookshop she will rotate from the position of a browser to being a buyer, then one of the translators of *Beowulf* and back to start.

Chloë Taylor Merleau reads this dream as an allegory for the inevitability of gendering. "The resistance to gendering is made painful by a homophobic culture," she argues, "and thus the resisters are mostly 'mutilated,' eventually forced into a circle and a wall anyway: gendering is inevitable, though the circle may be imperfect, the wall half-toppled down" (Taylor Merleau 91). I agree that the stone walls of the city represent the rigid boundaries of femininity and masculinity into which men and women are crammed, but I do not share the sense of automatic, tragic destiny with regard to Jeanette's passage into adulthood and her life as a woman, the sense of inevitability present in Taylor Merleau's interpretation. Jeanette's dream is very much a nightmare, resulting as it does from the ordeal of being forsaken by her community as well as by her lover. But as a nightmare, I suggest, it speaks of Jeanette's fears of the future, rather than of her present situation. It speaks of her fear of being mutilated in her struggle to define her gender identity according to her own inclination and wishes; the fear of wasting the chance to resist external pressures to deny her lesbian desire; the fear of making the fundamental mistake and giving up what she regards as her individuality in order to conform to societal conventions, and thus of suffering the final disappointment of endless cycles of performances of tasks dictated to her by convention.

It might seem surprising that the destination of final disappointment should be a bookstore where people browse, buy books, and translate a famous work of literature, given Jeanette's and Winterson's own fascination with literature and pleasure in books. But having to translate the much-translated *Beowulf* again and again maybe would not afford anyone much pleasure, especially not if one regards this text as a representative of the closed, male-dominated canon against which Winterson strains with her work. Jeanette has this nightmare at a time when she is only starting to understand the strictures of a gendered society. She has rebelled against one of the borders of the binary system of male and female: compulsory heterosexuality. Now she has to decide whether she will consent to using the conventional, hegemonic model of femininity – including marriage and motherhood – as a means of becoming an intelligible, speaking subject, or else create an identity through her resistance to the gendering practiced within her church. Her nightmare is the result of the struggle she fights subconsciously upon realizing the stark nature of the decision she needs to make.

Melanie's development after her public renouncment of her love for Jeanette demonstrates the nightmarish consequences of making a decision that is right according to societal norms and wrong in terms of one's own individuality. Not daring to leave the extended family she has found in Jeanette's church, she chooses the conventional option: She earns the privilege of belonging by resigning herself to being gendered female according to the norms of a hetero-patriarchal society. Startlingly, as she commits herself and her body to the process of gendering – indeed, as she actively engages in it – she changes physically and mentally. Shortly after the exorcism performed upon her, the formerly radiant Melanie looks "tired and crumpled like a balloon full of old air" (*Oranges* 109). The next time Jeanette sees her "[s]he had put on some weight and looked quite serene" (*Oranges* 118), and still later, just before getting married, "[Melanie] was serene, serene to the point of being bovine" (*Oranges* 119). Jeanette is dismayed and enraged by her former lover's metamorphosis into the plump, ununemancipated embodiment of the stereotypical self-denying mother, because she sees that Melanie virtually lives her nightmare. She has become one of the occupants of the city of Lost Chances, one of "those who chose the wall" (*Oranges* 110), someone who reads and re-translates *Beowulf* instead of fashioning her own identity and narrating her own life story. Melanie has chosen the easy safety of the confines of hegemony, over the uncertainty of having to determine her own notion of gender identity. Taylor Merleau speaks of the violence inherent in the discursive sexing/gendering of the body, a violence that is effaced in hetero-patriarchal society by being presented as normal (cf. 92). The changes occurring in Melanie and the ultimate arrest of her psychophysiological development in a state of bovine femaleness illustrate this violence: The church's sexing of her leaves her mutilated in body and mind.

Melanie's alarming example elucidates for Jeanette the necessity to resist the violence of being gendered in a way that would guarantee her a safe and comfortable life in the folds of her church. Yet, the intimidating alternative to acquiescing in a process of gendering that would produce an identity deemed "normal" is the identification with an abject subject position that would place her outside her community. Jeanette therefore asks herself whether it is "necessary to wander unprotected through the land?" (*Oranges* 110). This is the position she sees herself in after her relationship with another young convert is threatened to be revealed and Jeanette reports herself to the elders in an effort to protect her lover from what she has come to see as "the darker side of [her] church" (*Oranges* 128). The church council reacts to her "confession" by declaring the power wielded by women in Jeanette's branch of the church to be at the root of the problem. She is forced to resign all positions that would allow her what the pastors terms "influential contact" with the congregation (*Oranges* 132).

Jeanette's "inability to realize the limitations of [her] sex," as she herself sarcastically calls it, indicates her continual resistance to hegemonic gendering (*Oranges* 132). This resistance stretches from the field of language to that of desire, and in both spheres she reaches for privileges the society reserves for men: the power to use language to instruct and guide people in the former, the right to love and desire a woman in the latter. Consequently, Jeanette not only rejects the limits hetero-patriarchy places on "her sex," she also subverts the law of heterosexuality which stabilizes and naturalizes the binary of male and female. Such is the threat her resistance to gendering presents to her church that her alleged sin is taken as a pretext for the systematic withdrawal of rights and power from the entire female part of the church community. Moreover, in the face of one girl's revolt against a normative gender system that is deemed natural, the women connive at their own oppression by voluntarily handing their power over to the men.

Dismayed by this connivance of the oppressed with their oppressors and threatened with an exorcism more powerful than the first one, scheduled to render her abject, impossible identity intelligible and thus acceptable to the majority, Jeanette decides to leave her church. This decision places her outside the "stone wall" of hegemony, where she has to fend for herself without the nurturing of the tight-knit community that previously looked up to her for guidance and spiritual sustenance. It is Mother who leads the church women into insignificance by calling on the men to free them of their wrongfully usurped power. Mother also performs the split between her daughter and the church and thus herself: She ferrets out and burns all of Jeanette's books, love letters, and personal notes. After a church meeting she blames her for "taking on a man's world," of "flout[ing] God's law" and publicly renounces her (*Oranges* 131).

Jeanette tries to come to terms with the consequences of her decision by donning the identities of mythic or imagined persons and transferring her own struggle to the realities of these persons which she brings to life in acts of story-telling.[9] Thus, she temporarily becomes Sir Perceval and leaves the Round Table of the beloved King to embark on a quest for the Holy Grail, a quest that will keep Perceval restless and always searching. In the story of the young wizard Winnet Stonejar she recapitulates her own story – being taken into a community, groomed to fit her mother's purposes, and then expelled for loving "the wrong sort of people" (*Oranges* 125).[10] Winnet comes to live with a powerful sorcerer after he guesses her name. He cares for her as a parent and teaches her useful things, but eventually feels compelled to send her away as a punishment for her striking up a friendship with a stranger. One of the secrets the sorcerer teaches Winnet is that of the power of chalk circles to protect those who draw them around themselves from attacks of those on the outside.

For Jeanette, the image of the chalk circle relates to that of the stone wall in the same way as her subversive identity as a young lesbian woman relates to the hegemonic heterosexual femininity conventionally considered normal. In order to acquire subjecthood it is necessary to define the boundaries of one's self toward the outside. However, such boundaries must not become walls of stone, i.e., sealed tight against alternative subject positions, imprisoning those inside, and threatening and prohibitive to those outside. Rather, they should be like the chalk circle around young Winnet: drawn by oneself, light, with occasional openings, and even allowing for the possibility of its dissolution.[11] "It is necessary to distin-

---

[9]Palmer points out that Jeanette constructs for herself a series of shifting, fluid selves by means of acts of storytelling ("Postmodern Trends").

[10]Note that "Winnet Stonejar" is a near anagram of "Jeanette Winterson." Armitt suggests that by "[scrambling] the name" Winterson "[points] out the *limitations* of the character/author identification" (16).

[11]Taylor Merleau argues that the fact that the sorcerer threw Winnet the chalk with which to draw the circle means that Winnet's circle is not self-chosen and autonomous, but also an instrument of hegemonic order and restriction. In contrast, my reading emphasizes the necessity of the chalk circle, i.e., the need to define oneself against one's environment in order to become a person, a speaking "I."

guish the chalk circle from the stone wall," Jeanette philosophizes (*Or-anges* 111).

The next painful question Jeanette asks herself is whether a life in the state of homelessness is necessary in order to remain unmutilated and to retain her difference from the heterosexual norm. In the story of the young wizard, Winnet Stonejar is reluctant to leave the realm of her sorcerer father, but she heeds the warning of her favorite raven who did not have the strength to place himself outside hegemonic rule and who gives her his pebble-like heart as a reminder of the price he had to pay for staying. "You see, I chose to stay," the raven explains, "and my heart grew thick with sorrow, and finally set. It will remind you" (*Oranges* 144). Winnet leaves her home, and so does Jeanette who decides to "distinguish physics from metaphysics" (*Oranges* 111). She resolves to create for herself a home that is not dependent on physical surroundings or even a family but exists within herself, in the "cities of the interior" (*Oranges* 111). There, in her imagination, the principles for the construction of bodies and identities are different from those in her everyday reality: "[I]n the cities of the interior all things are changed. A wall for the body, a circle for the soul" (*Oranges* 111).[12]

But, if there are still walls and circles in "the cities of the interior," one might ask, where is the difference from hetero-patriarchal society? Taylor Merleau's reading of Jeanette's dream and the story of Winnet Stonejar is informed by her interest in Winterson's inventions of idioms to express the "silence of the victims of a wrong, a differend" (86).[13] She therefore regards both the wall and the circle as metaphors for "the damaging and erasure of gendering, or the 'soft-voiced' violence of sex" (90). I propose a reading of Winterson's first fiction that looks specifically into conflict-ing ideas and politics with which the author struggles. Such a reading ex-poses a tension between radical-lesbian, exclusivist notions reminiscent

---

[12] Jeanette's distinction between the body as the "wall" that stands for sex and the mind as the "chalk circle" that symbolizes gender follows Beauvoir's argumen-tation of the inevitability of sexing and the distinction of gender from sex, which allows the sexed body multiple genders.

[13] Using Butler's reading of Lyotard, Taylor Merleau defines women who love women as "differends" in the sense that they are people who are excluded through naturalized processes of othering and are thus denied subjecthood.

of Monique Wittig's writings on the one hand,[14] and the Foucaultian acknowledgment of the inevitability of gendering on the other, paired with
the realization that lesbian separatism neither works as a theoretical strategy, nor as a political one.

For Jeanette, the wall and the circle do not represent the same degree of oppression; the wall, though crumbling, is still rigid enough to
imprison people, whereas the chalk circle allows for a certain amount of
self-determination, as it is drawn by the person within it. By assigning the
wall to the body Jeanette recognizes the compulsory nature of gender and
criticizes it for its potentially crippling physical effects upon the body of
the gendered subject. The human body, Winterson seems to suggest, is
not a natural given. It is a product of mechanisms of gender assignment
through discourse and action, an assignment whose violence is concealed
and made to appear natural through the compulsory pairing of men and
women in heterosexual relationships, through the definition of desire as
directed toward the "opposite" gender. For the soul and mind surrounded
by a mere chalk circle, however, Winterson via Jeanette diagnoses and
proclaims the freedom to revolt, to reject the violent mechanisms of gendering and preserve the power to define one's own limits, desires, identifi-
catory characteristics.[15] A woman who loves another woman exposes and
therefore denaturalizes the interdependence of the binary gender system
and heterosexuality: female Jeanette is accused of "[a]ping men" (*Oranges* 125). In the eyes of the elders she paradoxically becomes male
although she never ceases to be a girl; she exhibits a non-identity that is
unintelligible to the heterosexual majority. Through her decision to live as
a lesbian Jeanette constructs a femaleness that is impossible and abject in
a community that defines women as exclusively desiring men. Lesbianism, therefore, is presented as an effective lever with which to unhinge
not only the inherently misogynist gender binary, but also the patriarchal
social order.

Yet the chalk circle of subversive lesbianism carefully leaves intact the
exclusive limits of the gender binary whose constructedness Winterson

---

[14]Read with Wittig, the lesbian Jeanette, in assuming speech, becomes a speaking
subject that is not bound by sex/gender and therefore is outside the discursive
system of gender.
[15]In a sense Winterson here reproduces the misogynist hierarchy of
mind/maleness/freedom versus body/femaleness/lack of freedom.

exposes so effectively in her text. To Jeanette, "a man is a man, wherever you find it" (*Oranges* 128), even if he happens to love another man. Loving a woman, teaching, and speaking in public will not render Jeanette less female; she understands herself to be a woman who "[sees] nothing else in common" between herself and men "apart from [her] never wearing a skirt" (*Oranges* 126).

Homosexuality is painted in equally essentialist colors in *Oranges*: Jeanette remembers that she "had never shown the slightest feeling" for men; as a child she saw something beastly in them, and the idea of having to marry a man gave her nightmares. But, although Winterson reproduces "the simple and restrictive binary terms ('you and us') of the struggle," as Doan describes it (146), her essentialism is an uneasy one already in her first fiction. Melanie marries, although there cannot be the slightest doubt that she once loved and desired Jeanette. Jeanette herself seems unable to decide whether her love for women is accidental or an act of willful resistance against heteronormativity and the gender identities produced by it. Although Winterson shows the disruptive potential of lesbianism in terms of the gender binary, she seems to recognize – and, indeed, regret – the fact that it is only thinkable in relation and opposition to heterosexuality, which in turn depends on the binary of male and female.[16] As Doan rightly points out, "[i]n *Oranges* binaries are revealed at every turn, though never erased or eliminated" (146). Winterson tackles the task of moving on to the erasure and elimination of binaries in her second fiction.

5.1.2 Villanelle

In *The Passion* borders are pointed out in order that they may be crossed, binaries revealed so that they may be transcended. Winterson here explores the idea of life as a series of choices from a reservoir of possibilities. In my discussion of the author's exploration of a diversity of imaginable identities and ways of living in this text I will concentrate on the concepts of gender and sexuality.[17]

---

[16]Doan calls the "continued reliance on the terms of heterosexuality" of the notion of the lesbian "troubling," "because the lesbian is still positioned within binary logic itself" (146).

[17]Other central concepts in this novel include those of time and space, which I briefly discussed in the opening chapter.

In its structure, *The Passion* cites and thereby highlights the dual set-up of heteronormative societies: There are two narrators, one male – Henri, the neck-wringer of chickens in Bonaparte's field kitchen – and one female – Villanelle, a Venetian card dealer sold into prostitution to the Grande Armée. On a scale measuring the degree of freedom of choice available to individuals in a society, Henri and Villanelle would occupy diametrically opposed positions. On the lower end, Henri, in need of a powerful father figure whose goals would lend his "lukewarm" life purpose and passion, becomes a soldier and follows Napoleon's despotic and ruthless leadership like a duckling that "will attach itself to whatever it first sees, duck or not" (*Passion* 147). During eight years of violence and deprivation he grows to hate the man he once adored and flees from the steppes of Russia toward Western Europe with his friend Patrick and the *vivandiére* Villanelle. He never reaches his home country, but, of his own volition, remains in a madhouse on the island of San Servolo, in the lagoon of Venice.

The high end of the scale measuring the availability of freedom of choice is represented by Venice, Villanelle's home and a place of shifting borders, deluding appearances, and unfixed rules: "the city of mazes" (*Passion* 49), "the city of disguises" (*Passion* 56), "the city of uncertainty" (*Passion* 58). For Henri, who is used to the regimental discipline of the French army, Venice feels somewhat unreal; he remembers that "[a]rriving at Venice by sea, as one must, is like seeing an invented city rise up and quiver in the air" (*Passion* 109). When he loses his way and asks Villanelle for a map, he is kindly reminded of the fact that "[t]his is a living city. Things change"' (*Passion* 113). Maps are useless in a place where "[c]anals hide other canals, alleyways cross and criss-cross so that you will not know which is which until you have lived here all your life"' (*Passion* 113). "This is an unusual city, we do things differently here," Villanelle explains to her friend, who, after hearing that in Venice boatmen are born with webbed feet and rumored to be able to walk on water, is secretly convinced that he is in "a city of madmen" (*Passion* 112).

The Venetians have adapted their ways of living to the changeable nature of their city and have integrated the liberties allowed by this variability into their relationships, including sexual ones. In Poland, Venice has become known as the "city of Satan" which supposedly houses "11,000 prostitutes all richer than the king" (*Passion* 104), and Villanelle, who has no interest in dispersing rumors such as this about her city, admits that "[s]ince Bonaparte captured our city of mazes in 1797, we've more or less abandoned ourselves to pleasure" (*Passion* 52). Indeed, not only is Venice full of casinos in which at times sexual services serve as wagers in games of chance, but these places of pleasure also provide "whipping rooms" for eager customers (*Passion* 125).

Villanelle revels in the freedom her city allows her. She earns a living as a card dealer in a casino and supplements her salary by picking the pockets and purses of partying strangers. During the summer months she basks in the sun on the hot stone stairs of Venetian churches, and in winter she revels in the sounds and sights of religion without bothering with religious rules and dogmas. Sex to Villanelle also seems a kind of basking in pleasure. She tells us early on that, in spite of her young age, she is "no stranger to love" (*Passion* 59), that she is "pragmatic" about it and "[has] taken [her] pleasure with both men and women" (*Passion* 60f.). After terrible years of forced prostitution she professes that she "[has] learnt to take pleasure without always questioning the source" (*Passion* 148). However, Villanelle distinguishes carefully between the excitements of casual sex on the one hand – as with the occasional customer of her casino, or even in the sisterly affection she feels for Henri and which she allows to lead to sex – and, on the other hand, love that steals the heart and produces passion.

In the "city of chances, where everything is possible" (*Passion* 90), Villanelle's uncomplicated bisexuality has little effect upon her emotional equilibrium. It does not seem unusual to her fellow-Venetians and is not met with sanctions that would lead readers to suspect that sexual encounters between people of the same sex are considered immoral or unnatural in Winterson's Venice. Therefore, when Villanelle falls in love with a married woman and experiences passion for the first time in her life, it is not the fact that she feels attracted to a woman that causes her anguish, but the fact that this woman is not wholly committed to her. "It was a game of chance I entered into and my heart was my wager," she realizes (*Passion* 94). With the Queen of Spades she risks her most valuable possession, her heart, true to her motto, "What you risk reveals what you value" (*Passion* 91).

In the sections of *The Passion* that are set in Venice, homo- or bisexuality are presented as valid choices for an individual. Heterosexuality is not compulsory; it is not enforced to become a law that naturalizes the gender binary; here, gender differences are comparatively loosely defined, a point which I will discuss in more detail further on in this chapter. But neither is heterosexuality ridiculed or made to appear grotesque *per se*, as was the case in *Oranges*. Henri's love and desire for Villanelle are as sincere and are portrayed as sympathetically as Villanelle's passion for the Queen of Spades. So, what (subversive) purposes does Villanelle's lesbianism serve in this work of fiction?

While in mercurial Venice sexualities and sexual preferences are representative features of freedom of choice and speak for an abundance of possibilities of leading one's life, such freedom is not available in Napoleonic France, let alone in the Grande Armée. Henri's mother escapes her aristocratic father and the marriage he arranged for his intelligent, independent-minded daughter and marries the quiet, gentle farmer who gave her shelter at his house. Women who are less determined to find their own way or less lucky in this pursuit fare worse in a patriarchal system based on war and male domination. Henri tells shocking tales of women who work as prostitutes in army camps:

> Napoleon himself ordered *vivandières* to be sent to special camps. *Vivandière* is an optimistic army word. He sent tarts who had no reason to be *vivant* about anything. Their food was often worse than ours, they had us as many hours of the day as we could stand and the pay was poor. [...] Unlike the town tarts, who protected themselves and charged what they liked and certainly charged individually, the *vivants* were expected to service as many men as asked them day or night. One woman I met crawling home after an officer's party said she'd lost count at thirty-nine. Christ lost consciousness at thirty-nine. (*Passion* 38)

In order to survive the sexual and physical violence of the soldiers who use them, the prostitutes rely on their solidarity – and their love for one another. During his only visit at an army brothel, Henri witnesses how the brutal cook attempts to beat a woman for spitting out his sperm: "He came forward with his fist raised but it never fell. My woman stepped forward and coshed him on the back of the head with a wine jar. She held her companion for a moment and kissed her swiftly on the forehead" (*Passion* 15). Lesbianism becomes a means of survival here; the two women's companionship provides the safety they need to preserve their basic emotional and physical wellbeing in the face of the constant threat of violation and annihilation, while their tenderness cushions off the hurt inflicted upon them by a representative of the sexist, masculinist system in which they live.

How much store Winterson sets by this trope of solidarity and love among women in defiance of male hegemony becomes apparent in the

fact that she takes it up again in *Sexing the Cherry*, where prostitutes con-
spire with the Dog-Woman to maim and kill their Puritan customers. Also
in *Sexing* we find an interlinking of two communities of women, the inhabitants of a harem and those of a nunnery, connected through a secret
under-water channel which allows them to come and go as they please
in their project of financing their future independent lives with the money
and artifacts they steal from the owner of the harem and his male friends.[18]

With the French occupation of Venice, the freedom to choose one's
way of living and loving in this city is challenged by agents of a society
organized along patriarchal principles. The text gives two striking examples of how a man reminds a woman of her inferior position in society
and of her predefined role as a woman. In both instances, sex is used as
the educational tool: One day after she had fallen in love with the Queen
of Spades, Villanelle loses to a soldier in a game of chance in which the
wager is his purse of money in the event of his defeat and his unhindered
access to her body, should the soldier win. Villanelle loses, and in one
lapidary comment she notes that "he was a man who liked his women
face down, arms outstretched like the crucified Christ" (*Passion* 70).

In the second instance, the cook who mistreated the prostitute while
he served in the French army, rapes Villanelle in the casino he frequents
to relax from his business of a meat supplier of Bonaparte's Grande Armée. He proposes marriage to her,[19] which Villanelle fatalistically accepts
when she realizes that the Queen of Spades will not leave her husband to
live with her: "I thought I might have a little game myself. Anything
now to relieve the ache of never finding her" (*Passion* 63). When the
cook ferrets out Villanelle, who tried to hide in order to escape his brutality, he punishes her by selling her to the French generals as a prostitute
and thus condemns her to a life of scheduled rapes. Aiming to assert not
only his own dominance over her, but also the overall dominance of men
over women, he forces this freedom-loving, independent-minded young
woman into sexually servicing men. By the time she is sold to the French
army, Villanelle has already experienced passionate love with woman and
has a history of cross-dressing for pleasure. The cook's punishment of her

---

[18]For a detailed analysis of all-female communities in Winterson's writing see
Stowers, "Communities."

[19]Taylor Merleau points out that for many rape victims marriage is the only "honorable" reaction to the abuse they endured (cf. 99).

can therefore also be read as a violent measure to "heterosexualize" her and thereby gender her female according to the binary gender system that is constructed and naturalized through cross-gender sexuality. Moreover, her sale into prostitution by a French ex-soldier constitutes a part of the colonialist enterprise of the Napoleonic France to root out traces of the original Venetian way of living, of which a self-determined sexuality and a comparative freedom of sexual object choice are important parts.

So far I have argued that a woman's freedom to express her sexuality freely and focus her desire on women as well as men signals the comparative freedom of choice and availability of multiple possibilities of constructing subject positions within the fluid boundaries of the city of Venice in *The Passion*. Yet, this observation is contrasted by the cautious, troubled nature of Villanelle's wooing of the Queen of Spades. The two women meet in the casino on a day when Villanelle wears men's clothes and a moustache. When she follows the older woman's dinner invitation, she hesitates to reveal her sex, fearing that the Queen of Spades might be attracted to her because of her apparent maleness, i.e., that the object of desire might be heterosexual. This begs the question of how unproblematic Villanelle's lesbianism – or lesbianism in general – really is in Winterson's Venice. Does it have a critical, political function apart from its important role of indicating freedom and heterogeneity in the city?[20]

When, on their way from Russia to Venice, Villanelle tells her traveling companions the story of her love for the Queen of Spades, she begins by asking them to admit that for a woman to love another woman "is not the usual thing" (*Passion* 94).[21] The unusual quality of her love seems to have been on her mind from the very beginning of her affair with the

---

[20]Pearce has raised the charge of universalism with regard to *The Passion*. She argues that "universalism is ensured by the inclusion of a broad spectrum of characters of different gender and sexual preference" and even ventures to suggest that "Villanelle's love affair cannot be said to be lesbian in any real political sense" (*Dialogics* 174). Contrary to this I regard Villanelle as a signifier of lesbian love who engages in sex with men under the pressures of compulsory heterosexuality or, as with Henri, as a token of affection that is effectively decoupled from passion. Rather than arguing for or against its veracity in terms of lesbian real-politics, my discussion of Villanelle's lesbianism explores possible subversive functions assigned to lesbianism in general in the text.

[21]To do justice to Pearce I want to add that in a different publication she admits that "[t]he acknowledgement that love between two women is 'not the usual

Queen of Spades, as her anxious question after their first night together suggests: "Could a woman love a woman for more than a night?" (*Passion* 69). The reason why this question even occurs to Villanelle, who knows that she is deeply in love with a woman, lies in the interdependence of gender and the law of heterosexuality. What she experiences with the Queen of Spades is more than the casual sexual adventures with women she alludes to. While in her city a woman can easily have short-lived affairs with other women, the privilege to love a woman and to commit oneself to her in a sincere, long-term relationship is reserved for men.

This connection between sexuality-*qua*-love and gender is emphasized by Villanelle's question that precedes the one quoted above. Staring into a canal she asks herself, "Could I walk on that water? Could I?" (*Passion* 69). Only boatmen and their male descendants are said to walk on water in Venice, due to the patrilinear physical anomaly of webbed feet. Villanelle was born with webbed feet, but as she is not a man, she is not quite certain that her feet will enable her to walk on water. As she succeeds, however, both in "walk[ing] across the canal like it was solid" (*Passion* 69) and in sustaining her love and passion for the Queen of Spades for many years after she ended their relationship, Villanelle questions with her body and her heart the supposedly biological foundations of the binary gender system. She exposes compulsory heterosexuality as a stratagem to naturalize gender differences and legitimize the subordinate position of women.

5.1.3   The Dancing Princesses

During his search for Fortunata, Jordan in *Sexing the Cherry* encounters eleven dancing princesses, Fortunata's older sisters who live together in one house. The stories they tell him of their lives and doomed loves present new endings to the fairy tale of the Twelve Dancing Princesses. They are endings that document women's determination to live their lives as they see fit. None of the princesses still lives with the husband she was forced to marry after the discovery of their illicit dancing excursions; Fortunata, the youngest, might not even have waited to be married, but "flew from the altar like a bird from a snare" to devote her life to dancing (*Sexing* 60). Winterson's re-writing of the tale of the Twelve Dancing Princesses

---

thing' offers an important corrective" to what she otherwise regards as a tendency to universalize lesbian love in *The Passion* ("Written" 163).

takes aim at the "happily ever after" of the traditional fairy story that allows fulfilment to women only within the patriarchal institution of matrimony and describes marriage as invariably leading to happiness. For the twelve dancers in Winterson's version heteronormative marriage represents confinement, and there is little doubt that it was utilized as a means to putting an end to their unruly, "unfeminine" mobility.

The sisters' stories take up important themes of the women's movement: domestic violence, husbands who destroy the happiness of their wives and endanger their health with their hazardous promiscuity, matrimony as an institution designed to subdue women and confine them to the domestic sphere, exploitation of women by husbands who view them as servants or sexualized play-things – in other words, a gender hierarchy that conceptualizes men as active subjects and rulers over women who are categorized as passive objects. However, while Winterson exposes the limiting, oppressive effects institutionalized marriage historically has had on women within a hetero-patriarchal system,[22] she proposes lesbianism neither as the only politically correct way of life for women nor as a panacea against the ills of sexism and patriarchy.[23]

Of the three sisters who lived with their women lovers, only one was able to save her relationship and is still enjoying it as she meets Jordan. It is the oldest princess, who fell in love with a mermaid while swimming and has lived in a well with her ever since, presumably undetected by the

---

[22]Winterson's re-written tales point out that marriage can be ill-suited to men, as well. One of the princes never touched his wife because he loved a man, another one neglected his princess because he felt imprisoned in his body and was incapable of love. Both die at the hands of their wives, the first in the embrace of his lover, the second at his own request.

[23]I do not share Gonzáles's view that "[l]esbianism, therefore, appears in the eyes of [...] Winterson [...] as the most revolutionary, radical and effectual weapon against patriarchy" (289). This reading seems reductive in so far as it fails to see lesbianism as one of many possibilities of exposing the constructedness of the binary gender system of hetero-patriarchal societies and one way among many of creating subversive and innovative subject positions. Gonzáles's essentialist claim that lesbianism in *Sexing* allows women "to discover their own true nature" (290) overlooks the evolution of Winterson's theoretical opinions from fairly essentialist identity politics in *Oranges* to a more postmodern, (de-)constructivist gender concept in *Sexing*.

larger society.[24] The other two lesbian love stories end in death and violation. The story of the fifth sister is a re-narration of the tale of Rapunzel. A
young woman refuses the arranged marriage to "the prince next door" in
order to live with an older woman in a tower (*Sexing* 52). To be safe from
attacks by the younger one's incensed family, the two lovers, now mythol-
ogized by the attackers as a girl in the claws of a wicked witch, seal every
entry to their home save a window through which they climb with the help
of a long braid and a wig nailed to the floor; "[b]oth of them could have
used a ladder, but they were in love" (*Sexing* 52). Their happiness ends
when the prince enters the tower disguised as a woman, overwhelms the
young princess waiting there and, upon her return throws the older one –
the fifth dancing princess – out of the tower. The sadistic prince forces his
pride-to-be to watch as he blinds her broken lover. In terms of drama and
violence the story of the seventh princess equals that of her older sister:
"The man [she] had married was a woman" (*Sexing* 54),[25] and the couple
spent eighteen happy years in an isolated castle, before their homosexual
relationship was discovered. The princess killed her lover "with a single
blow to the head" so that her pursuers would not burn her at the stake
(*Sexing* 54).

The relationships of the lesbian princesses thus do not fare much better
than the marriages of their heterosexual sisters; lesbian love clearly is not
immune to pain, loss, and betrayal in Winterson's writing. However, the
stories of the dancing princesses posit an important difference as to the
sources of mortal danger to homosexual and heterosexual relationships.
While the marriages seem structurally, internally flawed because partners
do not love one another or husbands abuse their wives, happy lesbian relationships are threatened and destroyed by external forces, in homophobic
attacks by the hegemonic powers. All of Winterson's dancing princesses
take control of their lives. They exhibit courage and resistance to patriarchal power by emancipating themselves from oppressive and unwanted

[24]The oldest princess's love for a mermaid – and not a mortal woman – might be
the reason why their relationship has remained undetected and unmolested.

[25]Note the irony in this phrase. It relies on the readers' knowledge that in the
seventeenth century, as well as in mythic fairy-tale time, and at the time *Sexing*
was written, same-sex couples were barred from marriage. Even today, after
homosexual partnerships were granted equal legal status with heterosexual ones
in some countries, the thought that in a marriage ceremony designed for a man
and a woman two women are unwittingly joined in matrimony is a comical one.

relationships with men. Again, the inevitable alliance of gender with het-erosexuality – here in the shape of the institution of matrimony – is ques-tioned; being a woman does not automatically entail sharing one's life with a man. Yet, while Winterson presents love among women as subver-sive and emancipatory, she does not champion a withdrawal into lesbian partnerships and separatism from larger society, as the tragic fates of some of the dancing princesses indicate.

While proclaiming same-sex relationships as a valid option for women, Winterson's re-writing of the tale of the Twelve Dancing Princesses is not concerned with an evaluative comparison of homo- and heterosexual ways of living.[26] Rather, it addresses the issue of violence done to women who do not submit to the mechanisms of gendering in hegemonic heteronormative patriarchy and women's refusal to put up with this violence. The risks attached to such resistance to the violence of gen-dering are illustrated in Zillah's tragic story. The young girl of that name was forced to build her own death tower for breaking the double taboo of incest and homosexuality in an affair with her sister. To prolong her life, she built a steep tower, but when Jordan chances upon her, isolation, longing for her sister, and hunger have driven her into madness and ren-dered her a haunting spectacle.[27] Her death cries are still tormenting the villagers years after the tower was razed to the ground.

Without the solidarity of other resisters, this story and those of the dancing princesses seem to say, it is nearly impossible to accomplish the feat of recognizing unconventional possibilities for the construction of identities and choosing from them. In Winterson's fictions, rebels look for the shelter of supportive communities: prostitutes in brothels orga-nize their defense against violent attackers or at times mingle with nuns in nunneries, the dancing princesses live together on their shared estate, For-tunata surrounds herself with dancing students, and even Jeanette engages

---

[26]Humphries makes a similar point when she writes that "rather than privileging lesbianism (good and natural) over heterosexuality (evil and unnatural), [Win-terson] reveals such notions to be constructs – relative rather than absolute" (9). She argues further that this perspective "opens up the possibility of a complete re-thinking of things" (9).

[27]My reading expressly challenges Pearce's argument that in *The Passion*, *Sexing the Cherry*, and *Written on the Body*, the constraints on protagonists who have to bear the historical and political consequences of their generation, gender, and sexual preferences "are apparently discarded" (*Dialogics* 174).

in a precarious alliance with the larger lesbian community. Villanelle and the Dog-Woman represent exceptions to this rule; but the former lives in a quasi-mythic city that fosters heterogeneity and many kinds of "shape-shifting," and the latter is self-sufficient to the extent of being autarkic. For the others, escape from oppressive patriarchal relationships, emancipation, and the search for alternative subject positions are invariably linked with the need of finding a home.

5.2   The Countermyth of Androgyny

The concepts of gender and sexuality are intimately and cross-referentially linked: In our binary gender system one of the foundations of the male-female dichotomy is the "law" that, in order to be recognized as male, men must desire women and in order to be intelligibly female, women must desire men. Therefore, when Winterson challenges hetero-sexuality as the normal and normative economy of desire, she also explores a variety of subject positions that subvert the binary opposition of male and female and "open up possible variations in personality and act" (Burns, "Powerful": 387). In the following I want to show that many of these variations are situated within the notion of androgyny; while they still cite the traditional two genders, they call into question the rigid boundaries between them.

Burns has described androgyny as "potentially Winterson's ideal voice" ("Powerful" 385), and for Schmidt it is one of the author's "new, positive countermyths [...] which replace the old ["male"] myths – the church, the state and the male-female dichotomy" (369). Winterson's presentations of androgyny have become more innovative and daring over the course of her first three major fictions. In *Oranges* we find what one might call a metaphysical androgyny: As I showed in the previous subchapter, Mother executes some of the gender roles and exhibits the gender-related behaviors expected of Father who in turn behaves in ways designated as typically female,[28] while Jeanette takes on the male privileges of speak-

---

[28]Father is the first and most inconspicuous of the non-sexist male characters Winterson creates in her early fiction, others being Henri and Jordan. Over the course of the three novels discussed here, these men go through their own processes of emancipation, Jordan being by far the most successful and most self-confident of them.

ing in public and desiring women. In *The Passion* and *Sexing*, however, androgyny – especially in women – combines metaphysical with physical androgyny. The question of how this is achieved in these two texts and to what gender-related effects now forms the scope of my analysis.

5.2.1   Villanelle and Henri

With its dual structure *The Passion* ostensibly cites the structure of the gender system; however, the text quickly proceeds to undermine this binarism by subverting the opposition of the real vs. the unreal initially associated with Henri and Villanelle, respectively, as well as the gender definitions represented by the narrators. Henri's "real" world is that of the battle-fields at Boulogne and the Russian taiga – a man's world that has use for women only as producers of young recruits and as prostitutes –, whereas Villanelle's Venice is a constantly changing, uncertain place that is "unreal" enough to allow both men and women the freedom to masquerade, play games of chance, and revel in feats of magic which abound in their city. As the story proceeds, the distinction between real and unreal, fact and fiction becomes increasingly blurred. Through his interaction with Villanelle and his residency in Venice, Henri comes to understand that the accurate account he attempts to give of his experiences during the Napoleonic wars is a collection of dreams, hopes, fears, and memories that is no more objective and "true" than the tendentious official historical accounts he had originally set out to rectify. As he thinks about his experiences in the French army during his voluntary confinement on San Servolo, Henri also begins to understand the fictitious nature of his image of the emperor, invented to answer his own needs for a strong fatherly figure. Now, on San Servolo, Napoleon occasionally crowds into his small room in the madhouse which is already filled with his dead mother and his friends who died during the Russian campaign. Henri's reluctant acceptance of historical and present reality as fiction and his rapidly decreasing ability and willingness to differentiate between reality and fiction form the theoretical background for the questioning of the "realness" of the male-female dichotomy in *The Passion*.[29]

---

[29] See also J. Morrison who states that "[b]y setting up Venice as a space of uncertainty/possibility, [. . .], the text destabilises the construction of sexes and genders as determinate, historically defined categories" (103).

This "realness," as well as the supposed naturalness of gender are most profoundly challenged by Villanelle's anatomy and her actions. In contrast to Henri, she seems highly conscious of her gender-bending faculties; she attributes them to the mythic customs regulating life in her home city and considers them fully in tune with the mercurial nature of Venice. In the "city of disguises [...] [w]hat you are one day will not constrain you on the next," she explains (*Passion* 150). As a positive consequence of this lack of constraint in people's choices of identities, so Villanelle points out, "you may explore yourself freely and, if you have wit or wealth, no one will stand in your way" (*Passion* 150). Villanelle's self-explorations are concerned with markers of gender which she disguises and reveals in true Venetian style. What starts out as a game, however, ultimately leads her to a serious questioning of the notion of identity.

In Venice card dealers are advised to cross-dress in order to render every aspect of a visit to the casino part of the enjoyment of gaming for the customers. On Bonaparte's birthday, a day of fancy-dress balls and excessive merry-making, Villanelle paints her lips bright red and applies white face powder. Her outfit consists of yellow breeches, boots, a loose shirt that conceals her breasts, and sometimes a codpiece to confuse her customers. "I dressed as a boy because that's what the visitors liked to see," she tells us (*Passion* 54). The masquerade she chooses enhances supposedly masculine physical features such as her boyish stature, and conceals those that are conventionally read as physical and symbolic marks of femaleness – her breasts. On the day she meets the Queen of Spades, Villanelle decides to add a moustache to her required "uniform" for "[her] own amusement" (*Passion* 55). In the casino, gender markers become "part of the game," the object of which is "trying to decide which sex was hidden behind tight breeches and extravagant face-paste" and in which employees engage just as enthusiastically as customers (*Passion* 54).

Villanelle's disguise is a subversive act of gender bending for various reasons: On a meta-level it mixes fact and fiction, reality and fantasy. The customers cannot determine what is "real" and what is "made up" about her exterior; they have to substitute their imagination for the "facts" that are deliberately withheld from them.[30] The cross-dressing card dealers

---

[30] Villanelle's name can also be read as an example of blurred or disguised geographic and cultural boundaries. An old Venetian crone tells her, "You're a Venetian, but you wear your name as a disguise" (*Passion* 54). Accord-

actively perform a gender identity by means of the garments and accessories they choose, as well as with their manner of speaking and acting.
By dressing "as a boy" and by imitating exterior features, speech, and behaviors that are understood to indicate masculinity, Villanelle, like Judith
Butler's cross-dressers and drag performers, reveals the imitative structure
of gender.[31] Her customers share in this subversive revelation, as they "decide" on the gender of the person they see before them. The cook, who,
despite several visits at the casino, remains uncertain as to Villanelle's
gender, decides that she is a woman. We do not learn on what basis he
makes his decision; it is possible that his wish to marry her and the legal
prerequisite for such a union, her femaleness in conjuction with his maleness, play a large part in it. The cook's decision makes Villanelle a woman
in his eyes. "Identity depends upon perception – what is foregrounded and
what it backgrounded," writes Gade (34). María del Mar Asensio stresses
the volitional side of gender attribution: "[W]hat someone 'is' depends
on what someone else wants her/him to be" (274). The boundaries of gender are destabilized, as performance, appearance, perception, and desire
construct an identity that is highly subjective, temporary, and variable.[32]

However, as Villanelle's above description of this "gender guessing"
shows, most of the participants in the "game" still assume that whosoever
guesses "right" will discover the true and identifiable sex that has been so
carefully covered up. For most Venetians the subversive destabilization of
gender boundaries thus is restricted to a specific place, e.g. the casino, or

---

ing Haslett, who cites the *Princeton Enclyclodedia of Poetry and Poetics*, "a
villanelle is a musical and poetic form, originally from Italy, introduced into
France in the sixteenth century" (45). Villanelle's name thus combines Italian
and French cultural influences.

[31] Doan points out that cross-dressing maneuvers the dresser into a position of
power, the power of knowledge and the ability to control perception, the power
and freedom to choose which gender to perform and to play with that choice (cf.
149).

[32] The question of the importance of appearance and perception in the assignment
of gender is raised again in the story of the seventh dancing princess in *Sexing
the Cherry*. Her lover had appeared to be a man and had been perceived as male
until after their marriage, when the princess found her husband to be a woman.

a particular time of the year, e.g. Bonaparte's birthday.[33] In contrast, Villanelle's partly required, partly voluntary disguise seems to have a lasting effect upon her conception of her own gender. Before she pays her first visit to the woman with whom she has fallen in love, she tries to decide whether to dress as a man or as a woman. The first option would present her to the Queen of Spades in the same disguise she had worn on their first encounter, while the second would reveal her to be a woman – or would it? "[W]hat was myself?" Villanelle asks herself. "Was this breeches and boots self any less real than my garters?" (*Passion* 66). Out of the fear that she might scare away the Queen of Spades with her lesbian desire, she twice opts for the breeches, only to turn back to the house of the beloved after her second visit and to confess, "I am a woman" (*Passion* 71). She lifts her shirt to reveal her breasts, but this physical "proof" of femaleness would not have been needed, as the Queen of Spades had guessed "right" all along.[34] Still, it serves to end the cautious kisses between the two women and initiates nine days and nights of passionate love-making.

Villanelle's doubtful question as to the "reality" of her "breeches and boots self" in comparison to her "garter self" grows out of the "double gender encoding" of her body (Doan 149). Due to her mother's imperfect execution of a rite to be performed in preparation of the birth of a boatman's child, Villanelle is born with webbed feet, the hereditary birthmark of the sons of boatmen. Among the boatmen and their families webbed feet are unquestioned markers of maleness; gendering via webbed feet is irreversible because of its innate foundation. This certainly holds true for Villanelle: "The midwife tried to make an incision in the translucent triangle between my first two toes but her knife sprang from the skin leaving no mark" (*Passion* 52). Villanelle was born a girl with feet that mark her as a boy – the first hermaphrodite in the community of boatmen: "There never was a girl whose feet were webbed in the entire history of the boat-

---

[33] This fact does not reduce the fundamental subversiveness of gender masquerade. See *Rabelais and His World*, Bakhtin's influencial study on the revolutionary carnivalesque in the Middle Ages.

[34] If the Queen of Spades was attracted to Villanelle not *in spite* of her male disguise but *because* of it, the two women temporarily presented a butch-femme couple with Villanelle performing the "masculine" part of the butch lesbian and the Queen of Spades the "feminine" part of the femme. As Butler has shown, in this constellation, too, gender norms and roles are parodied and revealed as constructed (cf. *Gender Trouble*).

men" (*Passion* 51). Villanelle's "male" feet are accompanied by every boatman's hereditary ability, or instinct, to expertly steer a boat through the canals of Venice. This is what she can do best and would most like to do for a living, but it is an occupation that is "closed to [her] on account of [her] sex" (*Passion* 53). The reigning conventions of gender roles and gender norms conflict with her genetic code.[35]

Yet this does not mean that *The Passion* argues from the position of biological essentialism. Rather, it points at the unreliability of biological criteria when used as points of reference for the differentiation between maleness and femaleness. In the face of this unheard-of confusion of gender characteristics in a baby girl, the midwife's reaction is a model of pious humility before higher forces and a testimony to the quasi-religious symbolic power of webbed feet: "'It's the Virgin's will [...]. No knife can get through that,'" she declares after blunting her knife on Villanelle's infant feet (*Passion* 52). With Venice's high level of tolerance for the unforeseeable and miraculous in mind, this exclamation can also be read as a beginning acceptance, if not recognition, of the idea that nature or biology neither support the imposition of rigid boundaries between the genders, nor should they be the basis of institutionalized gender norms.

Villanelle's stepfather is someone who already seems to take this notion for a fact: "He's never thought it odd that his daughter cross-dresses for a living and sells second-hand purses on the side. But then, he's never thought it odd that his daughter was born with webbed feet. 'There are stranger things,' he said" (*Passion* 61). We must not forget that Villanelle's stepfather is a baker by trade and thus does not belong to the community of boatmen. He probably would have reacted less calmly if he had been a boatman himself and Villanelle's biological father. The fact that Villanelle herself, the direct descendant of a boatman, agrees with this tolerant approach to her presumed abnormality therefore is more remarkable than the baker's liberalism: "And I suppose there are [stranger things than webbed feet on a baby girl]" (*Passion* 61).[36] At no point does Vil-

---

[35] Apparently, the exclusive maleness of the profession of the gondolier in Venice has persisted until June 2009. The city now has its first *gondoliera*, Giorgia Boscolo (cf. Chu).

[36] Ganteau sees in this "representation of androgyny in a natural, self-evident way" a sign of kinship of Winterson's work with magical realism ("Fantastic" 235).

lanelle exhibit the slightest anxiety about her own androgyny.[37] Instead, she uses it to her advantage and empowerment: In breach of the ban on working as a boatman imposed on women, she roams the city on land as well as on water, enjoying the mobility of any boatman. To save Henri and herself, she even walks on the canal and pulls their oar-less boat with her shaking friend away from the scene of his murder of the cook.[38] In a hetero-patriarchal society – fictitious Venice of the early nineteenth century as well as the readers' post-industrial Western or Westernized society – Villanelle's androgyny "invites cultural confusion and unintelligibility," as Doan observes (149), and thereby undermines the foundation of society, its rigid and hierarchically structured male-female dichotomy.[39]

---

[37] Kilian identifies "complete concealment" and "complete information" as the extreme options available to ambiguously gendered individuals for their stigma management and gender performance (159, my translation). Villanelle's careful hiding of her webbed feet with Kilian could be read as concealing the stigma of her abnormal gender ambiguity. However, as Villanelle has made very clear on several occasions, Venetian boatmen never take off their boots. The sight of her father's webbed feet proved fatal to the mental health of a tourist who foolishly bribed him to take his boots off and was sent to San Servolo after seeing the feet. What is more, it is quite possible that Henri's accidental look at Villanelle's feet might be the real cause of his growing mental disturbance. Villanelle's secrecy about her feet therefore is motivated by mythic taboos and the goodness of her heart. It is not a strategy to manage a troubling stigma.

[38] Haslett suggests that Villanelle walks on water in a "Christ-like fashion" (44). She reads this as an indicator for divine attributes of Villanelle's body and draws a connection between Winterson and feminist Biblical revisionism of the early 1990s.

[39] Del Mar Asensio reads the boatmen's webbed feet as phallic symbols and argues that "Villanelle is biologically marked by the phallus precisely to subvert patriarchy and phallocentrism" (270). See also Haslett who offers a reading of Villanelle's body as the fabulous and highly subversive body of a freak (44). Haslett also convincingly connects Villanelle's body with the poetic form of the villanelle, pointing out that "[t]he villanelle has been described as a plait of gold and silver threads into which is woven a third, rose-coloured thread; the metallic, unyielding character of the refrains is an emotional fact which the rose-coloured thread of the intellect, [...], tries in vain to escape. The lines of the rose-coloured thread have been characterized as attempting to withstand the conspiracy of the refrains and to assert change and mortality, thus having a peculiar poignancy and vulnerability. Her name thus gives Winterson's Villanelle

The reversal of gender roles between the male and the female narrtors of *The Passion* provides a further means of destabilizing the gender binary cited and highlighted in the novel. Villanelle leads her life in ways conventionally associated with maleness and masculinity. In Venice she has an occupation that leads her into the public sphere; she also engages in sexual relationships of her choice and desires women as well as men. She remains unmarried until she consents to the cook's marriage proposal; yearning for independence and self-determination, she soon leaves the cook and travels widely. After her husband's death she inherits his money and leads a financially secure life. In fact, as I explained earlier, her "masculine" independence and agility are perceived as such an affront by the representatives of the patriarchal social order that they attempt to forcefully gender her "female" according to their definition by means of rape and forced prostitution.

In contrast to Villanelle, Henri grew up in rural France, the only son of a quiet and gentle father and an independent-minded, ambitious mother. He inherited his father's attributes and, like him, adores his high-spirited mother. Henri never wanted to travel. His decision to join the Grande Armée was born out of a profound need for a strong guide who would give his life purpose and direction, which he felt unable to give it himself. Henri loathes violence. During his eight years of active service in the army he wrings the necks of countless chickens for the emperor, but he manages not to kill or maim a single person. Instead, he risks his life many times to rescue injured comrades from the battlefields. After he kills the cook in self-defense and in defense of Villanelle, hallucinations and states of panic push him deeper and deeper into schizophrenia. Thus, he suffers from an illness that for a long time has been exclusively associated with femaleness.

a form or structure, containing 'refrains' of recurring themes of obsession and destiny, and a 'rose-coloured thread' of change and mortality, which can be seen reflected in her body: her physical body echoes the body of the verse form. The most dominant refrains of Winterson's Villanelle, the 'plait of gold and silver threads,' are her webbed feet and games of chance, while her heart is the 'rose-coloured strand' of the villanelle, appearing again and again in different guises, always when Villanelle is attempting to counteract the control over her life maintained by the two dominant refrains" (45).

Henri has always felt safe in the company of women, and he increasingly associates himself with them.[40] He is ashamed of the brutish acts his fellow-soldiers commit against the prostitutes in the army brothel, senses and respects the love between the women, and critically raises the topic of compulsory heterosexuality in his narrative. Remembering the safety he felt when Villanelle bent over him for the first time to teach him how to make love to her, Henri writes: "She let [her hair] fall over me and I felt I was lying in the long grass, safe" (*Passion* 103). In Venice he once more experiences this feeling of profound safety in a female sphere. Villanelle asks him to steal her heart from the house of the Queen of Spades; she had not found the time to retrieve it from her lover before she was sent to Russia.[41] He finds her heart alive and beating in a sealed jar in the walk-in closet of the lady of the house, a womb-like space stacked with furs and sweet-smelling dresses: "A woman's room. Here, I felt no fear. I wanted to bury my face in the clothes and lie on the floor with the smell around me" (*Passion* 119).

A reversal of gender roles between Villanelle and Henri becomes particularly palpable in Henri's vision of the life they would lead if they ever married:

---

[40] Stowers speaks of "Henri's disobedient and contravening travels away from the masculine paradigm of Napoleon toward the fantastic – and decidedly female – Venice" ("Journeying" 143).

[41] Winterson has made it part of her artistic agenda to break up and re-enliven clichéd words and forms in the English language. In *Art Objects* she insists that "[a] writer has to get away from cliché and can never never call a spade a spade. To bring back to us starts of feeling that can volt through the thickness of the day means direct injections of language, undiluted, unmediated" (185f.). In *The Passion* she literalizes the romantic saying of "giving away one's heart" in love. Incredible though it is to Henri – and to the readers –, Villanelle's gift of her heart to the Queen of Spade leaves her own chest empty for eight years. Had not Henri succeeded in stealing it, the Queen of Spades would have woven the heart into a tapestry depicting the young woman in her male disguise, thus binding Villanelle to her for a life-time. As Henri gives the heart back to Villanelle, she takes possession of it amidst "terrible swallowing and choking noises" and re-gains complete control over her thoughts and emotions (*Passion* 120). With this episode Winterson gives her readers the "starts of feeling" that will remind them of the enormous emotional power of committed love. Importantly, it is the love between two women that possesses such immense power.

> She'd vanish for days at a time and I'd weep. She'd forget we had any
> children and leave me to take care of them. She'd gamble our house away
> at the Casino, and if I took her to live in France she'd grow to hate me.
> [...] She'd never be faithful. She'd laugh in my face. (*Passion* 123)

The behaviors and dynamics Henri lists here correspond entirely with the
stereotypical gender roles sanctioned in a hetero-patriarchal relationship.
The powerful but irresponsible husband neglects wife and children and
squanders his income to amuse himself in casinos and brothels, while the
faithful and caring wife makes do with what little is left for herself and the
children and waits for his return and attention, weeping. Only, in Henri's
vision Villanelle impersonates the active, no-good husband, and he represents the passive, long-suffering wife. Interestingly, this vision does not
create for us the image of a family in which the wife is fully emancipated
and both partners share in the responsibilities of work and child-care. Neither does it level out gender differences between the two protagonists.[42]
Rather, Winterson completely reverses the gender roles in a relationship
between a man and a woman and thereby indicates that behaviors and
character traits do not correspond with biological gender characteristics as
a matter of course. Through Villanelle's webbed feet the traditional feminist argument of the social construction of gender, developed as it was to
counter the notion of a biological determinism à la "Biology is Destiny,"
is complemented – and complicated – by the idea that biological maleness
and femaleness might in themselves be constructions.

5.2.2   The Dog-Woman and Jordan

In *Sexing the Cherry* the passages narrated by the Dog-Woman and Jordan
are marked by fruit icons that represent the narrators: The Dog-Woman is
represented by an unpeeled banana, her son Jordan by a pineapple.[43] With
these icons Winterson announces on the very first page of her text and
throughout the book that conventional cultural expectations of femininity
and masculinity will be frustrated in this fiction.

---

[42] In this point I disagree with Palmer, who diagnoses "the deconstruction of sexual
   difference" in *The Passion* ("Jeanette Winterson" 185).

[43] In the sections of the environmentalist and Nicolas Jordan the fruit icons are a
   half-pealed banana with its top cut off and left detached from the rest of the fruit
   for the former and the pineapple split in two for the latter.

In many ways, *Sexing* takes up the ideas about gender and narrative as well as content-related experiments to break up the male-female dichotomy that Winterson introduced in *The Passion*. What distinguishes the younger text from the older one is the rigor with which it pursues the notion of the simultaneity of masculinity and femininity within one individual, and the greater extent to which this simultaneity is conceptualized as part of a general undermining and blurring of binary oppositions of time and space.[44] It also offers a more radical alternative to the hierarchical two-tier gender system than its predecessor.

Through her very existence, the Dog-Woman renders absurd any conventional notion of femininity. As her name unmistakably points out, she is known to be a woman and also regards herself as a woman,[45] but hers is neither the weaker nor the fair sex. Her huge body enables her to perform greater feats of strength than any man: She catapults a full-grown elephant into the sky, kills scores of Puritans with her bare hands, and cannot be sexually satisfied even by the most experienced Casanova.[46] "How hideous am I?" is the question she asks before she gives a description of herself: "My nose is flat, my eyebrows are heavy. I have only a few teeth and those are a poor show, being black and broken. I had smallpox when I was a girl and the caves in my face are home enough for fleas" (*Sexing* 24). As she lives with fifty boarhounds on the stinking banks of the Thames and "hate[s] to wash, for it exposes the skin to contamination" (*Sexing* 35), her body-fumes make the hardiest men and women swoon.[47] Yet, she speaks of herself as a good woman, chaste and god-fearing, mod-

---

[44] Langland also sees Winterson's gender benders in this larger theoretical context: "In *Sexing the Cherry*, self and other, masculine and feminine, past and present, nature and culture are envisioned not as alternatives but as simultaneous and coexisting" (106).

[45] "The Dog-Woman" is an acquired name: "I had a name but I have forgotten it. They call me the Dog-Woman and it will do" (*Sexing* 11).

[46] Jago Morrison points out that *Sexing* "taps directly into [cultural anxieties about the attainment of a successful heterosexual femininity], playing on the potential instability and un-'naturalness' of 'sex' itself" (107).

[47] Referring to Bakhtin's description of grotesque body characteristics of Renaissance carnival imagery, Onega rightly emphasizes the grotesque nature of the Dog-Woman's body. She points out the Rabelaisian and Swiftean parentage of this huge creature who, by comparing herself to a mountain range, cites the Lilliputians' description of Gulliver as a "Man-Mountain" (cf. 303).

est in the company of her superiors, and gentle to those of inferior wit or strength.

While the Dog-Woman is aware of the discrepancy between her bodily features and the norms of femininity postulated not only by the Puritans but by society in general, she makes a particular show of her "womanliness" when she thinks it appropriate or worthwhile for herself or the few people she cares about. She performs femaleness when she has a use for it, but because of her anatomy this performance, complete with masquerade and role-acting, seems more of a gender parody than Villanelle's disguise.

A telling example of this strategic femininity-turned-parody is the Dog-Woman's scheme to trick the Puritan guards into granting her, Jordan, and Tradescant access to the public execution of the King. In a parodist spectacle reminiscent of a Monty Python movie, all three of them perform the version of femininity most likely to guarantee them admission to the spectacle: that of the common sinful woman ready to repent her countless transgressions and "in need of a pastor's touch" (*Sexing* 68). The Dog-Woman's masquerade consists of "rags, black as pitch," an old wig "begged from a theatrical," and a "specially reinforced wheelbarrow" in which she sits "like a heap of manure" (*Sexing* 68). Her acting consists of sighing, crying, and "rolling [her] eyes winningly," of "groaning and calling out to Jesus" (*Sexing* 69). The plot she has invented to enhance the credibility of her performance in the eyes of the soldiers is one of sinfulness, sickness, humility, and heart-felt repentance: "'I cannot [leave the wheelbarrow], sir,' I cried, 'for I have the Clap and my flesh is rotting beneath me. If I were to stand up, sir, you would see a river of pus run across these flags. The Rule of Saints cannot begin in pus'" (*Sexing* 69). In this charade Jordan and John Tradescant act the parts of "[her] daughter and [her] niece" who "have pushed [her] from Plymouth so that [she] can be redeemed" and will have to "[catch] any fluids that may flow from [her]," so as not to give offence to "the noses of the tender" with "the stench of a three days' dead dog" emitted by her body (*Sexing* 69). Her strategy proves highly effective, as the guards disgustedly wave all three of them through.

This scene is revealing in terms of the gender politics of *Sexing* not so much because of the cross-dressing chosen by Tradescant and Jordan as a means of disguising their identities as the King's gardener-discoverer and his assistant, but because of the "gender drag" performed by the Dog-Woman (cf. Langland). As she successfully acts out one particular kind of femininity that – although repugnant – is acceptable to and promulgated by the misogynist patriarchal regime of the Puritans, she highlights the political interests not only behind this specific gender construction, but exposes the mechanisms of naturalization of any constructed gender norm by means of politically motivated concepts, such as the notion of the inherent sinfulness of women and their natural subservience to men.

The Dog-Woman knows what feelings, thoughts, and behaviors are expected of her "as a woman." She enjoys exhibiting her knowledge of these gender norms and applauds herself for acting in accordance with them. Her confident declarations of her adherence to the rules of female gentleness are regularly contrasted with detailed accounts of instances in which she treats her enemies with wrathful violence. The Dog-Woman presents herself as being "gracious of nature" and willing to "allow [her]self to be led" (*Sexing* 25). Yet, almost in the same breath she states, "[B]odies mean nothing to me, dead or alive," betraying a decidedly "unfeminine" lack of feeling for her fellow-beings (*Sexing* 25). The only exceptions to this rule are the bodies of her hounds and, to a still higher degree, that of Jordan; she nurtures her adopted son with a fierce maternalism that spells danger to anyone who threatens him or does not hasten to help him. For instance, she bullies her witch-like neighbor into providing a remedy for the plague-ridden Jordan by threatening her with unnamed acts of violence.

The Dog-Woman's "maternal rage" (*Sexing* 140) is similar in its devastating effects to the rage she feels when she finds her house occupied by Roundheads after her lengthy absence and which induces her to kill some of them and leave some more with torn and broken limbs. After this eruption of violence she decides to spare the ringleaders and chooses to interpret their state of terrified petrifaction as sheer gratitude at this display of the goodness of her heart: "At my magnanimousness they were abashed, as even sinners must be in the presence of virtue" (*Sexing* 66). In other instances, she engages in bloody skirmishes with Puritans and then praises her – supposedly well-known – charitable impulse of not killing all of her attackers: "Out of charity, such as I am famed for, I left one or two to be crippled" (*Sexing* 84).

After countless murders – the first one having been her murder of her father who wanted to sell her to be exhibited as a curiosity when she was still a child – she blushes at being reminded that "'Thou shalt not kill' is a tenet of our faith" (*Sexing* 84). Yet, despite her undeniable tendency toward violence, she does not kill for the sake of killing or in order to rob her enemies of their possessions. She kills in the interest of honor and justice: "My actions are not motivated by thought of gain, only by thought of justice, and I have searched my soul to conclude that there is no person dead at my hands who would be better off alive" (*Sexing* 129).[48]

Thus, when this grotesque woman, who acts in ways conventionally assigned to the masculine, consciously masquerades as feminine, she problematizes the notion of femininity and flaunts the constructedness of gender.[49] Moreover, as she cites the gender norms of femininity such as graciousness, charity, magnanimity, and bashfulness "while threatening and performing mayhem" (Langland 102), she calls their meaning into question.[50] The Dog-Woman is a devoted mother, but a mother who is

[48] Of course, "honor" and "justice" are relational concepts and do not present absolute values. In *Sexing the Cherry*, the Dog-Woman sets the standards of what counts as honorable and just, but we as readers find ourselves eagerly accepting her standards and are inclined to agree with her self-satisfied assessment.

[49] Pearce acknowledges the revolutionary gender-bending role the Dog-Woman plays, but also stresses what she reads as reactionary, counterrevolutionary aspects in the parodist female body of this protagonist. She argues that the Dog-Woman also represents the "reactionary femaleness which draws clear parallels between women's traditional procreative role and the preservation of existing patriarchal institutions" (*Dialogics* 179). In contrast to this assessment I propose to consider the Dog-Woman's practice of citing reactionary gender roles as a precondition for her eventual destabilization of these roles. See also Langland's argument that "it is precisely the performative, citational dimension of Winterson's postmodern novel that allows it to be read *as* a feminist text, that allows it to move beyond the political ambivalence, its double encoding as 'both complicity and critique,' that, in Linda Hutcheon's theorization, disables the feminist political potential of postmodernism in general" (100). Moreover, read with Bakhtin, the Dog-Woman subverts hegemonic gender norms through the very grotesqueness of her female body (cf. Onega as well as Palmer, "Foreign Bodies").

[50] Unlike both Pearce and Langland, who regard the actions of the Dog-Woman as unconscious and unreflected, I read the her acts as conscious performances, much like consciously performed drag. While there is indeed no evidence in the text of her explicitly setting out to render female and male the same, the Dog-Woman constructs the supposedly feminine qualities for which she overtly praises herself and then gleefully points at their constructedness. Jordan describes his mother as "a fantasist, a liar and a murderer" (*Sexing* 92). The first

equipped with what she describes as a "natural capacity for murder" (*Sexing* 129). The "natural" capacities and features of this protagonist are so incongruent that they are rendered incompatible with the dichotomy of male and female. She demonstrates that nature provides a plethora of heterogeneous and variable characteristics which nonetheless have been instrumentalized for the construction and institutionalization of the binary of two distinct genders.

Furthermore, the Dog-Woman sweeps aside the patriarchal notion of women as docile, submissive beings and becomes a role-model of an invincible warrior-woman who fiercely fights for justice and yet is unashamedly loyal to her own interests. Her model-character is confirmed in the unreservedly positive portrait of her *alter-ego*, the environmentalist in twentieth-century London who lives the new kind of heroism Nicolas Jordan is looking for. This woman combines the strength, rage, and perseverance of her ancestress with an altruistic, eco-feminist commitment to the welfare of humankind in a healthy natural and social environment.

While the Dog-Woman's grotesque anatomy and her unfeminine actions undermine the gender binary, her son Jordan highlights its restrictive exclusivity and demonstrates the emancipatory power of imagination in his journeys of discovery of identities that include male and female components. By his own account, Jordan saw the King's gardener's request that he join his expeditions as a chance for "running away from uncertainty and confusion but most of all running away from [himself]" (*Sexing* 80). At home with his huge mother who seems entirely complete to him and in need of nothing and nobody, he feels sadly incomplete. He hopes that a journey will enable him to find "something [he] had lost," namely himself whom he believes he has "lost [. . .] in the gap between [his] ideal of [himself] and [his] pounding heart" (*Sexing* 100f.).

Having grown up in the care of a "mother [who] is bigger and stronger than [him] and that's not how it is supposed to be with sons" (*Sexing* 101), this thoughtful young man thinks that the part of himself that he has lost and must find again to make complete his ideal self is his masculinity. The confusion and uncertainty from which he feels the need to run away are caused by a fear of inadequacy with regard to the gender norms associ-

---

two characteristics confirm my reading of the Dog-Woman as a conscious performer of gender drag. As I will show, Jordan claims these for himself, as well.

ated with maleness, the fear of lacking true masculinity.[51] Consequently, Jordan's initial dreams of his ideal self reproduce stereotypical notions of what it means to be a "real man" in a masculinist patriarchal society:

> I want to be brave and admired and have a beautiful wife and a fine house. I want to be a hero and wave goodbye to my wife and children at the docks, and be sorry to see them go but more excited about what is to come. I want to be like other men, one of the boys, a back-slapper and a man who knows a joke or two. (*Sexing* 100f.)

As in seventeenth-century England traveling is the privilege of men and considered a heroic masculine occupation, Jordan hopes to become "a hero after all" and happily joins Tradescant on his journeys (*Sexing* 100).

Already long before he takes to the ship, Jordan knows a way of traveling that does not involve maps, globes or even a vehicle and that leads into another world – the realities of the imagination. He becomes obsessed with the discovery of journeys he could have made but had not in the everyday reality, journeys that remain unrecorded, "the path not taken and the forgotten angle" (*Sexing* 9). While his meticulously recorded voyages with Tradescant along carefully mapped routes earn him fame and honor according to the reigning conventions, they do not bring him the feeling of completeness he is looking for. But they hide within themselves the journeys of his mind on which he embarks whenever he can, in "[a]n effort to catch up with [his] fleet-footed self, living another life in a different way" (*Sexing* 80).[52]

On the first of these hidden journeys Jordan reaches the city of words where he is invited to dinner in a house without floors. There he meets and falls in love with a mysterious woman, the youngest of the twelve dancing princesses, as he learns later. This experience determines his interior journeys until he finds his beloved; it turns his journey into a quest for the dancer who might well be the beautiful wife he dreams of,

---

[51] Even after Jordan had long become a famous discoverer, his wish to "sit by the river and watch the boats" raises worries with the King's advisers that "he had gone mad in his thirteen years away" or that "his heart was broken" (*Sexing* 141). Obviously, such desires are not considered appropriate for a man, let alone a man of rank.

[52] Jordan's longing for journeys that are unmapped, unrepresented, infinite, and labyrinthine is reminiscent of "a curiosity (desire)" which, according to Pratt, is marked as "female and in need of control" (104).

and therefore into a quest for love. As he is looking for a woman, he thinks it wisest to inquire after her among women. His search leads him first to a community of prostitutes to whom he is only admitted in female disguise. Apparently, women's garments are becoming to Jordan: The prostitutes "praised [his] outfit and made [him] blush by stroking [his] cheek and commenting on its smoothness" (*Sexing* 30). He decides to "continue as a woman" without giving a specific reason for this decision (*Sexing* 31). But as he refers to "a number of people who, anxious to be free of the burdens of their gender, have dressed themselves men as women and women as men" (*Sexing* 31), we must assume that he, too, is anxious to be rid of the norms imposed upon him on account of his gender. Is Jordan's cross-dressing a device to relieve him of his difficult search for his maleness? At first it may have been, but it soon acquires a new relevance for him.

Jordan notices that his female disguise is not perceived as a disguise by the people he meets "as a woman." He actually passes for female. Not only does lonely Zillah in the tower believe that he is "the sister she had prayed for" and ask him to pass the night in bed with her, which he does "in some confusion" (*Sexing* 33). He also works at the vegetable stalls of a small market town among women who let him into the secret of their conspiracy against men. The longer Jordan's journeys of the mind last, the more he urgently he asks himself: "Was I searching for a dancer whose name I did not know or was I searching for the dancing part of myself?" (*Sexing* 40).[53] The successful and seemingly effortless cross-dresser realizes that his quest for Fortunata was not, as he had thought, part of his quest for traditional manliness, but rather for the feminine part of himself that neither his androgynous mother nor his masculinist peer group around John Tradescant had encouraged him to acknowledge and nourish. "[T]he running away from [uncertainty and confusion]" has been a "running towards" all along (*Sexing* 80): towards an alternative identity that includes an "alternatively defined gender" (Pearce, *Dialogics*: 179), in which a man can embrace aspects of his self that are understood to be feminine. This "running towards" according to Pearce is also "a quest for a new order of heroism: a heroism defined in terms other than conventional masculinity" (*Dialogics* 179), as he finds out as Nicolas Jordan some three-hundred years later in the brave London ecologist.

---

[53] In fact, it becomes increasingly obvious that Fortunata is a projection of Jordan's wishes and dreams, "a dancer who may or may not exist" (*Sexing* 80).

The insight that maleness can very well include feminine traits, however, is not the only insight Jordan enjoys. His quest for Fortunata, for the dancing part, the feminine part of himself, was guided by the notion of a possible and desirable completeness, to be attained so that "a person might live in peace" (*Sexing* 103). When he finds the dancing princess, to his intense disappointment she does not ask him to stay with her in the wilderness, nor will she come with him. Instead, Fortunata tells him to remember his wings whose "stumps are still deep in [his] shoulderblades" (*Sexing* 100).[54] Jordan's journeys of the mind will go on endlessly – "there is no end to even the simplest journey of the mind" (*Sexing* 102) – and instead of a completeness of identity he will only ever find selves that do not allow a fixed gender identity. His self-seeking travels will not uncover any unitary male self, but "a multiplicity of elusive selves" (Gade 32), in a variety of more or less imaginary lives. With a near-quote from Virginia Woolf's *Orlando* Jordan exclaims: "Our lives could be stacked together like plates on a waiter's hand. Only the top is showing but the rest are there, and by mistake we discover them" (*Sexing* 91).[55]

One of those alternative selves Jordan discovers is that of the young Navy officer Nicolas Jordan. The fact that he encounters this self in a different century leads him to an important realization: "The self is not contained in any moment or any place, but it is only in the intersection

---

[54]Fortunata's reference to wings can be read as an indirect citation of Angela Carter's famous winged creature, the *aerealiste* Fevvers of *A Night at the Circus*. With the giant Dog-Woman and the dancing-flying Fortunata, Winterson has created two protagonists who are each endowed with one of the marvellous characteristics of Fevvers: The Dog-Woman has her supernatural size an strength, and Fortunata possesses her ability to fly. By reminding Jordan of his wings, however, Fortunata alias Fevvers reminds him of his "feminine" powers, which – contrary to gender norms of the day – do include mobility.

[55]The corresponding passage in Woolf's *Orlando* reads as follows: "But it is not altogether plain sailing, either, for though one may say, as Orlando said (being out in the country and needing another self presumably) Orlando? still the Orlando she needs may not come; these selves of which we are built up, one on top of another, as plates are piled on a waiter's hand, have attachments elsewhere, sympathies, little constitutions and rights of their own, call them what you will (and for many of these things there is no name) so that one will only come if it is raining, another in a room with green curtains, another when Mrs Jones is not there, another if you can promise it a glass of wine – and so on; [...]" (143).

of moment and place that the self might, for a moment, be seen vanishing through a door, which disappears at once" (*Sexing* 80). Therefore, the selves of whom Jordan catches brief glimpses during his journeys are fleeting, momentary selves in different chronotopes. They are characterized by what Stowers calls "a flux of genders" ("Journeying" 142); he never acquires the predefined heroic masculine identity he set out to find.[56] The radical splitting of time in *Sexing the Cherry* coincides with a radical splitting of identity. This constellation "places a question mark over the supposed unity and 'in-dividability' of the 'individual' that underpins the idea of unified/determinate gender and sex," as Jago Morrison puts it (106).

In the three novels discussed so far, the protagonists most likely to engage in the 'nomadism of the mind' that enables them to construct subject positions with varying genders are the foundlings Jeanette and Jordan. Jago Morrison suggests that in Winterson's early fiction, "the subject born without the anchorage of a descent line becomes a wanderer, who is capable of travelling outside the boundaries of 'normalcy' and the known" (198).[57] Jordan's most graphic demonstration of this stepping outside of normalcy and the known is his embrace of the practice of grafting which he and Tradescant introduce to English botany after learning it from the French. He explains to his incredulous mother that

> Grafting is the means whereby a plant, perhaps tender or uncertain, is fused into a hardier member of its strain, and so the two take advantage of each other and produce a third kind, without seed or parent. In this way fruits have been made resistant to disease and certain plants have learned to grow where previously they could not. (*Sexing* 78)

Sensitized to the fragmented, multiple identities revealed in traveling and to the empowering, potentially liberating effects of the immersion in new realities of living and thinking, he begins to "[wonder] if it was an art [he] might apply to [himself]" (*Sexing* 78). In his musings about the moral

---

[56]Meyer links Winterson's "notion of an unfixed, mobile representation of selfhood" with Rosi Braidotti's concept of "nomadic subjectivity": "Nomadism, then, allows the character the necessary and useful facets of multiple homogeneous identities without being cornered by the bounded limits of a solitary one" (217).

[57]In *Lighthousekeeping* the gender-bending wanderer Silver is orphaned slightly later in life and has known her parents.

integrity of grafting and its possible social applicability he is confronted
with twofold scepticism. His mother regards the cherry he and Tradescant grafted as a "monster" that "[has] no gender and [is] a confusion to
[itself]" (*Sexing* 131). "Let the world mate of its own accord [...] or
not at all," she demands in yet another demonstration of the conventional
thinking of her time (*Sexing* 131).[58] Jordan's reply rings with confidence
and pride; its biblical language identifies the account of the grafting of the
cherry as a creation story: "But the cherry grew, and we have sexed it and
it is female" (*Sexing* 78f.).[59] The gardeners give the cherry a gender, but
it is not a "natural" one. As it is artificially created out of two "members
of a strain," the plant has an artificial, a constructed gender.

Encouraged by the success of his botanical experiments and by his experiences of living as a woman during his journeys of the mind, Jordan
considers for himself the grafting of a gender that is consciously constructed out of male/masculine and female/feminine components. As he
acknowledges the constructedness of gender, he can now envision the productive usage of the potential offered by construction, namely in the creation of alternative genders. Thus, while he continues to think of himself
as male, he claims for himself the freedom to construct his gender – possibly to construct it differently in every different situation. This is a technique the Dog-Woman has always used for herself, and her son has long
half-unconsciously envied her this independence from the ruling gender
norms. As Gade writes, "while sex is applicable to the characters of the
novel, in order not to make them 'a confusion to themselves', it is not a

---

[58] The Dog-Woman's apparent conservatism is seriously sabotaged by her own
account of her one sexual encounter with a man. Her description renders this
memorable act a clean parody of the "natural mating" between man and woman
she so vehemently advocates in her discussion with Jordan: "I cannot say that
I felt anything at all, though I had him jammed up to the hilt," she admits, and
recounts further that her friends, the prostitutes, "prised him out" of her with a
crowbar (*Sexing* 106).

[59] Note the stylistic similarity in the description in *Oranges* of the onset of a new
age for Jeanette after her first sexual encounter with Melanie – "And it was
evening and it was morning; another day" (*Oranges* 86) – and Jordan's above
account of the successful grafting of a female cherry. Both experiences are acts
of creation, which is reflected in their biblical language. What is created in each
is an identity that poses an alternative to the heteronormative gender identities
prescribed in societies that rely on a binary gender system.

determining characteristic. The flexible and multiple selves deconstruct stabilised sexual identities" (37).

Moreover, with his notion of grafting Jordan envisages procreation "without seed or parent," i.e., in a fusion of individuals that occurs outside of the "tired binarism of reproduction" (Langland 100), and therfore a new genesis of human life and human genders. Thus he counters the second sceptical view expressed by the goddess Artemis in Fortunata's story, namely the fear of finding the old mistakes repeated in new hierarchical set-ups – an exclusivist matriarchy, perhaps: "[W]hat if she travelled the world and the seven seas like a hero? Would she find something different or the old things in different disguises?" (*Sexing* 131). Jordan's grafting would create something different, a "third kind"[60] – neither "male" nor "female" in the traditional, prescriptive sense, but genders produced outside, beyond that dichotomy – which is stronger and more versatile than the original binary.[61] In effect, it anticipates a social order without binary oppositions, "brim[ming] with new gender configurations" (Doan 153).

However, underneath Jordan's revolutionary dreams about the construction of new genders an essentialism prevails with astonishing resilience. It is his essentialist perception of men and women: "I noticed that women have a private language," he informs us after his stint in the market town where he worked in female disguise (*Sexing* 32). He sees a chasm of estrangement and incomprehension dividing women from men, a chasm that is by no means mitigated by his passing for female: "In my petticoats I was a traveller in a foreign country. I did not speak the language. I was regarded with suspicion" (*Sexing* 31). The instructions his female co-workers give him about the nature of men in comparison to that of women reproduce biologist clichés such as, "Their noses are dull, [. . .].

---

[60]This recalls the "other sexes" envisioned by Virginia Woolf in *A Room of One's Own* (102).

[61] Meyer furthermore sees Winterson's text as grafted from male and female narrative strands: Jordan's and the Dog-Woman's narratives merge, complement, and sustain one another to form a new kind of narrative that offers new possibilities of writing, imagining, and living. She describes grafting as the "grotesque formation that serves as a metaphoric model for the intricate structure of the text" in which "two strains are fused and produce a third, that in turn allows for new possibilities" (Meyer 216). Palmer stresses Winterson's usage of the grotesque on the textual level in Villanelle's and the Dog-Woman's narratives ("Foreign Bodies").

They won't be able to mark a day-old lobster from a fresh one" (*Sexing* 32), as well as psychological truisms: "[A] woman, if cheated, will never forget and will some day pay you back, even if it takes years, while a man will rave and roar and slap you perhaps and then be distracted by some other thing" (*Sexing* 32). Jordan shows how much his own thinking revolves around the dichotomy of "them" and "us," locked in the old idea of war between the sexes: "This conspiracy of women shocked me. [...] I never guessed how much they hate us or how deeply they pity us. They think we are children with too much pocket money" (*Sexing* 32). Jordan's account of his adventures among women culminates not in the realization that he would make a rather good woman but in a ten-point list of cultural essentialisms about men accrued by the market women. It starts with men's constant craving for fresh delights, proceeds with damning verdicts about the shallowness, egotism, childishness, and unreliability of men, and finds its cynical climax in the observation that "[m]en deem themselves weighty and women light. Therefore it is simple to tie a stone around their neck and drown them should they become too troublesome" (*Sexing* 33).

Although he is "much upset" by this revelation, Jordan "concede[s] it to be true," after "observing [his] own heart and the behaviour of those around [him]" (*Sexing* 33). Apart from Jordan, John Tradescant, and the King, who in the Dog-Woman's narrative hovers above society like a benevolent but remote spirit, there are, indeed, no honest, likeable men in the mid-seventeenth century London of *Sexing the Cherry*. While it is true that most of the male heroes in Winterson's fictions are portrayed as sensitive, quiet, and caring men, to deduce from this that the author has a marked interest in the feminization of men is to repeat the essentialist fallacy of sorting characteristics that denote strength, power, sensitivity, or nurturing into male and female attributes (cf. Stowers, "Journeying"). Winterson's texts call for and advocate heterogeneity; an all-feminine social order would not fit this agenda. In *Oranges*, *Passion*, and *Sexing* women can be as tough, caring, or adventurous as men. Gender norms are not simply swapped between men and women so as to render women strong and ruthless, while men become weak and compassionate. Rather, protagonists search for alternative gender constructions that subvert the hegemonic prescriptions and offer multiple, varying subject positions. However, after Jordan's thirteen years of traveling on mapped and unmapped routes, after understanding the artificiality of gender norms and exploiting it to satisfy his wish for exploring life with diverse possibilities of identities, there is nevertheless no question in his mind that there are grave differences between women and men. While Jordan acknowledges the constructedness of gender, he still trips over the supposed "realities" of sex.

5.3   Fragmented Postmodern Subjects and the Unifying Force of Love

In her first three major fictions Jeanette Winterson explores gender as a significant facet of human identity and subjecthood. Her general vantage point is the critical inquiry into the traditional notion of a fixed, coherent identity embedded in specific, historically verifiable temporal and spatial realities. As she integrates a lesbian-feminist agenda and gender studies interests into this postmodern theoretical framework, she questions tenets of the patriarchal social order of post-industrial Western societies: the distinction of two genders positioned in binary opposition to one another, the prescription of heterosexuality as the normal economy of desire, and the definition of socio-cultural gender norms that supposedly follow from biological differences between the sexes. Winterson's work examines the concepts of lesbianism and androgyny as to their potential capacity for undermining the "heterosexual matrix" that is the "grid of cultural intelligibility through which bodies, genders, and desires are naturalized" (Butler, *Gender Trouble*: 194, fn. 6).[62]

Of the three fictions discussed here, *Oranges* most directly focuses on women's desire and love for women as a means of undermining the nexus of the male-female dichotomy and compulsary heterosexuality. Young Jeanette's uneasy, mystified ruminations on marriage and later, in contrast to this, her wholehearted embrace of her love for Melanie effectively denaturalize heterosexuality and expose its regulative purpose in a patriarchal society. The violent exorcism performed on Jeanette and her ex-

---

[62]For her concept of the heterosexual matrix Butler draws from Wittig's notion of the "heterosexual contract" and Rich's "compulsory heterosexuality." It characterizes "a hegemonic discursive/epistemic model of gender intelligibility that assumes that for bodies to cohere and make sense there must be a stable sex expressed through a stable gender (masculine expresses male, feminine expresses female) that is oppositionally and hierarchically defined through the compulsory practice of heterosexuality" (*Gender Trouble* 194, fn. 6).

pulsion from her community for being a lesbian point at the function of compulsory heterosexuality in the process of gendering. By desiring a person of the same sex, Jeanette in effect rejects the femininity society tries to impose on her in order to render her culturally intelligible as a woman. She selects instead an identity that is abject in the eyes of the majority and is ultimately punished by expulsion from the community. Yet, as Jeanette grasps linguistic and narrative agency, as she constructs herself as a subject by means of narrating her life story, she turns her abject lesbian identity and the "non-gender" assigned to her because of her lesbianism, into a viable, empowering subject position that subverts normative hegemonic notions of gender and sexuality.

Like *Oranges*, *The Passion* and *Sexing the Cherry* celebrate lesbian love as an emancipatory alternative to heterosexuality that renders problematic the claim to naturalness of cross-gender desire as well as the notion of gender itself. Both fictions bring into view the violence done to lesbians who resist the life-long process of gendering within a heteronormative social set-up. However, while *Oranges* merely reverses the labels "normal" and "natural" between homo- and heterosexuality, the latter texts question the very notions of the normal and the natural. Winterson gradually but decisively shifts her attention from a branding of the violence committed in the name of compulsory heterosexuality and a celebration of lesbian identity as a means of liberation and emancipation available to women toward the exploration of multiple subject positions in a variety of possibilities of gender and sexuality.

The author's increasing "refusal of totality" in terms of gender and sexuality and her interest in conveying to her readers a sense of the multitude of possibilities life offers for the construction of identities manifest themselves in her enthusiastic exploration of androgyny in her protagonists (Ganteau, *Fantastic*: 232). Embedded in narratives that blur the boundaries between "fact" and "fiction," Villanelle and Henri, the Dog-Woman, and Jordan question the natural as well as socio-cultural definitions of femaleness and maleness. Villanelle and the Dog-Woman in particular undermine the rigid and hierarchical male-female dichotomy by way of their respective physical unintelligibility in terms of reigning biological and cultural gender definitions. Villanelle's webbed feet question "the 'natural' and 'unchangeable' status of 'sex,'" indicating that Winterson's writing "collapses the sex/gender framework" (J. Morrison 109). The drag performances of both women – cross-dressing and a butch les-

bian identity for Villanelle, "gender drag" for the Dog-Woman – expose
sex and gender as "culturally mediated aspects of identity" (J. Morrison
109), and at the same time present alternative constructions of gender.

Winterson's protagonists share a position on the margins of society.
This status as outsiders confronts them with hegemonic gender norms they
experience as limiting and exclusive. The perception of their deviance
from these norms or from "the normal" initiates each of the protaginists'
search for their selves. However, by exploring possibilities of identity
in the realities of their imagination, Jeanette, Henri, and Jordan, the most
self-reflexive, analytical of the five, experience their selves as fragmented,
multiple, and variable; Villanelle and the Dog-Woman physically embody
fluid and inclusive gender identities. The quests for identity invariably
culminate in the realization that instead of a unitary, true self many nomadic identities are shaped and reshaped in an infinite process, "subject
positions whence existence may be perceived" (Gade 35). Although the
characters experience the choices arising from multiple subject positions
as liberating and emancipating, they yearn for wholeness and deep self-
knowledge.[63]

In Winterson's fictions, love is the one power capable of holding together and lending a kind of essence to the fragmented postmodern subject. Jeanette discovers her lesbian identity as indispensable to her becoming a speaking subject when she falls in love with Melanie. After Henri's
trust upon Napoleon is betrayed, his love for Villanelle renders his existence meaningful; and being loved and desired by the Queen of Spades, as
well as having herself loved and desired this woman, assures Villanelle of
her precarious femaleness. Jordan's love for Fortunata is the rallying point
for his imaginary selves, and the Dog-Woman's fierce maternal love for
her adopted son provides the focus of her disparate gender characteristics.
Winterson regards love – like art – as a transformative force: "[F]alling
in love challenges the reality to which we lay claim, part of the pleasure
of love and part of its terror, is the world turned upside down," she writes
(AO 15). At the same time that love challenges her protagonists' sense of
who they are and what reality they live in, it enables them to transform
reality so as to achieve a meaningful wholeness, "while respecting the in-

---

[63]Gade suggests that Winterson's characters "resemble the postmodernist subject
that does not know itself fully (*desidero*)" (35).

tegrity of each of the multiple discourses which come together in him or her" (Maagaard 152).

As a force of transformation love is potentially subversive. Love between women deconstructs compulsory heterosexuality and the hegemonic institution of marriage, a process that is supported by a reworking of imagery and texts with patriarchal associations. Thus, when Villanelle gives the Queen of Spades her heart, Winterson appropriates a trope of traditional heterosexual romance writing to represent the complexities of lesbian love.[64] Moreover, the enigmatic idea of passion is used to "[re-work] the boundaries of gender and sexual identity" (J. Morrison 103). "Somewhere between fear and sex passion is" (*Passion* 62), muses Villanelle, whose relationship with the Queen of Spades represents the chief example of passion in the fiction of the same title. In a text with an androgynous, cross-dressing lesbian heroine Winterson thus not only breaks up the heterosexual monopoly on passion in traditional romantic narratives, she also links the supposedly fixed categories of gender and sexuality with the unknowable, indefinable notion of passion.[65] Gender and sexuality, she seems to say, are as multifaceted, relational, and dependent on subjective feelings, experiences, and perceptions as passion.

So, how radical is Winterson's treatment of gender in her first three major fictions? Any answer to this question has to be as multi-layered as the author's novels: Winterson questions the binary gender system and undermines the rigid male-female dichotomy. She flaunts the constructedness of gender and uses it to envision new ways of constructing masculinities and femininities. With her androgynous protagonists she perforates the boundaries between male and female, advocating an inclusive concept of gender. Yet while Jeanette in *Oranges* deconstructs the nexus of gender and heterosexuality and invents herself by way of narrative as a speaking lesbian subject, she always remains recognizably female. Likewise, Henri and Jordan insist upon their maleness, even though they include characteristics in their gender identities that are considered female. The Dog-Woman is a grotesque woman who parodies conventional gender norms,

---

[64] Winterson's re-writing of romance will be one focus of the subsequent chapter. For her subversive appropriation of the motif of the heart as used in texts by Philip Sidney and John Donne see Ganteau's "Fantastic."

[65] In *The Passion* the importance of the motif of passion is underlined by its association with religion, a concept that receives the same – rather vague – definition as passion: "Religion is somewhere between fear and sex" (*Passion* 74).

but she proudly defines herself as a woman. Even web-footed Villanelle, who wonders about the realness of her gender, lives and thinks of herself as a woman. Pearce writes about *Sexing the Cherry* that its characters "never do 'transcend' their genders even though they may challenge their definition" (*Dialogics* 185).[66] The same is true for *The Passion* and most certainly for *Oranges*. In a similar vein, Burns "would not say that Winterson explodes the binary [...] so much as she puts it in a dialectical and problematizing relation. This dialectic is supposed to achieve – and often does – a transformative moment, a new opening in social understanding" ("Powerful" 375). These fictions reveal the processes of the construction of maleness and femaleness to be cultural instead of natural in kind, encouraging and engaging in alternative constructions of gender. Yet, sex remains an "applicable characteristic" (Gade 30), or, to use Villanelle's words as a case in point: "There are women of every kind and not all of them are women" (*Passion* 58). With sex intact as the frame of reference, gender boundaries can be shown to be relatively flexible and open to (re-)construction.

Jordan's notion of gender grafting represents Winterson's most daring vision of a human society created without reverting to heterosexual reproductive practice, i.e., without bodies that are defined as "male" and "female." In *Sexing the Cherry* this remains an idea mentioned almost by the way and over-towered by Jordan's acquiescence in the gender essentialisms spread by the market women. But it is an idea that continues to engage Winterson imagination. In *Written on the Body* she brings to the test the transformative and unifying force of love in the face of radical unintelligibility of gender.

---

[66] In a more radical reading Haslett sees in Villanelle the most powerful transgressor of the gender boundary in Winterson's early fiction. She suggests that the "fabulous body" of the Venetian is the body of a hermaphrodite or a transgender person.

6   Contesting Gender: *Written on the Body*

In *Oranges Are Not the Only Fruit*, *The Passion*, and *Sexing the Cherry* Jeanette Winterson presents gender as a concept that, by its very constructedness, offers individuals the possibility to create for themselves a flexible, inclusive, and ultimately empowering identity. While these early fictions successfully problematize and liquefy the notion of rigid gender norms replete with restrictive gender roles and reinforced by the law of heteronormativity, they leave intact the binary of maleness and femaleness. However, Winterson strains against the limits imposed by the notion of gender itself. The tension that is evident in Jordan's desire to apply the art of grafting to himself on the one hand, thereby creating a gender identity that would transcend the male-female dichotomy, and his paradoxical acquiescence with essentialist verdicts about men and women on the other, bespeaks the author's impatience with the stage the critical discourse on gender has reached in her novels by 1989. Undermining the boundaries of gender may effectively question the gender binary, but if the point of reference of this critical effort remains the idea of verifiable gender difference anchored in a dual system of sexes, effective epistemological and gender-political limits to deconstruction and to the construction of alternative identities persist.

Is there, thus, no breaking out of this cycle of re-constructing essentialist sexual difference even in the attempt to deconstruct gender differences in a literary work? In 1990, Winterson thinks there is and announces in an interview that "[t]he next book will be very different. It will have a genderless narrator and it will challenge the way that people read at all" (Kay 28/2). Laura Doan is one of few scholars who recognize and take seriously the author's resolve to break new ground in the transferal of theoretical insights of gender studies to literary production. She identifies the task Winterson had on her hands at the beginning of the 1990s as that formulated by Judith Butler in *Gender Trouble*. In her fiction, Winterson was to create "a thoroughgoing appropriation and redeployment of the categories of identity themselves, not merely to contest 'sex,' but to articulate the convergence of multiple sexual discourses at the site of 'identity' in order to render that category, in whatever form, permanently problematic" (Butler 128 qtd. in Doan 151f.).[1]

In *Written on the Body* Winterson's challenge to the way people read and make sense of what they read hinges upon the identity of her narrator – or more precisely, upon the absence of a specific sex and a gender identity in her narrator. The author answers Butler's call to problematize the category of identity in the most radical fashion, namely by creating an individual whose identity is clustered with converging "multiple sexual discourses" to such an extent as to leave it ultimately undefined by gender. As Winterson queries the idea of the inevitability of gendering – indeed, as she adopts as a working hypothesis the idea of the dispensability of gender identity for the creation of intelligible subjecthood, Winterson forces "the reconceptualization of alternative constructions" of identity Doan demands (151). The questions of how she attempts this, whether or not she is successful and to what effect will be the signposts of my analysis of *Written on the Body*.

6.1   The reluctance of accepting a genderless protagonist

Written on the Body is a mosaic of recollections, observations, and meditations of a first-person narrator who, after numerous affairs with both women and men, has fallen in love with beautiful, married Louise.[2] After learning of Louise's leukemia diagnosis, the narrator decides to leave her, in the hope of securing for her the expert care Louise's estranged husband, a renowned oncologist, promises to give her in exchange for the exclusive rights to his wife. Hiding away in a dilapidated cottage in the comparative

---

[1] Winterson has repeatedly stressed her independence of theoretical discourse, be it contemporaneous or older, insisting that her approach to gender issues in particular stems solely from her own imagination and from her immersion in literature, though not in what Turner calls "the current fashion for gender-transcending lesbian porn" (T18). Some doubt may be permitted as to the credibility of this statement; there is evidence that suggests that Winterson attempted in her fiction in 1992 what Butler called for in her groundbreaking gender-theoretical work two years earlier, as will be explored in the following.

[2] Jeanette Winterson, *Written on the Body* (1992; London: Vintage, 1993). All further reference is to this edition.

wilderness of the North York Moors, the narrator mourns love sacrificed to save the life of the beloved and embarks on a journey of the mind through Louise's embattled body. Through the reprimands of the empathetic bar-owner Gail Right, the narrator comes to realize the cowardice and cruelty of leaving Louise at her time of greatest need and returns to London in the – ultimately failed – attempt to find the beloved. The dream-like, open ending of the novel leaves to the readers' imagination whether Louise's appearance in the cottage is "real" or an illusion created by the narrator's desperate longing for her.

In significant ways, Winterson's 1992 fiction stands apart from the ones she wrote before and after its publication. On the surface, *Written* is a straightforward love story set in London and Yorkshire in the early 1990s.[3] It abstains from the excursions into the realms of fairytales, courtly epics, and adventure stories which critics and readers alike had come to expect as the author's handwriting; also, in this text the breaks with genre conventions are less disruptive of the main narrative than in its predecessors. However, I argue that what might on the surface seem to be Winterson's most conventional book must in fact be regarded as her most radical experiment with the categories of sex and gender to date: With her nameless genderless narrator she not only questions the binary gender system, but effectively offers an alternative to it.[4]

Quite predictably, most of the controversy that flared up after the publication of *Written on the Body* took its spark from the novel's narrator. Most of the critics and scholars who reviewed *Written* or included it in their studies found the narrator's genderlessness difficult to accept.[5] They refer to a "supposedly 'genderless narrator'" (Pearce, *Dialogics*: 173),

---

[3] As has become customary for scholarly texts on *Written on the Body*, I will occasionally abbreviate the full title to *Written*. In citations, the abbreviation will be *WoB*.

[4] For the use of romance as a tool for critique in Winterson's early novels, see for example Andermahr's "Reinventing," Ganteau's "Fantastic" as well as his "Hearts," Pearce's "Written," Onega, and the previous chapter of this study.

[5] Only four out of 22 reviews consulted for this study speak of a narrator without a gender. This ratio does not differ significantly in articles about *Written on the Body*. I have come across only few authors who treat the notion of genderlessness with the seriousness appropriate for a genuine concept, consciously employed by the author. See e.g. Børch, Gade, Haines-Wright and Kyle, Stevens, and most recently Haslett. Pearce appears undecided: In *Dialogics* she doubts the gender-

or to "a narrator whose gender was supposedly ambiguous" (Lambert, "I don't"). Others decide upon a gender for the narrator, sometimes after what seems like a quick glance at the text and at other times after complicated analyses of suggestive passages. Duncker takes a lesbian relationship between the narrator and Louise and therefore the narrator's femaleness for granted, even though she admits that the relationship is never openly named lesbian , while Palmer first notes the existence of "a narrator whose gender is unstated," only to refer to this narrator henceforth as "she" (*Contemporary* 112). Lambert unflinchingly links the gender of the narrator to that of the author, as she reproduces speculations about possible parallels between the novel and the author's biography – and therefore also gender and sexuality –, informing us that "the book was assumed by the literary London to be a *roman à clef* based on Winterson's own colourful sex life" (cf. "I don't").[6]

6.2   The Politics of Gendering the Narrator

From the beginning, Jeanette Winterson's oeuvre has been read as highly political, at times activist, both by her admirers and by her critics. Feminists in particular found their calls for powerful female figures answered and their hunger for sensitive men satisfied in *Oranges Are Not the Only Fruit*, *The Passion* and *Sexing the Cherry*. Lesbian feminists praised Winterson's critique of homophobia and chauvinism in Western societies and relished her portraits of assertive, self-confident, and attractive lesbians. It was these heroines – role models for modern and enlightened women and men and icons for the feminist and lesbian movements as well as for lesbian-feminist literary criticism – that reviewers and critics expected to encounter again in *Written on the Body*. Winterson's refusal to comply with the expectations of readers, activists, and scholars, her pursuit of her

lessness of the narrator, while she seems to grudgingly accept it in "Emotional Politics."

[6]Lambert is not the only critic who infers from Winterson's gender and lesbianism to that of the narrator. Gilmore, for example, includes *Written* in his study of limit-cases of autobiography. He argues that in this text, Winterson's "refusal to anchor the narrator through the name 'lesbian'" is the same as her refusal to anchor her "textual practice through the name 'autobiography'" (141). His broader argument is that this tactic "has allowed for a particular inquiry into the limits of intelligibility within the representation of identity" (141).

own theoretical and artistic agenda in terms of gender, identity, and constructions of 'reality' by means of a genderless protagonist in a love story was interpreted by the most disappointed as a betrayal of the feminist-lesbian cause or as selling out to the male literary establishment. Pearce declares that "[l]esbian readers, in particular, have experienced this 'sliding' of gendered and sexual identity – this refusal to 'name' – as a serious political betrayal" (*Dialogics* 173f.). Patricia Duncker mournfully describes *Written* as "a text full of lost opportunities" (85). She complains that "[b]y concealing the gender of the narrator, Winterson avoids writing a Lesbian text about the affair between two women shattering a rotten marriage, but a text which gives the (male) heterosexual reader plenty of room to feel smug. [...] He can imagine that Louise has chosen a better man" (81f.). Other commentators disparagingly call Winterson's ungendered narrator a "gimmick" (Miner 21/3; Kendrick), a "coy hermeneutic plot game" (C. Allen 49), a "tiresome conceit" (J. Smith; see also Stuart), or an "irritating ploy" by means of which "the author seems to be playing games with [the readers]" (Wingfield 66).[7] Wingfield irately accuses the author of addressing her fiction "not [...] to [...] feminists, lesbians or even the general public," but to "the (male) mainstream literati itself" (66), while Gerrard denies the text any gender-political ambition, let alone effect: "[I]n *Written on the Body* the fervent, keening love story was etherealised by having a narrator with no specified gender: love was made transcendent, depoliticised and gutted of credibility" ("Ultimate"). Quite clearly, a protagonist without an identifiable gender was deemed unworthy of either a lesbian or a feminist writer and generally unhelpful in the fight for women's liberation.

There are critics and scholars who cling to their preferred image of Winterson, for example, that of a writer of semi-autobiographic lesbian literature, or of a postmodern writer who deconstructs gender norms and thereby exposes their arbitrariness. They argue that, yes, the "real" gender of the narrator is hidden, but it is not beyond discovery. As a love story, *Written on the Body* does contain numerous passages that – to readers living in a society organized along the male-female dichotomy – appear to contain gender giveaways. Most of the critics who decide on a gender

---

[7]Out of the possible interpretations of *Written*, this is the one Winterson disliked most intensely: "It outraged me that it was being made out to be some frivolous, queer version of chick lit" (Jaggi).

for the narrator therefore do so after weighing what they regard as textual evidence. In the absence of a name and of personal or possessive pronouns, such traces of gender are transported by cultural stereotypes and gender-specific attributes: styles of clothing, actions, and opinions deemed appropriate or typical for a man or for a woman, or the kind of interaction going on between the lovers, rendering their relationship either "typically hetero" or "typically homo."[8] Ironically, such traces, or "gender clues," as Fludernik terms them (168), lend themselves to opposing interpretations.[9] Stowers, for example, states that the narrator's "rejection of masculine, heterosexual paradigms leaves [her] with little doubt that this narrator is indeed female" ("Erupting" 92), whereas Kendrick remarks that "[the narrator] broadcasts his current affairs without hesitation, even to near-strangers; it's difficult to imagine that such love is not heterosexual" (131).[10]

Some scholars read the narrator's genderlessness as a "*Leerstelle*" in the sense proposed by Iser, an information gap consisting in a valuable piece of information about the protagonist and the social or sexual relationships that protagonist engages in which the author intentionally denies the readers in order to encourage their individual imaginative contribution to the contract between the author and her readers (cf. Kauer).[11] After careful consideration, readers, if they hope to make sense of the narrative at all, must fill the information gap that blocks full intelligibility of the narrator. Proponents of the notion of genderlessness as a *Leerstelle* in *Written on the Body* argue that in order to be able to identify with the narrator and to understand the narrative, readers must decide upon a gender for the narrator. Then, in the attempt to infer the narrator's gender from textual details, i.e., from "gender clues" based on essentialist stereotypes,

---

[8]See Fludernik for a list of passages that characterize the narrator as "male," as "female," or that could be read as "inclusive" of maleness and femaleness. Fludernik seems to consider her list complete, but for those who search for indicators of the narrator's gender the text offers a great number of supposed clues, many more than Fludernik has identified.

[9]Berch also calls the issue of the narrator's sex "a hunt for clues" and wonders rather unappreciatively why the author "chose to be such a tease" about it (42).

[10]After a lengthy analysis of "gender clues" contained in the text, Fludernik comes to the same conclusion. Kauer, on the other hand, provides a similar list and decides, on the basis of her investigation, that the narrator has to be female.

[11]Cf. Iser, *Der implizite Leser* and *Der Akt des Lesens*.

readers will receive a host of inconclusive, possibly conflicting information. For example, is the fact that the narrator, in a flash of rage during
the search for Louise, smashes the jaw of Louise's deceitful ex-husband a
sign of manliness? Men are commonly deemed more liable than women
to beat up a rival over the imagined possession of a woman. However,
the narrator not only breaks a wrist bone in the action, but after the fight
"move[s] [Elgin's] head to a more comfortable position, fetching a cushion from the hall" (*WoB* 172). As physical weakness and vulnerability,
paired with the impulse to nurture connote femaleness in a patriarchal society, they level out the effect the narrator's initial outburst of violence
had on the reader's gender sensors. Thus, according to the proponents
of the *Leerstelle* theory, in the – necessary – process of deciding whether
the narrator is male or female, readers will recognize the arbitrariness and
artificiality of gender norms and will view essentialist gender roles and
norms critically. This will not prevent them from fixing the narrator's
gender in the course of their reading. Without a specific gender, so the
argument goes, the narrator would not be intelligible as a subject and the
love story would be "gutted of credibility," as indeed Gerrard claims it
to be. As gender is indispensable to the construction of identity, readers
will make a decision that has always already been included in the design
of the story. Therefore, the narrator "[wears] the mask of a gender-free
persona," to use Kauer's formulation, for one reason only (41), namely,
in order to unmask the constructedness of gender. Underneath that mask,
the narrator is a woman or a man, depending on the individual reader's
interpretation of the supposed narrative clues.

There are scholars, however, who strongly disagree with this notion of
a hidden but definite – and by implication essentialist – gender for the narrator. "When so many critics 'sex' the ungendered narrator of *Written on
the Body*," Humphries warns, "they specifically go against the intention of
the text to create a space in which the whole point is that gender may be
variously constructed, but is ultimately left indeterminate" (15). Gade also
insists on a reading that assumes the "construction of a narrator that is not
clearly gendered, as the narrative voice is not identified as either female or
male. Instead of stabilising the narrative position through sexing, the gender position of the narrator is perpetually constructed and deconstructed"
(30). Meyer takes up the idea of perpetual construction and deconstruction
and fuses it with Rosi Braidotti's theory of a postmodern nomadic subjectivity: The narrator "can be read as a nomadic subject who inhabits none

of these [gender] positions to the exclusion of the others," but "[holds] open numerous subject positions" (220). Moore and Lindenmeyer agree that Winterson's narrator does not have one fixed gender; this protagonist is a person who has different genders at different times and in encounters with different lovers (cf. Lindenmeyer). Both work with the notion of the narrator as a pastiche of differently gendered personae (cf. Moore).

As *Written on the Body* is widely received as a political text, or at least as a text created by an author with strong interests in the politics of gender, it is not surprising that reactions to the novel testify to the political agendas of those who utter them. Feminist-lesbian literary critics expressed their disappointment at what they perceived as a lack of solidarity with the women's cause and a betrayal of lesbian interests still in the late 1990s, the time when the most scathing criticism was published.[12] On the other hand, scholars who stress postmodern ideas in Winterson's work praise *Written* as a milestone in the deconstruction of essentialist gender boundaries.

Yet crucially, hardly one of the authors mentioned here so far contemplates the possibility that in her fifth fiction Winterson might try to undo gender in earnest.[13] Since we are living in a society that is clearly gendered, since women are still dominated by men in all but a few branches of this society and all too often are denied equal rights and equal treatment because of their sex, the abandonment of the notion of gender difference is decried as less than politically correct, or relegated to the realm of fairy tales. Neither Winterson's announcement prior to the publication of *Written* that she was going to create a genderless narrator, nor the text's refusal to assign a gender to its narrator are therefore taken quite seriously. Even Gade, who starts her article by announcing that "*Written* attempts to do away with sex and gender all together" (30), in her conclusion shies away from her radical point of venture: "In relation to sexual identities, Winterson's subversive fiction *may* push the boundaries of gendered identities to prove them *less fixed* than we think" (39, my emphases). Apparently, the

---

[12]Cf. Pearce (1998), Wingfield (1998), Lambert (1998). As recently as in 2007, Armitt, in her essay on "Storytelling and Feminism," expresses regret at what she interprets as Winterson's turning away from a previous "primary attachment to women" (15).

[13]This state of affairs seems slowly to change as more research has been conducted on Winterson's oeuvre. In a recent publication Jane Haslett reads the narrator's body as a body "which questions gender identity through a complete absence of gender identification" (43).

old argument that the deconstruction of social "realities" in postmodern theory and art excludes the possibility of a commitment to feminist – or any other – political goals, prevents scholars from acknowledging the full extent of Winterson's undoing of the concepts of sex and gender in *Written on the Body*. It also stops them from investigating the effects of such a radical experiment on our reading habits, our understanding of narration and its power, and on the discourse of gender and identity.

6.3   Narrating Genderlessness

Apart from political investments, another, substantial reason for the reluctance of the majority of reviewers and scholars to accept a genderless protagonist might be the difficulty of conceiving of and writing about a socially integrated person, however fictitious, as having no gender under the conditions of heteronormative Western society, a society that employs gender difference as a structuring principle and operates with a linguistic apparatus shaped by and ever reconstituting the gender binary. Is it possible, then, to write about genderlessness without using gendered language? What language can I as a scholar use in a study of Winterson's strategies to render her narrator genderless?

Wittig has stressed the central status of personal pronouns as engineers of gender in the English language, particularly in the third person singular (cf. 78f.). If I respect Winterson's effort to create a genderless subject, I cannot refer to that subject as "he" or "she" and thus engage in a process of gendering through language. Likewise, it is impossible to use forms like "he or she" or the shorter "s/he" as they would place the narrator within the binary of male and female. Stevens suggests that the narrator "could be described as the slash between 'she' and 'he' rather than as the two words on either side," but then – maybe out of an awareness that the slash still cites the gender binary – proceeds to use "she/he" and "her/his" as pronouns. Finally, the neutral "it" would deprive the protagonist of the status of a living being and an "absolute subject" that Wittig claims for all locators (78). The use of any of the personal and possessive pronouns the English language has at its disposal is clearly counterproductive when referring to a genderless protagonist. In order to avoid gendering the narrator when I specifically wish to analyze the genderlessness of that character, I therefore must rely on a very limited number of gender-unspecific nouns, all of which have already been used profusely in this chapter. Also, I must circumvent syntactic constructions that use personal and possessive pronouns to situate the narrator in the discourse with other characters. The result of these endeavors is a somewhat nominal style with rather many verbal constructions based on gerunds. Clearly, the English language poses stylistic limits to the discussion of a literary text with a genderless protagonist, limits which illustrate the very "stamping" and "[violent] shaping" of the social body and of the real through gendered language Wittig has pointed out so forcefully (78).

For *Written on the Body* Winterson carefully employs the linguistic means of a first-person narration and thus avoids the traps of imposing a gender on her protagonist through language: The "I" the narrator invents and presents in the narrative is not conclusively gendered. This does not mean, however, that the narrator abstains from self-descriptions that carry connotations of maleness or femaleness. On the contrary; one technique the author uses to render her narrator genderless can be described as an "overgendering" through an accumulation of gender clues that are contradictory. This "overgendering" occurs in the narrator's accounts of former love affairs and in descriptions of the relationship with and later the search for Louise. In the self-characterizations of the protagonist metaphors and titles rife with connotations of maleness or femaleness abound: In a bout of exasperation at the violence of love, that "big game hunter," the narrator asks: "How can you stick at a game when the rules keep changing? I shall call myself Alice and play croquet with the flamingoes" (*WoB* 10). When, in the early stages of their courtship, Louise calls to extend a seductive invitation, the still-liaised narrator feels duty-bound to turn it down and, after Louise disappointedly hangs up, "stare[s] at [the telephone] the way Lauren Bacall does in those films with Humphrey Bogard" (*WoB* 41). Later, a kiss of the beloved incites in the lover "Mercutio's swagger" (*WoB* 81), while further on in their relationship, Louise's loving attention makes the narrator "feel like a convent virgin" (*WoB* 93). When bitter doubts torture the narrator about the virtue of leaving Louise in order to gain for her the expert cancer treatment her husband Elgin promises to give her, the question, "Who do I think I am? Sir Launcelot?" does not elicit an answer in the unhappy lover's heart – and its potential as a gender give-away is speedily shattered: "Louise is a Pre-Raphaelite beauty but that doesn't make me a mediaeval knight" (both *WoB* 159).

Apart from a flaunting of stereotypical but contradictory gender characteristics, certain passages in *Written on the Body* illustrate thoughts and

emotions of the narrator that exhibit a deliberate ambiguity in terms of
the gender they may connote. Reminiscing about the shameful end of the
affair with a married woman called Bathsheba the narrator wonders, for
example, if "perhaps I should enlist [in the Army]" where "[they] are supposed to teach you [self-respect]" (*WoB* 46). Enlisting in the Army used
to be viewed as a very manly action, but the British armed forces ceased to
be an exclusively male domain decades ago and the process of opening up
to women had well started by the time *Written* was created. Neither is the
need of being taught self-respect restricted to male *or* female persons exclusively. Traditionally and stereotypically, a woman fighting for the love
of a married woman would be seen as suffering from a loss of self-respect
because of the undignified circumstances of their illicit relationship. But
in the Bathsheba episodes Winterson also plays with the popular trope
of the securely rich and married vamp who toys with her perhaps young,
male lover. As the gender of Bathsheba's lover remains ambiguous, a
psychological dimension moves into focus here and becomes clearly intelligible: the low self-respect of the narrator caused by the unwillingness
of the beloved to commit herself to her lover and to show her love openly.

As illustrated earlier, the narrator uses gendered language and clichés
of male and female behavior self-descriptively in a first-person narration
without creating in the readers' minds a picture of a conclusively gendered
person. We receive further personal information through the narrator's
accounts of interactions with former partners and current interlocutors.
What is significant in these accounts is that we cannot deduce from any of
the personal interactions the narrator tells us about that anybody considers
the protagonist to be a woman or a man. Through the filter of the narrator's accounts, former lovers, Louise's mother and grandmother, or Elgin
speak to us about the narrator's actions, thoughts, feelings, and words.
Significantly, in direct exchanges between these and other interlocutors
and the narrator – if they are related to us at all – they use, apart from the
neutral 'you,' terms that are pointedly unspecific as to the gender of the
addressee. A friend calls the narrator, who reluctantly admits the budding
affair with yet another married woman, a "bloody idiot" (*WoB* 32). In one
of the rare instances in which we witness one character talking to another
about Louise's lover, The Aged Pea, Louise's robust Australian grandmother, talks to her daughter about the bedraggled-looking caller at her
front door as about "this digger" and "this thing from the Disinfectant Department" (*WoB* 165). Voluminous and worldly-wise Gail Right addresses

her new friend and would-be Casanova simply as "love" or "honey" (*WoB* 147, 159), while for Louise her lover is "a pool of clear water where the light plays" (*WoB* 85).

Gender does not play into these terms of address. Rather, they reveal the history behind an action and the role the narrator plays in that history as seen by the friend who speaks to or about the protagonist: The "bloody idiot" has allowed another liaison with a married woman to blossom, although all the previous ones ended in heartbreak for one side or the other, and the friend is infuriated by such a blatant lack of self-control. They cut to the quick of the narrator's state of being at the specific moment of being addressed by others: The Pea is the narrator's last straw in the search for Louise, but this lady is an intimidating, well-armed fortress that needs to be taken in a frustrating and hopeless hunt for clues as to Louise's whereabouts. These adverse circumstances render the narrator a "thing," something that has become less than human because grief, guilt, and exhaustion have eaten away its humanness. The gender-unspecified "love" does not so much tell us anything about the addressee of this term of endearment than rather about middle-aged Gail Right's longing for someone who would be her own "love" at last, someone whom she could safely and justifiably call "honey" from the bottom of her heart. Finally, Louise sees through the unspectacular appearance and the inglorious personal history of the narrator with regard to previous relationships and sees in her lover purity, light, and freshness. In these interactions we receive a wealth of intimate information about the narrator, who nevertheless remains genderless. The pinning down of the narrator to one gender would not change any of these states or characteristics; gender becomes insignificant, a nonmarker, even though gender references might be used excessively at times in order to illustrate certain states of being or feelings.

Thus, as Winterson succeeds in characterizing her protagonist without resorting to a gender identity, she demonstrates the dispensability of this category as a means of personification and identification. A fixed gender identity, therefore, seems as redundant for the construction of the narrator's identity – or various, changing identities – as for the protagonist's assumption of a subject position. The narrator lives in an environment that is structured in terms of gender and has experiences that are shaped by interactions with people whose gender identity may be unorthodox and subversive but who are nevertheless gendered. However, when Winterson equips her narrator with characteristics, actions, or feelings that cite connotations of maleness or femaleness, she employs these citations with a deliberate lack of consequentiality, thus canceling out any gendering effects these connotations might possess. While readers are actively discouraged from deciding upon a specific gender identity for the narrator, they are invited to key into the narrator's feelings, ways of thinking, or motives in any given situation. Emotional and mental qualities are divorced from any specific sex and gender, but they are explored in detail and thus allow readers to form vivid images of the narrator's personality and develop a sense of sympathy or antipathy for this protagonist. Readers can do so without having to rely on preexisting notions of maleness and femaleness, notions that are shown to be illusory.

The device of the first-person narrative allows Winterson to do without pronouns, the primary engineers of gender in language. She does not pretend to have invented a genderless language with which to narrate her genderless lover. The narrator creates an "I" that is independent of the possession of a specific gender identity and therefore genderless. But the sociological and emotional components of such a genderless "I," the experiences and memories that form the identifying narrative, remain gendered, sometimes stereotypically so. To narrate genderlessness, i.e., the absence of a specific gender identity, thus seems possible only by means of gendered language – the only language we have at our disposal. While this fails to "cleanse" language of gender, it calls attention to the extent to which gender identities – as well as other identities – are discursively constructed. The fact that the narrator nevertheless resists gendering, poses a powerful challenge to the notion of gender as a binary opposition of female and male. It encourages readers to identify exclusivist, stereotypical language and to re-create it as inclusive and non-prescriptive. Furthermore, it offers an example of an identity and a subject position that functions without being moored to the limits of maleness and femaleness.

6.4   Effects of the Narrator's Genderlessness

6.4.1   Gender identities and sexualities of former lovers

Most of the narrator's numerous love affairs – with the exception of the relationship with Louise – are short-lived and relatively noncommittal. Yet, they are remarkable in so far as they offer the participants the freedom to define their sexuality and gender identities according to their individual needs and situations. In the various former girlfriends Winterson presents a range of very different interpretations of female gender roles in terms of professions, of power relations within the relationship, and of expressions of sexualities.

One lover is "addicted to starlit nights" and insists on having spontaneous sex only, preferably out in the public – a wish the narrator tries to accommodate in every possible way while their affair lasts (*WoB* 19). Not only does the girlfriend dictate time and place of their trysts, she also claims the traditionally male privilege of displaying and enjoying her sexuality publicly. The young Dutch woman Inge finds in the narrator a pliable helper for her "anarcha-feminist" terrorist assaults on urinals as "symbol[s] of patriarchy" (*WoB* 22). She defines herself as a terrorist, which – prior to the rise of female suicide bombings in the wake of the terrorist attacks of September 11 in 2001 – was an exclusively male domain.[14] Another girlfriend employs her lover as a source of inspiration during long nights of sneaking around rich people's dwellings and making up stories about the silent figures behind the windows. She sees herself as a burgeoning author who invariably will "become an alcoholic and forget how to cook" and thus turn into the stereotypical image of a (most likely male) writer (*WoB* 60). A girlfriend called Estelle does not only do business in the male domain of scrap metal, she also owns a Rolls-Royce, the patriarchal rich man's car *par excellence*, "with a pneumatic back seat" that has left a lasting impression on the narrator's memory for the macho love-making that had taken place on it. Judith, a botanist who breeds rubber plants in hothouses, insists on having her sexual needs satisfied between two and five in the afternoon, at the perpetual risk of being surprised by visitors of the Botanical Gardens. After an argument she ends the affair and locks the hothouse doors on the narrator who has to cross the city stark naked in order to get home. Bathsheba is a married woman with whom the narrator has an affair that stretches over several years. She is a successful dentist and a ruthlessly selfish lover, sacrificing her lover's self esteem and emotional well-being to her pleasures in a secret affair. Her successor, Jacqueline, works at the Zoo, "with small furry things that wouldn't be nice to visitors" (*WoB* 25). She treats the narrator "like a

---

[14]While outside of fiction female terrorists are the exception from the rule, there are literary predecessors of the "anarcha-feminist" terrorist. See for example the women of the city of Beulah in Angela Carter's *The Passion of New Eve*.

big cat in the Zoo" and seems satisfied with a minimal amount of attention from her partner (*WoB* 28). Louise, then, is a beautiful Australian art historian with a refined taste in high art and a cloud of admirers permanently around her, while the hard-drinking Yorkshire bar owner Gail Right intimidates the narrator with her yearning for physical intimacy and her enormous bodily expanse.[15]

Stevens rightly states that "[t]he extreme differences among these women function to expand traditional constructions of femininity, posing a challenge to the notion that there is, to use Cixous's words, 'a general woman' [...]." This is also true for Winterson's treatment of patriarchal notions of masculinity in the narrator's male lovers. They too are free to develop distinctly unorthodox gender identities:[16] Crazy Frank carries his midget-sized parents around with him on his shoulders. "They didn't need much room and they helped him to make friends. He explained that he was very shy" (*WoB* 93). The "midgets" are extensions of Frank's personality – the part of it that is small, shy, and in need of protection and therefore does not conform to the stereotypical characteristics of masculinity. Even his physique displays mixed gender signals: He sports a tall, muscular body and wears "huge gold hoops through his nipples" that give his body the image of a bull (*WoB* 93). Frank – accidentally or not – seriously undermines his exaggerated masculinity by joining the nipple hoops with a "chain of heavy gold links" which "looked rather like the handle of a Chanel shopping bag" – the epitome of clichéd femininity (*WoB* 93). Thus, by including drag accessories in his gender performance, Crazy Frank lacerates the construction of masculinity as the polar opposite of femininity.

Carlo, another boyfriend, leaves the narrator for "Robert who was taller, broader and thinner" (*WoB* 143). Importantly, it is not so much the biological sex that determines Carlo's choice of partner, but rather characteristics that apply to both men and woman. The narrator suggests that Robert is not preferred for his maleness but for his stature. In this

---

[15]Gail is one of the few sympathetic portrayals of older women in Winterson's oeuvre. (For others, see for example Elsie and the woman in the funeral parlor in *Oranges*). She shares an enormous body and a big heart with the Dog-Woman in *Sexing*.

[16]For a study on Winterson's masculinities in *Oranges*, *Passion*, and *Sexing* see Philip Tew. However, Tew is not interested in the male characters in *Written on the Body*.

respect Carlo shares his standards with Crazy Frank, who informs the narrator: "You'd be perfect if you were smaller" (*WoB* 93). In both cases sex and gender identity are not decisive for the selection of the object of desire. Winterson breaks the nexus between gender identity and sexual object choice: Men are not male because they desire women or because they are gay and therefore desire other men. Here we meet individuals called Frank and Carlo who select their sex partners on grounds of their physical height or the degree of their leanness. For Bruno, another former boyfriend of the narrator's, sex, gender, and sexuality lose their power to shape his identity altogether, a task that is taken over by an overwhelming sense of spiritual renewal after a near-death experience.

The narrator's genderlessness also has an effect on the identities of adversaries like Elgin. During the narrator's search for Louise in London, in the final, violent confrontation of the protagonist and Louise's divorced husband Elgin, descriptions of Elgin's attacks allude to stereotypical notions of both masculine and feminine styles of fighting: "Elgin punched me in the stomach and winded me against the wall. [. . .] Elgin kicked me in the shins" (*WoB* 170). Faced with an opponent who is "colt-mad" at him for having lied about helping Louise and keeping her lover informed about her condition (*WoB* 172), small, mole-like Elgin behaves like an actor cast for the male lead: He assumes a protective posture toward his new fiancée – first by stepping between the alleged assailant and the fiancée, then by sending the woman from the battleground in the house to the safety of the car – and proceeds to fight with all his might. The scene quotes familiar Hollywood images of two rivals locked in battle over a woman. In Winterson's cosmos, however, clichéd "manly" or "womanly" actions, such as breaking the opponent's jaw or bedding his head on a cushion to make him more comfortable, are rendered ambivalent. Not only is one of the actors an individual on whom labels such as male and female do not stick. Elgin, known as "the little rat" to The Aged Pea and her daughter (*WoB* 166), who needed Louise as a trophy wife to divert male rivals' judging gaze away from his 'unmanly' appearance, knocks the narrator to the ground, only to lie at his attacker's feet "in foetus position bleeding" a few moments later (*WoB* 172). Winterson's narrative execution of this sequence again calls into question the binary gender system, unhinging it in the case of the narrator and blurring the lines between stereotypical masculinity and femininity in Elgin; it also accentuates Louise's extraordinary importance for the narrator.

However, the "[denaturalization] of dominant conceptions of gender difference" which Stevens diagnoses, is not the only function of the wide array of gender identities expressed by the narrator's female and male lovers and other characters in the novel. These men and women receive and use the chance to invent their own gender identities as a direct effect of the genderlessness of their partner, the narrator. In their relationships with the protagonist women do not feel pressured into conforming to codes of behavior that govern the interaction with men or with other women and set tight limits to explorations of their individuality; men are free to acknowledge weaknesses within themselves and to express their gender identity in ways that blur the boundaries between maleness and femaleness. The ex-girlfriends and ex-boyfriends have no need to define themselves in contrast to "the opposite sex" or as similar to "the same sex" when their lover does not have a gender. The narrator's skilful sketching of the quirks and preferences of former lovers underlines the message that each relationship is as unique as the people who have a part in it.[17]

Furthermore, the fluidity of the gender identities of some of the ex-lovers and the narrator's own genderlessness undermine the notion of sexuality as being reducible to "gay" or "straight." The sexual relationships in which the narrator engages exist outside binary oppositions, "which are exposed, through their absence, as unduly regulatory and exclusionary," as Stevens puts it. The effect of such "genderless love" is liberating, as the respective couples neither have to grapple with the challenges of social stigmatization nor with the normalizing effects of belonging to a hegemonic stratum of society.

Thus, far from being a state of abjectness, of presenting the reason for casting a person out of human society to become the negative backdrop for "normal," gendered individuals, genderlessness endows the narrator with a conspicuous attractiveness. With the narrator, male and female lovers can be as unconventional, as untypical as they wish. In a relationship with an ungendered individual the partners can imagine and realize in their lives alternative variants of gender, variants that – maybe fleetingly – suit

---

[17] Stevens links her discussion of "the disparate characters in the text, exhibiting a range of gender possibilities" to Derrida's notion of the "sexual otherwise," "one sex for each time" and to Wittig's proposal that there are "not one or two sexes but many, as many sexes as there are individuals" (Derrida and Wittig qtd. in Stevens).

their individual erotic and/or emotional desires. Without the inherently normative dichotomy of male and female, subjects are free to identify with whatever gender variant they might feel comfortable with or to which subject position they might be attracted. And they enjoy the freedom of loving whomsoever they wish, because as Winterson said in an interview: "I don't think that love should be a gender-bound operation. It's probably one of the few things in life that rises above all those kinds of oppositions – black and white, male and female, homosexual and heterosexual" (Marvel 165/1f.).

6.4.2   The anarchic force of love

The arrival of Louise in the narrator's life marks the turning point in the psycho-emotional journey of her lover. Looking back to the period before Louise, the narrator expresses a sense of exhaustion induced by the hasty succession of love affairs "after years of playing the Lothario" (*WoB* 20). A self-description as "Lothario" is a quotation of the customary understanding of such a person as derived from canonic works of Western literature: Miguel de Cervantes's Lothario in the novella "The Impertinent Curiosity" in *Don Quixote* is the faithful friend who first refuses to and then consents to testing the fidelity of his best friend Anselmo's wife, in the process of which the two fall in love. In Nicholas Rowe's *The Fair Penitent* Lothario is a handsome, seductive lady's man. In the course of Western literary and cultural history the title of Lothario has come to be given to men who either have a strong interest in seducing and having short sexual relationships with as many women as possible or who are extremely seductive to women. Due to the literary forebears, such behavior is deemed excessively male. Thus, by using the name of Lothario as a self-descriptive alias, the narrator cites not only the clichés of Lothario-like manners but also highlights the practice of assigning a gender to an attitude or certain behaviors. Since the narrator is genderless, however, the exclusive maleness of acting like a Lothario is pulled into doubt. After all, what is so very "male" about such sexual behavior? Could not women behave like lotharios, as well, and don't some? Winterson questions and ultimately severs the presumed link between gender and love – both as an emotion and as a sexual activity – in order to shift the focus from presumed gender differences onto something else: It is not the supposed maleness of the Lothario in *Written on the Body* that is examined and exhibited in this short episode, but the behavior and way of living that merit this dubious title. The association with a Lothario calls attention to the comparatively superficial quality of the relationships the narrator had with the women and men who came before Louise and points to the completely different quality of the relationship with Louise.

Early on in the novel the protagonist philosophizes about the inevitable outcome of an affair with a woman who is firmly bound into the corsage and presumed security of marriage. In order to illustrate the relatively powerless position of the unmarried party in an illicit affair with a married woman, the narrator develops a dramatic conversation between a "lover" and a "naked woman." The wife admits to desiring her lover more than her spouse but declares that she loves her husband so much that she cannot bring herself to leave him in order to be with her lover (*WoB* 14f.). By unfolding this scenario Winterson cites a typical plot element of lesbian romance or melodrama: the frustrating and often futile fight of the lover for the loyalty of the beloved, who shies away from trading the security, prestige, and the comforts of married life for a risky life of love and passion lived on the precarious margins of society. By refusing to gender the "lover" the author brings to her readers' attention the clichés surrounding extramarital affairs and invites them to question the gender roles connected with these clichés. Yet this mini-drama has an even more important function within the novel: The stereotypical scene of an illicit affair is another negative backdrop for the relationship between the narrator and Louise. In contrast to the narrator's long-term affair with Bathsheba, the married dentist who enjoys the thrills of her affair but would not dream of leaving her husband, the relationship with Louise rests and depends on mutual respect and public acknowledgment.

The narrator's episode with Jacqueline, Louise's immediate predecessor, starts out as a pragmatic arrangement between equals. Jacqueline craves a home for herself, in connection with the sense of being needed by someone, while the narrator, feeling bruised by the affair with Bathsheba, "was tired of balancing blindfold on a slender beam, one slip and into the unplumbed sea. I wanted the clichés, the armchair" (*WoB* 26). While this passionless arrangement seems to satisfy Jacqueline's desires for as long as she deems herself the narrator's only and therefore indispensable partner, it soon turns boring for the narrator: "With Jacqueline I settled into a parody of the sporting colonel, the tweedy cove with line-up of trophies and a dozen reminiscences about each" (*WoB* 77). This parody of marriage paves the way for Louise's entry, but it proves difficult for the narrator to shed the habits of a Lothario and to commit to a potentially life-long partnership.

This difficulty is foreshadowed in the 'Amy episode.' The narrator thinks of Amy, a former girlfriend, after turning down Louise's invitation and after the miserable dinner with Jacqueline that follows this decision made out of a sense of responsibility for the current partner in a lukewarm quasi-marital arrangement. It is introduced by the statement: "During the night I had a lurid dream about an ex-girlfriend of mine who had been heavily into papier-mâché" (*WoB* 41). In this dream Amy frightened her amorous visitor with a papier-mâché snake inside the letter box attached to the front door "just at crotch level," in whose open mouth she had hidden a rat-trap (*WoB* 41). The narrator confesses to having hesitated before ringing because, "to reach the bell meant pushing my private parts right into the head of the snake" (*WoB* 41). Amy explained that "[i]t's for the postman. He's been bothering me," and, after demonstrating the construction's crippling mechanism on a leek and picking up the severed vegetable to put it into the soup to be eaten later in the evening, assures her lover that "[y]ou've got nothing to be frightened of" (*WoB* 42).

The rat-trap can hardly be trusted to distinguish between individual ringers; so, if according to Amy it presented no danger for the narrator, one is led to assume that it was either for the reason that there was no penis to be bitten off by this *vagina dentata*-like contraption, or that the narrator's behavior toward Amy was of a nature that did not warrant such a violent punishment.[18] Readers have no cause to doubt Amy's judgment of the danger for her lover; but then, why was the narrator nervous before ringing? The fact that this short episode takes place in a nightmarish dream puts another set of question marks behind the reason for the protagonist's hesitation in front of the door bell.

The dream about a leek chopped off in the toothed mouth of a snake is a reference to the notion of castration anxiety from classical Freudian psychoanalysis. This masculinist tradition reads dreams of cutting or even severing the phallus as showing men's subconscious fears of emasculation and a resultant loss of power and control. Significantly, it is also under-

---

[18] According to ethnographic explanations, legends about women with toothed vaginas in so-called primitive societies were told to deter young men from raping women.

stood to reflect the fear of losing an important person. The 'Amy episode' is full of allusions to stereotypical notions of maleness; it is an example of Winterson's playing with her readers' attempts at gendering the protagonist and of her – almost mischievous – subversion of theoretical constructions that shore up the binary gender system. In traditional psychoanalysis maleness and the possession of a penis are seen as the norm, while femaleness is seen as defined by the lack of a penis and therefore the desire for the phallus. With her genderless narrator, Winterson challenges this world view, and she downright ridicules it in the Amy episode.

On the one hand, the dream of a symbolic castration in a papier-mâché *vagina dentata* quotes patriarchal myths of men being devoured by deadly females, myths that betray a male horror of female sexuality and have resulted in many centuries of vilifying and marginalizing of women in patriarchal societies across cultures. Amy's reassuring explanation, on the other hand, contradicts and renders absurd allusions to maleness that exist in the dream sequence. As gender is thus declared a non-issue, the very conscious fears that torture the protagonist as Louise's intention and desire become more and more apparent move into the foreground: the fear induced by the prospect of abandoning oneself to the passion of another person – a person deemed desirable, but dangerously powerful – and thus giving up a large amount of one's own power; the fear of losing control over one's love-life, if not one's entire existence; the fear of losing the current partner in a passionless but safe relationship; the fear of never gaining the new lover who might be the ideal partner, and of ending up desperately lonely. Feelings of helplessness and powerlessness besiege the narrator who is confronted with a life-changing decision: "So what am I going to do? [...] How shall I know whether Louise is what I must do or must avoid?" (*WoB* 43). This uncertainty, which the sexually well-versed, seemingly independent narrator experiences as nightmarish, is what interests Winterson here. Thus, a dilemma of immense consequence to the narrator moves center-stage: the dilemma of laying one's life into someone else's hands, of giving up control in the hope of gaining fulfillment in love.

Written on the Body opens with the question, "Why is the measure of love loss?" (*WoB* 9). The mournful query indicates a renewed engagement with the notion of love as a game of chance, which is an important trope already in *The Passion*. "What you risk reveals what you value" (*Passion* 91), is Villanelle's motto in the earlier novel. It is shared by the narrator in *Written* who, in deciding to leave Jacqueline in order to be with Louise, risks a typical and valuable wager in the game of love: control. After their first lovemaking the narrator exclaims, "Louise, I love you," and is cautioned by the beloved: "Don't say that now. Don't say it yet. You might not mean it" (*WoB* 52). Against her lover's protests that "the effect" of Louise's presence is "that I am out of control" (*WoB* 53), Louise accuses the narrator of using the familiar three words in order to regain control: "'So you try and regain control by telling me you love me. That's a territory you know, isn't it? That's romance and courtship and whirlwind.' 'I don't want control.' 'I don't believe you.' No and you're right not to believe me" (*WoB* 53). Overwhelmed by an enormity of feeling never experienced before, the narrator takes refuge in the old behavior of the Lothario – and is promptly accused of "[t]rophy hunting," of seeing Louise as "another scalp on your pole" (*WoB* 53). Knowing that there is some truth to this claim, the accused is bewildered and eager to make concessions: "I wouldn't want to have much to do with me. [...] 'Tell me what you want and I'll do it'" (*WoB* 54). After years of playing the Lothario, of desiring many men and women, of leaving them after a brief affair or being left by them, the narrator craves constancy and guidance. Louise insists on constancy as a prerequisite of a new relationship, but the only guidance she is prepared to give is an allusion to the necessity to disentangle oneself from conventions that govern human interaction – to give up control.

Louise asks her lover to break with an internalized cliché of love as a relationship between two people that rests on a hierarchy of power and requires a strict management of control. One partner needs to be in control, needs to lead, while the other one allows her- or himself to be led. "Would Louise lead me so [like an angel leads the weary traveler]? Did I want to be led?" are the narrator's anxious questions at the outset of their relationship (*WoB* 54). The protagonist's conflicting desires to lead and to be led clash with Louise's powerful will for independence and self-governance. The array of the narrator's relationships represents an exemplary selection of other clichéd images of love (cf. Børch): There are variants of truant love presenting the illusion of freedom as expressed in reckless affairs with independent women and men, while the relationship with Jacqueline embodies the "saggy armchair" of sensible love in homeopathic doses, safely free of passion (*WoB* 10).

Finally, in the attempt to regain control over the onslaught of feelings after learning of Louise's illness, the lover turns to the cliché of self-sacrificing, narcissist love by giving up the beloved into the hands of her doctor-husband: "Our love was not meant to cost you your life. I can't bear that. If it could be my life I would gladly give it. [...] Please go with Elgin. He has promised to tell me how you are" (*WoB* 105f.). With this decision the narrator mimics Elgin's behavior toward his wife. Elgin regards Louise as his prized possession, his subject and domain over which he wields power and which earns him admiration in the eyes of his colleagues. Louise's and Elgin's relationship at this point serves as an illustration of the stereotypical imbalance of power between husband and wife in traditional marriages or heterosexual relationships. Elgin tries to instrumentalize Louise's illness for his scheme to regain power over her and bind her to him. The text even allows for a reading that suggests that Elgin makes up the cancer diagnosis or at least exaggerates the severity of Louise's illness in order to once more take control over his wife.[19]

To the narrator, who reproduces Elgin's patronizing behavior, giving up Louise presents an immense sacrifice that occasions much wallowing in self-pity and clinging onto the egoistic hope of doing the right thing. The narrator withdraws from the world into a ramshackle Yorkshire cottage that "was dirty, depressing and ideal" (*WoB* 107) and only stops to think of Louise's wishes and desires after Gail Right insists on "poking her nose into your shining armour [...]" and giving the depressed lover a piece of her mind: "You don't run out on the woman you love. Especially not if you think it's for her own good" (*WoB* 160). The narrator's decision to leave has deprived Louise of the freedom to choose for herself how she

---

[19]The name Elgin seems a deliberate choice indeed. It brings to the readers' minds the historical figure of Thomas Bruce, 7th Earl of Elgin who, as the British ambassador to the Ottoman Empire at the turn of the 18th century, acquired sculptures from the Parthenon and arranged for them to be brought to Britain where the Parliament purchased them from him and presented them to the British Museum. This collection of sculptures is often referred to as the 'Elgin Marbles.' Critics of Lord Elgin accused him of plundering the artifacts and then arguing that he was rescuing them. This alleged attitude more or less describes Elgin's plans with Louise and the deal he strikes with the narrator: He "plunders" her from her lover with the illusory promise to cure her of her cancer. The 'Elgin Marbles' suffered irreparable damage through the transport, and Louise certainly does not profit from Elgin's promise to 'rescue' her.

wants to deal with her illness, whether she wishes to continue her relationship with the narrator or go back to Elgin. The lover's macho desire
to lead the beloved, to control the end of a passionate relationship, proves
stronger than any trust in the power of their shared love.

This lapse into familiar patterns of dominance, however, serves as a
contrast to Winterson's otherwise optimistic explorations of the dynamics of a love that steers clear of the confines of hetero-patriarchal power
relations with the narrator's and Louise's relationship. Through the genderlessness of one of the lovers the nexus between gender and sexuality
is broken. This does not mean that the exercise of power in a relationship
does not play a role any more, but it is different in character and effect.
Both partners are equally unburdened of stereotypical gender roles and
matrices of relations of dominance versus submission in hetero- and homosexual relationships; they have an equal share in power over each other.
Love is presented as "this anarchic force sweeping up and down the world
to which no one is immune" (Winterson in Marvel 165/3), destroying hierarchical power relations between human beings.

The "anarchic force" of love is illustrated also in the narrator's subversive citation of the masculinist trope of the discovery of unknown lands
when referring to Louise's body:

> Louise, your nakedness was too complete for me, who had not learned the
> extent of your fingers. How could I cover this land? Did Columbus feel
> like this on sighting the Americas? I had no dreams to possess you but I
> wanted you to possess me. (*WoB* 52)

In a fashion that cites colonialist travel writing the protagonist compares
Louise's body to a newly discovered continent. But instead of staking
a claim in this 'colony' the lover relinquishes any rights of possession of
the beloved's female body. The exclusive authority of the woman over her
own body is thus acknowledged, and the lover's self-professed inability to
"cover this land" pays tribute to female strength and power.

There are indeed no hierarchies of power in the partnership of Louise
and the narrator. Both lovers possess and are possessed by one another;
the patriarchal idea of female submission or the notions of feminine weakness and lack of intelligence etc. in comparison to an imaginary male
standard become nonsensical. Various other passages underline the fact
that the narrator does not approach Louise as a conquistador, that there
is no monopoly of domination and submission here, as both are equally
possessive of and submissive toward one another: "Louise, in this single

bed, between these garish sheets, I will find a map likely as any treasure hunt. I will explore you and mine you and you will redraw me according to your will. We shall cross one another's boundaries and make ourselves one nation." (*WoB* 20).[20] Both lovers are shown to describe and read each other's bodies, to rouse and be roused by one another. They are equally subject and object of desire, thus overcoming hierarchical power relations, while they preserve their individual uniqueness (cf. Humphries), just like the narrator had once enviously noticed in an elderly couple: "Time hadn't diminished their love. They seemed to have become one another without losing their very individual selves" (*WoB* 82).

In *Written on the Body*, the rules of the risky game of love demand a canceling out of domination and possession in the relationship between two individuals, just as sexual passion as the bodily expression of love depends on mutuality, not mastery. Winterson therefore celebrates love as "an anarchic force" that is subversive of stereotypical gender-based, hetero-patriarchal modes of human interaction, a force that changes and shapes identities.

6.4.3   Narrative constructions of identity and the body

There is in *Written on the Body* a marked tension between what Miner disparagingly calls the "strangely disembodied, decontextualized charac-ter" of the narrator and excessively physical, socially fully contextualized Louise (21/3). I want to argue, however, that what Miner castigates as a lack of subtlety and a narrative flatness is part of a carefully structured, in many respects innovative exploration of the narrative production of the body and of identity.

We know indeed only few details about the protagonist, a professional translator of Russian with an emotional attachment to the old reading room of the British Library, who owns a flat in London but has no car and usually wears "a pair of shorts with RECYCLE tattooed across one leg" (*WoB* 12). The narrator volunteers no description of physical detail beyond recurrent mention of the shorts, but talks at length about a colorful collection of male and female ex-lovers in a fragmented, discontinuous

---

[20]My reading refutes Duncker's argument that Winterson has to reproduce hetero-sexual clichés, such as the cliché of male mapping and possession of the female body, "if she is to preserve the possibility of her narrator being a man" (84f.).

narration that provides a wealth of information about the protagonist's own emotional conditions. None of the narrator's lovers and acquaintances gives or demands a definition of gender and sexuality and none is given by the narrator. While the idiosyncrasies of the former lovers are described in detail, the protagonist's own sexuality and sexual preferences remain obscure. In Winterson's universe, the adoption of a certain gender identity and sexuality is not mandatory; in fact, "sexuality had been dislodged from both gender and identity in Winterson's fictional world" (Stevens), in which neither heterosexuality nor indeed the declaration of any sexual identity are normative. The narrator's "subversive performances" of gender – of the shyness of a convent virgin or Mercucio's swagger, for example – "disrupt any coherence between body, gender and identity" (Gade 38).

From early on in the novel the narrator assumes that the readers know they are dealing with an unreliable narrator: "I can tell by now that you are wondering whether I can be trusted as a narrator" (*WoB* 24). Such skepticism on the readers' part seems appropriate, given the fact that two former lovers' claims that the narrator makes up "truths" about famous writers and artists, namely Renoir and Henry Miller, remain undisputed (cf. *WoB* 22, 60). The narrator's self-confessed unreliability explicitly highlights the inherent fictionality of the narrative. In Winterson's fictional world, gender too is a fiction, something the protagonist makes up like stories about people and events without a guarantee of truth, or indeed something that is left out altogether.

With a protagonist who randomly wears allegedly masculine and feminine gender labels, but ultimately defies integration into the binary systems of gender and sexuality, Winterson experiments with the notion of intelligibility of bodies itself. She imagines a world in which the subject status of a human being is not contingent upon the adoption of a certain gender or sex, and in which genderless bodies matter. Haslett suggests that "[t]he lover's body is invisible to any objectifying gaze" (43). And indeed, this "non-specific body" (43) may have significant consequences for the readers' very conceptions of the body. Depending on the interpretation of the text, the lover may be read as "female, male, hermaphroditic, transgendered, differently abled, from any culture in the world, with any sexual preferences, or any combination of the above," as Haslett points out (43). The first-person narrative of the protagonist, then, highlights the textuality of the narrator's body.

Louise contributes her own narrative layer to the palimpsest that is the protagonist's body. She describes her lover as "the most beautiful creature male or female I had ever seen" (*WoB* 84). It is a compliment that is immediately and wholeheartedly rejected by the narrator: "I don't lack self-confidence but I'm not beautiful, that is a word reserved for very few people, people such as Louise herself" (*WoB* 85). If a bodily identity is discursively constructed, this suggests, if it can be deconstructed and created anew, the fiction of one's identity can also be deciphered and re-written. Louise asks her lover to "come to me without a past. Those lines you've learned, forget them. Forget that you've been here before in other bedrooms in other places. Come to me new" (*WoB* 54). For a genderless narrator who is not weighed down by clichés and conventions knotted to gender and sexuality, re-birth or self-invention seem possible. The risks involved in such a radical new beginning are considerable, but they are risks the narrator is willing to take because of the prospect of re-invention of the self in a loving relationship with Louise: "I know what it will mean to redeem myself from the accumulations of a lifetime. I know and I don't care. You set before me a space uncluttered by association" (*WoB* 81).

Winterson draws the picture of a body formed by a past, i.e., by the fictional narratives that accumulate into a personal history and create identities. However, she also envisages the possibility of freeing oneself or being freed of inherited, restraining narratives of gender and sexuality and creating one's own versions of identities. The narrator experiences such a rebirth under Louise's loving hands:

> Written on the body is a secret code only visible in certain lights; the accumulations of a lifetime gather there. In places the palimpsest is so heavily worked that the letters feel like braille. I like to keep my body rolled up away from prying eyes. Never unfold too much, tell the whole story. I did not know that Louise had reading hands. She translated me into her own book. (*WoB* 89)

By "translating" the narrator into her own book, Louise writes her lover's identity anew. This act of creation does not involve the conclusive gendering of her partner,[21] nor does it lead to the definition of their sexuality. It does, however, mark the beginning of the narrator's own emancipation

---

[21] Jago Morrison suggests that the narrator is someone "on whom sex has yet to be written," presumably by Louise (113). Here I disagree. There is no suggestion in the text that the narrator is lacking a gender and therefore in need of gendering.

from damaging effects of potentially exploitative affairs in the past and a self-invention as a lover in a committed relationship with Louise.

In sharp contrast to the genderless narrator, Louise is presented as beautiful, as excessively female, a woman whom Elgin regards as his trophy. But her body too undergoes a narrative rebirth. When cancer infringes upon Louise's physical integrity, the narrator re-creates the body of the absent beloved through language.

> If I couldn't put Louise out of my mind I would drown myself in her. Within the clinical language, through the dispassionate view of the sucking, sweating, greedy, defecating self, I found a love-poem to Louise. I would go on knowing her, more intimately than the skin, hair and voice that I craved. (*WoB* 111)

Citing from anatomy books, the protagonist describes "THE CELLS, TISSUES SYSTEMS AND CAVITIES OF THE BODY," "THE SKIN," "THE SKELETON," and "THE SPECIAL SENSES" of Louise's body at war with itself (*WoB* 114-39). Inspired by grief and longing, the lover utilizes the cool, impersonal terminology of medicine and science to re-imagine the beloved in a language that is unfettered by gender conventions.[22]

"As your lover describes you, so you are," says the ninth princess in *Sexing the Cherry*, who killed her hunter-husband like a falcon after he insisted that she was falcon-like (*Sexing* 56). Through the narrator's description Louise's cancerous body is restored and turned over to the narrator, although the beloved may be as far away as Switzerland.[23] "The body is the direct locus of domination and it only becomes intelligible through discourse," writes Gade (28). The narrator's narrative evokes Louise's body, even as it is locked in battle with the cancer within her, so that Louise lives

---

[22]See Rubinson's analysis of Winterson's challenge to "the totalizing and authoritative characteristics of scientific discourse" ("Body Languages" 219).

[23]Lucie Armitt takes issue with the narrator's re-writing of Louise's body as ungendered from a feminist perspective. Armitt suggests that through this act of ungendering the only female voice in the novel is written away, a voice that has never been a very strong or individual woman's voice, since Louise speaks through the narrator only (cf. 20). While Armitt grants that Louise body is narrated with a language that is ungendered in Wittig's tradition, she warns that "writing on the body can actually make women disappear" (21).

inside her lover's imagination regardless of whether or not she has died of her illness:[24]

> From the kitchen door Louise's face. Paler, thinner, but her hair still mane-wide and the colour of blood. I put out my hand and felt her fingers, she took my fingers and put them to her mouth. The scar under the lip burned me. Am I stark mad? She's warm. (*WoB* 190)

Both the narrator's and Louise's bodies are re-written by their lovers, and they are re-written outside the conventions of gender. Winterson thus offers a radical subversion of presentations of sex and gender. She treats these categories as non-normative arrays of possibilities of identifications and presents genderlessness as a viable subject position. As bodies are re-imagined as palimpsests covered with texts in *Written on the Body*, identity is presented as fluid and subject to continual discursive re-invention.

6.4.4 Narrative, romance, and reading

Toward the end of the novel a well-meaning friend tries to comfort the narrator by calling the relationship with Louise "the perfect romance" (*WoB* 187). And *Written on the Body* is indeed a romance, albeit a subversive one. With the love story between Louise and the narrator Winterson presents a re-writing of heterosexual romance. She uses the genre designed to transport heterosexist notions of love as a power play in order to expose them as harmful clichés. The narrator therefore quotes from the "rule book" of "wise old hands": "Settle down, feet under the table. She's a nice girl, he's a nice boy," only to warn that "[i]t's the clichés that cause the trouble" (*WoB* 71).

In her seminal work on feminism and the Western narrative, *Alice Doesn't*, Teresa de Lauretis points out that Western narrative primarily seeks to establish the difference of sex (cf. 119). With a love story, or romance, that has a genderless protagonist Winterson thus not only challenges the binary gender system but also the foundations of Western narrative and "the way people read at all" (Winterson in Kay 28/2). From the very first page, *Written* presents itself to its readers as a love story, possibly a tragic one:

---

[24]Cokal even suggests that Louise might have been a figment of the narrator's imagination all along.

> Why is the measure of love loss? [...] You said, 'I love you.' [...] 'I love
> you' is always a quotation. You did not say it first and neither did I, yet
> when you say it and when I say it we speak like savages who have found
> three words and worship them. I did worship them but now I am alone on
> a rock hewn out of my own body. (*WoB* 9)

Readers who have grown up and live in a society that is organized along
gender differences expect the protagonists of a romance to be clearly, even
stereotypically gendered and consequently will try to discern the narrator's sex. Winterson plays with the expectations of her readers and she
frustrates our attempts to apply misleading gender assumptions to the narrator so that this love story may fit into established habits of reading and
comprehension. Our reading practices reflect our world views, and the
author confronts us with the fact that we picture reality as structured by
binary oppositions such as the binaries of male and female, and frame our
narratives accordingly. In *Written* Winterson claims that gender should
and can be inconsequential to narration.[25] She encourages her readers to
imagine with her a world in which the status of a subject is not dependent
upon the assumption of an intelligible and socially sanctioned variant of
gender and sexuality and where the genderless body matters.

Winterson tasks her work with changing people's views on the world
and thus with changing the world, because literature renders alternatives
to oppressive discourses that surround us imaginable: "We are constantly
threatened in life, it's true. But once you are alone with a book, [...], all
these defenses drop and you can enter into a quite different space where
you will learn to feel differently about yourself" (Bilger 87). *Written on
the Body* undermines one of the most regulatory and restrictive social
concepts, the gender binary, offering empowering and liberating food for
thought.

---

[25]Cf. Rubinson, "Body Languages."

Conclusion: Difference Undone?

> I call upon us to reject what seemed to be positive social iden-
> tities. I'm suggesting that we should work to undermine those
> forces that make being a man, a woman, or a member of a
> racialized group possible; we should refuse to be gendered
> man or woman, refuse to be raced.
>
> Sally Haslanger

Toni Morrison's texts reflect a two-fold concern of hers: From a theoretical starting point that thinks race as a phantasm, an arbitrarily constructed
category invented to create, justify, and preserve the ideology of White
supremacy they unveil motives for and mechanisms of racialization, rendering palpable the deleterious consequences of a notion of race that is
grounded in folk beliefs of biologically founded essentialisms for the interaction of human beings. Yet the constructedness of race does not mean
that race is not a reality. For many African Americans and other people
of color, who – because of their racial background – are disadvantaged
in a hierarchically structured society that privileges whiteness in terms of
access to full employment, health care, higher education, and political and
economic participation in general, it is a source of pride and an empowering means of identification. Thus Morrison's writing also examines the
emancipatory potential of racial identity for African Americans. In all of
this, her texts pose and explore the question of how to live with and what
to do with race in the United States.

The trope of racial authenticity has played a major role in Toni Morrison's writing in the larger context of the importance of racial identity
for African Americans; indeed, in her early novels, *The Bluest Eye*, *Sula*,
Song of Solomon, and *Tar Baby*, the protagonists' search for identity revealed the discovery of an "authentic blackness." Thus, *The Bluest Eye*
explores the terrible psychological consequences for Pecola of attempting
to suppress her blackness in order to achieve what can only ever be an
inauthentic whiteness. *Sula* takes up the discussion opened by its prede-

cessor of a certain inexplicable funkiness that signals blackness. Milkman in *Song of Solomon* travels to the South in search of what he believes to be his grandfather's gold and finds his roots in the community of Shalimar, where the men are still real hunters, the women know intuitively how best to interact with their men, and the children are singing songs that refer to Africans and the home continent of their forebears. *Tar Baby* contrasts Jadine Childs's unsettling feeling of having an insufficiently authentic racial identity – which here stands for Jadine's entire sense of personhood – with the self-assured "true" blackness of the woman in the yellow dress in a French supermarket and with the tight-knit, race-based community of Son's presumably authentic home town in Florida.

In *Playing in the Dark*, Morrison exposes whiteness as a cultural construct devoid of biological essence that depends directly on the definition and pejorative characterization of Black otherness. Construction excludes authenticity and the idea of a definitive essence it rests upon, which makes whiteness per se inauthentic. The author's first four novels, however, illustrate her hope – as if against better theoretical judgment – for both authenticity and essence in Black identity, a distinctive Black difference. Thus, in Morrison's thinking of that period, "whiteness may be a construction, but blackness is at least possibly an essence" (Duvall 16), an essence that is positively connoted. John Duvall calls the motivation to fill essential blackness with positive meaning "epistemological affirmative action" aimed at subverting the positive meaning attributed to whiteness as it constructs itself as the opposite of "evil" blackness (16).

Although written within this early phase of Morrison's career, the short story "Recitatif" breaks with this celebratory exploration of authentic blackness. Instead, it may be read as an analytical text about the concept of race: Firstly, it discusses racialization in general as an interactive process of construction through attributing racial meaning to individuals. Confronted with the statement of racial difference between the two protagonists, readers are tempted to assign racial identities to Twyla and Roberta by construing arguments for one or the other option out of cultural attributes the text offers which are not directly related to race. As race is one of the most powerful markers of difference in Western culture, there is a strong impulse to racialize characters whose racial identity is not clearly identified. Morrison's text thus points our attention to how we "do race" and illustrates our individual complicity in the act of racialization.

However, a reading of the short story that resists the temptation to fix racial identity on inconclusively raced characters and accepts the impossibility to decide on the protagonists' racial identities highlights a second layer of critique in the text, a critique which is no less important for being less openly presented: "Recitatif" identifies race as an oppressive discourse of difference that silences other discourses which may be equally important, if not more so in specific contexts. Twyla's and Roberta's conflict does not arise out of their different racial backgrounds – even though for the largest part of the narrative Twyla, the narrator, seems convinced that it does. What fuels their friendship as well as their conflicts is a childhood trauma the protagonists have in common: the abandonment they both experienced at the hand of their mothers. Their shared history of neglect, the hardship of growing up motherless and indeed parentless in a world hostile to young girls, be they "real" orphans or not, Black or White, outweighs their experience of racial difference. As Morrison demonstrates the power of the race discourse to dominate our thinking, she also unmatters race by exposing its inherent arbitrariness and underlining the relevance of other facets of the self and of experiences of sameness for social relationships.

While in *The Bluest Eye*, *Song of Solomon*, and *Sula* the characters' essentialist – and thereby implicitly racialist – search for authenticity seems unquestioned by the author, *Tar Baby* is the first of Morrison's novels that reflects her engagement with constructivist ideas by calling into question and describing as highly problematic the restrictive narrowness of the all-Black community in Eden, Florida.[26] In this respect, Eden is a forerunner to Ruby: a place that excludes outsiders and restricts the personal development of its own inhabitants on grounds of racial purity. Yet significantly, while in the earlier novel Black authenticity seems potentially possible for anybody with African American ancestors, however remote that ancestry may be, in *Paradise* the idea of racial authenticity is questioned as radically as the meaning of the Black ancestor (cf. Christian, "The Past": 422). Moreover, the notion of Black racial purity becomes as problematic as the phantasm of pure whiteness.

The all-Black town of Ruby is Morrison's exemplary racialized community which allows her to explore aspects of the performative construc-

---

[26]This fictitious all-Black town cites Zora Neale Hurston's town of Eatonville in *Their Eyes Were Watching God* of 1937.

tion of blackness. Two insights stand out most clearly here: Firstly, race is a matter of belief; it is constructed "religiously" by the town elders and their fellow citizens to the effect that a catechism – in the sense of a body of religious beliefs and practices – of racial purity is created to regulate a community founded on the "religion" of pure blackness.

The second insight grows out of this quasi-religious doctrine of racial purity upheld by force of regulatory laws or commandments: This doctrine needs and therefore creates an impure counterpart against which the community of the pure 8-rocks materializes, a counterpart that threatens racial pollution from the inside of the community as well as from the outside. The New Fathers of Ruby spell out the "pollution rules" Ian Hacking identifies as inevitable characteristics of "every stable group:" These rules "define who one is not, and hence provide a sense of self-identity and self-worth: *we who are not polluted*" ("Why Race" 114/2) – the creators of and dwellers in an earthly paradise of racial purity and moral integrity.

Morrison shows that gender and gender rules are integral elements of the "concept of the defiling other" Hacking describes, which informs the notion of racial purity (114/2). For the leading members of the community of Ruby, women are the primary agents of pollution. Therefore, not only must women who live within the town be strictly guarded and firmly guided throughout their lives, but women from Out There must be treated with suspicion and best kept outside the walls of the settlement. Moreover, the sexuality of Ruby's men and women has to be closely regulated so as to prevent emotional entanglements and sexual encounters that would pollute the community and thus threaten its identity and sense of self-worth. *Paradise* demonstrates lucidly how the laws of heterosexism are employed for the purpose of producing an "ideal race."

Most obviously, however, the elders of Ruby see in the women who live in the neighboring Convent incarnations of the "defiling other" that threatens the racial purity of the town from the outside. The list of incriminating evidence Ruby compiles to prove the alleged evilness of this community is long: The group of women is identified as racially mixed and therefore impure, since according to the logic of racial purity equaling moral integrity they are already morally corrupt in the eyes of the New Fathers.

As a homo-social, all-female community the Convent violates the hetero-patriarchal rules regulating both race and gender in Ruby. Not only does this group of women neither want nor need male leadership, not only are some of them seen as sexually aggressive and self-determined. The relationships among the women are also interpreted as – at least potentially – lesbian in kind. While there is some truth to this judgment with respect to Seneca and Gigi, it is wrongly transferred onto all of the women and provides the final reason the Rubyites need to decide to assault the Convent. "Especially at those junctures in which a compulsory heterosexuality works in the service of maintaining hegemonic forms of racial purity, the 'threat' of homosexuality takes on a distinctive complexity," Butler argues (*Bodies That Matter* 18). Toni Morrison underpins this theoretical insight with her narrative exploration of the complex interaction between an all-Black town fighting for the survival of what it holds to be its racially pure paradise and an all-female community the town considers racially mixed; thus she adds a significant element to her complex analysis of race and of mechanisms and effects of racialization.

But does the Convent community represent Morrison's vision of a raceless society, as I proposed cautiously at the outset of this study? Clearly, as the women live in a racialized world, they are also racially categorized by others – sometimes quite blatantly, sometimes less obviously so. The citizens of Ruby, who identify a "white girl" among the women, cannot but view the Convent as a racially polluted place; before them Sister Mary Magna and her fellow nuns classify the child Consolata as "certainly not white." In a society that is racially structured people will be categorized in terms of their presumed racial background. Yet, within the walls of the Convent the women do not join in this practice. It seems that the old mansion provides a space for its inhabitants to develop identities that do not rely on the assignment of a racial category. However, this does not happen coincidentally. Rather, the Convent community shows characteristics that make the absence of race as a marker of difference thinkable and practicable. As a transcultural contact zone it enables the interaction and cross-fertilization of Anglo-American, Arapaho, African Brazilian, and African American cultural traditions and spiritualities. While these different traditions together lend the community new and idiosyncratic features, they remain noticeable as distinct and revered influences that do not dissolve in a multicultural melting pot.

The Convent community does not congeal into a fixed group identity but remains in flux, in a perpetual process of evolving that continues even beyond the end of the narrative. Under the guidance of the spiritually awakened and religiously eclectic Consolata, five traumatized women of different ages, socio-economic and intellectual backgrounds move from an uneasy coexistence in the absence of better options to relationships of confessional openness, mutual understanding, forgiving, and shared em-powerment. While each of the women bares her soul and narrates her life to the others, racial attributes are divested of their capacity to assign meaning to a person's story. As no one refers to herself or any of the other women in terms of race, as no one therefore performs acts that would racialize herself or others and the "racial gaze" is "eclipsed [altogether]" ("Home" 9), this category loses its regulatory power. The Convent be-comes a safe haven of racial equality, appreciation of distinct cultural tra-ditions, and recognition of individual uniqueness, yet unlike Ruby it is not a safe haven that is hermetically sealed off from outside influences. This uncompromising openness of the Convent eventually hastens the violent destruction of the community, but significantly, the women continue to live in this precarious earthly paradise outside the walls of the mansion, in the midst of wider US society.

Then, does this community of women represent Morrison's vision of a "racial home"? As I have argued, the Convent is indeed "a-world-in-which-race-does-*not*-matter" to the people who inhabit it, although it *does* matter extremely to those who surround the community and interact with it. Among themselves the women have succeeded in "depriving [race] of its lethal cling" ("Home" 5), and even though race proves lethal for them, they stimulate a fundamental change in the mental framework of one of the most powerful men in Ruby, a change that can be read as an indicator that the "racial house" of Ruby may in time be "[transformed] completely" so as to become "a race-specific yet non-racist home" for its citizens. In its heterogeneity, inclusiveness, and lack of essentialist thinking the Con-vent presents a fictional illustration of Morrison's idea of a "third [. . .] world" of race ("Home" 12). This idea is reminiscent of Homi Bhabha's notion of the Third Space which, through its politics of inclusion rather than exclusion, "initiates new signs of identity, and innovative sites of collaboration and contestation" (1). The Third Space is a mode of iden-tification inherent to hybridity which "enables other positions to emerge [. . .], displaces the histories that constitute it, and sets up new structures of authority, new political initiatives [. . .]" (Rutherford 211). Thus, Mor-rison's fictional "third world" of race is the non-hierarchical, inessentialist "racial home" she envisages in her essay.

However, is race minus the capacity to forcibly regulate social interaction, to evaluate people and create hierarchies of power still identical with race as the folk concept defines it? No, it is not. Rather, Morrison envisages a notion of race that is comparable to Joshua Glasgow's "race*," a concept that he develops a decade after the publication of *Paradise* in a philosophical effort which

> acknowledges that race is an apparition, attempts to adequately face the facts on the ground, retains some of the conceptual resources necessary for understanding, repairing, and ending our seemingly overwhelming legacy of racial injustice, recognize the centrality of race to people's identities, and envisions a world with something very much like race but with neither racial injustice nor biological racial discourse. (155)

Significantly, Glasgow expresses the fear of being too optimistic with his own project to develop a concept of race* that is "race-specific yet non-racist," to stay with Morrison's words; he is afraid that "this might be asking for too much, for a utopia of sorts," and worries about it being "foolish or naïve to seek to accommodate hope, truth, and justice in one package" (155). As we have seen earlier, Morrison entertained similar doubts and was eager to distinguish her own writing about "a place where race both matters and is rendered impotent" from traditions that, in her view, relegate a world without racial discrimination to utopian thinking ("Home" 9). With *Paradise*, however, she offers a confident literary vision of "race without dominance – without hierarchy" ("Home" 11): race*.

From the beginning, Jeanette Winterson's fictions have been preoccupied with the exploration of the interrelatedness of gender, identity, and the body or, more generally, reality. Her novels denounce the subjugation of women, lay open the means by which male domination has been achieved historically and is still safeguarded today; they undermine masculinist worldviews by parodying clichés of maleness and femaleness, thus taking a decidedly feminist stance. Over time, however, they express an increasingly critical view of the very notion of gender.

Winterson focuses on several sites of subversion of traditional gender norms and boundaries, opening up possibilities of gender through a variety of means. Sexuality is one such site of subversion: Jeanette in *Oranges Are Not the Only Fruit*, Villanelle in *The Passion* and some of the dancing princesses in *Sexing the Cherry* desire and live with women,

and although they experience marginalization and ostracism from hegemonic society, they defy the gender norms of compulsory heterosexuality
and insist on the extension of the category of intelligible, livable bodies to
include lesbian bodies. Far from being an unfortunate sexual confusion or
fateful malfunctioning that leads to the social death of women who love
women, lesbianism in these first three fictions is celebrated as another
valid, empowering sexuality. While lesbianism is not portrayed as better
or less complicated than heterosexuality, it serves at times to highlight the
impossibility of reaching the ideals of (heterosexual) love and at times
becomes a mode of resisting and surviving male violence.

     Narration itself is another site of subversion in Winterson's texts. Not
only does the author re-write traditional texts like fairy tales and narratives of romance by telling a tale from perspectives of formerly marginalized characters or including their views, or by transforming tropes such
as journeying and true love in ways that render female characters active,
self-assertive, and powerful. Her protagonists also narrate their own lives,
drawing from their own memories and the memories of others as well as
from historical or literary texts, and thereby take control of their own identities. Narrating one's identity here is presented as an act of empowerment
and emancipation. Significantly, it also underlines the constructedness of
identity and therefore its inherent lack of essence.

     While in *Oranges* the traditional binaries of gender and sexuality re-
main largely intact, *The Passion* and *Sexing the Cherry* call into question
the opposition of maleness and femaleness and challenge the boundaries
and social consequences of these categories. In the cases of Villanelle
and the Dog-Woman the site of a radical questioning of essential gender
norms and boundaries is the human body. Villanelle's webbed feet are
insignia of maleness on her female body; like men, she is able to steer
the black boats through the narrow Venetian canals and to walk on water.
Her hermaphroditic body points to the unreliability of physical "evidence"
of maleness or femaleness and argues against the use of biological criteria
for the construction of gender categories. Yet, non-biological, discursively
negotiated criteria like garments, styles of dressing, and body language are
revealed to be just as arbitrary: Villanelle cross-dresses for professional
reasons at the casino as well as for her own pleasure in private and is able
to pass as male.

     With her gigantic, immensely strong and unkempt body the Dog-
Woman, on the other hand, parodies norms of womanhood in Puritan

England. Her strategic enactments of rites of femaleness and femininity serve the purpose of gaining her access to male-only public venues, while her faithful citations of laws of heterosexuality ridicule these laws and damage those they are designed to privilege – men who seek pleasure and power. The Dog-Woman's performative agency and especially Villanelle's androgyny thus enable the "new possibilities of gender" Judith Butler calls for (*Gender Trouble* 185). While as abject, unintelligible bodies they constitute the necessary 'outside' of gender as we know it, they haunt the domain of intelligible bodies "as the spectre of its own impossibility, the very limit to intelligibility" (Butler, *Bodies That Matter*: xi), challenging existing essentialist notions of gender:

> When such categories [of man and woman] come into question, the reality of gender is also put into crisis: it becomes unclear how to distinguish the real from the unreal. And this is the occasion in which we come to understand that what we take to be 'real,' what we invoke as the naturalized knowledge of gender is, in fact, a changeable and revisable reality. (Butler, "Preface": xxiii)

Both Villanelle and the Dog-Woman claim for themselves the status of legitimate subjects in spite of their apparent failure to materialize as bodies that matter in the hegemonic heteronormative sense. Thus, Winterson's heroines "insist upon the extension of ... legitimacy to bodies that have been regarded as false, unreal, and unintelligible," meeting the only normative goal that Butler allows for her own endeavors with *Gender Trouble* ("Preface" xxiii). They defy regulatory measures to contain bodies within the narrowly defined boundaries of male and female.

With her male protagonists in *The Passion* and *Sexing the Cherry* Winterson also explores alternative modes of identification and new possibilities for gender. Henri presents a powerful example of determining his own identity by narrating memories of his relationships with various objects of love: his mother, Napoleon, and most importantly, Villanelle. Crucially, his relationship with the abject Villanelle does not compel Henri to strive for a gender identity that confirms the laws of heteronormativity. For his sense of self he rather looks to his mother and Villanelle for orientation, taking Napoleon and the cook as negative, repulsive examples of normative maleness.

In a similar vein, Jordan subverts gender norms by claiming his mother as his standard for maleness. But with this protagonist Winterson complicates and expands the notions of gender and identity further than in *Or-*

anges and *Sexing*. As Jordan goes on imaginary journeys through alternative realities, he not only encounters worlds that defy the laws of gravity and render absurd received notions of time and space. He also lives as a woman, looks for and appreciates female aspects of his own being, and begins to hope for gender options outside of the essentialist binarism of maleness and femaleness. The horticultural technique of grafting becomes the mental vehicle for this move away from the gender binary; yet it is a move that is not realized outside of botany, only envisioned. "The third is not given," Jordan tells his mother in Fortunata's words (*Sexing* 131), pondering that there might be an option other than "male" and "female" that is not – or not yet – quite imaginable or visible. Instead, as he thinks about grafting genders, Jordan wishes for himself to have "some of Tradescant grafted on to me so that I could be a hero like him" (*Sexing* 79). The King's chief explorer is the model man of his time in England, and Jordan, feeling less than fully male, does not build upon a "third" possibility of gender, but instead dreams of becoming hegemonically male like Tradescant. In a later era Jordan's alter ego, Navy officer Nicolas Jordan on the *HMS Gauntlet*, still strives for a hero's life and, dissatisfied with the male models of neo-capitalism, looks to the environmentalist, Dog-Woman reincarnate, for purpose and guidance. Once again "the third" shines through as a possibility, but it is not given.

The fluid identity Jordan's name connotes thus is only invoked and not yet realized in *Sexing*. However, in *Written on the Body* Winterson explores gender fluidity and presents an alternative concept of identity in the course of the novel. Like Jeanette, Villanelle, Henri, and other earlier Wintersonian characters the narrator creates a narrative identity. But in *Written* identity evolves specifically through narratives of memories of the first-person narrator's numerous love affairs and relationships which are marked as reciprocal.

Thus, on the one hand the lovers' gender identities and sexualities are influenced positively by the narrator's genderlessness. Both male and female partners are able to develop variants of gender that differ from prescribed norms of masculinity and femininity; they also define their individual sexualities according to personal quirks and preferences and independent of normative labels such as "perverse," "homosexual," or "heterosexual." On the other hand, the narrator's identities are shaped in and through intimate relationships. As Winterson does not assign a gender to the narrator and gives readers only the most rudimentary details about the narrator's biography, profession, physical appearance, likes and dislikes, we meet a protagonist who, prior to Louise's appearance, is primarily defined as an eclectic lover. Each of the partners adds details, and gender is constructed as fluid, not to be pinned down as male or female, or even at times male and at times female. The exclusive positions of male and female, gay and straight do not correspond with the information we derive from the narrator's interactions with others; clearly, this protagonist is not intelligible within the heteronormative concept of gender as a construction based on binary notions of sex and sexuality. Crucially, in *Written on the Body* the narrator's unintelligibility and abjection within the framework of the hegemonic system does not lead to marginality and powerlessness in society. Rather, it highlights the restrictiveness of the heteronormative notion of gender by allowing those who interact with the genderless narrator to construct for themselves empowering alternative identities.

With her narrator Winterson thus explores identity as interactive and relational, in contrast to conservative notions of identity as a composite of inherent bio-psychological essences. Identity in the sense of self-sameness or "self-constancy" is the result of the narrator's memories of relationships with others and the narrative that gives shape to them. Haines-Wright and Kyle describe the Ricoeurian notion of "self-constancy" as the capacity for fidelity and "a function of memory marked by communication" (177). Out of the narrator's multiple love affairs, the relationship with Louise is most powerfully marked by fidelity. It therefore defines the narrator's identity most strongly: The protagonist's sense of self-sameness is engendered through fidelity to the beloved and through memories of a relationship marked by fidelity which are communicated in a narrative. Moreover, as the narrator fully commits to Louise at the end of the novel, the beloved responds to this commitment by appearing in the cottage which at that moment encompasses the entire world. In *Written on the Body*, mutual fidelity in love is the unifying force that produces intelligible subjecthood regardless of the laws and standards of heteronormativity.

Furthermore, Winterson highlights the link between identity and the body by figuring the narrator's memories through bodies: Louise's body, which the narrator describes in various states of health and sickness, honing language that is celebratory and unhegemonic, and the protagonist's own body, whose skin is a "palimpsest" covered with "accumulations of a lifetime," translated and rendered intelligible under Louise's "reading hands" (*WoB* 89). Thus, while the narrator remembers Louise's body and shapes her identity through narrative, Louise reads her lover's body and "translate[s] [the narrator] into her own book" (*WoB* 89). The task of creating a narrative of Louise's memories and thus of the identity of the narrator, however, is left to the readers, who create meaning in the process of reading the novel.

Difference Undone?

In this study I hope to have shown that Toni Morrison has no interest in the obliteration of racial difference, while Jeanette Winterson problematizes gender differences without eliminating them outright. Both authors attempt to recover the notion of difference from essentialist ideologies that are structured along binary oppositions and rely on the idea of fixed identities. Apart from theorizing racial and gender difference as social constructions of an irreducibly political quality that are manufactured in performative reiterations and citations, Morrison and Winterson investigate mechanisms of the construction of racial and gender differences respectively, as well as their effects on hierarchies of power in human society. Moreover, within the contexts they are most interested in they share the goal of rearticulating difference, to "iterate difference that is prized but unprivileged," as Morrison phrases with regard to the concept of race ("Home" 12).

Paradise, in my view, represents Morrison's most radical questioning of the notion of race to date. While with her creation of all-Black Ruby she exposes race as a socio-historical, quasi-religious construction with potentially deadly consequences for those relegated to a lower stratum of a given racial hierarchy, in her literary vision of the Convent as a racially egalitarian community she succeeds in her effort to "develop nonmessianic language to refigure the raced community, to decipher the deracing of the world" ("Home" 11). As the "social divisive forms and consequences of 'race thinking'" Lucius Outlaw identifies are rendered impotent in the community of women (82), race remains socially and individually valuable without creating hierarchies of power. The Convent, therefore, although ravaged by the racialist extremism of the New Fathers of Ruby, is itself free of racism – without, however, being raceless.

In the context of gender, Winterson rearticulates difference "as that which disrupts the coherence of any postulation of identity," to use Judith Butler's words ("The End" 202f.). Jordan's insight at the end of *Sexing the Cherry* that "even the most solid of things and the most real, the best-loved and the well-known, are only hand-shadows on the wall" (144), in *Written on the Body* is revealed to be relevant even for the "well-known truths" of sexual difference and different sexualities. Winterson's genderless narrator demonstrates not only our own participation in repetitive acts of gendering – our performances of hand-shadows of femininity and masculinity – but also presents to us alternative possibilities of gender and sexuality which subvert the hegemonic, essentialist binarisms that structure our realities. Winterson furthermore invites us to re-articulate identity as relational and reciprocal instead of fixed and essential, based on a sense of self-constancy that grows out of fidelity toward loved ones and is expressed in narratives that communicate memories of relationships. The nexus of memory and identity, together with the construction of the human continue to engage the author. *The Stone Gods* of 2008 discusses the consequences of the loss of memory to an individual's sense of self-hood and calls into question fixed boundaries of humanness. As she explores the question of whether an intelligible biological body as we know it is a necessary precondition for being human, and indeed for love, Winterson takes on Butler's call to "think through the debates on the body, since it may or may not be true that cultural construction effaces both sexual difference and bodily process" ("End of Sexual Difference" 202). With Spike, the Robo *sapiens* who learns to love, we are encouraged to ask: "[I]s human life biology or consciousness? If I were to lop off your arms, your legs, your ears, your nose, put out your eyes, roll up your tongue, would you still be you? You locate yourself in consciousness, and I, too, am a conscious being" (*Stone Gods* 76). Because, finally, "[n]othing is solid, [. . .]. Nothing is fixed" (111).

In the texts discussed here, Toni Morrison and Jeanette Winterson offer lucid analyses of prevailing effects of race and gender upon our conceptions of bodies, identity, and social life. As they visualize the discriminatory potential inherent in both of these categories, denouncing injustices done to individuals and groups of people through regulatory processes of racialization or gendering, they also point out the subversive potential of the performative construction of race and gender.

Yet Morrison's and Winterson's texts also reveal the significantly different agendas of their authors: For Morrison, a blurring of race boundaries or stretching of limits of, say, blackness or whiteness in order to question a supposed race binarism is meaningless, and – conscious of the stark realities of race in contemporary US society – she certainly does not promote the elimination of race as a marker of difference. Instead, based on insights of Critical Race Studies about the artificiality of this concept, she proposes a notion of race that appreciates racial differences as variable, non-essential, and potentially empowering constructions without endowing them with the authority to create hierarchies of power. Morrison, therefore, endorses Haslanger's urgent call to "refuse to be raced" to the extent that she challenges the folk concept of race and denounces racialization on the basis of essentialisms; she does not propose the elimination of race thinking altogether.

Winterson, on the other hand, anticipates Butlerian theories of citations and reiterations of gender rules and translates them into activism that challenges heteropatriarchal worldviews and constructions of society by calling into question and, indeed, dissolving binaries of gender and sexuality. Without disappearing as categories of identity, maleness and femaleness are presented as fluid and relational, subject to multiple acts of construction and re-construction.

In contrast to Morrison, who retains race and re-imagines it as an eclectic, non-discriminatory concept, Winterson proposes a notion of relational, reciprocal identity grounded in fidelity that entails a fundamental redefinition of gender, away from binaries and fixed sexes, toward new possibilities of intelligibility. In their novels, neither of the authors eliminate racial nor gender difference completely. Rather, they rearticulate the notions of race and gender to represent differences without hierarchies of power. While they do not regard a world without differences of race or gender as feasible or even desirable, in their writing they envision realities that encourage non-discriminatory, empowering possibilities of race* and gender*.

Works Cited

Primary Literature

Morrison, Toni. *A Mercy*. New York: Alfred A. Knopf, 2008.
——. *Beloved*. 1987. London: Picador, 1988.
——. "Home." *The House that Race Built: Original Essays by Toni Morrison, Angela Y. Davis, Cornel West, and Others on Black Americans and Politics in America*. Ed. Wahneema Lubiano. New York: Vintage Books, 1998. 3–12.
——. "Introduction: Friday on the Potomac." *Race-ing Power, En-gendering Justice: Essays on Anita Hill, Clarence Thomas, and the Construction of Social Reality*. Ed. Toni Morrison. New York: Pantheon Books, 1992. vii–xxx.
——. *Jazz*. New York: Signet, 1992.
——. *Love*. New York: Alfred A. Knopf, 2003.
——. "Nobel Lecture, 7 December 1993." *The Georgia Review* 49.1 (1995): 318–30.
——. *Paradies*. Trans. Thomas Piltz. Reinbek bei Hamburg: Rowohlt, 1999.
——. *Paradise*. 1997. London: Chatto & Windus, 1998.
——. *Playing in the Dark: Whiteness and the Literary Imagination*. 1992. London and Basingstoke: Picador, 1993.
——. "Recitatif." *Confirmation: An Anthology of African American Women*. Ed. Amiri and Amina Baraka. New York: William Morrow, 1983. 243–61.
——. *Song of Solomon*. 1977. London and Basingstoke: Picador, 1989.
——. *Sula*. 1973. New York et al.: Signet International, 1993.
——. *Tar Baby*. 1981. New York et al.: Signet International, 1983.
——, ed. *The Black Book*. New York: Random House, 1974.
——. *The Bluest Eye*. 1969. London and Basingstoke: Picador, 1986.
——. "Trouble With Paradise." *Berliner Lektionen*. Berlin: Bertelsmann and Berliner Festspiele, 17 Oct. 1999.
——. "Unspeakable Things Unspoken: The Afro-American Presence in American Literature." *Michigan Quarterly Review* 28.1 (1989): 1–34.

Winterson, Jeanette. *Art and Lies: A Piece for Three Voices and a Bawd*. London: Vintage, 1994.
——. *Art Objects: Essays on Ecstasy and Effrontery*. London: Vintage, 1996.

Winterson, Jeanette. *Boating for Beginners*. 1985. London: Vintage, 1999.
——. "Books and Family." ABC Arts Online (21 Sept. 2001) 10 Apr. 2005 <http://www.abc.net.au/arts/books/stories/s424267.htm>.
——. "Books in the Digital Age." ABC Arts Online (21 Sept. 2001) 10 Apr. 2005 <http://www.abc.net.au/arts/books/stories/s424271.htm>.
——. "Internet Discussion." *Guardian Unlimited* (7 Sept. 2000) 2 May 2006 <http://www.guardian.co.uk/Archive/Article/0,4273,4060792,00.html>.
——. *Lighthousekeeping*. London and New York: Fourth Estate, 2004.
——. *Oranges Are Not The Only Fruit*. Filmscript. Dir. Beeban Kidron. London: BBC2, 1990.
——. *Oranges Are Not The Only Fruit*. 1985. London: Vintage, 1994.
——. "Second Hand Pleasures." ABC Arts Online (21 Sept. 2001) 10 Apr. 2005 <http://www.abc.net.au/arts/books/stories/s424260.htm>.
——. *Sexing the Cherry*. 1989. London: Vintage, 1996.
——. *Tanglewreck*. London: Bloomsbury, 2006.
——. *The Passion*. 1987. London: Vintage, 1996.
——. *The Stone Gods*. 2007. London: Penguin, 2008.
——. *Weight*. Edinburgh, New York, Melbourne: Canongate, 2005.
——. *Written on the Body*. 1992. London: Vintage, 1993.

Secondary Literature

Abel, Elizabeth. "Black Writing, White Reading: Race and the Politics of Feminist Interpretation." *Feminisms: An Anthology of Literary Theory and Criticism*. Ed. Robyn R. Warhol and Diane Price-Herndl. New Brunswick, NJ: Rutgers University Press, 1997. 827–52.
Acker, Kathy. *Don Quixote Which Was a Dream*. New York: Grove Press, 1986.
Aguiar, Sarah Appleton. "'Passing On' Death: Stealing Life in Toni Morrison's *Paradise*." *African American Review* 38.3 (2004): 513–19.
"Alex Haley." Thomson Gale Data Bases. 19 June 2005 <www.galegroup.com/free_resources/bhm/bio/haley_a.htm>.
Allen, Brooke. "The Promised Land: *Paradise* by Toni Morrison." *The New York Times Book Review* (11 Jan. 1998): 6–7.
Allen, Carolyn. *Following Djuna: Women Lovers and the Erotics of Loss*. Ed. Teresa de Lauretis. Theories of Representation and Difference. Bloomington and Indianapolis: Indiana University Press, 1996.
Andermahr, Sonya. "Reinventing the Romance." *Jeanette Winterson: A Contemporary Critical Guide*. Ed. Sonya Andermahr. London and New York: Continuum, 2007. 82–99.

Angelo, Bonnie. "The Pain of Being Black: An Interview with Toni Morrison." *Conversations with Toni Morrison*. Ed. Danille Taylor-Guthrie. Jackson: University Press of Mississippi, 1994. 255–61.

Anshaw, Carol. "Into the Mystic: Jeanette Winterson's Fable Manners." *Village Voice Literary Supplement* 86 (1990): 16–17.

Anzaldúa, Gloria E. *Borderlands/La Frontera: The New Mestiza*. 1987. San Francisco: Aunt Lute Books, 1999.

Armitt, Lucie. "Storytelling and Feminism." *Jeanette Winterson: A Contemporary Critical Guide*. Ed. Sonya Andermahr. London and New York: Continuum, 2007. 14–26.

Ashley, Kathleen M. "Toni Morrison's Tricksters." *Uneasy Alliance: Twentieth Century American Literature, Culture and Biography*. Ed. Hans Bak. Amsterdam and New York: Rodopi, 2004. 269–84.

Bakhtin, Mikhail M. *Rabelais and His World*. 1965. Cambridge, Mass.: M.I.T. Press, 1968.

Barnhart, Robert K., ed. *The Barnhart Concise Dictionary of Etymology*. New York: Harper Collins, 1995.

——, ed. *The Dictionary of Etymology*. New York: The W.H. Wilson Company, 1988.

Barthelme, Elizabeth. "Fantastical & True: Author and Nobel Laureate Toni Morrison." *Commonweal* (9 Oct. 1998): 24–25.

Belsey, Catherine. "Postmodern Love: Questioning the Metaphysics of Desire." *New Literary History* 25.3 (1994): 683–705.

Bemrose, John. "Trouble in Utopia: *Paradise* by Toni Morrison." *MacLean's* 111.13 (1998): 65.

Bengtson, Helene. "The Vast, Unmappable Cities of the Interior: Place and Passion in *The Passion*." *Sponsored by Demons: The Art of Jeanette Winterson*. Ed. Helene Bengtson, Marianne Børch, and Cindie Maagaard. Agedrup: Scholar's Press, 1999. 17–26.

Bennett, Juda. "Toni Morrison and the Burden of the Passing Narrative." *African American Review* 35.2 (2001): 205–17.

Bent, Geoffrey. "Less Than Divine: Toni Morrison's *Paradise*." *The Southern Review* 35.1 (1999): 145–49.

Berch, Bettina. "Briefly Noted." *Belles Lettres* 8.3 (Spring 1993): 42.

Bhabha, Homi K. *The Location of Culture*. London: Routledge, 1994.

Bilger, Audrey. "The Art of Fiction CL: Interview with Jeanette Winterson." *Paris Review* 145 (1997): 68–112.

Bloom, Harold. *The Western Canon: The Books and School of the Ages*. New York et al.: Harcourt Brace, 1994.

Bold, Christine. "'An Enclave in the Wilderness:' Rev. of *Paradise* by Toni Morrison." *Times Literary Supplement* No 4956 (1998): 22.

Børch, Marianne. "Love's Ontology and the Problem of Cliché." *Sponsored by Demons: The Art of Jeanette Winterson.* Ed. Helene Bengtson, Marianne Børch, and Cindie Maagaard. Agedrup: Scholar's Press, 1999. 41–54.

Brooks, Libby. "Power Surge." *The Guardian* (2 Sept. 2000) 3 Apr. 2003 <http://www.jeanettewinterson.com/pages/content/index.asp?PageID=214>.

Brown, Dan. *The Da Vinci Code.* New York: Doubleday, 2003.

Brown, Helen. "A writer's life: Jeanette Winterson." *Daily Telegraph* (3 Oct. 2003) 15 Mar. 2006 <http://www.arts.telegraph.co.uk/arts/main.jhtml; jsessionid=P5EHCSJOZWP35QFIQMFSFFWAVCBQ0IV0?xml=/arts/2003/10/05/bowinterson.xml>.

Bryant, Jerry H. *"Born in a Mighty Bad Land:" The Violent Man in African American Folklore and Fiction.* Blacks in the Diaspora. Bloomington & Indianapolis: Indiana UP, 2003.

Bryce Bjork, Patrick. *The Novels of Toni Morrison: The Search for Self and Place in the Community.* New York et al.: Peter Lang, 1992.

Burns, Christy L. "Fantastic Language: Jeanette Winterson's Recovery of the Postmodern Word." *Contemporary Literature* 37.2 (1996): 278–306.

——. "Powerful Differences: Critique and Eros in Jeanette Winterson and Virginia Woolf." *Modern Fiction Studies* 44.2 (1998): 364–92.

Butler, Judith. *Bodies That Matter: On the Discursive Limits of 'Sex'.* New York: Routledge, 1993.

——. "Conversational Break: A Reply to Robert Gooding-Williams." *Race.* Ed. Robert Bernasconi. Malden, Mass.: Blackwell, 2001. 260–64.

——. *Gender Trouble.* New York: Routledge, 1990.

——. "Passing, Queering: Nelly Larsen's Psychoanalytic Challenge." *Bodies That Matter: On the Discursive Limits of "Sex".* New York and London: Routledge, 1993. 167–85.

——. "Preface 1999." *Gender Trouble.* New York and London: Routledge, 1999. vii–xxxiii.

——. "The End of Sexual Difference?" *Undoing Gender.* New York and London: Routledge, 2004. 174–203.

Calvino, Italo. *If on a Winter's Night a Traveller.* 1979. London: Vintage, 2002.

——. *Invisible Cities.* 1972. New York: Brace, Harcourt, Jovanovitch, 1974.

Campbell-Johnston, Rachel. "Into Cyberspace." *The Times* (6 Sept. 2000) 2 Apr. 2003 <http://www.jeanettewinterson.com/pages/content/index.asp?PageID=215>.

"Candomblé." Wikipedia. 27 Oct. 2005 <http://www.en.wikipedia.org/wiki/Candmbl\%C3\%A5>.

Carter, Angela. *Nights at the Circus.* London: Chatto & Windus, 1984.

——. *The Bloody Chamber and Other Stories.* London: Gollancz, 1979.

——. *The Passion of New Eve.* 1977. London: Virago, 1982.

Christian, Barbara. *Black Feminist Criticism: Perspectives on Black Women Writers*. New York: Pergamon Press, 1985.

——. "'The Past is Infinite': History and Myth in Toni Morrison's Trilogy." *Social Identities* 6.4 (2000): 411–23.

——. "The Race for Theory." *The Nature and Context of Minority Discourse*. Ed. Abdul R. JanMohamed and David Lloyd. New York, Oxford: Oxford University Press, 1990. 37–49.

Chu, Henry. "Venice's First Female Gondolier Pushes Off Into Uncharted Waters." *LA Times* (21 July 2009) 21 July 2009 <http://www.latimes.com/news/nationworld/world/la-fg-venice-gondolier21-2009jul21,0,5944354,full.story>.

Clewell, Tammy. "From Destructive to Constructive Hauting in Toni Morrison's *Paradise*" (2002) 20 May 2005 <http://www.sfu.ca/west-coast-line/clewell_morrison.pdf>.

Courlander, Harold. *The African: A Novel*. New York: Crown Publishers Inc., 1967.

Crenshaw, Kimberlé, Neil Gotanda, Gary Peller, and Kendall Thomas, ed. *Critical Race Theory: The Key Writings that Formed the Movement*. New York: New Press, 1995.

Cronon, Edward D. *Black Moses: The Story of Marcus Garvey and the UNIA*. Madison: University of Wisconsin Press, 1955.

Crouch, Stanley. "The Roots of Huckster Haley's Great Fraud." *Jewish World Review* (18 Jan. 2002) 27 July 2006 <www.jewishworldreview.com/cols/crouch011802.asp>.

Curti, Lidia. *Female Stories, Female Bodies: Narrative, Identity, and Representation*. New York: New York University Press, 1998.

D'Aguiar, Fred. *The Longest Memory*. 1994. London: Vintage, 1995.

Dalsgård, Katrine. "The One All-Black Town Worth the Pain." *African American Review* 35.2 (2001): 233–48.

Darroch, Fiona. "Re-Reading the Religious Bodies of Postcolonial Literature." *The Politics of English as a World Language: New Horizons in Postcolonial Cultural Studies*. Ed. Christian Mair. Amsterdam and New York, NY: Rodopi, 2003. 203–8.

David, Ron. *Toni Morrison Explained: A Reader's Road Map to the Novels*. New York: Random House, 2000.

de León, Alfonso. *Racial Frontiers: Africans, Chinese, and Mexicans in Western America, 1848-1890*. Ed. Ray Allen Billington. Histories of the American Frontier. Albuquerque: University of New Mexico Press, 2002.

De Lauretis, Teresa. *Alice Doesn't: Feminism, Semiotics and Cinema*. Bloomington: Indiana University Press, 1984.

De Zordo, Ornelia. "Larger Than Life: Women Writing the Excessive Female Body." *Textus* 13.2 (2000): 427–48.

del Mar Asensio Arostegui, Maria. "Recurrent Structural and Thematic Traits in Jeanette Winterson's *The Passion* and *Sexing the Cherry*: Time, Space, and the Construction of Identity." Diss. Universidad de la Rioja, 2008.

del Mar Asensio, María. "Subversion of Sexual Identity in Jeanette Winterson's *The Passion*." *Gender, I-Deology: Essays on Theory, Fiction and Film*. Ed. Chantal Cornut-Gentille D'Arcy and José Ángel García Landa. Vol. 16. Postmodern Studies Series. Amsterdam, Atlanta: Rodopi, 1996. 265–78.

do Nascimento, Abdias. *Brazil - Mixture or Massacre? Essays in the Genocide of a Black People*. Dover, Mass.: The Majority Press, 1979.

Doan, Laura. "Jeanette Winterson's Sexing the Postmodern." *The Lesbian Postmodern*. New York: Columbia UP, 1994. 137–55.

Donahue, Deirdre. "Morrison's Slice of *Paradise*." *USA Today* (8 Jan. 1998) 10 Jan. 1999 <http://www.usatoday.com/life/enter/books/b128.htm>.

D'Souza, Dinesh. "Is Racism a Western Idea?" Christian Ethics Today: Journal of Christian Ethics (005 1996) 30 July 2009 <http://www.christianethicstoday. com/issue/005/IsRacismaWesternIdeabyDineshD'Souza_005__.html>.

——. *The End of Racism: Principles for a Multiracial Society*. New York: Free Press, 1995.

Du Bois, W.E.B. *The Souls of Black Folk*. Chicago: A.C. McClurg & Co., 1903.

Duncker, Patricia. "Jeanette Winterson and the Aftermath of Feminism." *'I'm Telling You Stories': Jeanette Winterson and the Politics of Reading*. Ed. Helena Grice and Tim Woods. Amsterdam: Rodopi, 1998. 77–88.

Durrant, Sam. *Postcolonial Narrative and the Work of Mourning: J.M. Coetzee, Wilson Harris, and Toni Morrison*. New York: SUNY Press, 2004.

Duvall, John Noel. *The Identifying Fictions of Toni Morrison: Modernist Authenticity and Postmodern Blackness*. New York et al.: Palgrave, 2000.

Elia, Nada. *Trances, Dances, and Vociferations: Agency and Resistance in Africana Women's Narratives*. New York: Garland, 2001.

Eliot, T.S. "Burnt Norton." 1969. *T.S. Eliot: The Complete Poems and Plays*. London and Boston: Faber & Faber, 1989. 171–76.

Ellison, Ralph. *Invisible Man*. New York: Random House, 1952.

Estor, Annemarie. *Jeanette Wintersons's Enchanted Science*. The Hague: Talkingtree, 2004.

Farnsworth, Elizabeth. "Interview with Toni Morrison." PBS Online Newshour. (9 Mar. 1998) 16 Feb. 2005 <http://www.pbs.org/newshour/bb/entertainment/jan-june98/morrison_3-9.html>.

Farrar, Stacy. "Writing on the Body." *Sydney Star Observer 704* (11 Mar. 2004) 15 Mar. 2006 <http://www.ssonet.com.au/archives/display.asp?articleID=3754>.

Farwell, Marilyn R. "Chapter 6: The Postmodern Lesbian Text: Jeanette Winterson's *Sexing the Cherry* and *Written on the Body*." *Heterosexual Plots and*

Lesbian Narratives. Ed. Marilyn R. Farwell. New York: New York University Press, 1996. 168–94.

——. "The Lesbian Narrative: 'The Pursuit of the Inedible by the Unspeakable'." *Professions of Desire: Lesbian and Gay Studies in Literature*. Ed. George E. Haggerty and Bonnie Zimmerman. New York: MLA, 1995. 156–68.

Felski, Rita. *Literature After Feminism*. Chicago and London: University of Chicago Press, 2003.

Fetterman, Eric. "The Celebrated 'Roots' Of A Lie." *New York Post* (2002): 025.

Field, Michele. "Jeanette Winterson: 'I Fear Insincerity'." *Publishers Weekly* (20 Mar. 1995): 38–39.

Fludernik, Monika. "The Genderization of Narrative." *Publication des Groupes de Recherches Anglo-Américaines de l'Université François Rabelais de Tours (GRAAT)* 21 (1999): 153–75.

Fraile-Marcos, Ana María. "Hybridizing the 'City upon the Hill' in Toni Morrison's *Paradise*." *MELUS* 28.4 (2003): 3–33.

Frankenberg, Ruth. *White Women, Race Matters: The Social Construction of Whiteness*. Minneapolis: University of Minnesota Press, 1994.

Franklin, Jimmie Lewis. *A History of Blacks in Oklahoma, Journey Toward Hope*. Norman: University of Oklahoma Press, 1982.

Fultz, Lucille P. *Toni Morrison: Playing with Difference*. Urbana & Chicago: University of Illinois Press, 2003.

Furman, Jan. *Toni Morrison's Fiction*. Ed. Matthew Bruccoli. Understanding Contemporary American Literature. Columbia: University of South Carolina Press, 1996.

Gade, Bente. "Multiple Selves and Grafted Agents: A Postmodern Reading of *Sexing the Cherry*." *Sponsored by Demons: The Art of Jeanette Winterson*. Ed. Helene Bengtson, Marianne Børch and Cindie Maagaard. Agedrup: Scholar's Press, 1999. 27–39.

Ganteau, Jean-Michel. "Fantastic, but Truthful: the Ethics of Romance." *The Cambridge Quarterly* 32.3 (2003): 225–38.

——. "Hearts Object: Jeanette Winterson and the Ethics of Absolutist Romance." *Refracting the Canon in Contemporary British Literature and Film*. Ed. Susana Onega and Christian Gutleben. Amsterdam: Rodopi, 2004. 165–85.

Gates Henry Louis, Jr. "When Candidates Pick Voters." New York Times. *New York Times* (23 Sept. 2004) 24 Sept. 2004 <http://www.nytimes.com/2004/09/23/opinion/23gates.html>.

——. "Writing 'Race' and the Difference It Makes." *"Race," Writing, and Difference*. Ed. Henry Louis Gates, Jr. Chicago and London: The University of Chicago Press, 1985. 1–20.

Geertz, Clifford. *The Interpretation of Cultures*. New York: Basic Books/Harper Collins, 1973.

Gerrard, Nicci. "The Ultimate Self-Produced Woman." *The Observer* 5 June 1994, sec. The Observer Review: 7.

Gilmore, Leigh. *The Limits of Autobiography: Trauma and Testimony*. Ithaka and London: Cornell University Press, 2001.

Gilroy, Paul. *The Black Atlantic: Modernity and Double Consciousness*. London: Verso, 1993.

Glasgow, Joshua. *A Theory of Race*. New York: Routledge, 2008.

Goldberg, Michelle. "Utopia Lost and Found: *Paradise* by Toni Morrison." *Metroactive Books* (1998) 16 Feb. 2005 <http://www.metroactive.com/papers/metro/02.26.98/lit-morrison-9808.html>.

Goldstein-Shirley, David. "Race and Response: Toni Morrison's 'Recitatif'." *Short Story* 5.1 (1997): 77–86.

——. "Race/(Gender): Toni Morrison's 'Recitatif'." *Journal of the Short Story in English* 27.Autumn (1996): 83–95.

González, Susana. "Winterson's *Sexing the Cherry*: Rewriting 'Woman' Through Fantasy." *Gender, I-Deology*. Ed. Chantal Cornut-Gentille D'Arcy and José Ángel García Landa. Vol. 16. Postmodern Studies Series. Amsterdam, Atlanta: Rodopi, 1996. 281–94.

Gooding-Williams, Robert. "Race, Multiculturalism and Democracy." *Race*. Ed. Robert Bernasconi. Malden, Mass.: Blackwell, 2001. 237–59.

Gordon, Avery F. and Chistopher Newfield. "Introduction." *Mapping Multiculturalism*. Ed. Avery F. Gordon and Chistopher Newfield. Minneapolis and London: University of Minnesota Press, 1996. 1–16.

Gray, Paul. "Paradise Found." *TIME Magazine* 151.2 (19 Jan. 1998). <http://www.cgi.pathfinder.com/time/magazine/1998/dom/980119>.

Grice, Helena and Tim Woods. "Reading Jeanette Winterson Writing." *'I'm Telling You Stories': Jeanette Winterson and the Politics of Reading*. Ed. Helena Grice and Tim Woods. Amsterdam: Rodopi, 1998. 1–11.

Griffin, Gabriele. *Heavenly love? Lesbian images in twentieth-century women's writing*. Manchester and New York: Manchester University Press, 1993.

Guillaumin, Colette. "The Changing Face of 'Race'." *Racism*. Ed. Martin Bulmer Solomos and John. Oxford and New York: Oxford University Press, 1999. 355–62.

Hacking, Ian. "Making up People." *Reconstructing Individualism*. Ed. Thomas C. Heller, Morton Sosna, and David Wellbery. Stanford: Stanford University Press, 1986. 222–36.

——. "Why Race Still Matters." *Daedalus* 134.1 (2005): 102–16.

Haines-Wright, Lisa and Tracy Lynne Kyle. "From He and She to You and Me: Grounding Fluidity, Woolf's *Orlando* to Winterson's *Written on the Body*." *Virginia Woolf: Texts and Contexts*. Ed. Beth Rigel Daugherty and Eileen Barrett. New York: Pace University, 1996. 177–82.

Haley, Alex. *Roots*. Garden City: Doubleday, 1976.

Hamilton, Cynthia. "Multiculturalism as a Political Strategy." *Mapping Multiculturalism*. Ed. Avery F. Gordon and Chistopher Newfield. London and Minnapolis: University of Minnesota Press, 1996. 167–77.

Hamilton, Kenneth Marvin. *Black Towns and Profit: Promotion in the Trans-Appalachian West, 1877-1915*. Urbana and Chicago: University of Illinois Press, 1991.

Hancock, Ann. "Jeanette Winterson." *British Novelists Since 1960: Third Series*. Ed. Merritt Moseley. Detroit, Washington, D.C., London: Gale. A Bruccoli Clark Longman Book, 1999. 301–08.

Harding, Rachel E. "Candomblé: A Religion of the African Diaspora." *Prometra* (2002) 26 Mar. 2003 <http://www.prometra.org/Report_on_Candomble.htm>.

Harding, Wendy and Jacky Martin. *A World of Difference: An Inter-Cultural Study of Toni Morrison's Novels*. Vol. 171. Contributions in Afro-American and African Studies. Westport, Conn., London: Greenwood Press, 1994.

Harris, Andrea L. *Other Sexes: Rewriting Difference from Woolf to Winterson*. New York, NY: SUNY Press, 2000.

Haslanger, Sally. "Gender and Race: (What) are they? (What) do we want them to be?" *Noûs* 34.1 (2000): 31–55.

Haslett, Jane. "Winterson's Fabulous Bodies." *Jeanette Winterson: A Contemporary Critical Guide*. Ed. Sonya Andermahr. London and New York: Continuum, 2007. 41–54.

Higgins, Therese E. *Religiosity, Cosmology, and Folklore: The African Influence in the Novels of Toni Morrison*. New York and London: Routledge, 2001.

Hill, Mike. *After Whiteness: Unmaking an American Majority*. New York, NY: New York UP, 2004.

Hinds, Hilary. "*Oranges Are Not The Only Fruit*: Reaching Audiences Other Lesbian Texts Cannot Reach." *New Lesbian Criticism: Literary and Cultural Readings*. Ed. Sally Munt. New York: Columbia University Press, 1992. 153–72.

Homans, Margaret. "Representation, Reproduction, and Women's Place in Language." *Literary Theory: An Anthology*. Ed. Julie Rivkin and Michael Ryan. Malden, Mass. and Oxford: Blackwell Publishers, 1998. 650–655.

Hong Kingston, Maxine. *China Men*. New York: Alfred J. Knopf, 1980.

———. *The Woman Warrior*. New York: Vintage International, 1975.

Humphries, Louise Horskjær. "Listening for the Author's Voice: 'Un-Sexing' the Wintersonian Oeuvre." *Sponsored by Demons: The Art of Jeanette Winterson*. Ed. Helene Bengtson, Marianne Børch and Cindie Maagaard. Agedrup: Scholar's Press, 1999. 3–16.

Hurston, Zora Neale. *Their Eyes Were Watching God*. Philadelphia: J.B. Lippincott, 1937.

Hutcheon, Linda. *A Poetics of Postmodernism: History, Theory, Fiction.* New York and London: Routledge, 1988.

Iser, Wolfgang. *Der Akt des Lesens: Theorie Ästhetischer Wirkung.* München: Fink, 1976.

———. *Der Implizite Leser: Kommunikationsformen des Romans von Bunyan bis Beckett.* München: Fink, 1972.

Italie, Hillel. "Toni Morrison's 'Paradise': Novelist savors her success." *Standard Times* (2 Jan. 1998) 16 Feb. 2005 <http://www.s-t.com/daily/02-98/02-01-98/e07ae211.htm>.

Ivry, Benjamin. "Interview with Jeanette Winterson." *Wall Street Journal* (Mar. 2003) 2 Apr. 2006 <http://www.jeanettewinterson.com/pages/content/index.asp?PageID=216>.

Jaffrey, Zia. "The Salon Interview." *Salon* (2 Feb. 1998) 12 Apr. 2004 <http://www.salonmagazine.com/books/int/1998/02/cov_si_02int.html>.

Jaggi, Maya. "Jeanette Winterson: Redemption Songs." *The Guardian* (29 May 2004) 8 Mar. 2006 <http://www.jeanettewinterson.com/pages/content/index.asp?PageID=272>.

Johnson, M.K. "'Stranger in a Strange Land': An African American Response to the Frontier Tradition in Oscar Micheaux's *The Conquest: The Story of a Negro Pioneer.*" *Western American Literature* 33.3 (Fall 1998): 228–52.

Jones, Jill C. "The Eye of the Needle: Morrison's *Paradise.*" *Faulkner Journal* 17.2 (2002): 3–23.

Joyner, Louisa. *Toni Morrison: The Essential Guide.* Ed. Jonathan Noakes and Margaret Reynolds. Vintage Living Texts: The Essential Guide to Contemporary Literature. London: Vintage, 2003.

Jörns, Klaus-Peter. *Notwendige Abschiede: Auf dem Weg zu einem glaubwürdigen Christentum.* Gütersloh: Gütersloher Verlagshaus, 2004.

Kakutani, Michito. "'Paradise': Worthy Women, Unredeemable Men." *Books of the Times, New York Times* (6 Jan. 1998): E8.

Katz, William Loren. *The Black West.* Garden City, NY: Doubleday & Company, Inc., 1971.

Kauer, Ute. "Narration and Gender: The Role of the First-Person Narrator in Jeanette Winterson's *Written on the Body.*" *'I'm Telling You Stories': Jeanette Winterson and the Politics of Reading.* Ed. Helena Grice and Tim Woods. Amsterdam: Rodopi, 1998. 41–51.

Kay, Jackie. "Unnatural Passions." *Spare Rib* 209 (Feb. 1990): 26–29.

Keating, AnaLouise. "Investigating 'Whiteness,' Eavesdropping on 'Race'." *JAC: A Journal of Composition Theory* 20.2 (2000 Spring): 426–33.

Kella, Elizabeth. *Beloved Communities: Solidarity and Difference in Fiction by Michael Ondaatje, Toni Morrison, and Joy Kogawa.* Uppsala: Uppsala University, 2000.

Kendrick, Walter. "Fiction in Review." *The Yale Review* 81.4 (Oct. 1993): 124–37 (131–33).

Kilian, Eveline. *GeschlechtSverkehrt: Theoretische und Literarische Perspektiven des Gender-Bending*. Königstein/Taunus: Ulrike Helmer Verlag, 2004.

King, Karen L. *The Gospel of Mary of Magdalene: Jesus and the First Woman Apostle*. Santa Rosa, Cal.: Polebridge Press, 2003.

———. "Why All the Controversy? Mary in the Gospel of Mary." *Which Mary? The Maries of Early Christian Tradition*. Ed. Stanley F. Jones. Leiden & Boston: Brill, 2003. 53–74.

Klinghoffer, David. "Black Madonna: Toni Morrison's Popularity Is Less a Matter of Literary Taste Than of Mass Psychology - Critique of Adulation of New Morrison novel, 'Paradise'." *National Review* (9 Feb. 1998) 16 Feb. 2005 <http://www.findarticles.com/p/articles/mi_m1282/is_n2_v50/ai_20191277>.

Krumholz, Linda J. "Reading and Insight in Toni Morrison's *Paradise*." *African American Review* 36.1 (2002): 21–34.

Kubitschek, Missy Dehn. *Toni Morrison: A Critical Companion*. Critical Companions to Popular Contemporary Writers. Westport, Conn., London: Greenwood Press, 1998.

Kuitert, Harminus Martinus. *Kein Zweiter Gott: Jesus und das Ende des kirchlichen Christus*. Düsseldorf: Patmos-Verlag, 2003.

Lacan, Jacques. "The Symbolic Order." *Literary Theory: An Anthology*. Ed. Julie Rivkin and Michael Ryan. Malden, Mass. and Oxford: Blackwell Publishers, 1998. 184–89.

LaCapra, Dominick. "Trauma, Absence, Loss." *Critical Inquiry* 25.4 (1999): 696–727.

Lainsbury, G. P. "Hubris and the Young Author: The Problem of the Introduction to *Oranges Are Not the Only Fruit*." *Notes on Contemporary Literature*. 22.4 (1992): 2–3.

Lambert, Angela. "I don't want to boast, but." *The Independent* 29 June 1994, sec. Comment: 17.

———. "Jeanette Winterson." *Prospect Magazine* (Feb. 1998) 4 Mar. 2006 <http://www.prospect-magazine.co.uk/articles_details.php?id=4295&issue=0>.

Langland, Elizabeth. "Sexing the Text: Narrative Drag as Feminist Poetics and Politics in Jeanette Winterson's *Sexing the Cherry*." *Narrative* 5.1 (1997): 99–107.

"Langston, Oklahoma." African American Registry. 20 May 2005 <http://www.aaregistry.com/african_american_history/2095/Langston_Oklahoma_a_FUBU_Black_town>.

Lanser, Susan S. "Queering Narratology." *Ambiguous Discourse: Feminist Narratology & British Women Writers*. Ed. Kathy Mezei. Chapel Hill and London: University of North Carolina Press, 1996. 250–61.

Le Guin, Ursula K. "Introduction." *The Left Hand of Darkness*. New York: Ace Books, 1976. i–vi.

Lee, Alison. "Bending the Arrow of Time: The Continuing Postmodern Present." *Historicité et Métafiction dans le Roman Contemporain des Iles Britanniques*. Ed. Max Duperray. Aix-en-Provence: Université des Provence, 1994. 217–229.

Lehmann, Elmar. "Remembering the Past: Toni Morrison's Version of the Historical Novel." *Lineages of the Novel*. Ed. Bernhard Reitz, Eckart Voigts-Virchow. Trier: WVT Wissenschaftlicher Verlag Trier, 2000. 196–203.

Lemke, Cordula. *Wandel in der Erfahrung: Die Konstruktion von Welt in den Romanen von Virginia Woolf and Jeanette Winterson*. Vol. 35. HORIZONTE: Studien zu Texten und Ideen der europäischen Moderne. Trier: Wissenschaftlicher Verlag Trier, 2004.

Lenz, Günter H. "Toward a Dialogics of International American Studies: Transnationality, Border Discourses, and Public Culture(s)." *The Futures of American Studies*. Ed. Donald E. Pease and Robyn Wiegman. Durham & London: Duke University Press, 2002. 461–85.

Lindenmeyer, Antje. "Postmodern Concepts of the Body in Jeanette Winterson's *Written on the Body*." *Feminist Review* 63 (Autumn 1999): 48–63.

Link, Jürgen. *Versuch Über Den Normalismus: Wie Normalität Produziert Wird*. Opladen, Wiesbaden: Westdeutscher Verlag, 1999.

Lorber, Judith. "'Night to His Day': The Social Construction of Gender." *Paradoxes of Gender*. New Haven: Yale University Press, 1994. 13–36.

Lubiano, Wahneema. "Introduction." *The House that Race Built: Original Essays by Toni Morrison, Angela Y. Davis, Cornel West, and others on Black Americans and Politics in America*. New York: Vintage Books, 1998. vii–ix.

"Lucius Annaeus Seneca, [the Younger]." European Graduate School. 19 Sept. 2005 <http://www.egs.edu/resources/seneca.html>.

Maagaard, Cindie Aaen. "Jeanette Winterson: Postmodern Prophet of the Word." *Literary Canons and Religious Identity*. Ed. Erik Borgman, Bart Philipsen and Lea Verstricht. Aldershot and Burlington: Ashgate, 2004. 151–61.

"Macumba/Candomblé." Religious Movements, University of Virginia. 1996. 27 Oct. 2005 <http://religiousmovements.lib.virginia.edu/nrms/macu/html>.

Mantel, Hilary. "No Disco, No TV, No Diner, No Adultery: *Paradise*." *Literary Review* (1998) 16 Feb. 2005 <http://www.users.dircom.co.uk/~litrev/199804/Mantel_on_Morrison.html>.

Marcus, James. "This Side of Paradise" (1998) 12 May 2003 <http://www.amazon.com/exec/obidos/tg/feature/-/7651/t/102-9477403-4454509>.

Marvel, Mark. "Jeanette Winterson: Trust me. I'm telling you stories." *Interview* 20 (1990): 165, 168.

Matus, Jill. *Toni Morrison*. Manchester and New York: Manchester University Press, 1998.

McGuire, George Alexander. "Universal Black Men Catechism." ca. 1920.

McKenzie, Marilyn Mobley. "Spaces for Readers: The Novels of Toni Morrison." *The Cambridge Companion to the African American Novel*. Ed. Maryemma Graham. Cambridge: Cambridge University Press, 2004. 221–32.

Menand, John. "War Between Men and Women: The Sixties Come to an All-Black Town in Oklahoma." *The New Yorker* 73.42 (12 Jan. 1998): 78–82.

Mendoza, Robert. "Our Lady of Regla." *Azodnem* (2004) 18 Oct. 2005 <http: //azodnem.com/Cauldron/Yemaja.htm>.

Menzies, Diane. "Disturbing Picture of Paradise." *Edmonton Sun* (22 Feb. 1998) 19 Apr. 2003 <http://66.249.93.104/search?q=cache:VsbbunoCkzcJ:www. ottawalynx.com/JamBooksReviewsP/paradise_morrison.html+menzies, +diane,+edmonton+sun+paradise\&hl=de\&lr=\&strip=0>.

Messmer, Marietta. "Intra-American Internationality: Morrison Responding to Faulkner." *Internationality in American Fiction: Henry James, William Dean Howells, William Faulkner, Toni Morrison*. Ed. Armin Paul Frank and Rolf Lohse. Frankfurt/Main: Peter Lang, 2005. 187–242.

Messud, Claire. "The Body Politic." *The Guardian* 26 Aug. 1992, sec. Feature: 29.

Meyer, Kim Middleton. "Jeanette Winterson's Evolving Subject: 'Difficulty into Dream'." *Contemporary British Fiction*. Ed. Richard J. Lane, Rod Mengham and Philip Tew. Cambridge: Polity, 2003. 210–25.

Mihan, Anne and Thomas O. Haakenson. "Standard Deviation: An Interview with Jürgen Link. Modernity and the Reign of Normalism." *Cabinet* 15 (Fall 2004): 83–7.

Miner, Valerie. "At Her Wit's End: Rev. of *Written on the Body*." *The Women's Review of Books* 10.8 (May 1993): 21.

Moore, Lisa. "Teledildonics: Virtual Lesbians in the Fiction of Jeanette Winterson." *Sexy Bodies: The Strange Carnalities of Feminism*. Ed. Elizabeth Grosz and Elspeth Probyn. London: Routledge, 1995. 104–27.

Mori, Aoi. *Toni Morrison and Womanist Discourse*. New York et al.: Peter Lang, 1999.

Morrison, Jago. *Contemporary Fiction*. London: Routledge, 2003.

"Nazi-Symbole: Zahlen." Hyperlinks Gegen Rechts. 19 July 2005 <http://www. hyperlinks-gegen-rechts.de/nazi_symbole.html#zahlen>.

Nelson, Dana D. "The 'White Problem': The Critical Study of Whiteness in American Literature." *Modern Language Studies* 32.1 (2002): 5–178.

Nicol, Kathryn. "Visible Differences: Viewing Racial Identity in Toni Morrison's *Paradise* and "Recitatif"." *Literature and Racial Ambiguity*. Ed. Teresa Hubel and Neil Brooks. Amsterdam and New York: Rodopi, 2002. 209–231.

Nunn, Heather. "*Written on the Body*: An Anatomy of Horror, Melancholy, and Love." *Women: A Cultural Review* 7.1 (1996): 16–27.

Obama, Barack. *The Audacity of Hope: Thoughts on Reclaiming the American Dream*. New York: Vintage, 2006.

"Oklahoma's History." State of Oklahoma. 2 Mar. 2005 <http://state.ok.us/asfdocs/stinfo2.html>.

"Omolu and Mary Star of the Sea." The Quiet in the Land. 18 Oct. 2005 <http://www.thequietintheland.org/brazil/category.php?id=janine-antoni>.

Onega, Susana. "Jeanette Winterson's Politics of Uncertainty in *Sexing the Cherry*." *Gender, I-Deology*. Ed. Chantal Cornut-Gentille D'Arcy and José Ángel García Landa. Vol. 16. Postmodern Studies Series. Amsterdam, Atlanta: Rodopi, 1996. 297–313.

O'Reilly, Andrea. *Toni Morrison and Motherhood: A Politics of the Heart*. Albany, NY: SUNY Press, 2004.

Othow, Helen Chavis. "Comedy in Morrison's Terrestrial Paradise." *CLA Journal* 47.3 (2004): 366–73.

Outlaw, Lucius (1990). "Toward a Critical Theory of 'Race'." *Race and Racism*. Ed. Bernard Boxill. Oxford and New York: Oxford University Press, 2001. 58–82.

Page, Philip. *Dangerous Freedom: Fusion and Fragmentation in Toni Morrison's Novels*. Jackson: University Press of Mississippi, 1995.

———. "Furrowing All the Brows: Interpretation and the Transcendent in Toni Morrison's *Paradise*." *African American Review* 35.4 (2001): 637–67.

Pagels, Elaine. *The Gnostic Gospels*. New York: Random House, 1979.

Painter, Nell Irving. *Exodusters: Black Migration to Kansas after Reconstruction*. New York: Alfred A. Knopf, 1977.

Palmer, Paulina. *Contemporary Lesbian Writing: Dreams, desire, difference*. Gender in Writing. Buckingham, Philadelphia: Open University Press, 1993.

———. "Foreign Bodies: The Grotesque Body in the Fiction of Jeanette Winterson." *Gramma* 11 (2003): 81–93.

———. "Jeanette Winterson: Lesbian/Postmodern Fictions." *Engendering Realism and Postmodernism: Contemporary Women Writers in Britain*. Ed. Beate Neumeier. Vol. 32. Postmodern Studies. Amsterdam and New York: Rodopi, 2001. 181–89.

———. "Postmodern Trends in Contemporary Fiction: Margaret Atwood, Angela Charter, Jeanette Winterson." *Postmodern Subjects/Postmodern Texts*. Ed. Jane Dowson and Steven Earnshaw. Vol. 13. Postmodern Studies. Amsterdam & Atlanta, GA: Rodopi, 1995. 181–99.

Pearce, Lynne. *Feminism and the Politics of Reading*. London: Edward Arnold, 1997.

———. *Reading Dialogics*. London et al.: Edward Arnold, 1994.

———. "The Emotional Politics of Reading Winterson." *'I'm Telling You Stories': Jeanette Winterson and the Politics of Reading*. Ed. Helena Grice and Tim Woods. Amsterdam: Rodopi, 1998. 29–39.

——. "'Written On Tablets Of Stone'? Jeanette Winterson, Roland Barthes, and the Discourse of Romantic Love." *Volcanoes and Pearl Divers: Essays in Lesbian Feminist Studies*. Ed. Suzanne Raitt. London: Onlywomen Press, 1994. 147–68.

"People & Events: Booker T. Washington." PBS Online. 22 July 2005 <http://www.pbs.org/wgbh/amex/garvey/peopleevents/p_washington.html>.

Phipps, Keith. "Toni Morrison, *Paradise*." *The Onion A.V. Club* (2004) 16 Feb. 2005 <http://avclub.theonion.com/review.php?review_id=2978>.

Piercy, Marge. *Woman on the Edge of Time*. New York: Fawcett Books, 1976.

Pratt, Mary Louise. *Imperial Eyes: Travel Writing and Transculturation*. London, New York: Routledge, 1992.

Pykett, Lyn. "A New Way With Words? Jeanette Winterson's Postmodernism." *'I'm Telling You Stories': Jeanette Winterson and the Politics of Reading*. Ed. Helena Grice and Tim Woods. Amsterdam and Atlanta, GA: Rodopi, 1998. 53–60.

Quadflieg, Helga. "Feminist Stories Told on Wastewaters: Jeanette Winterson's Novels." *Anglistik & Englischunterricht* 60 (1997): 97–111.

Raddatz, Fritz J. "Ich Bin Keine Amerikanerin: Ein Zeit-Gespräch Mit Toni Morrison." *DIE ZEIT* (Aug. 1998): 33f.

Ramsey, Tamara Ann. "Producing Queer Affiliations: Feminist, Lesbian, Aesthetic, and Queer Reading Practices." *Virginia Woolf and her Influences: Selected Papers from the Seventh Annual Conference on Virginia Woolf*. Ed. Laura Davis and Jeanette McVicker. New York: Pace, 1998. 275–81.

Rayson, Ann. "Decoding for Race: Toni Morrison's 'Recitatif' and Being White, Teaching Black." *Changing Presentations of Minorities East and West: Selected Essays*. Ed. Larry E. Smith and John Rieder. Honolulu: Colleges of Languages, Linguistics, Literature. University of Hawai'i, and East-West Center, 1996. 41–46.

"Red, Black and Green." UNIA-ACL. 5 Oct. 2005 <http://www.unia-acl.org/history/flagstor.htm>.

Reynolds, Margaret. "Interview with Jeanette Winterson." *Jeanette Winterson: The essential guide*. Ed. Margaret Reynolds and Jonathan Noakes. Vintage Living Texts: Contemporary Literature in Close Up. London: Vintage, 2003. 11–29.

——. "Interview with Toni Morrison." *Toni Morrison: The Essential Guide*. Ed. Jonathan Noakes and Margaret Reynolds. London: Vintage, 2003. 11–19.

Reynolds, Margaret and Jonathan Noakes. *Jeanette Winterson: The essential guide*. Vintage Living Texts: Contemporary Literature in Close Up. London: Vintage, 2003.

Richards, Constance S. *On the Winds and Waves of Imagination: Transnational Feminism and Literature*. New York and London: Garland Publishing, Inc., 2000.

Robinson, Susan. "The Black Panther Party." *Gibbs Magazine* (14 Nov. 2005) 19 July 2005 <www.gibbsmagazine.com/Black\%20Panther\%20Pty.htm>.

Roether, Diemut. ""Radikal Bin Ich Nicht, Aber Unabhängig": Interview Mit Toni Morrison." *die tageszeitung* 0 6./7. Nov. 1999, sec. Kultur: 15.

Roth, Phillip. *The Human Stain*. London: Vintage, 2000.

Rottenberg, Catherine. "Passing: Race, Identification, and Desire." *Criticism* 45.4 (2003): 435–52.

Rubinson, Gregory J. "Body Languages: Scientific and Aesthetic Discourses in Jeanette Winterson's *Written on the Body*." *Critique* 42.2 (2001): 218–32.

——. *The Fiction of Rushdie, Barnes, Winterson and Carter: Breaking Cultural and Literary Boundaries in the Work of Four Postmodernists*. Jefferson, NC, and London: McFarland & Company, 2005.

Rutherford, Jonathan. "The Third Space: Interview with Homi Bhabha." *Identity: Community, Culture, Difference*. Ed. Jonathan Rutherford. London: Lawrence and Wishart, 1990. 207–221.

Satchidanandan, K. "That Third Space: Interrogating the Diasporic Paradigm." *Indian Literature* 45.3 (203) (2001): 5–9.

Saxton, Ruth O. *The Girl: Constructions of the Girl in Contemporary Fiction by Women*. New York: Palgrave MacMillan, 1998.

Schappell, Elissa and Claudia Brodsky Lacour. "The Art of Writing Fiction CXXXIV." *The Paris Review* 129 (1993): 83–125.

Scheck, Denis. "Im Gespräch: Toni Morrison. Die Aufklärung Hat Erst Begonnen." *Deutsches Allgemeines Sonntagsblatt* (7 Jan. 2000) 23 Apr. 2003 <http://www.sonntagsblatt.de/artikel/2000/11-s4.htm>.

Schmid, Susanne. "Contemporary Women Writers and Their Use of Myth." *Proceedings: Anglistentag 1996, Dresden*. Ed. Uwe Böker and Hans Sauer. Trier: Wissenschaftlicher Verlag, 1997. 363–71.

Schmidt-Haberkamp, Barbara. "The Appropriation of the Third Space: Considerations Upon the Mediating Function of Migrant Writers." *Anglistentag 1999 Mainz: Proceedings*. Ed. Bernhard Reitz and Sigrid Rieuwerts. Vol. 21. Proceedings of the Conference of the German Association of University Teachers of English. Trier: Wissenschaftlicher Verlag, 2000. 301–11.

Schur, Richard. "Locating *Paradise* in the Post-Civil Rights Era: Toni Morrison and Critical Race Theory." *Contemporary Literature* 45.2 (2004): 278–99.

Scott, Suzanne and Lynne M. Constantine. "Belles Lettres Interview." *Belles Lettres* 5.4 (1990): 24–26.

Segar, Jennifer. "Arapaho." *Minnesota State University, Mankato* () 23 Mar. 2005 <http://www.mnsu.edu/emuseum/cultural/northamerica/arapaho.html>.

"Seneca Nation of Indians." Seneca Nation of Indians. 19 Sept. 2005 <http://www.sni.org>.

Shockley, Evelyn E. "Toni Morrison, *Paradise*: Review." *African American Review* 33.4 (1999): 718–9.

Smith, Dinitia. "Toni Morrison's Mix of Tragedy, Domesticity, and Folklore." *The New York Times* (8 Jan. 1998): E1.

Smith, Joan. "Grazed Anatomy." *The Independent* 13 Sept. 1992, sec. The Sunday Review Page: 26.

Sollors, Werner and Maria Diedrich. *Black Columbiad: Defining Moments in African American Literature and Culture.* Cambridge: Harvard University Press, 1994.

Spillers, Hortense. "Mama's Baby, Papa's Maybe: An American Grammar Book." *Literary Theory: An Anthology.* Ed. Julie Rivkin and Michael Ryan. Malden, Mass. and Oxford: Blackwell Publishers, 1998. 656–72.

Staples, Brent. "Eden, Oklahoma: Trouble in Toni Morrison's *Paradise*" (14 Jan. 1998) 29 July 2009 <http://www.slate.com/id/3039>.

Stein, Gertrude. *The Autobiography of Alice B. Toklas.* New York: Brace, Harcourt, Jovanovitch, 1933.

Stevens, Christy R. "Imagining Deregulated Desire: *Written on the Body*'s Revolutionary Reconstruction of Gender and Sexuality" (15 Dec. 1997) 8 Mar. 2006 <http://www.ags.uci.edu/\%7Eclcwegsa/revolutions/Stevens.htm>.

Storace, Patricia. "'The Scripture of Utopia': *Paradise* by Toni Morrison." *The New York Review of Books* XLV.10 (11 June 1998): 64–69.

Stowers, Cath. "Journeying with Jeanette: Transgressive Travels in Winterson's Fiction." *(Hetero)sexual Politics.* Ed. Mary Maynard and June Purvis. London and Bristol, PA: Taylor & Francis, 1995. 139–58.

——. "'No Legitimate Place, No Land, No Fatherland': Communities of Women in the Fiction of Roberts and Winterson." *Critical Survey* 8.1 (1996): 69–79.

——. "The Erupting Lesbian Body: Reading *Written on the Body* as a Lesbian Text." *'I'm Telling You Stories': Jeanette Winterson and the Politics of Reading.* Ed. Helena Grice and Tim Woods. Amsterdam: Rodopi, 1998. 89–101.

Stuart, Andrea. "Terms of Endearment: *Written on the Body* by Jeanette Winterson." *New Statesman and Society* (1992–09–18): 37f.

Suggs, Henry Lewis, ed. *The Black Press in the Middle West, 1865-1985.* Westport, CT.: Greenwood Press, 1996.

Tally, Justine. "Reality and Discourse in Toni Morrison's Trilogy: Testing the Limits." *Literature and Ethnicity in the Cultural Borderlands.* Ed. Jesús Benito and Ana María Manzanas. Vol. 28. Rodopi Perspectives on Modern Literature. Amsterdam and New York, NY: Rodopi, 2002. 35–49.

——. *Toni Morrison's (Hi)Stories and Truths.* Hamburg: Lit-Verlag, 1999.

Taylor Merleau, Chloë. "Postmodern Ethics and the Expression of Differends in the Novels of Jeanette Winterson." *Journal of Modern Literature* 26.3/4 (Summer 2003): 84–102.

Taylor, Quintard. *In Search of the Racial Frontier: African Americans in the American West, 1528-1990.* New York, N.Y.: W. W. Norton & Company, 1998.

Teall, Kaye M. *Black History in Oklahoma*. Oklahoma City: Oklahoma City Public School System, 1971.

Terzieva-Artemis, Rossitsa. *Stories of the Unconscious: Sub-Versions in Freud, Lacan and Kristeva*. Frankfurt/Main: Lang, 2009.

Tew, Philip. "Wintersonian Masculinities." *Jeanette Winterson*. Ed. Sonya Andermahr. London and New York: Continuum, 2007. 114–29.

"The Thunder, Perfect Mind." Nag Hammadi Library. 21 Nov. 2005 <http://www.gnosis.org/naghamm/thunder.html>.

Timehost. "Time 25: Toni Morrison." Internet chat. TIME Magazine (1998) 9 Sept. 2003 <http://www.time.com/community/transcripts/chattr012198.html>.

Tolson, Arthur L. *The Black Oklahomans: A History 1541-1972*. New Orleans: Edwards Printing Company, 1974.

Took, Thalia (alias Mary Crane). "Yemaya" (2004) 18 Oct. 2005 <http://www.thaliatook.com/AMGG/yemaya.html>.

Turner, Jenny. "Portrait: Preacher Woman." *The Guardian* 17 June 1994, sec. The Guardian Weekend Page: T 18.

Turner, Patricia. "Paradise Lost: A Black Community Tears Itself Apart in Toni Morrison's Latest Novel." *San Francisco Chronicle. Book Review* (11 Jan. 1998): 1.

"Unia History." UNIA. 23 Mar. 2005 <http://www.unia_acl.org/info/historic.htm>.

Verdelle, A.J. "Paradise Found: A Talk with Toni Morrison About Her New Novel." *Essence* (Feb. 1998) 10 Jan. 1999 <http://www.findarticles.com/cf_0/m1264/n10_v28/20187690/print.jhtml>.

"Violence Against Women." 2009. UNIFEM 26 Nov. 2009 <http://www.unifem.org/gender_issues/violence_against_women/>.

Walker, Barbara G. (1985). *The Crone: Woman of Age, Wisdom, and Power*. San Francisco: HarperSanFrancisco, 1988.

Walker, Margaret. *Jubilee*. Boston: Houghton Mifflin, 1966.

Washington, Booker T. *Up From Slavery*. New York: Doubleday, 1902.

West, Cornel. *Race Matters*. 1993. New York and Toronto: Vintage Books, 2001.

Whitton, Natasha. "Toni Morrison's *Paradise*." *Women Writers* (20 Aug. 1999) 16 Feb. 2005 <http://www.womenwriters.net/bookreviews/whitton2.htm>.

Williams, Nudie Eugene. "Oklahoma: Genesis and Tradition of the Black Press, 1889-1980." *The Black Press in the Middle West, 1865-1985*. Ed. Henry Lewis Suggs. Westport, Conn.: Greenwood Press, 1996. 267–296.

Wilt, Judith. "'Down Here in Paradise': Toni Morrison's Americas." *The Puritan Origins of American Sex: Religion, Sexuality, and National Identity in American Literature*. Ed. Tracy Fassenden, Nicholas F. Radel, and Magdalene J. Zaborowska. New York & London: Routledge, 2001. 273–92.

Wingfield, Rachel. "Lesbian Writers in the Mainstream: Sara Maitland, Jeanette Winterson and Emma Donoghue." *Beyond Sex and Romance? The Politics of Contemporary Lesbian Fiction.* Ed. Elaine Hutton. London: The Women's Press, 1998. 60–105.

Wittig, Monique. "The Mark of Gender." 1985. *The Straight Mind and Other Essays.* Boston: Beacon Press, 1992. 76–89.

Wood, Michael. "Sensations of Loss." *The Aesthetics of Toni Morrison: Speaking the Unspeakable.* Ed. Marc Conner. Jackson: University of Mississippi Press, 2000. 113–24.

Woolf, Virginia. *A Room of One's Own.* 1928. London: Penguin Books, 2004.

——. *Orlando: A Biography.* 1928. London: Chancellor Press, 1994.

Youngs, Tim. "Introduction: Context and Motif." *Writing and Race.* London and New York: Longman, 1997. 1–30.

Yukins, Elizabeth. "Bastard Daughters and the Possession of History in *Corregidora* and *Paradise*." *Signs: Journal of Women in Culture and Society* 28.1 (2002): 221–47.

"Zeichen." Hilchenbacher Bündnis für Toleranz und Zivilcourage. 19 July 2005 <http://www.hilchenbacherbuendnis.de/zeichen.htm>.

Zucker, Marilyn. "Virginia Woolf and Jeanette Winterson." *Virginia Woolf Miscellany* 61 (Fall 2002): 4–5.